Shaping Africa's Talent

ENDORSEMENTS

"Talent management as a discipline has never been more important.

"It is pleasing to see HR professionals in South Africa responding to this business priority of ensuring that organisations have the required talent to not only navigate these challenging and complex times, but to thrive in them. *Shaping Africa's Talent* is therefore a timely contribution to the ongoing education of HR professionals and indeed business leaders about examples of the best practices we have in our country on Talent Management.

"Congratulations to the contributors who wrote the chapters of this book and I hope this is the beginning of a trend of HR practitioners in South Africa informing the world about the best that we have to offer in Human Resources Management in our country."

Mike Brown, Chief Executive: Nedbank

"One of the key challenges in 21st-century leadership is talent management. The challenge in Africa is heightened by the large diversity of the continent. *Shaping Africa's Talent* offers both a context and appreciation of the emerging challenges and strategies to address these. Whilst acknowledging the opportunities of new technology and enhanced communication systems, there is also a strong emphasis on employers developing strong employer brands that are attractive to employees and that can withstand the appeal and the pull of the international companies, which are also seeking to attract the very same talent."

Mmasekgoa Masire-Mwamba, Executive Director of TMMO, Botswana
Mmasekgoa served two terms as Deputy Secretary-General for the Commonwealth

"Africa's future development will depend on the development of its talent. *Shaping Africa's Talent* goes a long way towards providing companies doing business in Africa with a roadmap to manage and develop talent in a more focused and professional manner.

"The case studies and best practices featured in *Shaping Africa's Talent* also offer excellent guidelines to learn from and shape your own talent strategies in Africa."

Antoinette Irvine, Human Resources Vice President – Global Supply Chain – Unilever

"At last! An honest and comprehensive look at Africa's vast talent pool – at once a platform for Africa taking its rightful place in the world as a hub of diverse talent, but also looking at the need for ongoing talent development that is relevant to current challenges of automation, where the world of innovation presupposes a tomorrow where an unskilled workforce will be replaced by robots, or an influx of a skilled Diaspora, that will further preserve the current talent pool status quo that is largely unskilled and undeveloped."

Nene Molefi, Managing Director – Mandate Molefi HR Consultants

"Africa's wealth and true potential can only be unlocked if the vast talent pool of this continent is developed to its fullest potential. *Shaping Africa's Talent* is the guidepost to achieve this goal. Here you will find the required talent development frameworks, best practices and strategies to assist organisations to attract, retain and develop the best talent possible."

Pearl Maphoshe, Pick n Pay – HR Director

"The continent of Africa does not have the 'luxury of time' to ponder, pilot and re-design transformative and transactional interventions for business, including the critical work of Human Resources. It for this reason that *Shaping Africa's Talent* is of great value to all business leaders and HR professionals as in each chapter world-class gold nuggets of information regarding successfully proven theories and methodologies are shared that can easily be replicated in whatever industry you may find yourself in or in whatever country. *Shaping Africa's Talent* shows how it has worked for others and hence how it will work for you in Africa."

Heather Montgomery, VP Global Organisational Effectiveness, Anglo Gold Ashanti

"Knowledge Resources has published a must-read for anyone needing to consider and define a Talent Management strategy in Africa. Read this book – and learn from the best. It takes an in-depth look at the trends and policies shaping the talent landscape in Africa, drawing on experts in this field, and presents several compelling and insightful case studies. It further sets out leading talent processes in Africa that look at the role of business schools, building technical and vocational skills, and deliberates on graduate to leadership programmes. For leaders and HR professionals responsible for talent acquisition and development in Africa, this book is essential reading."

Professor Shirley Zinn, Group HR Director, Woolworths

"Indeed a timely and perhaps overdue publication that effectively addresses both the current and emerging realities of managing talent in the African context. A balanced range of recognised thought leaders and experienced practitioners provide valuable perspectives on the very nature and complexity of this challenge, and offer actionable insights spanning the entire talent management value chain, based on solid experiences gained in multiple industries. A strongly recommended read for those employer organisations already operating across Africa who wish to optimise the execution of their respective talent management strategies as well as for those who are planning to expand their operations into the continent."

David Conradie: Key Account Director, Mindcor Consulting

"A rich resource that will be of enduring value, *Shaping Africa's Talent* brings the science, art and actual practice of talent management into a single, substantial offering. While each chapter offers unique, stand-alone value, the work as a whole will take you on an enriching journey in which each stage adds value to the next. From the strong contemporary focus on fundamentals to the generous insights into their proven application within highly admired organisations, this is a book to buy once but to refer to time and again."

Penny Milner-Smyth, Human Resources Executive, South African Sugar Association

"Africa has a critical role to play in the global arena, but first its home-grown talent needs to find African solutions to Africa's problems. The continent is filled with dynamic and creative young people who, through technology, are now more liberated than ever before. This book provides important insight into how we might best shape Africa's talent."

Ilke Dunn, Head Leadership, Culture and Young Talent - RMB

"This timely book revolves around the critical C's that will matter strategically for the Continent of Africa from a talent perspective. The Continent has all the Capability to be a future world leader on condition that it becomes talent-driven. Using a seamless Combination of Conceptualisation and Cases in an insightful way, the book covers in a well-informed and argued way the significantly Challenging, Changing, Complex, Chaotic Context demanding Competitiveness through Continuity – expressed as sustainability – and Collaboration. Key to future Competitiveness is the dedicated, well thought through and ongoing Cultivation of Capital, in particular People Capital. Cultivating People Capital demands the right Culture to build Capacity and Commitment – people, organisationally and institutionally wise – to make Africa a great talent Continent. This book will make you 'Cee' what is required to equip yourself and your organisation to make your much needed talent Contribution towards making Africa the future place to be."

Prof Theo H Veldsman, Department of Industrial Psychology and People Management,
Faculty of Management, University of Johannesburg. Work Psychologist.

"Doing business on our wonderful continent is not without its challenges. Facing these challenges and making reality your friend will enable you to enjoy the many rewards Africa has to offer. The acquisition of and retention of critical talent is one of the key levers of success for any business – getting it right requires the right mix of understanding the context in which you operate and appreciating the availability of the requisite talent. I am passionate about what Africa has to offer and this book gives a sobering and realistic view of what it takes to succeed in accessing and attracting talent. There are too many myths surrounding talent in Africa. Terry skilfully works through the facts so that leaders and HR practitioners can act with confidence and impact."

Darryl Wright, Group HR Executive, AVI Head Office

First published in 2016

ISBN: 978-1-86922-625-1
ISBN: 978-1-86922-626-8 (ePDF)

Published by KR Publishing
P O Box 3954
Randburg
2125
Republic of South Africa

Tel: (011) 706-6009
Fax: (011) 706-1127
E-mail: orders@knowres.co.za
Website: www.kr.co.za

Printed and bound: HartWood Digital Printing, 243 Alexandra Avenue, Halfway House, Midrand
Typesetting, layout and design: Barbara Hirsch, barbieh@mweb.co.za
Cover design: Marlene de Villiers, marlene@knowres.co.za
Editing and proofreading: Elsa Crous, getitedited@mweb.co.za
Project management: Cia Joubert, cia@knowres.co.za

Shaping Africa's Talent

Enabling Africa's Potential

Edited by

Terry Meyer

publishing

2016

TABLE OF CONTENTS

ABOUT THE EDITOR

Terry Meyer, an independent consultant, academic, author and keynote speaker, holds a Master's of Management (HR) degree from Wits Business School. As a consultant with 20 years' experience he has worked at executive levels, facilitating solutions to organisational problems. He has extensive experience in strategy facilitation (business and human capital strategy); organisational design and capability building; executive effectiveness, succession and development; talent and skills development and reinventing HR (designing the "next generation" HR function).

Terry has worked in a variety of sectors and industries in South Africa and elsewhere in Africa. Previously, he was a full-time faculty member of Wits Business School, where for eight years he taught organisational behaviour and was responsible for the highly regarded Master of Management in HR programme. He is the current Programme Director of the HR Executive Leadership Programme run by Stellenbosch Business School – a programme which he designed, in addition to teaching on a variety of leadership programmes. For the past five years he has run the Wits Business School International Executive L&D Study Programme, leading a number of senior HR and L&D professionals to engage with top global companies and business schools in the United States and Europe.

Terry currently lectures on the Unisa SBL MBL programme, having previously taught on the Executive Development Programme (EDP). Much of his writing focuses on disruptive leadership in a connected world. He has written or co-edited six important books and has contributed articles to a number of journals. He is currently finalising a book entitled *Shaping Africa's talent,* which is due for release in August.

A former board member of the Institute of People Management (IPM), Terry is registered as a Master HR Professional with the SABPP (South African Board for People Practices). He has received numerous professional awards, including the IPM Presidential Award (2008), an award at the International HRD Congress in Mumbai (2009) and a Lifetime Achievement Award from the SABPP (2012).

Terry has the ability to blend extensive academic thought leadership with his practical experience in a corporate role and as a consultant. He is considered a leading thinker and advisor in his various fields of expertise. His primary theoretical basis is grounded in systems thinking, and he has the ability to approach organisational problem solving from a multi-disciplinary perspective.

ABOUT THE CONTRIBUTORS

Lisa Ashton, who holds an M.Com in Human Resources Management (Industrial Psychology), is a senior industrial psychologist. She has accumulated a wealth of consulting experience from a wide range of Human Resource and Organisational Change projects and interventions.

Lisa joined Third Foundation Systems (TFS) in 1996 prior to the formation of BIOSS SA. She has worked with CPA (career-path appreciation) and the Matrix of Working Relationships since 1993, and has been with BIOSS Southern Africa since 1996, where she now holds the position of Managing Director. She has worked extensively in Africa, South America, Eastern Europe and the United States.

She has also lectured at the University of Johannesburg in Strategic Personnel Management, Organisational Behaviour and Psychometrics. Previous positions include Principal Consultant (MAC Consulting), primarily as part of large-scale organisational change projects, and corporate roles in the banking and telecommunications industries.

Her areas of specialty include executive assessment, succession planning, talent management, human resources development, strategic human resource planning, and coaching. She has a special interest in diversity management, leadership and decision making in the face of complexity. She has learnt that leadership is about creating conditions for others to be successful. Her particular area of expertise is in the development of people strategies to deliver on the strategic intent of organisations.

Zia Attlee currently heads up the research division at KR. She is the former manager of the Psychometric Advisory Services Department at JvR Psychometrics.

Zia holds a BA (Hons) in Psychology and a Master of Management from Wits Business School. Her present role at KR includes managing the research team in producing and publishing in-depth and comprehensive research on human capital, and labour trends and developments in various African countries.

Sarah Babb facilitates leadership and organisational identity change. Many global companies grapple with how to refocus around customer-centricity, innovation and collaboration, and this demands significant changes from leadership. Sarah consults, runs programmes and coaches executives across EMEA (Europe, the Middle East and Africa) countries and companies working with these transitions. During the past year, she worked in Tanzania, Zambia, Zimbabwe, Kenya, Namibia, South Africa and India, and with executives from the Kingdom of Saudi Arabia and Europe. Sarah is currently doing her PhD in Leadership Identity Change, having completed an MBA (Cum Laude) in 2004, and a postgraduate Diploma and BA in Industrial Psychology and Industrial Sociology. Sarah also founded and ran a multimillion rand business in development for ten years. She enjoys writing and presenting, and has attended numerous conferences in her area of specialisation.

Chantal Butler, who holds an MA in Psychology from the University of Cape Town (UCT) and an MBA from USB (the University of Stellenbosch Business School), is registered as a psychologist with the Health Professions Council of South Africa (HPCSA).She started working at Woolworths in 1999, and has 20 years' experience as an HR professional and leader. She finds her purpose in the belief that everything we do should be about leaving the world in better place, having built a brighter future for the next generation.

Outside of work, she is the proud mother of two children, and has a passion for music, art and theatre.

Lydia Cillie-Schmidt is an independent consultant and owner of "The Talent Hub", whose focus areas are the design and implementation of talent management processes and strategy across the employee lifecycle, including acquisition, deployment, development and engagement. The Talent Hub is the implementation partner for Learning Paths International, as well as Appraisal Smart in South Africa. These processes are supported by leadership development programmes, assessment centres, psychometric assessments, the design and presentation of training programmes, coaching, mentoring, performance management and succession development.

Lydia has more than 30 years' experience as an industrial psychologist, working as a permanent employee for organisations such as Vodacom, Sasol, the SABC (South African Broadcasting Corporation) and the Department of Post and Telecommunications. As an independent consultant, Lydia gained experience in organisation design, as well as the design of career paths, learning paths and training games. She has experience in policy design and medico-legal report-writing. She developed a toolkit on Workforce Planning and has presented several workshops on topics such as integrated talent management, HR as a strategic business partner, workforce planning and succession management. A registered industrial psychologist, she completed a doctorate in Industrial Psychology, focusing on the use of narrative technique in management development.

Wilhelm Crous, who has a B.Com Honours in Industrial and Organisational Psychology, obtained an MBA from the University of Stellenbosch Business School (UBS). He has been a guest lecturer at various universities and business schools and has received numerous special awards, including the Lifetime Achievement Award from the South African Board for People Practices (SABPP) for his outstanding contribution to the Human Resources Management profession and a Chancellor's Medal from the University of Pretoria for his contribution to Human Resources Management. Wilhelm was one of the founders of the SABPP and is a member of the Academy of Management. He is currently the lead editor of the 'Human capital and labour report' series.

Debbie Farnaby is currently a partner in the Heidrick & Struggles' Johannesburg office, where she leads the Global Technology Services practice for sub-Saharan Africa. Her corporate expertise spans 25 years in technology functions in mining and manufacturing organisations, with extensive experience at the Exco level.

Her last corporate role was as Group Director for Shared Services for the De Beers Group, where she was responsible for providing a range of shared services to the group's global operating entities. These shared services included technical mining consulting services, ICT, and financial, security, supply-chain and facilities management. She also served as the Group Director of Information Technology (CIO) for the group. Previously, Debbie also served at the global executive level for Sappi Ltd as Group Director for Technology and Information Services.

She has served in both executive and non-executive director roles on both listed and unlisted company boards, including Sappi Europe, De Beers Consolidated Mines, Debswana, Element 6 and Palabora Mining.

Debbie has an MSc in Computer Science from the University of Stellenbosch, and a BSc in Computer Science, a GDE in Mechanical Engineering and a PDE in Educational Technology from the University of the Witwatersrand.

Jacques Haworth is currently the Director: Business Management at Bioss Southern Africa, and has formed part of the Bioss team since 2004. He has extensive experience in the areas of assessment, assessment centres, training, coaching, competency design, organisational design, talent management, career development and succession planning.

He has over 20 years' experience working in the human resources field, both locally and globally across various industries including mining, financial services, pharmaceuticals, transportation, fast-moving consumer goods (FMCG) and government. He has led projects focusing on total organisational redesign and development, and has supported clients in the design and development of assessment centres, competency design, talent management models and processes, assessment practices, as well as the design and delivery of various bespoke interventions aimed at empowering clients to build their skills internally.

Jacques lives in Johannesburg. He is an avid reader, a nature lover and a keen student of the work of Carl Jung. He is passionate about designing requisite and flexible organisations that allow for the optimal utilisation of people as a competitive advantage. He holds a B.Com Hons degree in Industrial Psychology.

André Horak is an established speaker, consultant and thought leader on social business, social collaboration and enterprise social networking. He is also an IBM Champion for Social Business – a global programme which recognises and rewards innovative thought leaders in the IBM community.

André has been part of the IBM ecosystem for over 18 years, focusing primarily on designing and delivering collaborative solutions to dozens of customers in South Africa and the rest of Africa. Between 2012 and 2015, André was employed by IBM South Africa as Sales Lead for IBM's Collaboration Solutions, including the industry-leading IBM Connections and IBM Digital Experience platforms.

His vast experience in delivering collaborative solutions across various industries and lines of business has uniquely positioned him to help customers understand how social collaboration tools can be applied and integrated with existing systems and processes to drive business results.

In his current role at i1 Solutions (a premier IBM business partner), André assists South African companies to become leading social businesses by helping them to successfully implement and adopt their enterprise social networking tools, while integrating social collaboration and exceptional digital experiences with existing business processes and enterprise applications.

James Hu, Unilever Talent Manager – Southern Africa.

James began his career at Unilever in 2012 as an HR graduate on the Unilever Future Leaders Programme, after completing his studies at the University of Cape Town. Through Unilever's rotation-based graduate programme, he was able to develop experience and insights across the HR spectrum. After completing HR roles in the Marketing and Supply Chain functions, James embarked on a short-term international assignment in Kenya, where he worked in a leadership development role for East Africa. Since returning, James has been responsible for talent management for the southern African region. As part of Unilever's Bright Future agenda, James leads youth employability initiatives across the continent. He also currently sits on the board of directors of Engineers Without Borders South Africa.

Madeline Lass holds a BA (Translation) and a three-year Primary Teachers' Diploma. She has more than 20 years' experience in the publishing industry as a book editor, writer and production manager. She has worked for some of the most prestigious publishers in South Africa, including Juta & Co and Jonathan Ball, in the fields of law, economics, entrepreneurship, business strategy and engineering. Shell South Africa and Shell Oil Products Africa retained her as an internal communications consultant for ten years. Apart from the numerous articles she has written, she has also researched, written and produced three major family histories for the founders of Foschini, Gundle Plastics and BL Williams Construction.

Johan Ludike, an Executive Human Resource Practitioner, gained the majority of his experience within the financial services (RBS, Barclays, FNB, Mashreq Bank), retail (Sainsbury's), telecoms (MTN, Emirates Telecommunications) and, more recently, the hospitality industries (Yum Brands!).

Shortly after completing a Master's in Human Resource Management and Occupational Psychology, he pursued and obtained international multinational HR experience in London, Europe, the Middle East and Asia. He contributed to the following publications:

- *The role of the CHRO* (2014)
- *Human capital trends – building a sustainable organisation* (2011) and
- *Managing human resource development: an outcomes-based approach* (2007).

Johan has been fortunate to present papers at several conferences, to lecture at business schools and attend seminars and workshops, both locally and internationally, on strategic leadership talent management and human resource management.

Nazrene Mannie joined Transman as Training Executive for the group in April 2014. She was previously employed as Skills Development and Human Capital Executive at SEIFSA and at the National Business Initiative (NBI) in the capacity of Programme Manager: Skills Development. She has held various positions within the management consulting, HR and banking sectors.

Nazrene previously served on the Accounting Authority and related sub-committees of the Manufacturing, Engineering and Related Services Sector Education and Training Authority (MERSETA) and is currently involved in structures resorting under the Services Seta.

She serves on a number of national and ministerial bodies within the skills development environment, including the National Skills Authority Board and is an exco member of the Technical Working Group of the Human Resource Development Council (HRDC) and Business Unity South Africa's (BUSA) education-related committees. As a member of the board of the Federation of African Professional Staffing Organisations (APSO), her portfolio focuses on the professionalisation of employees in the staffing industry.

Morné Mostert is Director of the Institute for Futures Research at Stellenbosch University. He advises globally on executive decision-making and cognitive development for senior leaders and has worked in Paris, London, Dubai and several African countries.

Subsequent to obtaining a PhD in the Management of Technology and Innovation, he has specialised in futures thinking, strategic thinking, systems thinking and creative innovation. He is the Chairman of the global think tank World Leadership Day and the Founding Chairman of the media tech start-up Africa Business Radio.

A regular keynote speaker and frequent guest on radio and television in the business media, Morné is also the author of the influential book *Systemic leadership learning – leadership development in the era of complexity*, which has been the prescribed text for several international programmes on strategic leadership.

Samuel Njenga is an experienced process facilitator who has worked in the areas of leadership development, change management, corporate sustainability and strategic alignment. His interests include how organisations create and share knowledge, how to promote organisational learniprofng, and how to lead and manage change processes.

Samuel, who has worked in corporate social investment (CSI), now consults and lectures on corporate sustainability and on leadership for sustainable local economic development. A student of systems thinking, he is passionate about enabling business and organisational leaders to better manage the complex situations they face, by using applied systems thinking. Samuel is also a visiting faculty member at the University of Stellenbosch and the Henley Business School, where he lectures on systems application to organisational issues like leadership development, change management, project management, management roles and team performance.

Apart from holding a BEd (Hons) from Kenyatta University, Samuel obtained an MA in Organisational Leadership (Eastern University, USA) and an MCom in Organisational Management and Systems (UKZN). He is the co-author, with A.T. Smit, of *Leading the way through CSI: A guidebook for corporate social investment practitioners.*

Terrence Taylor is a leadership development executive who specialises in developing strategies and initiatives that touch, change and empower people to change the game and meaningfully contribute to changing the world. He focuses on bench strength building, building effective teams, business impact measurement, executive development, experiential programmes design, coaching and mentoring, learning as a service, transformative facilitation and scalable development.

Terence is the General Manager: Talent, Analytics and Leadership and Learning at Discovery in Johannesburg. From 2012–2013 he was Head of Ecobank Academy and Group Learning and Development at Ecobank, Lome, Togo. Prior to that, he worked at Standard Bank in Johannesburg as Director: Senior Designer Leadership and Learning Since 2004 he has been affiliated to the Gordon Institute of Business Science (Gibs) in Johannesburg, where he designs and facilitates management and leadership courses for corporates.

Tracy Potgieter, HR Director: International Division (Coca-Cola Beverages Africa), is a seasoned HR professional leader and registered industrial psychologist with over three decades of HR experience in retail, manufacturing, tele-communications and the FMCG industry. Tracy has worked for Coca-Cola Sabco (Pty) Ltd for the past 14 years as part of a dynamic senior HR leadership team, led by Cathy Albertyn, which develops and builds HR capability across the organisation.

A registered industrial psychologist with a passion for developing people to fulfil their full potential and purpose, Tracy enjoys using innovation to enable business strategy and, over the years, has been deeply involved in the architecture of building and growing various HR processes and systems. Tracy's proudest achievement is founding Wings and Wishes in 2006, an organisation committed to transporting critically ill children to specialist medical care, and having assisted over 3 000 patients since its inception (www.wingsandwishes.org).

Jenali Skuse pursued a double Bachelors at Stellenbosch University between 2004 and 2008, eventually leaving the Wineland town with a PPE (politics, philosophy and economics) and a degree in English and Sociology. Jenali subsequently completed a postgraduate degree in Politics. In Germany, she completed a fellowship in gender and genocide at the University of Oldenburg. Upon returning to Johannesburg she managed a successful rock band, completed a Master's and lectured in Political Studies at Wits. After two years of never-ending pressure, Jenali used her meagre savings to explore the mountains, beaches and jungles of South America for six months. After learning exactly two Spanish phrases, "Donde esta el bano?" and "Un cerveza grande, por favour", getting lost in many Andean cities and eating far too many plates of rice and beans she returned to South Africa where her employer branding journey began.

As Research Manager for Magnet Communications, Jenali was responsible for collecting, processing, analysing and presenting research for the South African market. She held this position for three years before moving into the role of Employer Branding Consultant at Universum. She now works directly with some of the top local employers on defining, refining and implementing their employer branding strategies in order to become more attractive employers. Jenali was recently promoted to Country Manager for Universum South Africa. In her spare time, you are likely to find her climbing a mountain, hanging off a rock or trying to get the adventure club she runs 'un-lost'.

Abe Thebyane is Group Executive: HR for Nedbank. He has almost 30 years of extensive Human Resources and overall business experience in various senior and executive positions, in several large corporations and across a range of industries. Some of his most notable leadership positions include Executive Head: HR at Anglo Platinum Ltd and Executive Director: HR at Iscor Ltd.

Through his experience in executive as well as other consulting positions, Abe has built up a wealth of knowledge and expertise in the HR sphere, especially in HR strategy, skills development, employee relations, employee diversity, talent management, workforce planning and change management.

Abe holds a B.Admin degree from the University of the North, a postgraduate Diploma in Management (HR) from Wits Business School, an MBA from De Montfort University and an MSc in Banking Practice and Management from IFS University College.

FOREWORD

Prof Frik Landman, USB-Ed

Africa is the richest continent. Africa is the poorest continent.

The former refers to our majority global share of arable land, natural resources, fantastic youth population, etc. The latter refers to our seeming inability to turn our endowment into wealth for all, to take up our place on the world stage. To resolve this by searching for a missing link or a panacea would be to err on the side of over-simplicity.

The *problématique* of the continent is complex and demands a systems perspective and approach. When you intervene in any large complex system you are confronted with the reality of boundaries (you cannot do everything for everyone at once) and you therefore – with your best understanding of the system (e.g., a social system) you are faced with – are forced to seek a high leverage point. This is where a systemic variable such as talent presents itself as a significant game changer. As stated in the recent Global Competitive Index, "strong institutions, available talent, and a high capacity to innovate hold the key for the success of any economy". [1]

Since the *Economist* in September 2011 proclaimed on its front page the fact of 'Africa rising', evidence has been forthcoming that the continent is indeed performing much better than not only its own past but also the developed world would seem to indicate. Yet, there is an economic narrative that the current growth trajectory is mostly based on the trade of our commodities and is therefore fickle and not sustainable. Frankly, it is viewed as jobless growth.

An increasingly louder call is heard for the beneficiation of our commodities to forge a more sustainable future for our incredible youth demographics. The reality is that "today 40% of the continent's population is under the age of 15, and it is estimated that young adults (15– 29) will make up a further 28% of the population in a decade". [2] In the absence of economic growth and opportunities, this potential youth dividend can turn into a human disaster. Our youth want to own part of this continent's wealth and, in the absence thereof, great frustration will set in, as is already being witnessed in various regions.

A Chinese proverb comes to mind: If you want one year of prosperity, grow seeds. If you want ten years of prosperity, grow trees. If you want 100 years of prosperity, grow people. This proverb hosts the seed of the core of talent development, which is its ethos. As Africans we want to and can contribute to a global societal ethos by demonstrating the courage to protect our humanity, our environment, as well as our economy as an integrated whole. This hinges on how we answer the ethical question of what kind of Africa we choose to build together, given the immense resources we have at our disposal. [3] This is an ethos that requires agreement amongst three important stakeholders, namely the public sector, the private sector and civil society. Talent development in Africa requires the synergy of the collective.

The call for collective action is echoed by the United Nations Conference on Trade and Development (Unctad): "Countries also need to improve the capacity-building efforts of regulatory bodies with regard to *human resources*, to enhance performance, which may be supported regionally through shared training programmes, twinning arrangements and information sharing arrangements to more effectively disseminate best practices and benchmark regulatory performance."[4]

African society is in need of a serious effort, on the part of all stakeholders, to develop talent in order to help the continent move towards a sustainable future. It is therefore necessary to design research which could elegantly generate the requisite information to be shared and applied towards talent development. Different and diverse stakeholders need to effectively collaborate to provide accessible and beneficial research and talent development interventions.

Observing the challenges Africa faces, the vast natural resources the continent has been endowed with, and the talent potential it holds, requires an incessant drive and imperative to maintain an effective, future-oriented, sustainable talent development agenda.

This book is a reflection of that intent.

Endnotes

1   Klaus Schwab, The Global Competitiveness Report 2014-2015, *World Economic Forum*, Retrieved 1 August 2016, http://www3.weforum.org/docs/WEF_GlobalCompetitivenessReport_2014-15.pdf, p xiii
2   The Legatum Prosperity Index, 2013, *Legatum Institute*, Retrieved 1 August 2016, http://media.prosperity.com/2013/pdf/publications/PI2013Brochure_WEB.pdf, p 21
3   *George Bernard Shaw said:* We are made wise not by the recollection of our past, but by the responsibility for our future.
4   Unctad, *Economic Development in Africa Report 2015,* retrieved 30 June 2016, <unctad.org/en/PublicationsLibrary/aldcafrica2015_en.pdf>

References

The Legatum Prosperity Index, 2013, *Legatum Institute*, Retrieved 1 August 2016, http://media.prosperity.com/2013/pdf/publications/PI2013Brochure_WEB.pdf, p 21

Unctad, *Economic Development in Africa Report 2015,* retrieved 30 June 2016, <unctad.org/en/PublicationsLibrary/aldcafrica2015_en.pdf>

Schwab, K, The Global Competitiveness Report 2014-2015, *World Economic Forum,* Retrieved 1 August 2016, http://www3.weforum.org/docs/WEF_GlobalCompetitivenessReport_2014-15.pdf, xiii

INTRODUCTION

Africa is a continent of great potential. Collectively, its nations constitute one of the fastest-growing economies in the world, with one of the largest populations of young people eager to help realise and be part of the potential that awaits them.

Africa is a very diverse continent comprised of many countries, cultures, economies and challenges. It is far from homogeneous.

Nevertheless, to achieve its potential, African economies need to collaborate on a number of issues to facilitate investment, trade and economic development in a way that will improve the lives and opportunities of its people, communities and societies. Of notable importance is the need for infrastructure development, the removal of obstacles to the cross-border movement of goods and people, and political stability based on sound governance and ethical principles.

For this potential to be realised, more than anything else Africa needs to grow (and keep) its talent and leadership capability at all levels and in all sectors of its many economies and societies. Countries around the world are competing for talent. If you consider the number of highly qualified people in the African diaspora who live and work in numerous countries around the world, you cannot help but ask: Why are they there and not in their home countries? It is accepted that skills will, and should, migrate to garner global exposure and experience. However, Africa needs those skills, and countries and cites need to develop competitive strategies to make themselves *talent attractive*. Furthermore, where there is talent, investment will follow.

One of the consequences of home-grown skills is reduced reliance on expatriates and imported skills.

This book constitutes an attempt to share many of the strategies and tools that have been effective in building talent and leadership ability in the African context, with the intention of assisting organisations to build the talent pool that the continent needs. Although there are many great insights and examples of effective talent development throughout the book, a number of gaps need to be acknowledged.

First, most of the chapters are written by South Africans. This is not intentional; it is simply a fact that my own network did not extend into Africa, although I would have welcomed contributions from the many thought leaders and organisations across the continent. That said, all the contributors have extensive experience working or engaging with clients in various African countries, and are therefore supremely qualified to speak knowledgeably of the continent.

Furthermore, all of the company case studies are about organisations with operations throughout the continent, and their experience is highly relevant beyond their home bases.

There are three more gaps in respect of key talent issues which resulted purely from a lack of time, access and space in the book. Those are

- the role of women as a key source of talent and leadership;
- the role of the disabled as a source of talent and leadership, and the importance of proactively providing opportunities and access to skills, information and networks for people with disabilities; and
- the importance of building Africa's entrepreneurs, as it is in this space that job creation and economic development are likely to have the greatest impact.

I am sure there are many other omissions, but the reality is that there is just so much time to access experts and a limit to the number of chapters that a book such as this can accommodate. Perhaps a future publication will be written as a result of emerging needs.

Most importantly, there is a need to acknowledge the knowledge, insights, experience and commitment of the contributing authors. They are a blend of academics, consultants and corporate leaders who have taken time out of their hectic schedules to share with leaders and HR professionals across the continent. Writing a chapter for a book is no small task, and they have more than lived up to this challenge in their area of expertise.

The book is divided into roughly three sections: the first adopts a wide-angle perspective and addresses high-level strategic issues confronting the talent and leadership landscape on the continent, including in organisations. The second comprises a number of case studies of leading companies that have demonstrated the impact of talent and leadership development as key strategic business imperatives. Finally, the third section contains a number of chapters that address specific talent processes in a very practical way.

This book subsequently aims to provide a strategic perspective as well as practical examples and tools to assist talent professionals and leaders in managing and growing their talent.

I would like to take this opportunity to thank the authors, Knowledge Resources and all the support staff who played such a key role in making this book possible.

My own ultimate vision is that the countries and cities of Africa will become globally *talent attractive*, because where talent resides investment follows. If this book or my company is able to help achieve this vision, then the effort to bring it to fruition will have been worth it.

I wish you all pleasant reading. I would be happy to engage with individuals and organisations on an ongoing basis through my website, www.leadershipsa.com. Leadership SA has extensive experience in the fields of strategy facilitation, organisational design, talent and skills development, executive effectiveness and succession, and the reinvention of HR. Although it is a small business in its own right, it has extensive access to thought leaders, consultancies and other institutions in a variety of areas of expertise (such as the authors of chapters in this book) with which it partners to provide customised solutions for clients. Hence the strong focus on leadership in a connected world.

The hope is that this book will provide a basis for a broader and long-lasting movement that it will establish networks aimed at supporting African talent development, and will offer all those involved a vehicle to collaborate and share experiences, to the benefit of this great continent and its people.

PART 1

CHAPTER 1

TALENT MANAGEMENT IN AFRICA – A CONTEXTUAL OVERVIEW
Wilhelm Crous and Zia Attlee

In this first chapter, Wilhelm Crous and Zia Attlee set the context for shaping Africa's talent.

Context is one of the most important factors when developing any kind of strategy or organisational system. For leaders and HR professionals responsible for talent acquisition and development in Africa, this chapter is essential reading not only for building talent at an organisational level, but also for enabling those who influence national skills policies and strategies to understand the bigger picture and make informed choices. Skills development starts at primary school and is affected by almost all socio-economic systems within an economy. As such, a holistic approach to skills development is necessary at a national level.

This chapter provides a wealth of information about the continent in general and talent specifically. It identifies the strengths and weaknesses of African countries in respect of their talent pool and resources. Apart from being a reservoir of facts, this chapter also provides important analyses and insights into the need for talent development on the continent.

From the analysis, Wilhelm and Zia identify eight "messages" and ten recommendations which emerge from the available information. To make decisions at organisational or national levels, accurate and comprehensive information is essential. In the African talent space, such information tends to be fragmented and spread across a number of different studies and reports. This chapter makes a great start towards pooling the relevant information, so that decision makers are able to see the bigger picture and make informed policy and strategy decisions.

Knowledge Resources has an extensive research capability and has conducted wide-ranging research into a number of African countries – the reports of which are available for scrutiny.

Introduction

This chapter provides the context for discussing talent management in Africa. First, an overview of Africa's progress over the past ten years is presented, along with the challenges facing future economic growth and the renewed focus on industrialisation. Second, a broad overview is given of sub-Saharan Africa's human capital and talent, rather than a detailed country-by-country analysis – doing the latter might be dangerous, because the continent is made up of 54 different countries and is highly heterogeneous, with over 2 000 different languages being spoken! Although the emphasis is on human capital and talent on a macro level, the talent-related challenges facing different countries are more or less the same.

The African continent is so large, the US, China and India would fit inside its borders, with room to spare for a few European countries too! For decades, Africa's deterioration or lack of economic growth was caused by weak governance, autocratic and corrupt leaders, ethnic conflict, widespread nationalisation and a slump in food and commodity prices during the 1970s and 80s. One could add to the list the negative legacy of colonisation, independence and liberation wars and, in South Africa, apartheid.[1]

Over the past decade the situation has changed substantially. Africa is more peaceful today than ever before. Yes, Somalia, South Sudan and the Central African Republic are failed states, and attacks by radical Islam do take place in Nigeria and East African countries, but overall sub-Saharan Africa is safer than it was 20 years ago. The continent is also more democratic, with regular elections being held in many nation states. The respective economies are better managed, with inflation under control, central banks making independent decisions and economic reforms leading to less red tape and better protection for countries than a decade ago.[2] As new political democracies are established, and political and investor risk decreases, investors are on the lookout for resources and producers are targeting the fast-growing group of middle-class consumers. No wonder that the lead articles in *The Economist* have, over the past 13 years, told vastly different stories:

- 13 May 2000 edition: *The hopeless continent*
- 3 December 2011 edition: *Africa rising*
- 2 March 2013 edition: *Aspiring Africa*

As recently in April 2016, the *The Economist* published an article entitled "Making Africa work", calling on the continent to focus on industrialisation in order to create more jobs for a burgeoning young population.[3]

International companies such as Barclays, Vodacom, Siemens, Unilever, GE, Walmart and TATA have all increased their presence in Africa. In addition, South African home-grown brands such as MTN, Shoprite, Woolworths, Sasol, Econet, FNB and Dangote Cement have all expanded their operations across Africa.[4]

The explosion in mobile technology has seen the rise of innovations such as M-Pesa, a mobile money system widely embraced in Kenya and Tanzania, which allows users to make purchases and send cash transfers via cell phone. M-Kopa and Milvik are two more examples of financial services offered on mobile platforms.[5]

There are doubts, however, about whether the recent commodities boom will translate into sustainable and inclusive socio-economic development. Two characteristics of the boom are alarming: first, thus far growth has not had the desired effects on employment, income and human development – it has not translated into sufficient jobs, and most employment expansion has occurred in the informal economy, usually at very low levels of productivity. Low labour absorption rates in particular continue to affect new entrants to the labour market. Second, there is little indication of structural change towards productivity-driven economies. Growth has mainly been driven by the exploitation and export of natural resources: between 2000 and 2011, petroleum and mineral resources accounted for more than two-thirds of exports, and agriculture for an additional ten per cent. The revenues from commodity exports stimulated domestic consumption, creating spill-over effects into wholesale and retail activities and real estate products, but little progress has been made in terms of manufacturing and production-orientated services. Manufacturing is currently decreasing as a percentage of GDP and exports.[6] However, as the commodities super cycle has come to an end, some of Africa's oil-producing and metal-rich giants now face a difficult future. Countries relying on the export of commodities (especially oil) have been adversely affected by low oil prices and a drop in demand from China for virtually every commodity. Countries such as Nigeria, Angola, Ghana, Zambia and South Africa have witnessed a dramatic slowdown in economic growth: the World Bank predicts that economic growth across the continent will slump to about three per cent in 2016, down from 7–8 per cent a decade ago. That will be slightly higher than the population growth rate of 2.7 per cent.[7]

Deindustrialisation is also hitting Africa hard. According to *The Economist*,[8] this is mainly due to the following factors:

- Weak infrastructure drives up the costs of producing and transporting goods;
- Africa's rich natural resources brought about the "Dutch disease", where increased exports of oil and other natural resources tend to drive up exchange rates, making it cheaper to import goods and more costly to produce and export locally; and
- Africa's geography is problematic: manufacturing is moving from China to neighbouring countries such as Bangladesh and Vietnam, instead of "distant" Africa.

These trends will have to be reversed quickly, if Africa is to sustain economic growth, eradicate poverty and create meaningful jobs. According to Amadou Sy, Director and Senior Fellow at the Brookings Institution's Africa Growth Initiative, African countries will need to achieve "quality economic growth" and rely more on "engines of growth such as agriculture and manufacturing, than exports of oil and other commodities".[9] Or, as *The Economist* in its editorial of 16 April 2016 puts it: "Africa's past has long been defined by commodities, but its future rests on the productivity of its people. By 2050 the UN predicts that there will be 2.5 billion Africans – a quarter of the world's population. Given good governance, they will prosper. The alternative is too dire to imagine."[10]

Nonetheless, some African countries are breaking the mould. Ethiopia's manufacturing sector saw average growth of over ten per cent a year for the period 2006–2014. Tanzania and Rwanda are following suit. Again, it is imperative that African countries shift workers into more productive industries if the continent hopes to grow rapidly. Infrastructure and incentives for manufacturing firms need to be set up to harness the wealth of human capital available in Africa.

Industrialisation now a priority

Despite recent high economic growth rates, Africa is not maximising its potential, having failed to translate this into meaningful job creation or the broad-based economic and social development needed to reduce high levels of poverty and inequality. Many institutions such as the African Union and UN Economic Commission for Africa have called on African countries to start transforming their economies through increased value addition in the primary commodity sector, and to invest more in higher productivity employment-generating sectors, with a focus on manufacturing and technologically advanced services.[11] While industry (manufacturing in particular) has traditionally been a source of considerable employment generation in economies, Africa's share of global manufacturing output between 1970 and 2013 fell from three to two per cent, and as a share of sub-Saharan Africa's GDP, manufacturing has shrunk from about 20 per cent to roughly half that. A case in point is South Africa, the continent's most advanced economy, where manufacturing accounts for 13 per cent of GDP, while manufacturing in Thailand contributes 28 per cent of GDP.[12] The obstacles confronting Africa are myriad and complex: the availability of an uninterrupted power supply is a major constraint; as are poor road/railroad infrastructure; major obstacles to trade; red tape; lack of venture capital and access to capital. Add to that corruption at various levels and it is clear that the road to industrialisation will not be easy.[13]

The situation is further aggravated by low labour productivity, which increased by an average of 1.6 per cent during 2000–2011 and by 2.3 per cent in 2012–2013, compared to East Asia's 7.5 per cent. This rate is expected to drop to a cumulative 1.9 per cent during 2014–2016, mainly due to inadequate investment in financial and human capital.[14]

Singapore, which is ranked second on the Global Talent Competitiveness Index (GTCI), views the future growth of human capital as essential for sustaining the country's impressive economic growth into the future.[15] If that is the case for Singapore, a highly developed and competitive economy, it should be even more so for African countries. The focus for Africa – and specifically its governments and policy makers – must therefore be on improving and increasing its human capital and talent stock, in order to move from a commodities-based economy to manufacturing and high-level services aimed at eradicating poverty and improving employment levels.

Human capital and talent

Africa's riches and potential are locked up not only in minerals and commodities, but even more so in the opportunities and challenges that diversity and human capital offer. In fact, it is human capital that makes the difference. Brian Keeley from the Organisation for Economic Cooperation and Development (OECD) indicates: "Economic success crucially relies on human capital – the knowledge, skills, competencies and attributes that allow people to contribute to their personal and social well-being, and that of their countries". Raising human capital refers not only to education and training, but also to the improvement of health levels, community involvement and employment prospects.[16]

Of the 12 pillars which make up the Global Competitiveness Index (GCI) compiled by the World Economic Forum (WEF), four pillars are directly related to human capital, namely health; primary and higher education and training; labour market efficiency and innovation. This indicates clearly that a nation should focus on the consistent development and upgrading of human capital at a national level.[17]

Keeley states that the link between human capital and economic growth is real and significant. This has been confirmed by evidence from the OECD, which shows that if the average time spent in education by a population increases by one year, then economic output per head of population should grow by between four and six per cent in the long run.[18] This is, however, where Africa is at a disadvantage. There is a tremendous lack of high-level skills, despite the vast potential pool of talent that exists on the continent. For example, a major weakness of Africa as a whole is the low level of management-related skills, which lies at the heart of low productivity and service delivery inadequacies. According to Pfeffermann, a lack of management skills and knowledge are the main reasons why aid and investment money disappear, and service programmes fail.[19] In fact, two leading economists of the World Bank, Shantayanan Devarajan and Wolfgang Fengler, state that despite some catch-up over the past decade, countries in sub-Saharan Africa still have the lowest levels of human capital in the world.[20] In taking a closer look at human capital and talent, it is necessary to focus on the living standards of selected African populations, before studying the continent's economically active populations and employment trends, as well as the quality of its talent stock.

Living standards

An analysis of the living standards of a country's population provides a context for the socio-economic circumstances within which the labour pool functions. For the purposes of this chapter, the Human Development Index (HDI), compiled by the United Nations Development Programme (UNDP) is used, as well as some research compiled by Afrobarometer. The HDI is a composite index measuring achievement in the basic dimensions of human development – a long and healthy life, education, and a decent standard of living. Table 1.1 indicates the ranking of specific African countries out of a total of 186.

Table 1.1   Human Development Index for selected African countries[21]

Country	HDI ranking	Average annual HDI growth (1990–2014) as a percentage
South Africa	116	0.29
Ghana	140	1
Zambia	139	1.57
Kenya	145	0.62
Angola	149	1.1*
Rwanda	163	2.89
Nigeria	152	1.06*
Tanzania	151	1.44
Uganda	163	1.89
Mozambique	180	2.74
Botswana	106	0.74
Namibia	126	0.35

Note: * Average annual HDI growth, 2010–2014

Apart from South Africa (ranked 116th) and Botswana (106th), the remaining countries rank in the bottom quarter compared to the rest of the world, despite most countries having improved substantially over the past 20 years. The fact is, the HDIs for African countries are still very low, as can be confirmed by analysing basic poverty factors such as access to medication/medical treatment, clean water for home use, or cash income. Research conducted by Afrobarometer (compiled by researchers from Michigan State University in cooperation with African NGOs and other research institutions) indicates that in most African countries a large percentage of the population goes without basic necessities. About 36 per cent have gone "several times to always" without clean water in Zambia, 33 per cent in Tanzania and 80 per cent in Uganda. With regard to access to medicines/medical treatment, 35 per cent or more have "several times to always" gone without it in Tanzania, 94 per cent in Uganda and 39 per cent in Zambia.[22]

It is therefore clear that the findings of the HDI and Afrobarometer indicate an average to low standard of living in virtually every African nation. Employers should take cognisance of this situation, as these are the circumstances in which the majority of the working population functions. Investing in the social environment through social responsibility programmes is therefore a priority for foreign investors.

Size of the labour market

The economically active population (EAP) in sub-Saharan Africa is large and growing quickly – Tables 1.2 and 1.3 provide examples from selected African nations to confirm this. Over a nine-year period, the EAP growth rates for Tanzania, Kenya and Uganda exceeded 30 per cent, while most other countries remained in the 20 per cent-plus range. Only South Africa, with a growth rate of ten per cent, is substantially lower.[23] (This will change, as the population growth rate is now rapidly increasing after the HIV/Aids tragedy of the 1990s and early 2000s.) The EAP in sub-Saharan African countries is made up of youths and will remain so for several decades to come. This is where the demographic dividend comes in: Africa can offer a large pool of labour, especially for labour-intensive industries and services, at low cost. But herein lies a danger, though: with the world moving quickly towards robotics, automation and artificial intelligence, that demographic dividend can develop into a demographic curse, unless the right policy decisions are not made now. (More about this in the latter part of the chapter.)

Table 1.2   Size of EAP in millions for selected countries[24]

Country	EAP %
Nigeria	55.8
Tanzania	25.3
South Africa	20.0
Kenya	17.5
Uganda	15.1
Mozambique	12.5
Ghana	11.4
Zambia	6.7
Rwanda	5.6

Table 1.3   Growth rates in EAP for selected countries[25]

Country	Growth %	Period
South Africa	10.0	2005–2014
Ghana	16.3	2006–2011
Zambia	25.0	2005–2014
Nigeria	28.0	2005–2014
Sub Sahara	29.0	2005–2014
Tanzania	31.0	2005–2014
Kenya	32.5	2005–2014
Uganda	34.0	2005–2014
Rwanda	19.2	2008–2013
Mozambique	12.6	2008–2013

The biggest bulk of the working population has, of necessity, to find some form of employment in the informal sector (see Table 1.4). Except for South Africa (24%) and Nigeria (54%), in almost all other African countries over 80 per cent of the population is employed in the informal sector, of whom eight in ten work in the agricultural sector. In most cases it is a matter of survival, hence subsistence farming is widely practised.

The informal sector also absorbs the semi- and unemployed population. This scenario is aggravated because virtually no social networks are in place, whereas in South Africa the unemployed can claim unemployment insurance, social grants, etc. The flip-side is that a strong entrepreneurial spirit prevails among these population groups.

Table 1.4   Formal vs. informal employment in selected African countries[26]

Country	Formal sector %	Informal sector %
Ghana	14.0	85.0
Kenya	13.0	86.0
Zambia	17.0	83.0
Tanzania	6.5	93.0
Uganda	15.0	85.0
Nigeria	46.0	54.0
South Africa	76.0	24.0
Mozambique	5.1	94.9

Quality of human capital and talent

The quality of human capital and talent on a macro level is determined by the level of education and schooling, tertiary education, vocational training and obviously the quality of the education system. It is clear from Table 1.5 that, excluding South Africa, the education levels of adult populations in Africa are quite low. Secondary education levels are between ten and 20 per cent of the adult population for most countries, and tertiary well below ten per cent.

Table 1.5   Education levels as percentage of adult population [27]

Country	Secondary %	Tertiary %
Ghana	10	2
Kenya	14	8[2]
Tanzania	19	–
Uganda	5	2
Nigeria[1]	32	12
South Africa	84[3]	5
Mozambique	2	1[2]
Rwanda	11	2

1 Employed
2 Post-secondary and tertiary
3 South Africa – secondary (all grades)

Over the last ten to 20 years the situation has improved rapidly: gross enrolment rates at primary education level have increased substantially to almost 100 per cent in many countries. The opportunity is still there to substantially increase these rates for the secondary and tertiary levels (see Table 1.6).

Table 1.6   Gross enrolment rates for secondary and tertiary education levels[28]

Country	Secondary	Tertiary
South Africa	110.8	19.7
Ghana	67.1	12.2
Kenya	67.0	4.0
Nigeria	43.8	10.4
Tanzania	33.0	3.9
Rwanda	32.6	6.9
Uganda	26.9	4.4
Mozambique	26.0	5.2

The quality of the education system in African countries can still be vastly improved (see Table 1.7). Countries such as Ghana, Uganda, Tanzania, South Africa and Nigeria will have to pay urgent attention to this deficit. Many countries on the continent aspire to reach middle-income status over the next decade and a half, but that will not be achievable with bad and/or deteriorating education systems.

Table 1.7   Quality of education systems – international ranking[29]

Country	Ranking
Zambia	35
Kenya	36
Rwanda	45
Botswana	77
Uganda	81
Namibia	96
Tanzania	98
Mozambique	119
Nigeria	125
South Africa	138

The international ranking of universities in African countries (excluding South Africa) is also low, with the best university of the remaining countries ranking below no. 1 000 in the world. The quality of the education offered by any of the universities ranking below that, is questionable (see Table 1.8).

Table 1.8   University rankings[30]

University	Ranking
University of Cape Town	332
Makerere University	1 215
University of Nairobi	1 698
University of Ghana	1 757
Addis Ababa University	1 976
University of Dar-es-Salaam	2 220
University of Nigeria	3 367

Vocational and managerial training

According to the WEF, the quality of staff training and management schools in Africa is generally better than the quality of the respective education systems (see Tables 1.9 and 1.10). As expected, South Africa ranks far above its counterparts, to place among the best in the world. Countries within the Southern African Development Community (SADC) region are currently streamlining their vocational training to align their accreditation system with that of South Africa. Namibia and Botswana, for example, have progressed substantially with their respective vocational education and training (TVET) systems. Ethiopia follows the German model by staffing its TVETs with German specialist technicians. There are, however, acute shortages of professionals in the healthcare, financial services, engineering, IT and agriculture sectors.

Table 1.9   Quality of management schools[31]

Country	Ranking
South Africa	24
Ghana	48
Kenya	56
Zambia	58
Rwanda	74
Uganda	93
Nigeria	102
Tanzania	123
Mozambique	136

Table 1.10   Quality of staff training[32]

Country	Ranking
South Africa	19
Kenya	46
Rwanda	57
Nigeria	62
Ghana	64
Zambia	72
Uganda	107
Tanzania	116
Mozambique	125

Some of the reasons for the low quality of the education systems can be found in the rapid growth in total student numbers from primary to tertiary level, which has caused major backlogs in infrastructure and resource provision to schools. In addition, growing and developing high-quality, experienced teachers and other educational personnel takes time. The fact that, for example, teachers are badly paid (sometimes not at all), have access to few resources and are overwhelmed by large classes, aggravates the situation.

The output at university level is totally skewed towards the social and behavioural sciences, with very few students following engineering, medical and other scientific routes. The number of postgraduate students is also low.[33] As a result, productivity levels in African countries, as measured by output per worker, have been very low since 1990 (see Table 1.11). The same applies to growth rates in human capital stock: output per worker increased by only 1.66 per cent per annum for Africa as a whole in the 2000s. Central and Western Africa posted rates below one per cent. Growth rates in human capital stock were below one per cent for the continent as a whole during the 2000s, with North and West Africa being slightly above average with 1.1 per cent growth.

Table 1.11   Average growth rates of output per worker, capital stock per worker and human capital by subregion and decade[34]

Subregion	Growth of	1990s %	2000s %
East	Output per worker	0.4	3.0
	Capital per worker	1.4	4.2
	Human capital	1.0	1.0
Central	Output per worker	-3.4	0.4
	Capital per worker	0.3	1.8
	Human capital	0.9	0.6
South	Output per worker	0.7	1.7
	Capital per worker	3.7	2.8
	Human capital	0.9	0.8

➡

Subregion	Growth of	1990s %	2000s %
West	Output per worker	-1.7	0.9
	Capital per worker	3.3	0.3
	Human capital	0.9	1.1
North	Output per worker	1.5	2.5
	Capital per worker	6.6	4.8
	Human capital	1.3	1.1
Africa (All)	Output per worker	-0.4	1.6
	Capital per worker	3.3	2.4
	Human capital	1	0.9

The GTCI[35]

Insead, the Adeco group and the Human Capital Leadership Institute compile an annual GTCI. South Africa is currently the highest-placed African nation on the index, ranking 57th out of 109 countries (see Table 1.12). Despite that, South Africa still ranks below Malaysia, China and the Philippines. Of note are Botswana (65th), Tunisia (73rd), Namibia (74th) and Kenya (86th). In analysing the low ranking of various African nations it is clear that, to modernise African economies, policy makers and employers need to do far more to improve the talent stock. This is confirmed by the "messages" which can be derived from the 2015–2016 findings (see Table 1.12).

Table 1.12   The GTCI 2015–2016 for selected countries[36]

Country	Rank	Overall score
Switzerland	1	72 648
Singapore	2	71 456
Luxembourg	3	68 978
United States	4	67 902
Denmark	5	67 865
Malaysia	30	54 039
China	48	46 600
Philippines	56	44 229
South Africa	57	43 726
Botswana	68	41 041
Namibia	79	38 092
Kenya	86	36 190
Rwanda	87	36 098

➡

11

Country	Rank	Overall score
Morocco	93	33 227
Senegal	99	31 097
Uganda	101	29 848
Ghana	102	29 698
Mali	105	27 212
Tanzania	106	26 623
Ethiopia	107	26 608
Madagascar	109	22 726

Source: The Global Talent Competitiveness Index 2015–16

Compiling the GTCI[37]

The GTCI is a composite index which relies on a simple yet robust input-output model composed of six pillars (four on the input side, two on the output side).

1. **The talent competitiveness input subindex**
   Composed of four pillars, it describes the policies, resources and efforts that a particular country can harness to foster its talent competitiveness. **Enable** (pillar 1) reflects the extent to which the regulatory, market and business environments create a favourable climate for talent to develop and thrive. The other three pillars describe the levers of talent competitiveness, which focus respectively on what countries are doing to **Attract** (pillar 2), **Grow** (pillar 3) and **Retain** (pillar 4) talent.

2. **The talent competitiveness output subindex**
   It aims to describe and measure the quality of talent in a country that results from the above policies, resources and efforts. Composed of two pillars, it describes the current situation of a particular country in terms of **Labour and Vocational** (pillar 5) and **Global Knowledge** (pillar 6) skills.

The main findings of the GTCI 2015–2016, with relevance to Africa

The GTGI for 2015–2016 had eight main messages, based on the findings.[38]

Message 1

Mobility is a key ingredient of talent development. The new context of talent mobility leads to a different paradigm, i.e., from brain drain and brain gain to "brain circulation". The benefit of internationally mobile people for both countries plays out in remittances, diaspora investments, the acquisition of know-how and experience via networks and the innovations and entrepreneurship qualities acquired through mobility by successful returnees.

Message 2

The migration debate needs to move from emotions to solutions. History can help here, as it shows how much benefit has been generated from the circulation of talent across borders. With growing inequalities, one tension that requires attention is that between mobility for the privileged and lack of opportunity for those lower on the social pyramid. Those who are not part of the talent pool or creative class may not be willing to support the immigration of highly skilled professionals and students, despite the clear rationale, unless their own children have the opportunity to get ahead, regardless of socio-economic background.

Message 3

Management practices make a difference in attracting talent. One important difference is the quality of management practices, which is a function of whether (or not) management is professional and attributes positions on merit rather than kinship/friendships, and the attention paid to employee development.

Message 4

While people continue to move to new jobs and opportunities, jobs are moving to where the talent is. Corporations are beginning to move strategically important product development and research and development (R&D) activities to countries that employ quality talent at low cost. This is facilitated by efficient international communications and the diffusion of technology. China, South Korea, the Philippines, Slovenia, Turkey and Vietnam in particular are benefiting from this trend, while Africa is largely excluded, for the time being.

Message 5

New talent magnets are emerging: apart from the US, Switzerland and Singapore, talent is increasingly being drawn to countries such as Chile, South Korea, Rwanda and Azerbaijan.

Message 6

Low-skilled workers will continue to be replaced by robots, while knowledge workers will be displaced by algorithms. As technological innovations increase the number and array of activities and professions that can be automated, they will affect knowledge workers as much as technicians and manual workers. With new business models being introduced, some employees may work virtually, from home, for different employers, while others will have to retrain or move far away to secure jobs.

Message 7

In a world of talent circulation, cities and regions are becoming critical players in the competition for global talent. Talent continues to be attracted by the usual enablers:

1. High-quality infrastructure;
2. Competitive market conditions and business environment;
3. An existing critical mass of talent with excellent networks and cooperation possibilities; and
4. Superior living conditions.

Cities are using increasingly adaptive and proactive strategies to attract global talent, and can differentiate and brand themselves through local capabilities.

Message 8

Scarce vocational skills continue to handicap emerging countries – even those which have invested in higher education have neglected this training band, including BRICS countries such as China, India and South Africa.

Implications and recommendations

1. Fast-growing labour pools in African countries need to be absorbed in productive jobs, preferably in the formal sectors of the economy;

2. The potential for growth in the mining and extraction sectors is limited, especially given current and foreseeable international demand. Industrialisation, and specifically the commercialisation of the agricultural sector, therefore seems to be the best way forward. Apart from the high-level human capital required, governments will also have to improve infrastructure, eliminate trade barriers, free up economies by reducing red tape, and curb corruption in order to enable industrialisation.

3. To improve the quality of human capital and talent, the quality of education systems must be addressed through appointing better-qualified teachers in greater numbers, improved facilities and resources, and greater emphasis on the vocational and technical streams.

4. Tertiary education needs urgent attention. The growth in student volumes is placing tremendous pressure on existing infrastructure. Again, more and better-qualified academic personnel are required. More students should be encouraged into the science, technology engineering and mathematics (STEM) disciplines.

    Upgrading the infrastructure and providing better-qualified personnel will take a decade or two. Time is, however, of the essence. In the meantime, technology can be used to team up with top-class universities and other academic institutions to offer high-quality tuition to students across Africa. Universities can also collaborate more closely with their overseas counterparts, to conduct research and offer specialised academic programmes.

5. Talent mobility should be encouraged. Opportunities and incentives should be increased to encourage members of the diaspora to return, invest and work in Africa. Restrictions on expatriates with specialised skills should be relaxed, as they constrain economic growth. Obviously, programmes should be in place to transfer knowledge and skills to locals in such cases.

6. There should be greater focus on vocational and technical skills. Too many secondary and tertiary students follow the "soft" social science route. The quality of vocational and technical skills training must be improved as well. Again, collaboration with the best in the world, for instance the German, South Korean and French technical and vocational training systems and content, could be considered and modified to suit local needs.

7. The gap between the world of work and educational institutions should be addressed. Too many resources go to waste through outdated and irrelevant training and education methods and curricula. The gender gap also needs to be closed as a matter of urgency.

8. The continent has an acute shortage of managers and professionals. This shortage can be addressed through better collaboration with top-notch business schools on the continent and abroad. Employers should also invest more in training a greater number of managers and specialists. More specialised skills in the mining and agriculture sectors could improve productivity and competitiveness, and in so doing create more job and development opportunities for employees.

9. Various development agencies, think tanks, policy advisors and government departments and officials talk glibly about the need for a higher quality of human capital, if the continent is to progress up the value chain of economic development. The reality is that it is a very difficult process which will take a generation or two and will require substantial investment. Various economic development plans already outline the road(s) to economic growth, but they totally underestimate the level of management and specialised skill required to make it happen. A better understanding of this reality will help us formulate more realistic policy decisions and implementations, however urgent they may be.

10. The elephant in the room, which receives little attention from government policy makers, investors in Africa and employers, is the impact that the Fourth Industrial Revolution or Second Machine Age will have on plans for industrialisation, job creation and poverty eradication. Robotics and artificial intelligence are not science fiction anymore, but are very real.

The Boston Consulting Group predicts that the price of industrial robots and their enabling software will drop by 20 per cent over the next decade, as their performance improves by five per cent each year. The percentage of tasks handled by such machines will rise from the current eight per cent to 26 per cent by the end of the decade. Even China has joined in the race:[39] China's manufacturing sector is turning to automation in a government-backed, robot-driven industrial revolution on a vast scale. Chinese manufacturers bought 66 000 of the 240 000 industrial robots sold globally. The impact on developing economies will be severe; as *The Financial Times* puts it:

> Developing countries from India to Indonesia and Egypt to Ethiopia have long hoped to follow the example of China and Japan, South Korea and Taiwan before them: stimulating job creation and economic growth by moving agricultural workers into low-cost factories to make goods for export. Yet the rise of automation means that industrialisation is likely to generate significantly fewer jobs for the next generation of emerging economies.[40]

Today's low-income countries will therefore not have the same possibility of achieving rapid growth by shifting workers from farms to higher-paying factory jobs. It is now a race against the machines, with these countries likely struggling to create sufficient manufacturing jobs before they are wiped out by the gathering robot army of China and its cohorts.[41]

The Financial Times quotes Tom Lembong, Indonesia's Trade Minister, as stating: "Many people don't realise we're seeing a quantum leap in robotics. It's a huge concern and we need to acknowledge the looming threat of this new industrial revolution. But as political and business elite, we're still stuck on debates about industrialisation that were settled in the twentieth and even nineteenth centuries."[42]

The reality for Africa is similar. Governments, employers and trade unions will have to address the new reality of the Fourth Industrial Revolution as a matter of extreme urgency!

Conclusion

Africa's development priorities in terms of talent and otherwise are numerous and significant. Herein lies a tremendous opportunity for entrepreneurs, investors, innovators and businesses to contribute and make a difference. In concluding, a few focus areas are highlighted, despite the list not being exhaustive.

1. Multinational corporations investing in Africa should embrace a development psyche/attitude. The colonial mindset of extracting and exploiting resources before exiting, belongs to the bad old days. It is now all about developing the country and especially its people. Multinational corporates can play a significant role in uplifting skills levels and reducing poverty through social responsibility programmes. What is even more important is that they utilise their expertise, innovative skills and resources to create a better world for the inhabitants of the continent.
2. Companies in African countries that implement strategies and policies to enhance industrialisation will experience heightened competition for high-level talent and specialised skills. These employers will therefore have to invest far more in talent development through learning and development initiatives, bursary schemes, and technical and vocational training.
3. As part of the industrialisation initiatives, governments and specifically policy makers need to take serious cognisance of the arrival and impact of the Fourth Industrial Revolution. This is not science fiction anymore, but a present-day reality. Among the questions to be answered are: How will this revolution impact the country's drive towards industrialisation? Is it still a viable option, given the advent of 3-D printing and robotics? How will it impact job creation? Are African education systems geared to provide the skills and knowledge required to create opportunities in a "new", digitised world?
4. Corruption, bribery, corporate theft and a disregard for ethical conduct in some organisations must be eliminated. Corporations (especially multinationals) can provide leadership in this regard. Instilling good corporate ethics and values, living them, and educating employees on the moral and

tangible benefits thereof could instigate a turning point in many countries. The present situation in countries such as Nigeria and even South Africa, to an extent, inhibits economic growth and stifles the development of their citizens.

5.   Employers in both the private and public sector should invest disproportionately in the development of leadership and management skills, where the multiplier effect will be tremendous: service delivery and productivity will increase, and in so doing will improve the overall competitiveness of companies and countries as a whole. That will, in turn, draw more investment and create jobs, improve standards of living and provide the energy and momentum to establish a positive loop.

Endnotes

1   KR Research, 'Human Capital and Labour Research Portal', n.d., retrieved 6 May 2016, <http://www. hcresearchportal.com/>.
2   *The Economist*, 'Making Africa work', 16 April 2016, p. 7.
3   Ibid.
4   KR Research, op. cit.
5   'Making Africa work', op. cit.
6   T Altenburg & E Melia, *Kick-starting industrial transformation in sub-Saharan Africa*, International Labour Organisation, Geneva, 2014.
7   'Making Africa work', op. cit.
8   *The Economist*, 'More a marathon than a sprint', 7 November 2015, pp. 35–36.
9   CN Chonghaile, 'Commodities on a slippery slope', *Mail & Guardian*, 15–17 January 2016, p. 17.
10   'Making Africa work', op. cit.
11   United Nations Economic Commission for Africa, *Economic report on Africa*, Dynamic Industrial Policy in Africa, Addis Ababa, Ethiopia, 2014, p. 29.
12   *The Economist*, 'Not making it', 16 April 2016, p. 9.
13   Ibid.
14   United Nations Economic Commission for Africa, loc. cit.
15   CIPD and Human Capital Leadership Institute, *The future of talent in Singapore 2030*, Chartered Institute of Personnel and Development, London, March 2016, p. 4.
16   B Keeley, *Human capital: How what you know shapes your life*, OECD Publishing, Paris, 2007, p. 97, retrieved 5 May 2016, <http://images2.ehaus2.co.uk/oecd/pdfs/free/0107101e.pdf>.
17   KR Research, op. cit.
18   Keeley, op. cit., p. 34.
19   KR Research, op. cit.
20   Ibid.
21   United Nations Development Programme (UNPD), *Human development report 2014: Sustaining human progress – reducing vulnerabilities and building resilience*, 18 November 2014, retrieved 5 May 2016, <http://hdr.undp.org/en/human-development-report-2014>.
22   KR Research, op. cit.
23   Ibid.
24   Ibid.
25   Ibid.
26   Ibid.
27   Ibid.
28   Ibid.
29   Ibid.
30   Ibid.
31   Ibid.
32   Ibid.
33   Ibid.
34   United Nations Economic Commission for Africa, op. cit, p. 32.
35   Insead: Adecco Group, *The global talent competitive index 2015-2016*, Human Capital Leadership Institute, Singapore, 2015, pp. 32, 36–37, 38–41.
36   Ibid.
37   Ibid, p. 32.
38   Ibid, pp. 36–37.

39   B Bland, 'March of machines', *Financial Times*, 1 May 2016, pp. 1, 18.
40   Ibid.
41   Ibid.
42   Ibid.

References

Altenburg, T & E Melia, *Kick-starting industrial transformation in sub-Saharan Africa*, International Labour Organisation, Geneva, 2014.

Bland, B, 'March of machines', *Financial Times*, 1 May 2016, pp. 1, 18.

Chonghaile, CN, 'Commodities on a slippery slope', *Mail & Guardian*, 15–17 January 2016, p. 17.

CIPD and Human Capital Leadership Institute, *The future of talent in Singapore 2030*, 15–17 January 2016, p. 4, retrieved 6 May 2016, <http://www.cipd.asia/media/The-Future-of-Talent-in-Singapore-report_tcm1038-6888.pdf>.

Insead: Adecco Group, *The global talent competitive index 2015-2016*, Human Capital Leadership Institute, Singapore, 2015, pp. 32, 36–37, 38–41.

Keeley, B, *Human capital: How what you know shapes your life*, OECD Publishing, Paris, 2007, p. 97, retrieved 5 May 2016, <http://images2.ehaus2.co.uk/oecd/pdfs/free/0107101e.pdf>.

KR Research, 'Human Capital and Labour Research Portal', n.d., retrieved 6 May 2016, <http://www.hcresearchportal.com/>.

The Economist, 'More a marathon than a sprint', 7 November 2015, pp. 35–36.

The Economist, 'Making Africa work', 16 April 2016, p. 7.

The Economist, 'Not making it', 16 April 2016, p. 9.

United Nations Development Programme, *Human development report 2014: Sustaining human progress – reducing vulnerabilities and building resilience*, 2014, retrieved 18 November 2014, <http://hdr.undp.org/en/human-development-report-2014>.

43   United Nations Economic Commission for Africa, *Economic report on Africa*, Dynamic Industrial Policy in Africa, Addis Ababa, Ethiopia, 2014, p. 29.

Additional reading

UNAIDS, 'AIDSinfo, 2014', retrieved 20 November 2014, <http://www.unaids.org/en/dataanalysis/datatools/aidsinfo>.

UNAIDS, 'HIV and AIDS estimates, 2014', retrieved 20 November 2014, <http://www.unaids.org/en/regionscountries/countries/southafrica/>.

United Nations Development Programme (UNDP), 'Multidimensional poverty index, 2014', retrieved 19 November 2014, <http://hdr.undp.org/en/content/multidimen-sional-poverty-index-mpi>.

United Nations Educational, Scientific and Cultural Organisation (Unesco) World Heritage Convention, South Africa, 2014, retrieved 30 March 2014, <http://whc.unesco.org/en/statesparties/za/>.

PART 1

CHAPTER 2

TALENT FRAMEWORK AND ISSUES IN TALENT MANAGEMENT
Terry Meyer

The purpose of this chapter is to provide an overarching framework for talent management by setting the context for many of the chapters in this book. In addition to providing a broad framework, it discusses a number of key issues in talent management.

I have facilitated several courses in talent management, both for HR professionals and for leaders of organisations up to Exco level. Most participants understand or are grappling with specific issues within the talent strategy; many require a high-level framework to make sense of not only these, but also the processes they are required to deal with.

It has been my privilege to engage with a number of leading global organisations in the US, Europe and Africa. In almost all instances, the differentiating factor that enables them to attract, engage and retain top talent is the quality and commitment of top leadership. Leaders in these organisations realise that appointing top talent is a fundamental requirement for the execution of strategy and ensuring organisational competitiveness.

This chapter sets out a framework that HR practitioners and leaders can apply to ensure that effective policies and processes are implemented in a holistic manner in their organisations. It therefore acts as a high-level "blueprint" for a comprehensive talent strategy.

I was also privileged to facilitate a workshop for a large company with operations throughout Africa as part of a business school programme. It soon became evident that the HRD manager had composed a particularly well-conceived talent management policy for the organisation, and he kindly allowed me to use this as an illustration of what a comprehensive policy entails – on condition of anonymity. Having worked with many organisations to facilitate the creation of a talent policy, this is certainly one of the most thorough outlines I have seen, and it is closely aligned with the framework used in this chapter.

The aim here is to set out the context for the book as a whole. Therefore, the chapter is written in a manner that is practical and easily understandable, without extensive jargon. The thinking behind the chapter is nevertheless based on substantive theoretical rigor.

Introduction

In this chapter I provide a comprehensive framework for talent management that is relevant to almost all organisations and which has, to some degree, informed the structure of this book. This framework will be similar to those used by organisations with sophisticated HR systems. There are, however, many organisations that do not have such advanced processes and policies in place, and in many instances these processes and policies are not always applied effectively. The aim is to make this framework comprehensive yet simple, so that it can be applied in organisations of any size or level of sophistication.

I subsequently address several key issues involved in designing and implementing a talent management strategy for an organisation. In my view, talent management – like leadership – is both an art and a science. In too many organisations the established talent processes are institutionalised, to the point where they have become mechanical "tick box" exercises.

A talent management framework

When designing a talent strategy, it is important to use a framework that offers a coherent picture of the various talent processes and interventions. The following is the framework I use with clients when the aim is to ensure the alignment of all aspects of the talent strategy and processes.

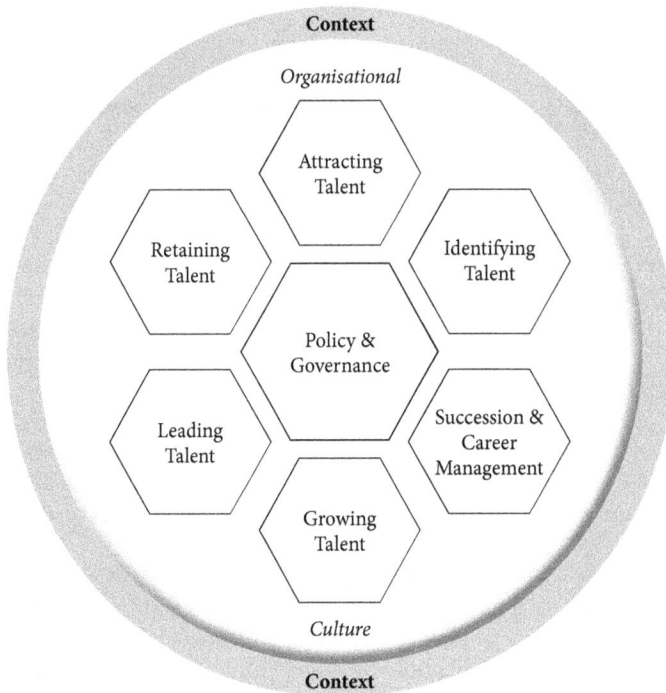

Context

Organisational

Attracting Talent

Retaining Talent

Identifying Talent

Policy & Governance

Leading Talent

Succession & Career Management

Growing Talent

Culture

Context

Figure 2.1   A comprehensive talent framework

It is prudent to investigate each element of the framework.

Context

Clearly, for an effective talent strategy it is important to evaluate the context or external environment in which the organisation operates. Information that needs to be collected and analysed includes details of the labour market dynamics in the industry or particular skills grouping (e.g., supply and demand of nurses or engineers), within a particular geographical location or within specific age profiles, etc.

In some cases it is not enough to merely analyse the local labour market: many occupations are governed by a global labour market, as is the case with engineers and accountants. They are a global "commodity" and will generally work where the remuneration offered and quality of life meet their needs.

It is vital to indentify and interpret a number of other factors that will impact the attraction and retention of talent, including the social and political context of the country involved, the demand for local skills, the cost of living and safety issues.

Such an analysis must be relevant to the needs of the organisation, in addition to being comprehensive. This is, in effect, a risk analysis of the external factors influencing the availability of talent.

Culture

It is often said that organisations hire for competence, then fire people for lack of cultural fit. It is imperative that an organisation articulate its culture and that future talent be recruited in line with that culture. Organisations have an "immune system" that, over time, "ejects" individuals who do not integrate into the culture. That is why some South African organisations, in particular, spend so much time and effort ensuring that prospective employees will thrive in their (often highly performance-focused) culture, and that the culture will be perpetuated. These organisations view their culture as a significant asset to be protected. Rand Merchant Bank[1] and Discovery Health[2] are two South African firms that place great emphasis on their culture, as it shapes their talent strategy.

Occasionally, the talent strategy may require the organisation to change its culture to increase the likelihood that a potential talent will "fit in", for instance, a male-dominated organisation that wishes to attract more female talent. In this case an intervention to create a climate in which women are effectively integrated would need to be undertaken to ensure equality and inclusivity in the workplace. Similarly, an organisation with a history as a public sector culture, that wishes to become more effective and competitive, will need to hire people (possibly from the private sector) to create a new culture in line with the organisation's strategy. A number of state-owned enterprises (SOEs) in Africa currently face this challenge. In their case, talent selection will become a vehicle for cultural transformation.

Policy and planning

As is the case with any system, a talent policy must be developed to ensure consistency and outline clearly the principles governing the talent management process and strategy. Note that a talent strategy may change over time as dynamics change, but a well-written policy should remain fairly constant in terms of the principles involved.

There are a number of questions that a *talent policy* should address, for example:

- What does the organisation mean by "talent"? Does it include everyone, or is it restricted to those few individuals who will take the organisation into the future?
- How will talent be assessed to determine potential? Will psychometric assessments be used and in what way will the information influence appointments?
- Which structures and processes will govern the system (see below)?
- What are the roles of the different role players in the system?
- What principles will be applied in establishing career paths and planning the career development of individuals?

An example of a well-written talent policy is attached as an appendix to this chapter.

Key to formulating a *talent strategy* is an understanding of the current state of talent in the organisation. Increasingly, in sophisticated organisations data analytics provide important details about the extent and nature of the current workforce. More and more, such analytics are being driven by a new generation of software that enables broad analysis, as well as deep cutting to understand the specifics of the state of talent at that moment in time.

Such analytics can provide both current and predictive information on, amongst many other things,

- skill levels;
- demographic profiles;
- psychographics;
- talent attractors;
- skill and succession gaps;
- performance profiles;
- engagement levels;
- stress levels and health information; and
- why employees stay or leave.

According to Bersin's 2016 predictions[3] the emergence of new generations of technology with new real-time analytical capabilities will transform HR in general, and talent management in particular. These and many other issues will need to be addressed in a comprehensive talent policy and strategy.

Governance

As in any large organisational system, talent management requires effective governance. This is especially true because much of the information that it deals with, is highly confidential and frequently sensitive in nature.

Most organisations have talent panels/boards that oversee the talent process. Depending on the size of the organisation, there may be an executive talent panel and various divisional panels or, in the case of smaller organisations, a single panel for the entire company. These panels are made up of the relevant senior managers/executives, including the CEO, and their role is generally to

- determine the future talent and skills needs of the organisation/division, based on the future strategy;
- identify talent and skills gaps/risk in the organisation and take appropriate action;
- identify high-potential staff who are considered future leaders or specialists and ensure that they are included in succession plans;
- facilitate the compilation of succession plans and approve them;
- ensure that succession plans consider staff outside divisional or functional silos;
- ensure that the identified talent compile comprehensive development plans and that these are executed;
- track the progress of identified talent in the organisation; and
- deal with any other talent issues that require policy decisions.

Roles

The talent system involves numerous role players, each of whom needs to play his/her part to make the system work. Like any system, if one role player does not properly fulfil his/her role, the system becomes less effective. Key role players include

- **the CEO and Exco**: In my experience in engaging with top global organisations, these role players are indispensable to a talent strategy. They need to recognise that the talent, skills and leadership capability of the organisation are prerequisites for executing the strategy. This cannot be outsourced to HR, thus providing outstanding leadership is a key responsibility of executives. Remember: *HR processes and systems will never compensate for a lack of leadership*;
- **Line managers**: It is said that talented people leave managers, not necessarily the organisation. They usually exit the organisation in one of two ways: either by departing from the organisation, or staying and remaining disengaged. The role of line managers is to fulfil their leadership obligations and ensure the effective engagement of skilled people;

- **HR:** Different silos in HR have different roles, but overall they need to establish the systems, processes and technology necessary to reinforce the talent strategy. They have a key role to play in advising line managers and executives on ways to attract, engage and retain talent. In this regard, the application and interpretation of analytics is a key HR function;
- **Employees:** Employees play a vital role in driving their own careers, in ensuring that they continuously develop themselves, and in taking advantage of the opportunities their organisations offer.

Attracting talent

Attracting the right talent requires an organisation to build an employer value proposition (EVP). This aspect, which differentiates an organisation from its competitors in the talent market, is often linked to the corporate brand. Organisations that are considered best companies to work for by skilled people or graduates have a compelling EVP.

In a diverse workforce, however, a single EVP may not suffice, as most organisations have between three and four generations of employee working for them. As in the case of a customer base, different employee populations will have different psychographics which must be considered when attempting to attract and retain skilled staff.

It goes without saying that organisations need to be visible to attract prospective talent. The emergence of social media has significantly changed the talent attraction landscape. Prospective employees have access to huge amounts of information about companies in the marketplace, and they invariably access this data when making career choices. On the flip side, reputational damage can instantly go viral.

The development of an EVP is expanded on in the chapter "Developing a Compelling Employer Value Proposition to Attract Africa's Talent".

Identifying talent

It is easy to assess performance; it is less easy to assess potential. There are many ways of assessing potential, yet the more information that can be gleaned about an individual, from a variety of sources which provide a consistent "story", the greater the confidence one can have in any judgement made about someone's potential.

Psychometric assessments, in conjunction with track record and management assessments – if they are consistent – can thus offer some degree of confidence in judging an employee's potential. Of course, where this information is not consistent, further fact finding is necessary.

It is important to identify potential in terms of people's strengths. Effective assessment provides information about the kind of role an individual is best suited to assume, and placements should be made accordingly. An example would be determining whether a candidate is better suited to a management or a specialist role.

It must be emphasised that the consequences of ill-conceived appointments can be catastrophic to the individual, the organisation and co-workers. Decisions about appointments should therefore not be taken lightly.

The issue of assessment of potential is explored in greater detail in the chapter "From Potential to Performance: Assessing Talent and Leadership Potential".

Succession and career management

Succession is at the heart of talent deployment. The selection of successors is based on assessments of potential, and informs employees' development plans. It also is central to talent and skills risk analyses. In my view, succession is often treated as a mechanical exercise in organisations. This presents a significant challenge, and should be avoided at all costs.

When I run strategy or top talent/succession workshops, I spend time discussing the future challenges facing the organisation. This includes the growth strategy, the impact of market or digital disruption on the design of the organisation, diversity and a number of other factors that will shape their world in days to come. I end off with these questions:

• What will your leadership team(s) need to look like five years from now? and
• Where are they now?

This is the level at which a discussion with Exco finally gains traction and focuses their attention. The people who make the organisation successful today may not be the ones who will lead it into the future.

The next question concerns the identification of a replacement for the CEO or an Exco member. This may be an uncomfortable discussion to have. All too often, HR provides a checklist of competencies against which potential candidates are evaluated. This is the stuff of nightmares!

It has to be emphasised that the gap between being a CFO and a CEO is enormous. The same chasm exists between the roles of Chief Accountant and CFO, for example.

Deep discussions need to be held to ensure that the requirements of the role of, say, the CEO of the future are clearly understood in terms of the envisaged strategy and environment of the business. This, in itself, gives rise to crucial discourse on the role of the CEO in the organisation. It forces the organisation to ask whether that role should be primarily externally facing, with a focus on strategy – in which case the position of a COO, who runs the business operationally, may be needed.

It is unacceptable to look at a single Exco position in isolation. It would be better to look at the team and ensure that the required strengths and mental models are present in the collective. If diversity is an issue, then the diversity reflected in the team as a whole is a factor that must be considered in appointments. Issues such as political and government networks, localisation pressures and the ability to lead people from a variety of cultures may well affect organisational effectiveness, particularly in developing economies such as those in Africa.

A final important point is that at this level the structure and roles of Exco should take into account the strengths and motivations of individuals. Traditional HR practice assumes that structures and roles are predetermined, and that individuals should be appointed to fit into the boxes created by the structure. I have a contrary view, namely that it is better to build jobs around talented people, to enable them to apply their strengths, than it is to try to fit them into such boxes. This applies at levels where discretion is a major feature of a role, and is a significant way to develop and retain talent. Let them do what excites them! The proviso is that within the team or larger collective, the necessary skills and roles must be accommodated.

Once potential executives have been identified, they must be properly developed. This includes potential job rotation, international exposure and, importantly, the opportunity to build an extensive general business network rather than a narrow, professional one.

Developing talent

Too often high-potential talent is identified and a development plan is drawn up, only to discover the following year that no progress has been made and allowing the same plan to roll over to the next year.

High-potential talent move at an accelerated pace, therefore their skills development needs to keep abreast if they are to be sufficiently prepared for their future roles. Key to developing talent is to ensure that personal development plans offer a variety of learning experiences, ranging from course attendance to experiential learning. A key trend is to focus on experiential learning, which entails employees being given stretch assignments, with the necessary support, to build their abilities in environments outside their comfort zones. It does not mean giving them a role in which they have to keep the seat warm. They need to be given a mandate to drive change and must be evaluated on their ability to do just that.

In global organisations, high-potential talent is sent to different parts of the world to gain experience in different cultures and in places far outside of their comfort zone. This builds resilience and adaptability, amongst other critical leadership skills. At a 2013 Insead presentation, a professor explained that neuroscience has shown that learning through adversity actually creates changes in the brain. Organisations that do not have access to international postings can create opportunities to challenge leaders and stretch them in situations that will take them out of their comfort zones. Whilst it is important to create challenges, there is an equal need to provide support and opportunity for reflecting on experiences. As a result, coaching is increasingly used as a development process in which trained coaches "hold up a mirror" to reflect behaviour and assist learners in gaining personal insight into their actions and the consequences of those actions. This is discussed in detail in the chapter "Coaching for Leadership Impact".

Leading talent

For talented people to grow and be effective, they need strong leadership. Leadership development in an organisation has a symbiotic relationship to talent management. In all the top firms I have engaged with globally, and in Africa, the distinguishing factor has been the quality of the leadership at all levels of the organisation. This not only refers to individual leadership effectiveness (although that is important), it also pertains to the building of a *leadership culture* in an organisation that creates chemistry and an environment in which talented people can excel.

No matter how good the HR talent processes and practices are, they will never replace high-quality leadership. It follows that for a talent strategy to be effective, the building of individual and organisational leadership is imperative. This is expanded upon in the chapter "Growing Leaders for a Connected World".

Retaining talent

If all of the above factors are in place, the likelihood of retaining top talent is great. Paradoxically, the organisations that lose much of their talent are those that invest most heavily in leadership and talent development.

Successful firms recognise that by having a pipeline of top talent passing through the organisation they can access the best talent available, and when individuals leave they have a full replacement pipeline in place. They keep in touch with talent that has left – people who are normally ambassadors for the company – and if they need them back after a period, there is a good likelihood that they will return and bring with them all the experience they have gained in the interim.

There are, of course, a number of financial incentives aimed at retaining people, but that topic is beyond the scope of this chapter.

Key issues in talent management

Whilst the above framework is generally followed by sophisticated organisations in Africa and around the world, many are not yet at a stage where they have adopted a holistic talent framework. Even in sophisticated organisations, a number of issues concerning talent management may arise, that warrant further discussion.

Shift from individual performance to organisational capability and effectiveness

In my experience, key issues on which talent managers focus are the sourcing, deployment and development of individual talent. Yet, if one looks at talent through a strategy rather than an HR lens, it becomes clear that the end result of talent management should be a combination of organisational capability and individual effectiveness.

While it is quite true that an organisation does require top talent, this in itself seldom represents a competitive advantage. Merely having talented individuals in a team does not necessarily result in that team winning the game. What talent managers and organisational leaders need to concern themselves with, in addition to individual talent attraction and development, is creating chemistry which allows talented people to perform effectively and in such a way that the performance of the whole is greater than the sum of its parts.

We all know that a group of highly skilled and competent people, when constituted as a team, can either be extremely effective or supremely toxic. This chemistry is the result of the culture of the organisation.

Simply attracting and developing great talent does not necessarily mean that the organisation as a whole will be effective. Yet this is the end game of all these activities – the effectiveness of the organisation as a whole, so that it can win in whatever strategic context it competes.

Furthermore, human capital (talent) can be bought, but at a price. Much as technology is acquired in any modern business environment, so skills can be bought locally or globally. What cannot be bought or copied, however, is the *organisational capital* that is the chemistry and culture of any effective company. This is clearly demonstrated in all the corporate case studies included in this book.

This argument suggests strongly that *talent managers need to consider their role as extending well beyond the acquisition and development of individual talent.* It has to incorporate the entire arena of organisational effectiveness, of which traditional talent management is but one component. It is true that many organisations have an organisational development (OD) function to deal with issues of culture. If this is the case, then talent management should report within the OD function to ensure that there is an integrated strategy for building organisational capability and guaranteeing organisational effectiveness. In fact, there is an argument to be made for the entire function to resort under the strategy function, as organisational effectiveness is the basis for strategy execution.

Talent management, as part of leadership, is both a science and an art

The science of talent management is fairly self-evident; it comprises those processes and systems (described above) which are largely run by HR. The art of talent management, like leadership, is derived from the realms of intuition and wisdom. It is a subject requiring deep thought and insight. It certainly has no place for the "tick box" approach that one finds in many organisations today, fuelled as it is by technology and short-term thinking.

At senior levels in particular, deep thought needs to be given to the future challenges facing the organisation, as well as the composition of the leadership team(s) of which the future "talent" will form part. The importance of future challenges is based on the assumption that the type of leader who made the organisation a success in the past, is not necessarily the same type who will take it to new levels with a different strategy in a different world. The future challenges – and consequent capability – of future leaders require considerable reflection and a significant degree of objectivity from everyone involved.

As indicated earlier, people do not function in isolation. They are part of a "team" and it is often the team that should be the subject of scrutiny, rather than individuals. Senior teams require a strong balancing process to ensure that they have the collective ability required to face the future with confidence. This balancing act may be dependent on, amongst others, the cultural, gender, racial, age, nationality, discipline and experience mix of the team, to name but a few. By only focusing on individuals rather than the collective, these factors are excluded from effective decision making. Understanding this and the implications for an organisation is where wisdom plays a vital role.

I have served on far too many talent panels where the conversation was superficial and resulted in checking competency "tick boxes", rather than facilitating deep dialogue about important matters. It must be recognised that talent management (including succession planning) is a highly political process in most organisations where *there are competing factions and even competing ideologies about the future;* often it is simply related to how different players see the world. It is in these arenas that the *art* of leadership plays a significant role.

Talent management as a transformational process

Effective leaders who serve on the executive or on boards will understand that top leadership appointments may be part of a significant transformational agenda to reinvent the organisation. *When strategy changes, the appointment of the right people to drive the new strategy is essential.*

In my experience, the following are some of the transformational strategies that organisations on the continent are implementing at present:

* A shift from being a local player to becoming a pan-African or global player;
* A move from an operational focus to becoming highly customer focused;
* A shift to incorporate disruptive technology;
* A shift in which innovation becomes a competitive advantage;
* Changes in the product or customer base; and
* Changes to operating models and organisational structures.

All these strategies require organisational transformation and new capabilities, therefore the talent process must be strategic and must build on new organisational capabilities that will drive the transformational agenda.

It's all about leadership

I have had the privilege of engaging with a variety of top global companies that are recognised as best companies to work for in Europe, the US and South Africa. Whilst they all have talent and HR systems, processes and technologies, the common thread that differentiates them is leadership-related. As I have already indicated, the quality of leadership is the most important factor in attracting, engaging and retaining talent.

Leaders in high-performing organisations recognise that the execution of their business strategy is largely dependent on the quality of the talent and the leadership culture that defines the organisation. Such organisations value individual leaders, but also build a leadership culture that is reflected at all levels. They therefore ensure that talented people within the organisation are challenged and given an opportunity to develop and grow. Working for such organisations is therefore demanding – they expect results. But for talented people it is a rewarding and enriching experience.

A key success factor in such organisations is the importance of creating a purpose and a set of values that talented people can identify that, and which aligns with their own purpose and values.

Management and specialist career paths

Most organisations that excel in talent management offer people with skills the opportunity to grow their careers in management as well as in specialist roles. They recognise that specialists in a particular field are as important as those who progress in a management career. Such organisations avoid a common problem, which is for skilled people to progress in their careers and grow their earnings potential, they need to move into management. The consequence of moving specialists into management roles for the sake of career progression, is that the organisation loses such specialists and often has to accommodate weak leaders and managers, with all the concomitant damage this inflicts.

Specialists should be valued both in terms of remuneration and benefits, and their status in the organisation should be recognised.

Conclusion

If Africa is to unlock its economic potential and reap the resulting social rewards, the priority should be to identify and grow talent on the continent. Africa should no longer rely on expatriates from the East and West, but should rather foster a culture of developing African talent.

The current practice in many countries, of instituting immigration legislation to force localisation, is not sustainable. Rather, such countries need to establish a talent pool that public, private and other sectors can draw on to build institutional capacity and economic competitiveness. Each country has to answer the question: *What needs to be done to ensure that we as a country attract talent which will meet our own skills needs in the future?*

Much commendable work is being done by various developmental organisations and academic institutions on the continent, but in the final analysis it is individual organisations – primarily in the private sector – that will have the greatest impact on technical and leadership talent and skills development.

The development of a talent pipeline for countries begins at primary school level and continues through further and higher education and into the work environment. At a national level, growing talent for economic and social prosperity requires a holistic policy framework that is effectively instituted. It is only in this way that the potential of Africa will be realised.

Appendix: Example of a talent policy

Document Type and Title		
Human Resources Policy		
Talent Management		
Document Information		
Originator: Head of Training and Organisational Development	**Activity:** Organisational Development	**Type of Document:** Human Resource Policy

TABLE OF CONTENTS

Purpose

The purpose of the Talent Management Policy is to govern the talent management process in the company.

Scope

The Talent Management Policy and Procedures apply to all employees within the company, as well as to those persons or entities doing work on behalf of the company.

General

Reference documents

Reference	Description
ISO 9001	Quality Management System
CPM 001	Company Policy Manual
SABPP HRMS	National Human Resource Management Standards

Definitions/Abbreviations

Abbreviations

Abbreviation	Description
HR	Human Resource
HRD	Human Resource Development
IDP	Individual Development Plan

Definitions

Keyword	Definition
Company	Any company or subsidiary within the group
Successor	High-performing employee with the potential to fulfil a future core, critical, scarce or risk position in the company
Talent	High-potential employees in core, critical, scarce or risk positions that sustain and improve organisational performance
Talent pool	Selection or group of high-potential employees to be developed for core, critical, scarce or risk positions in the company
Core position	Operational position needed to generate revenue
Critical position	Essential position to sustain organisational performance
Scarce position	Position difficult to fill in the company or the industry (an imbalance in the demand for and supply of a particular skill)
Risk position	Core or critical position to be replaced in the short term (1–2 years), medium term (3–4 years) or long term (5 years)
Personal development plan	A document indicating the training activities or learning path of an employee

Authorisations

Position	Authorisation
Talent Committee	Approve talent pools Approve succession plans Approve personal development plans of talent pool members

Policy

Talent committees

A talent committee must be established for each division in the company. Sub-committees for each department will be established for the corporate division. The board will act as a talent committee for executive positions.

- Talent committees consist of the following employees:

- HR manager
- Executive / Managing Director / General Manager / Head of Department
- Head of Training and Organisational Development
- Other committee members nominated by the executive / Managing Director / General Manager / Head of Department

The function of talent committees is to

- identify current and future talent needs in a division;
- establish a talent sourcing strategy;
- nominate possible internal successors;
- approve talent pools and succession plans;
- establish and drive a talent culture;
- support the talent development process; and
- monitor and track the development progress of successors.

Talent needs

Talent committees must conduct a talent needs analysis annually. The Head of Training and Organisational Development is responsible for coordinating and facilitating the talent needs analysis and review process. The talent needs analysis must be in line with the strategic mandate of the company to identify current and future talent needs. Talent needs must focus on the core, critical, scarce and risk positions in the company.

Talent identification

Talent committees are responsible for developing a talent sourcing strategy to address the talent needs identified.

Possible talent sourcing strategies include:

- Build: Develop internal high-potential employees;
- Buy: Recruit external talent if internal talent capacity is lacking;
- Borrow: Outsource operational activity or create strategic partnership with other companies;
- Birth: Create long-term talent pipelines;
- Bridge: Develop a temporary solution for loss of skill;
- Bounce: Move employees from another part of the organisation; and
- Bind: Implement retention strategies in the short term.

Talent committees must nominate employees for core, critical, scarce or risk positions identified in the talent needs analysis. This must be done in consultation with line and HR management. The nomination process must be done in line with the *Employment Equity Act*.

A talent assessment system must be used to evaluate nominated employees to establish a final talent pool for each division.

Talent Assessment System

The Head of Training and Organisational Development is responsible for developing and maintaining a talent assessment system within the company. The talent assessment system must consist of two talent assessment components, namely

- past performance; and
- future potential.

Past performance is measured by the following:

Dimension	Measurement tool	Evaluator	Weight
Qualifications Job-relevant qualifications Other qualifications	Certified copies of qualifications	HR Manager	20
Work experience Years of service at the company Total work experience	Employee records	HR Manager	20
Work performance	Performance review records on the HRIS	HR Manager	40
Work behaviour	Internal 360° questionnaire (Work Behaviour Scale)	Superiors, colleagues, subordinates	20
TOTAL SCORE			**100**

Future potential is measured by the following:

Dimension	Measurement tool	Evaluator	Weight
Future job requirements • Qualifications • Years of experience • Type of experience • Technical skills and knowledge set • Key competencies	Correlation assessment (future job profile)	HR Manager	20
Cognitive ability	Cognitive Process Profile (CPP)	Internal / external psychologist	60
Person–job fit attributes of future job profile	Hogan Personality Inventory (HPI)		
Stress behavioural tendencies	Hogan Developmental Survey (HDS)		
Values	Motives, Values, Preferences Inventory (MVPI)		
Integrity	GIOTTO		
Leadership capability	Servant Leadership Survey		
Emotional intelligence	EQ-I 2.0		
Performance potential	Internal 360° questionnaire (Performance Potential Scale)	Superiors, colleagues, subordinates	20
TOTAL SCORE			**100**

A final talent score is calculated as follows:

- Performance score + Potential score = Final score
- Final score ÷ 2 = Talent score

The following grid is used to plot performance and potential scores:

Performance	**Excellent**	**Coaches or trainers**	**Good potential, urgent development**	**High potential, urgent development**
	Good	**Key contributors**	**Good potential for development**	**High potential for development**
	Low	**Movement needed**	**Job enrichment needed**	**Direction or support needed**
		Misplaced	**Emerging**	**High**
		Potential		

Talent committees must use this grid as a guideline to finalise a succession plan for each division and to determine development actions for talent pool members.

Talent pools

Talent committees must finalise and approve talent pools for each division using talent assessments results.

Succession plans

Talent committees are responsible for developing and maintaining a succession plan for each division in the company. The succession plan must indicate at least one successor for each core, critical, scarce or risk position identified by the talent needs analysis. Successors must be selected from the approved talent pool. The succession plan must be updated annually.

Talent development

An Individual Development Plan (IDP) must be developed for each talent pool member. The Head of Training and Organisational Development and the Training Coordinator are responsible for developing IDPs in consultation with talent committees. The talent committee must approve the IDPs of talent pool members.

The IDPs of talent pool members must include the following:

- Training activities aligned to the managerial competency framework of the company;
- Training activities aligned to the specific positional competency framework;
- Employee-specific training;
- Mentor and coaching sessions; and
- Experiential learning activities (job rotation, enrichment and shadowing, etc.).

Mentors

Talent committees are responsible for assigning a mentor to each talent pool member.

The responsibilities of mentors include

- providing mentorship to talent pool members;
- coordinating the IDP activities of talent pool members;
- monitoring and tracking the development progress of talent pool members;
- applying corrective actions if development is behind schedule; and
- submitting quarterly mentorship reports to the talent committee.

Talent deployment

Talent pool members must successfully complete all training activities listed in their IDPs and must prove competence before they may be deployed or promoted. Deployment of talent can only be done when a position becomes available. No guarantees of promotion should be made to any successor or talent pool member. In case more than one successor was earmarked for a position, the talent committee must select the most capable successor for the position when it becomes available. This selection process must include competency-based interviews with each successor, psychometric assessments, a job profile correlation, simulation exercises, reference interviews with mentors, and a review of talent development records.

Talent retention

Talent pool members must complete climate, culture, and work-wellness assessments annually, to identify possible talent retention risks.

Climate, culture, and work-wellness assessments must diagnose the following employee experiences:

- Supervisory relationships;
- Collegial relationships;
- Role clarity;
- Management style;
- Performance management (goal setting and feedback);
- Growth and development;
- Person job fit;
- Employee's perceived competence;
- Perceived career paths;
- Remuneration satisfaction;
- Availability of physical resources; and
- Leave and overtime management.

Climate, culture, and work-wellness assessments must diagnose the following talent retention risks:

- Employee turnover;
- Burnout;
- Disengagement;
- Over-commitment;
- Stress and related ill health; and
- Corporate citizenship behaviour.

The Head of Training and Organisational Development and the HRD Practitioner are responsible for conducting climate, culture, and work-wellness assessments annually on talent pools. Feedback and recommendations must be provided to mentors, talent committees and talent pool members.

Mentors must apply or coordinate the recommended corrective actions to limit or eliminate the talent retention risks identified.

Procedures

Talent identification and development procedure

Description

This is the procedure to follow to identify and develop talent within the company.

Objectives

- Establish a talent committee;
- Identify core, critical, scarce and risk positions within the company;
- Finalise a talent pool for each division;
- Finalise a succession plan for each division;
- Finalise talent development plans; and
- Monitor and track talent development plans.

Responsibilities

Position	Responsibility in the particular procedure	Standard form(s) to be used
HR Manager	• Complete the HR questionnaire of the Talent Assessment System • Coordinate internal 360 assessments of the Talent Assessment System • Submit assessment results to the Head of Training and Organisational Development	• Talent Assessment System
Head of Training and Organisational Development	• Set up talent committees for each division • Schedule kick-off meetings for talent committees • Consolidate assessment results • Provide feedback to talent pool members on assessment results • Provide feedback to the talent committee on consolidated assessment results • Create personal development plans for talent pool members • Conduct annual talent development reviews	• Talent Assessment System
External / Internal Psychologist	• Conduct psychometric assessments • Submit psychometric assessment results to the Head of Training and Organisational Development • Provide feedback to talent pool members on individual psychometric assessment results	• Psychometric Request Form

Position	Responsibility in the particular procedure	Standard form(s) to be used
Talent committee	• Conduct talent needs analysis annually • Nominate possible internal successors for core, critical, scarce and risk positions identified • Finalise a talent sourcing strategy • Select and approve talent pool members • Approve talent development plans	• Talent Needs Analysis Form • Talent Assessment System • Succession Plan
Successor	• Complete learning activities of the personal development plan • Participate in mentoring sessions	• IDP
Mentor	• Provide mentorship to talent pool members • Coordinate IDP activities of talent pool members • Monitor and track development progress of talent pool members • Apply corrective actions if development is behind schedule • Compile quarterly mentorship reports	• IDP • Mentor Report

Endnotes

1   'RMB at a glance – RMB | Traditional values, innovative ideas', 2012, retrieved 25 February 2016, <http://www.rmb.co.za/aboutglance.asp>

2   'Introduction and about Discovery', 2012, retrieved 25 February 2016, <https://www.discovery.co.za/discovery_coza/web/linked_content/pdfs/about_us/introduction_and_about_discovery_2012.pdf>

3   'Predictions for 2016: A bold new world of talent, learning …', 2015, retrieved 3 February 2016, <http://www.bersin.com/News/EventDetails.aspx?id=19402>

References

'Introduction and about Discovery', 2012, retrieved 25 February 2016, <https://www.discovery.co.za/discovery_coza/web/linked_content/pdfs/about_us/introduction_and_about_discovery_2012.pdf>

'Predictions for 2016: A bold new world of talent, learning …', 2015, retrieved 3 February 2016, <http://www.bersin.com/News/EventDetails.aspx?id=19402>

'RMB at a glance – RMB | Traditional values, innovative ideas', 2012, retrieved 25 February 2016, <http://www.rmb.co.za/aboutglance.asp>

PART 1

CHAPTER 3

STRATEGIC THINKING – AN IMPERATIVE FOR AFRICA'S LEADERSHIP TALENT

Income Prescripts 5i – a framework for strategy formulation and strategic review

Morné Mostert

For organisations in Africa to navigate the changes and complexity of the environment in which they operate, leaders will need advanced skills in strategic thinking.

While operational excellence is a critical competence of organisations, the absence of strategy can easily result in them doing the wrong thing, and doing it well! What is required is a strategic framework that enables leaders to make sense of the complexity of their business environment and develop appropriate strategies.

The pressures for operational excellence through increased cost cutting and continuous attempts to do more with less have a profound impact on the engagement of leaders and talent at all levels in the organisation.

A further challenge to strategic thinking, which is by definition holistic, is the emergence in the 20th century of "specialisation", which has translated into organisational design dominated by specialist silos. As mentioned in a number of chapters in this book, the 21st century will be defined by collaboration across silos. However, this requires what the author refers to as a transdisciplinary mental model.

This chapter by Morné Mostert, Director of the Institute for Futures Research (IFR) at Stellenbosch Business School, positions the need for strategic thinking and provides a practical framework to assist leaders in building their organisation's strategy in a fast-changing, complex world. The IFR has a history of growing leaders in strategic and systems thinking, and Dr. Mostert is one of the continent's most knowledgeable academics in the field. His insights into the restrictions that linear and operational thinking imposes on leaders and their organisations, and the consequences thereof, are extremely valuable. He provides practical ways in which strategic thinking can enable leaders and organisations to deal with the complexity they face in a changing world. A quote from his chapter summarises its essence: "In the future of Africa, such complex problems will occur with increasing regularity, and such strategic competence will therefore become a valued intellectual asset."

This is an impactful chapter, eloquently written and blending intellectual rigor with practical insights into the critical strategic thinking competencies that are essential for Africa's future talent – particularly its leaders.

Africa and the Era of More – what it means for leaders

Africa is more. Its people, its talent, its resources and its natural beauty present a canvass of potential, a bounty of opportunity. But Africa is also complex, its fortunes and image ebbing and flowing with every budget cycle. It has claimed as victims both the arrogant who wish to copy and paste foreign models, and the naïve who believe a good heart is the only requirement for success here. I humbly submit that in the next few decades, Africa will indeed offer more, but it will also require more from its talent and those who wish to engage with that talent.

We are currently in the Era of More: more revenue; more customers; more value; more of a global footprint; more technology and more innovation. The paradigm of growth seems so intuitive, its very mention appears superfluous. But 'more' also means more complexity; more uncertainty; more competitors; more dilemmas, paradoxes, dichotomies, oxymorons and conundrums. And this means more intensive demands on the mind of the modern manager – a mind which is already under heavy strain. Conceiving of intelligent strategy with such a stretched mind taxes the intellect, to the point of diminishing returns. In the Era of More, one unintended consequence that is fast emerging is more strategic disengagement by the very talent that organisations once held dear.

Strategic thinking is, of course, a form of thinking – a cognitive processing of multiple inputs with endless interactions and possibilities. In recent times, however, the art of thinking has appeared to move to the background, and has been surpassed in intention and intensity by a focus on emotional competencies or a form of determination characterised by action-orientation. Critical self-awareness and socially interactive competencies are the staple of leadership development diets. This has created yet another perfect storm for leaders: at the same time that complexity has exploded, cognitive competence appears to have lost ground to affective skills development. This has left many managers in tune and sensitive, but simultaneously deeply defective in terms of their cognitive processing abilities.

In addition, due to accelerating frequencies of change, strategy has come under severe and intensive scrutiny. Gone are the days of determining 30-year (or even ten-year) plans, communicated with confidence to abiding, trusting and subordinate staff. Businesses have realised that the art of prediction is growing ever more tenuous, and plans are best made with the requisite environmental awareness and responsiveness to market demands, the latter being vitriolic and occasionally apparently random. Not only are things changing (if only that could change!), but the rate of change is accelerating, and that makes strategy a delicate art.

Long-term, waterfall and top-down-type strategy has dissipated in favour of heuristic options. The very meaning of 'long-term' has changed. Pre-designed, pre-packaged and pre-prepared solutions all have desperately short shelf-lives and readers at the top are starting to be challenged like never before.

At the same time, middle and even senior managers are coming under increasing operational pressure. The global financial crisis appears to have had little educational value, given the way boards and executives set targets. While many were hoping for a review of how we do business, most boards appear to have interpreted the global slowdown as an annoying retardation in profit generation. Targets have kept going up. Yesterday's personal best is tomorrow's minimum requirement, as organisations grapple with the legacy of the crisis, which they often consider a loss of easy profit. For this reason, managers are under increasing pressure to produce at rates hitherto unseen. Old methods of conceiving of strategy are running out of steam. Cost cutting only gets you so far.

With the strategic space further threatened by observable and dramatic organisational failure, middle and even senior managers have grown increasingly disillusioned with both strategy and erstwhile big company job security. With severe company failures and retrenchments, employment at a large firm no longer offers any more of a secure future than smaller companies or even self-employment do. It is clear that when the dynamics of spectacular failure and continuous change collide, faith in the certainty of strategy wanes at a rapid rate. This has led many managers to experience a desperate sense of disengagement from strategic formulation and review.

Strategic disengagement is further exacerbated by a management response used in self-defence: as a counter-measure to strategic uncertainty and failure, managers often revert to their specialisation, favouring the status of their technical expertise over the value of seniority gained from a management title. This, in turn, accelerates the lack of engagement in complex realities as it produces a constant reductionist specialisation. As a result, strategic blind spots increase in size, while contextual awareness diminishes even further. Many managers have simply opted out of strategic participation and passively await the annual strategic translation into business unit objectives and individual key performance indicators.

Such inward specialisation has had yet another consequence for strategic complexity: the resulting silo-sitis that besets many large organisations. Despite calls for holism, teamwork, shared mental models and 'alignment', large departments within the same organisation often resemble limbs from various organisms – uncoordinated and governed by apparently separate decision-making processes. A vicious and self-reinforcing cycle often leads to a widening strategic distance between separate business units, and the customer suffers the consequences until a surprising competitor lures him/her away with promises of 'simplicity'.

Even for those leaders convinced of the merits of scanning the strategic landscape (as opposed to simple internal manoeuvring) the mental demands are increasing exponentially. While the Era of More has meant more customers, predicting the behaviour of those customers has become akin to star-gazing and consulting a crystal ball for certainty. Some may already be trying the magic 8-ball. Customers have more power. They have more choice. And more competitors are broadening their focus over more of the already complex market terrain.

Enhanced customer force in the customer–provider power differential has indeed also had positive effects. Companies that are customer conscious know the extent of knowledge which customers can access. Many companies are more respectful of customers, and the design of products and their service packaging exert further mental drag on the available cerebral horsepower of leaders.

Paradoxically, despite an overly operational approach on the part of many managers, strategic translation into operability remains problematic. As managers increase their ability to 'drill down and unpack' their specialisations, they become more operationally astute, but suffer greater strategic myopia. Operations are measured with exactness (a curse of the analytical mind), and check boxes are ticked. But strategic progress remains limited despite operational excellence. Arguably, it is precisely such strategic disengagement that threatens the operationalisation of strategic intent.

Thus, the mind of the manager is under continuous attack from the vagaries, uncertainties and cunning conundrums of participating in, formulating and reviewing organisational strategy. A clear need therefore exists to cope with such strategic complexity.

The need for transdisciplinarity

One of the dominant developments of the 20th century has been specialisation. Small, holistic providers of services have given way to trades in large organisations. As information became increasingly democratised, talented leaders gained differentiation through hyper-specialisation. While this accelerated the development of knowledge in specific fields, it had several unintended consequences, including a downward separation of discreet, ever-miniaturising particles of expertise. The transition curve of that evolution is shown below.

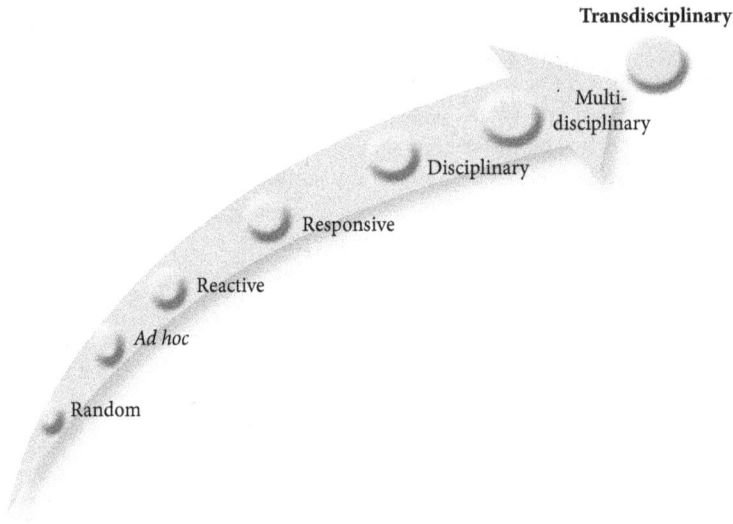

Figure 3.1   Transdisciplinary transition curve

The diagramme illustrates how knowledge development for talented leaders has evolved to a point where, given current levels of strategic complexity, such leaders must think in transdisciplinary ways. In this context, transdiciplinarity may be defined as

> a social approach to thinking for new knowledge development, in complex problems, that transcends single-discipline and multi-discipline approaches in order for a holistic challenge in a larger system to be addressed, in a manner that also contributes to each individual field.

Participants in such strategic thinking processes are therefore required not only to contribute their own specialised knowledge individually, but to do so in a manner that assists in solving problems which are larger than those present in their own fields of expertise. *In the future of Africa, such problems will occur with increasing regularity, and strategic competence will therefore become a valued intellectual asset.*

The framework proposed here attempts to present a vantage point for such thinking in the review and formulation of strategy.

Towards a workable framework for strategy

Making complex matters too simple is naïve and dangerous; just as dangerous as over-complicating simple ideas. This framework aims to engage with the mind of the manager in a delicate dance of balance and poise – on the one hand, it wishes to communicate the full complexity of strategy, and on the other it aspires to provide a practical framework for real-world application by managers with real-world objectives.

This strategy framework aims to address managerial strategy disengagement by offering an accessible framework for both

- strategic review, and
- strategy formulation.

For review, we may consider current levels of consciousness and sufficiency, and our satisfaction with the status quo. For formulation, we should consider in more detail the ideal state.

The framework is intended as an instrument for examining the strategic landscape. For that reason it contains a broad spectrum of dimensions in the interest of panoramic environmental scanning. It is presented as a mnemonic device which also serves as a meaningful acronym, in order to

- enhance recall and
- increase the probability of strategy-level discourse.

A cautious premise for steps towards tolerable levels of uncertainty

No model or framework can present the entire gamut of possibility in any field, but a broad perspective offers particular value in the domain of strategic thinking. It is noteworthy to observe that the framework is NOT aimed at strategic planning, nor at strategic implementation. It is unashamedly (yet humbly) offered in the interests of enhancing the quality of strategic *thinking and ideation* – essential precursors for any action.

The framework offers strategic **PRESCRIPTS** (fundamental principles) for **InCOME** (revenue). The acronym represents the following 15 dimensions:

- **In**novation, noesis, change and learning
- **C**ompetition
- **O**utlook, opportunity, scope and potential
- **M**arkets and customers
- **E**conomic and financial
- **P**hilosophical, paradigmatic and ethical
- **R**egulatory and voluntary coding
- **E**nvirons
- **S**ystemic interconnectedness
- **C**ultural and social
- **R**isk and mitigation
- **I**dentity, image, brand and messaging
- **P**olitical and geopolitical
- **T**echnology and cybernetics
- **S**ustainable futures

The dimensions above are not presented for linear application – they may be appraised in any order. But the aim is to find a balance between strategy as over-simplified and strategy as overwhelmingly complex.

For each dimension, a series of questions act as guides to both formulate new strategic options and review current strategy.

Innovation, noesis, change and learning

- Is it old or new? (There is always one or the other)
- Do we value innovation?
- Do we discuss it?
- Are we allowed to experiment?
- How do we treat failure?
- Do we co-create?
- What has recently changed?

- What else needs to change?
- What would we like to change?
- What is about to change?
- What are we trying NOT to change?
- What do we need to learn?
- Where should we benchmark?
- What can we learn from cross-sighting?
- What is our sense of noesis (nous, common sense, intellect, mind, reason, understanding, consciousness)?

Competition

- Are we competitor-conscious?
- Who is trying to kill us? (Our clients?) Who are our main competitors?
- Who will win what?
- What makes them better (let's be honest!)?
- Where are we better?
- Do we have a USP (unique selling proposition)/UVP (unique value proposition)?
- What do we have or do that our competitors would love to get their hands on/envy/admire?
- Who are our strategic alliances and why?
- Who is the competition likely to be in the future? Vendors/suppliers, smaller/larger companies/ government/internal?
- Do we value differentiation and/or cost leadership?
- Who are the fast followers? Are we? Should we be?
- What are our competitors signalling?
- Is there opportunity and sense in competition?

Outlook, opportunity sensing, scope and potential

- Where could we grow?
- Are we growing in the right areas?
- Are we missing opportunities?
- Where should we pay more/less attention?
- How much more is there?
- Are we casting the net too widely or too narrowly?
- Can we see the opportunities available to us or do we have strategic blind-spots?
- How saturated is the market?
- How much appetite is left?
- How likely is success?
- Would you invest in this organisation and why (why not)?

Markets and customers

- Who is the customer?
- Whom do we serve? How do we serve them and why?
- Are we creating raving fans or grudge-buyers?
- Who else should be our customer(s)?
- Which customer communities are we targeting?
- Who is being mistreated?
- Do we know enough about these communities?
- Why would they buy from *us*?
- What else do they buy?

- How do we build loyalty? Have we formed a tribe?
- Do we have the right levels of customer intimacy?
- Are we customer-centric, or barely customer-tolerant?
- How do we blend product, service/communication and emotion?
- How do we create value for the customer, where value may be defined in terms of
  a. money
  b. time
  c. effort
  d. anxiety?
- Can we think 'outside in' to meet their needs?
- What is our fun-theory?

Environs

- In our organisation, is green simply the colour of money?
- What is our intended relationship with the environment?
- Do we know our carbon footprint?
  a. Do we prefer not to know?
  b. Do we care?
  c. Are we working on reducing it?
- Do we have sophisticated green criteria for procurement?
- How active are we in footprint reduction?
- Do we consider communities around us?
- Do we externalise damage responsibility to suppliers and customers?
- How do we navigate the operational, transactional, contextual and intra-cognitive environments?

Philosophical, paradigmatic and ethical

- What do we believe about the need for our service?
- Which world-views dominate our discourse and conduct?
- Do we keep our promises?
- What guides our conduct?
- How alive are our values?
- How ethical are we in our relationships with stakeholders?
- Is governance simply about compliance, or do we engage for commitment?
- Is there a correlation between our espoused theory and our theory in use?

Regulatory

- Do we know and understand the rules?
- Do we respect the rules?
- What is being reregulated and deregulated in our favour, or to our disadvantage?
- Do we know, mimic or write the rules of the game?
- Do we differentiate between internal and external rules?
- Do we appreciate the impact of explicit as well as tacit/implicit rules?
- Meta-rules: Who gets to make the rules about making rules, who gets to break the rules?
- Do we blindly implement or tactically manoeuvre?

Economic

- Do we have congruence between 'It's all about the money' and 'It's never about the money'?
- How do we (and should we) treat financial matters?

- How do we balance profit orientation with other differentiators, like quality?
- Do we follow a 'value vs. money' or 'value FOR money' approach?
- What is the general state of our cash flow?
- Do we invest enough in research and development?
- What are the dominant trends?
- What is the macro-outlook
  a. globally
  b. regionally
  c. locally
  d. for the industry
  e. for the sector
  f. for our company
  g. for the business unit
  h. for our team?
- Does everyone understand our basic business model?
- Funding: How are we funded and what do we fund in turn?
- Pricing: Are we transparent and correctly priced for our value proposition?
- What excites us: revenue or margin management?
- Are we more interested in cost management or simply cost cutting?
- Cost: Benefit – is the money going to the right expenditure?

Systemic interactivity

- Are we connected?
- Where are the nodes?
- Which patterns are we exhibiting?
- Do we behave holistically?
- Do we sense opportunities for connective redefinition?
- Do we challenge strategic boundaries?
- Do we appreciate and grow critical new relationships?

Cultural and social

- How do we and our related communities typically behave?
- Do our typical patterns of behaviour match those of our clients?
- What are the patterns?
- Who are the external and internal communities?
- What is the quality of our relationships with them?
- Are some stakeholders more equal than others?
- How we integrate with suppliers?
- What can we learn from staff behaviour?
- Whom do we see as peripheral, e.g. CSI partners, franchisees?
- Do we favour certain customer segments?

Risk and mitigation

- What are the major threats?
- Can these be averted or overcome?
- What are our levels of risk aversion/tolerance?
- Can we see danger for what it is?
- Is it acceptable to point out risk?

- Are we afraid of the right things?
- Does fear paralyse us or do we respond with agility?
- Do we try to avoid all risk by pretending it is a machine, or can we manage the human factor?
- Do we study probability as well as impact?
- How rational or irrational are our fears?

Identity, image, brand and messaging

- How are we perceived?
- Who exactly are we?
- Who owns us?
- Where did we come from?
- Do our friends define us?
- What defines us?
- Do we have the right brand for our strategy?
- Are all our stakeholders brand ambassadors?
- What is our personality?

Political and geopolitical

- What are our key political relationships?
- How do we acquire, retain and manage political power?
- What is the extent of geopolitical stability in our domiciled and target regions of operation?
- Who are our friends?
- Who are our foes?
    - Who are the friends of our enemies and
    - The enemies of our friends?
- How well do we integrate micro, meso and macro dynamics and regional considerations?

Technology and cybernetics

- Is this a differentiator for us?
- Are we investing appropriately in technology?
- Are our managers and leaders engaged with the right technology?
- Do we make optimal use of the technology we already have?
- Are our managers and staff techno-savvy?
- Can we spot and manage socio-technical challenges?
- Do we upgrade wisely?
- Can we create the technology we need but cannot buy?
- Cybernetics: Does the right information flow in the right way?
- Is technology helping us to engineer the future?
- Are we using technology for design?
- Are we automating the right things?

Sustainably strategic futures

- Are we building sustainable competence?
- What is the prognosis for our long-term survival?
- Are we migrating to our preferred state?
- How long can this last?
- Cannibalism: What do we need to destroy about ourselves in order to ensure our survival?
- Are we balancing profit, people and planet?

The above questions offer a powerful conceptual tool for high-level reflection and are likely to allow for the emergence of shadow insights and blind-spot opportunities.

The framework addresses the current need for implementation and excellent execution by testing each of the 15 dimensions against five application areas, lending the 5i to the nomenclature of the framework. For each dimension, the strategy review team asks:

1. What is our key **insight**?
2. Based on this insight, what is our **intent**?
3. To support this intent, which **initiative(s)** should we explore?
4. Based on these initiatives, what can we commit as **investment**?
5. Based on these initiatives and investments, what are the systemic **implications**?

For further clarity on implementation, each dimension may be viewed at a range of levels, including the level of

*   activity – day-to-day processing;
*   operations – short-term monitoring and engagement;
*   tactics – decisions of process and structure redesign to overcome operational challenges;
*   tactical strategy – linking structural and procedural dimensions to pure strategy;
*   strategy – a selection and creation of intent.

A matrix view of the complete framework appears in Table 3.1.

Table 3.1   InCome PRESCRIPTS 5i – Matrix view

		In	C	O	M	E	P	R	E	S	C	R	I	P	T	S
Insight	Internal															
	External															
Intent	Internal															
	External															
Initiative	Internal															
	External															
Implications	Internal															
Systemically	External															
Investment	Internal															
	External															

It is clear that the matrix view shows the potential expansiveness of the framework. It offers 15 dimensions, to be applied to the 5i areas of application, i.e., already comprising 75 dimensions. Each application area may also be examined for internal and external implications, which means there are 150 options in total.

The intention is not for every strategic dialogue to cover all 150 areas. Instead, organisations and talented strategists may use it as a frame. Some clients even use it as a 'sanity check' to ensure that their strategic thinking takes cognisance of elements beyond the classical 'increase targets by X% and cut costs by Y%'. Africa already possesses a holistic outlook. This framework offers a structured engagement, with a range of prerequisite strategic dimensions, that elevates the quality of the strategic discourse.

Strategic thinking as a form of cognitive processing

The dominant containing system for the framework is the Cognitive Suite of Competencies. While affective factors cannot be denied, the framework aims to enhance cognitive processing competence in the field of strategy. While strategy is always contained by leadership, the framework does not primarily seek to examine strategy in the context of individual consciousness and leaders' critical self-awareness. Instead, the quality of strategic cognitive engagement is the focus, with leadership in support. One motivation for the subordination of leadership in this context is the democratisation of strategy in emerging methodologies, such as design thinking. Other cognitive elements in the containing system include systems thinking, future thinking, innovation/creative thinking, analytical thinking and others, as illustrated in the preliminary cognitive bricolage diagramme below.

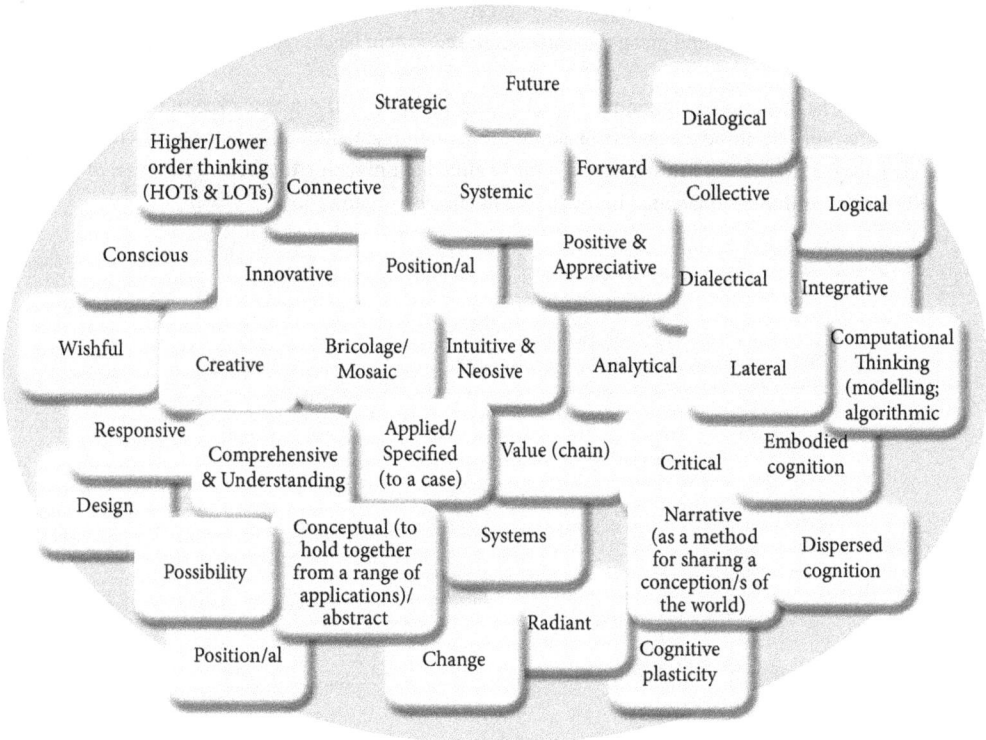

Figure 3.2   Cognitive bricolage

Bricolage is simply the notion of construction with what is at hand; somewhat ad hoc, but nevertheless somehow forming a cohesive whole. It is a principle of design in complexity – a key characteristic of the current strategic landscape. The collection of thinking modalities listed above simply aims to stimulate. It is a tool for attempting alternative modes of thinking, which is the only way in which talented people may conceive of creative ideas for advantage through innovation.

Conclusion

Africa will not follow the traditional trajectory of economic development which North America and Western Europe did during the 20th century; it will leapfrog many developmental stages and is likely to present several sudden emerging opportunities as it evolves. For that reason, talent in Africa needs to be alert to the strategic opportunities the continent has to offer.

With complexity increasing globally, high-quality thinking is essential for success. To continue favouring a bias for action, insisting on the implementation imperative of strategy may paradoxically inhibit opportunity sensing. The generation of high-quality ideas by high-quality talent is an opportunity that is now available to organisations on the continent. Africa does not have to make the same mistakes as its other global competitors – it can cherry-pick good practice globally and grow its talent into a leadership corps that appreciates the value of a broad strategic perspective. Africa already has a tradition of dialogue; the social exchange of high-order thinking is an obvious next step to ensure that African talent remains engaged and approaches the challenges facing the continent in a strategic way.

The InCOME PRESCRIPTS 5i framework provides the landscape for such dialogue. It is expansive in its design, but not prescriptive in its application. Organisations and individual talents may use it both to review current strategies and design new strategies. It is a canvass of reflection and opportunity that connects Africa's talent so as to identify and grasp the potential the continent has to offer.

While it may be true that implementation is critical to strategic success, the quality of cognition that precedes implementation will determine the quality of action taken on implementation. Talent across Africa needs to be actively engaged in high-calibre strategic discourse aimed at unlocking the fecund potential of strategic possibility located within both talented individuals and talented organisations.

PART 1

CHAPTER 4

TALENT AND TECHNOLOGY – YOUR BUSINESS SHOULD BE SOCIAL
André Horak

This is one of my favourite and most important chapters in the book.

It speaks to a future that few organisations have yet embraced but which will, before long, become the new normal of talent management.

Like others, I have stated in many parts of the book the importance that collaboration, and the destruction of boundaries and silos, will play in successful organisations of the future.

While outside the workplace employees of all generations are embracing social media as the preferred form of communication, in most organisations legacy technologies – be they emails or HR information systems – dominate.

The use of social technology has profound implications not just for technology, but for driving an organisational culture of transparency, collaboration and engagement that is highly talent attractive.

In most organisations the marketing people "get this". They understand and implement the power of "social" as their customer base expects it – even to the point of using crowdsourcing to drive product development and innovation. Yet few organisations have embraced the power of "social" internally.

There is little doubt that the use of social platforms and technologies will become a competitive factor in generating collective knowledge, collaborative innovation and organisational agility in a fast-changing and disruptive world. A significant proportion of younger generations of employees use social media as their primary vehicle for communication in their day-to-day lives; those organisations that facilitate this internally, will be demonstrating an employee value proposition that will have great appeal for that age group.

Whilst the early adoption of new technology and the social consequences thereof involves certain risks, those who lag behind in a rapidly changing world will soon find themselves at a significant disadvantage. The challenge is not the technology as such; it is the potential social fall-out of that technology that leaders and HR professionals should be exercising their minds about. I engage with many HR professionals and very few of them actively conceive of a future dominated by social technology and behaviour.

As a consultant who works extensively with IBM social and collaborative technology, André has the ability to help organisations prepare for a future that is already the present. This chapter is simply written, yet should create discomfort amongst readers – particularly leaders who are responsible for shaping their organisations' future.

Most of us are already engaged in social networking

We live in the Social Era. Social media and social networking have become part of everyday life. Now, more than ever, an increasing number of people are actively using social technologies in their daily lives. Think about the social tools and networks we all use regularly (if not daily) for sharing and communicating. Tools like WhatsApp, Facebook and Instagram allow us to "live out loud" – to share our views, thoughts and life experiences through posts, pictures and video in real-time with our networks of friends and family, allowing them to engage with us through likes and comments.

"Social media" has also changed the way we make decisions about purchases and travel. It is now easier than ever to tap into the wisdom of crowds, view feedback from others about products they have bought, places they have stayed and airlines they traveled with. We are more informed and we can learn from the experiences of others.

Knowledge is easily accessible. Take YouTube, for example, where thousands of videos are shared daily. It is easier than ever to share the knowledge we have with the world, and for the world to find and consume that knowledge. Everyday questions, such as "How do I ...?" are not only answered, but backed up by step-by-step instructions showing us exactly "how to ...". And the best part? You can access this information whenever you are ready to learn, wherever you are. You can watch a clip over and over until you are comfortable with doing something yourself.

What about our professional lives? Like most people, you probably have a LinkedIn profile. When I'm about to meet a new customer, I search their profile on LinkedIn to get to know more about them beforehand. But LinkedIn is so much more than just a platform for building professional networks: it has become one of the preferred platforms for finding talent. It seems that recruiters and headhunters are increasingly relying on LinkedIn to find suitable candidates, and they are also tapping into the networks of their prospects by asking for referrals, should the prospect not be interested in the position they have on offer.

Despite your company's views and policies on social networking, your employees are already social, and sticking your head in the sand will not make it go away.

LinkedIn has changed the playing field

Today it is harder than ever to "hide" the top talent in a company. All your top talents have profiles on LinkedIn or similar public social networking sites, which means they are effectively "in the market" all the time.

I am sure that most of you already use LinkedIn to find experts and talent when you need to fill positions or grow your skills base, but have you considered the fact that everyone else out there is doing exactly the same? All the talent you source and recruit from LinkedIn remains on LinkedIn and is targeted by headhunters and recruiters on an ongoing basis.

With that in mind, here are a few things to think about:

- Do you know how many of your top people have profiles on LinkedIn?
- How often do they receive notifications about exciting new opportunities?
- How do you ensure that you retain your top talent despite all the opportunities they are presented with?
- If you do not believe this is a real concern, maybe you should make a point of asking the people who leave your company, whether their new job was presented to them via LinkedIn or any other social network.

The home-to-office time warp

When it comes to using modern tools and technology, I find it fascinating that most companies are still stuck in 1996.

Social media marketing and recruitment are the most obvious applications of social technologies within organisations. Many companies think that engaging in social media marketing makes them a social business – they couldn't be more wrong!

Your ability to find and hire the best talent is a key differentiator which gives you the edge over your competitors, but these days everyone strives to find the best people in order to become (or remain) the leader in their industry and beat the competition. Having the best people is simply not enough. Your ability to bring new talent on board quickly, to expose your experts to everyone in your organisation so that they can share their expertise, and to retain not only your top talent but also their knowledge, are what really differentiates you from your competitors.

Your top talent use social networking in their personal lives to quickly and effectively share and engage with people outside of your organisation. In fact, it is probably their active participation in social networks like LinkedIn that exposed them to you in the first place. Those who truly understand the power of social media will most likely blog about their subject matter expertise or share knowledge through videos on YouTube to build their personal brand.

The sad reality is that when they are at the office, they "time warp" back to 1996. The tools we offer our top talent are not only 20 years old, they are also completely inadequate for effective sharing and collaboration. I remember using email and shared drives as far back as 1996, and today the majority of companies still primarily rely on these platforms for sharing and collaboration amongst their workforce.

When you compare the collaboration tools you have in the workplace with those you use in your personal life, you may suddenly realise that it is impossible to find and connect with experts in your organisation. The sharing of experience, content and knowledge becomes difficult and ineffective, and collaboration is limited to teams who work closely together or who can meet in the same boardroom.

I often ask my customers when last they sent an email to a family member or friend, or whether they tend to wait until Monday morning to mail photographs of their great weekend to their intimate circle. They usually look at me as if I'm out of touch with reality, before laughingly pointing out that they share these experiences instantly, using Facebook, Google+ or Instagram. Yet, when they arrive at the office on Monday morning, the only way they can share content, ideas or experiences with colleagues, is by sending mails or saving files on shared drives.

How talent gets lost in translation

A great deal of effort goes into the recruitment process. Recruiters spend hours identifying the best candidates, and candidates spend hours showcasing their skills, expertise, work experience and ambitions. Their comprehensive CVs contain pages of information about themselves: their qualifications, where they've worked, the positions they've held, what duties they were responsible for, their achievements and awards, what other languages they speak, their hobbies and more.

Then, once the candidate's application is successful and they are hired, the company exchanges their comprehensive CV for a job title – something like "Team Leader" or "Product Manager", and the CV containing detailed information on how that new talent can add value to the organisation is filed away somewhere, never to be looked at again.

The reality is that next time the organisation requires a specific skill, it will most likely start looking externally – often with the help of consultants – while a talented individual who has all the skills and expertise to do the job is sitting at a cubicle around the corner. The inability to locate experts inside the organisation costs much more than just the consultant's fee of the person hired to do that job. It often leaves individuals inside the organisation feeling as if they are being overlooked. The reality is that most companies do not have the ability to identify experts inside their business, and the larger the organisation and the more geographically dispersed it is, the harder it becomes to do so.

Your top talent want to build their brand in the organisation, they want the ability to showcase and share their expertise and knowledge, but in most cases there is no internal platform where they can build a professional profile like they already do on LinkedIn.

Imagine being able to quickly find an expert in your business who can help you solve a problem, or who holds the answer to a burning question. Imagine being able to access the knowledge these experts share, without even speaking to them. Imagine being able to identify individuals who have the right skills and experience to drive a new business initiative. Becoming a social business will enable you to achieve all this, and more.

What is a social business?

A social business embraces social technology to allow the people inside the organisation to connect quickly and easily, in order to share and collaborate with the people around them.

Becoming a social business involves far more than simply deploying enterprise social networking within the organisation. It is a journey which involves infusing social into the DNA of the business, making social part of the way you work every day and embedding it into your daily business processes.

I have met numerous customers who have tried a "build-it-and-they-will-come" approach with enterprise social platforms, but I am yet to identify one which has made a success of it. The biggest mistake companies make is to think that just because their employees use social networking in their personal lives, they will know how to use it for business purposes. The reality is that without guidance, people start using enterprise social networking tools in the exact same way they use Facebook, with devastating results. We all know that most people use Facebook and other social networks as platforms for sharing (sometimes negative) thoughts, status updates about what they had for lunch, or even what they are planning to do during the weekend. Sharing this type of nonsense on an enterprise social network quickly results in people disengaging and deeming the network "just another waste of time".

Another scenario which I frequently encounter, sees enterprise social networking software being installed and deployed by the IT department, prior to IT simply sending everyone a mail instructing them to use the tool which is now at their disposal. In this scenario there is usually some adoption of the tool by the IT department, but no one else in the business really knows what they are supposed to do with it, and after logging in for the first time they never bother again because they cannot see the benefit.

The reality is this: your employees want to be more social at work, they want a better way of sharing and collaborating, and if you fail to provide the tools, they will find their own solutions. One of these is to use free cloud-based enterprise social networking tools, which results in "pockets" of social networking outside the control of corporate IT, and may put sensitive corporate information at risk. As a consequence, different departments start using different tools, and in the end you miss the opportunity to move away from the current silo-ed approach to sharing and collaboration. Your challenge is to provide your employees with a single enterprise social networking platform that is aligned with your long-term social business strategy and goals, but, more importantly, to combine this with the necessary implementation plan and change management, to ensure that you achieve the required adoption and business results.

Adoption is the key to social business success, but that is a topic for another day.

Working out loud

How do you maximise the reach and impact of the top talent and experts in your organisation? The talent you hire bring new ideas and experience, but often their impact on the business is limited because it is difficult to share their experience and ideas with those around them. This becomes even more fraught when the organisation is geographically dispersed.

Think about how often you reinvent the wheel by spending time solving problems which others in the business have already solved, or how much time you waste in answering the same questions over and over again.

Imagine your top talent and experts being able to share what they are working on and the problems they solve with everyone in the organisation, and doing so easily and in a transparent manner. By allowing everyone to share what they are working on, the problems they have and the solutions to those problems, you allow more people to benefit and learn from such experiences.

A social business achieves this through the use of status updates, posts, blogs and wikis. We call this "working out loud".

Recognising employees out loud

Employee recognition systems offer a great way for big and small companies to motivate employees and drive specific behaviour. Many companies use software to implement and manage their employee recognition systems, thereby providing a platform for employees and managers to give recognition to colleagues.

I see a couple of shortfalls in this approach. First, this is normally a separate system (another silo) – people hardly ever access the employee recognition system unless they want to give or receive recognition themselves. Beyond this, there is no real reason for, or benefit to be derived from, accessing the system in the course of a normal working day. Second, notifications from these systems are usually sent via email. Typically, the person being recognised receives a mail, and his/her manager is copied.

Imagine being able to amplify these recognition messages far beyond just the recognised employee and his/her manager? By integrating your employee recognition system with your enterprise social network you can amplify and exponentially increase the value of this process. By posting notifications to the profiles of the initiator, the employee and the employee's manager, these three people – along with everyone in their networks – will take note of such recognition. In addition, anyone who sees the post on the enterprise social network can interact with it by liking, commenting on or sharing it, thus extending the reach of the post to everyone in their network.

Gamification is another way of amplifying employee recognition. By integrating gamification with your enterprise social network and employee recognition, employees can earn badges which may be displayed on their social profile for all to see, thus adding to their personal branding within the organisation.

Badges (which effectively represent specific achievements) can be linked to individual challenges. These challenges, in turn, can be linked to specific behaviours, effectively supporting the organisation's vision, mission and values.

By recognising your top talent and experts out loud, you increase the value and effectiveness of the recognition given, resulting in improved employee retention, while allowing employees to strengthen their brand within the organisation.

Crowdsourcing ideas and solutions

Innovation is a key success factor in business today. The ability to come up with "the next best thing" before your competitors do, and to take those ideas to market within the shortest period of time, gives you that edge you need to stay on top.

This is also one of the reasons why organisations look for the best and brightest talent when hiring. The reality is that when it comes to innovation, this function often ends up in the hands of a select group of people, and companies miss the opportunity to tap into the collective knowledge and potential of all the bright minds they employ.

Your next big idea might already exist without an effective way of surfacing and reaching the right decision makers. Imagine being able to reach out to all your talent and experts when scouting for innovative ideas and solutions, giving everyone a voice as well as the ability to collaborate around potential solutions. Imagine being able to share your ideas with everyone in the business, and quickly getting their feedback and being able to identify the best ideas by allowing more people to vote for the ideas they like.

The ability to crowdsource ideas and solutions gives a social business the edge. It allows them to effectively tap into their entire talent pool, to identify and find the best new ideas. In doing so, they increase the value derived from the talent they hire, while making everyone feel that they have a voice which is being heard.

Knowledge lives inside people's heads

Think about the places where you currently share documents and content in your organisation. The first and most obvious platform for sharing is email. Think about the language you use: "Can you please send me the file?" You "send" the same files multiple times, effectively creating multiple copies of the same document which is stored in various mailboxes, resulting in multiple versions of the truth. This diminishes the value of the content, because you can never be sure whether the copy in a specific inbox is actually the latest version of the file.

Another popular method is using shared drives. Think about this for a minute: How many files are stored on shared drives which you seldom access? How many of those files are older than five years, or perhaps even older than ten years? Do you ever open those files?

The reality is that when you detach the "knowledge" from the expert, it immediately starts losing value. Why don't you ever look at those "old" files on the shared drive? Well, frankly, because you don't "trust" them.

You don't really know who created the file, who accesses the file, how often it is accessed, and what people are saying about the file and the value of its content.

Knowledge does not live in documents, emails or file attachments; it lives inside of the heads of people – your experts. The ability to identify the expert allows you to access the knowledge that experts can share. By retaining the connection between the experts and the knowledge they share, you retain "trust" in the content.

In a social business, everyone in the organisation helps to highlight the valuable content, thus assisting others in identifying the appropriate content and establishing trust in that content. They use simple social networking and tracking capabilities, like tracking the number of times a file has been downloaded, when last anyone perused the content, the number of likes the content received, and even conversations around/comments about the content.

What does the future hold?

The concept of social business is nothing new, and many organisations across the world are reaping the benefits of working more transparently, and having a more connected and engaged workforce. The concepts described in this chapter explain some of the more common usage patterns for enterprise social networking. But what else can a social business achieve, and what does the future hold as more and more businesses adopt social collaboration and embed it into the culture of their organisation?

I think the possibilities are endless, and the potential of what can be achieved will depend purely on an organisation's ability to embrace and implement exciting new ways of working.

Imagine being able to innovate more aggressively, by allowing people in your business to volunteer their time and skills to work on the projects they are most interested in, effectively crowdsourcing the skills required to take new, exciting ideas to market? Think about what this does for employee satisfaction and retention, and how this contributes to your employee value proposition and the company becoming an employer of choice …. Not to mention the improved productivity and efficiency you will experience when people work on the things they truly enjoy!

Conclusion

Becoming a social business can help you to attract, engage and retain the best talent. As a social business you can maximise the impact of your top talent and experts by allowing them to connect quickly and effectively, to share and collaborate with colleagues and stakeholders, thus allowing everyone to benefit from the knowledge and experience they bring to the organisation.

Becoming a social business is a journey. As is the case with any journey, you will require a plan showing the milestones you need to reach along the way, as well as a means of measuring your progress.

If you truly want your organisation to be a people-centric business, you should become a social business. Have you started your social business journey?

PART 1

CHAPTER 5

LEADING IN A CONNECTED WORLD
Terry Meyer

Just as leaders strategise for their organisations, so it is crucial that they identify a leadership agenda based on key related challenges emerging from the world around them.

This chapter begins with a discussion of the important global leadership challenges that will impact leaders in all organisations. Most of these issues already appear in well-thought-out leadership agendas.

The next issue under study relates to the kind of organisations that will be successful in a modern, connected and disrupted economy. The focus is on the importance of entrepreneurial mindsets, innovation and agility as key organisational success factors and the need for these attributes to be reflected in the leadership of an organisation.

Within the environmental and organisational context, a new framework for leadership is provided. This in no way negates all other leadership theories, but positions leaders as stakeholder-centric, where the greater organisational purpose – rather than specific team goals – is emphasised. This positions network creation and collaboration as the most important leadership attributes.

Finally, there is a discussion about how future leaders can be developed to be effective within such an environment. This shifts the emphasis from formal development to building networks that connect people to other people, ideas and institutions. André Horak's chapter on the impact of social and collaborative technology provides the backdrop for leadership and leadership development in the organisation of the future.

As demonstrated in the title of this chapter, two key game changers in the future leadership space are disruption and connectivity. To be effective in this space, leaders will need not only conventional skills (which are still important!) but also a mindset/mental model that views the world through a very different lens. How we see the world determines our behaviour, and this is certainly also the case with leadership.

This chapter is important for those involved in building Africa's future leaders if they are to be effective in a disruptive and connected world. This does not only apply to HR professionals – leaders are by far the most important developers of future leaders in particular, and talent in general.

Introduction

Throughout history, more books and papers have arguably been written and courses run about leadership than almost any other subject, yet we continue to find spectacular failures of leadership – in society, amongst politicians, and in the realm of business. This chapter is concerned with leadership in public and private sector organisations, rather than in the social and political spheres.

Michael Porter, in his landmark 2014 article in the *Harvard Business Review*,[1] states that "business has lost legitimacy". In the years since then the problem seems to have increased, judging from the questionable organisational behaviour manifested during the financial crisis and in the continuing acts of non-compliance being perpetrated by massive organisations which are household names and which the public had come to trust.

It can be said that, for whatever reasons, the world, and business in particular, is experiencing a crisis of leadership. Whilst there are many exceptional leaders of exceptional organisations, they stand out in the crowd as the exception rather than the rule.

In Africa, if organisations are to achieve their potential and contribute to the economic and social development of the continent, leadership must be a key requirement.

> Africa's development challenge – be it governance, water and sanitation, education, health, energy, infrastructure, gender equality, trade and investment and usually, a combination of all these factors given that they are inextricably linked – has been attributed to one major factor: a lack of effective, cohesive and ethical leadership, across all levels and sectors of society.[2]

Yet with all of the writings on leadership, why is there still no consensus on what leadership means? Furthermore, is leadership in the connected world of the 21st century different from how it was practised in the past? Does it need to be?

One thing we can say about leadership, that few would dispute, is that it is contextual. The effectiveness of leaders depends on the context in which they lead – the kind of organisation involved, the nature of "followers" and, of course, the societal culture in which it occurs.

I generally introduce lectures on leadership with the statement that "whatever anyone says about leadership, it is likely that the opposite is also true".

We live in a world in which "social" technology is disruptive. Like disruptive technologies throughout history (such as the telephone, electricity, the internal combustion engine and the steam train) this technology, which enables unlimited connectivity, is changing the nature of both society and the economy. Different leadership models are required to create organisations that will compete and thrive in a connected and disruptive world.

This chapter focuses on leadership in the context of a connected world; a world in which disruption is accelerated by technology and which is embracing a culture of openness and transparency. The argument made here, is that in a connected world a different leadership framework is required – one involving multiple stakeholders and organisational collaboration, rather than traditional team leadership. This does not negate any of the traditional leadership theories or approaches, but it does provide a different contextual framework in which they need to be applied.

The aim here is to address the following questions:

- What are some of the key leadership challenges, facing leaders globally at all levels in organisations, that should shape a leadership agenda?
- How will organisations need to be designed to be effective and competitive in a connected world?
- What will leadership in this world be about, and what is a relevant framework that will enable leaders to understand and define their role?
- What do organisations need to do to grow leaders who will make a difference in a connected world?

Key leadership challenges

Each year a number of large consulting and other organisations publish research into the challenges facing CEOs and other C-Suite leaders.[3,4,5,6] A number of common themes have emerged from these findings and from general observations of the leadership environment. The following are several of the more important such findings and their implications. Note that these are *leadership* rather than business challenges.

The importance for leaders is that these challenges should shape their future leadership agendas. Each of these is discussed briefly.

Market disruption

No business can proceed on the basis of business as usual. Increasingly, new business models and technologies are enabling organisations to "steal the cheese" of traditional businesses. In South Africa, companies such as Capitec, Outsurance and Discovery are redefining the business sectors in which they operate. Elsewhere in Africa, for instance, Econet in Zimbabwe is challenging the traditional banking sector by offering full banking services via cell phone to rural and urban users, who can now tap into solar power to recharge their phones and hence do not have to walk long distances to town to do their basic banking. The M-Pesa banking service in Kenya is one of the most successful mobile banking operations in any emerging market.[7]

Globally, a number of organisations are challenging traditional business models. Uber (the world's largest taxi company) owns no vehicles; Facebook (the world's largest social media platform) creates no content; Alibaba (the world's most valuable retailer) owns no inventory; and Airbnb (the world's largest provider of accommodation) owns no real estate.

Organisations thus need to either create disruption or at least have the necessary defences to adapt rapidly when others do. This requires certain key organisational attributes which leaders need to create and which challenge many traditional processes and mental models, including

- *entrepreneurship*, in which organisations continually find and exploit opportunities faster and better than their competitors;
- *innovation*, specifically in respect of business models, which see effective organisations continuously finding ways to do things better or differently to stay ahead of the competition. This needs to be embedded in the organisational culture, and not be constrained by unnecessary rules and procedures;
- *agility*, which refers to the ability to respond rapidly to new opportunities/threats in the market, without being impeded by traditional bureaucracy and entrenched processes. In fact, it requires the capability to completely reinvent the organisation, so as to instantly take advantage of, or respond to, market changes.

The only way that organisations will be able to build these attributes is by appointing and nurturing leaders who reflect exactly these attributes. The same applies to talent throughout the organisation. *It is about a collective mindset that is continuously on the edge of chaos and is comfortable with being there.* It must be emphasised that this not only applies to the private sector. Increasingly, private sector organisations are taking over functions and services provided by public sector departments or state-owned enterprises. Education, healthcare, energy and postal services are just a few of many examples.

Technological disruption

Technology in every sphere is the great disruptor.[8]

Recently, while I was teaching a business school programme for middle/senior managers in the construction industry, this issue came up. Nobody could think of anything that would disrupt the basic nature of construction, until I informed them that I had recently seen a picture of the first digitally printed building. This was incomprehensible to them. Their mental models had filtered out anything that challenged their traditional view of technology in their industry.

Yet this is the world we live in. There is no sector in which technology of some sort is not redefining the nature of the business, including the public sector. In a field such as education, technology will be a game changer.

Leaders of the future need to be scanning their radar screens to understand what new technology is on the edge of their screen, and what threats or opportunities this presents. Simply put, such technology can help organisations work smarter, or it can completely disrupt the business model or sector structure.

Diversity

Diversity is a global challenge. In a connected world, leaders need to be able to provide leadership to people with divergent world-views, needs and expectations. Leading the workforce of the future will increasingly include

- leading multiple generations;
- leading in a multicultural and multinational context;
- dealing with multiple religious persuasions which, at times, will reflect global religious tensions in the workplace;
- promoting equal treatment of women in the workforce and adapting to the needs of different genders;
- providing opportunities for people with disabilities so that they can move from being marginalised to contributing to the effectiveness of organisations; and
- accommodating linguistic diversity. Language is related to culture and the ability to relate to people who speak different languages and represent different cultures will become imperative.

The increasing need to lead diverse teams or organisations has significant implications for leaders. It requires that they create a culture of inclusiveness in which people from diverse backgrounds, with diverse mental models, feel *included* in their team and the organisation as a whole.

In their recent outstanding book, *Leading in a changing world*,[9] Keith Coats and Graeme Codrington put forward the notion of *invitational leadership*. This is an important concept which implies that leaders in diverse organisations/teams need to ensure that everyone, whatever their differences, is "invited" to be part of the team. Members need to be drawn into the inner circle, not marginalised at the edge of social interactions within the organisation/team. Creating a culture of inclusion calls for high levels of sensitivity to the subtle dynamics that, often unconsciously, foster exclusion and marginalisation.

The future of work

The trend of telecommuting is well established in leading organisations. There are, however, many other factors that will impact the future world of work, from redesigned careers to new office and spatial configurations.[10]

Increasingly it is accepted that knowledge workers in particular will have what Charles Handy calls a portfolio of work.[11] My portfolio of work, for example, includes the roles of consultant, academic/educator, presenter, author, photographer, husband, parent and property manager. Time for all the different dimensions of "self" needs to be included in a "work" portfolio. People already perform multiple roles in their daily lives, and through technology they can generally work anywhere, at any time. Employees already have multiple work arrangements with their employers, from full-time to part-time employment and a number of variations in terms of engagement. The line between employee and provider is narrowing, which is causing stakeholders to consider the implications for labour law and the protection of different categories of "contract" worker.[12]

The key challenge for many people is to bring their (often competing) life roles into balance. In fact, one of the most important leadership challenges is to help people manage that balance. Corporations are home to many workers who are highly stressed, and this affects their engagement, their productivity and their ability to innovate. Such stress tends to be exacerbated by constant organisational restructuring – generally another term for "doing more with less", which heightens employees' sense of insecurity.

While technology has many advantages, it also means that people are at work 24/7. All these factors, combined, require that leaders assist employees in balancing their lives, to the benefit of all concerned.

The fact that leaders often only meet with their diverse staff intermittently or virtually, problematises a team's cultural cohesion. The result of such a very fluid work relationship is that leaders need to be flexible and treat each individual in a way that balances his/her needs with those of the organisation. A shift is required, from performance management that is time and task orientated, to one that focuses on results and is oiled by trust. Traditional managers have difficulty rewiring their mental model to accommodate this flexibility and, in many cases, a new psychological contract between the organisation, the leader and the employee is necessary.

Figure 5.1 provides a useful illustration of recent shifts in the world of work.

The evolution of the employee

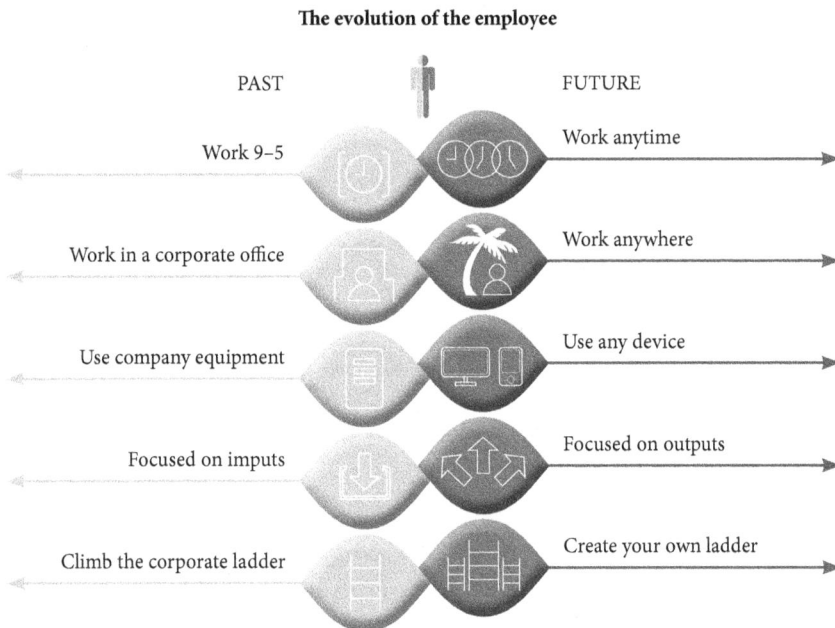

PAST	FUTURE
Work 9–5	Work anytime
Work in a corporate office	Work anywhere
Use company equipment	Use any device
Focused on imputs	Focused on outputs
Climb the corporate ladder	Create your own ladder

Figure 5.1   Recent shifts in the world of work[13]

Sustainability

Ensuring sustainability is traditionally a task allocated to a specialist, whose job it is to find good causes, whether through corporate social investment (CSI) or environmental monitoring. The role of such specialists is also to arrange photo-shoots for executives, for inclusion in annual "People, Planet and Profits" reports (integrated reporting) as part of building their reputation as good corporate citizens.

It is my view that the conversation needs to change in two ways: first, sustainability needs to be an integral part of organisational strategy. Unilever is an outstanding example of how the CEO has insisted that everything the company does be sustainable and create value for the organisation and the world at large.[14] The company has set tough targets in a variety of areas; this makes good business sense and takes corporate citizenship to a different level. Their sustainability framework illustrates their approach.

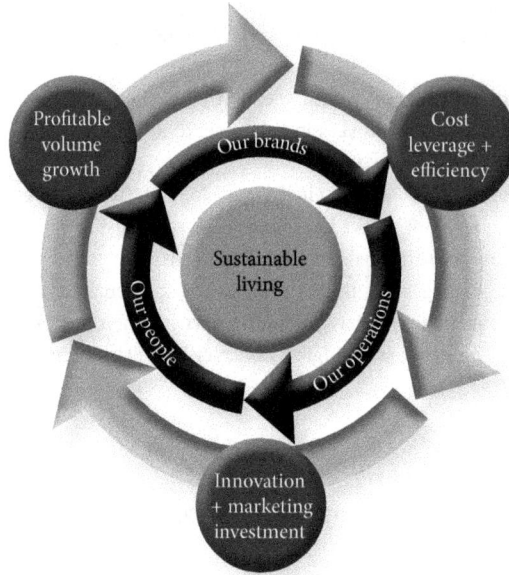

Figure 5.2   The cycle of sustainable living[15]

Second, an emerging conversation has to be about the role of business in society. In a world where there are so many social issues, the role of business has changed from being about making profits for shareholders, to adding value for a wide range of stakeholders. Making money is the result of such value, rather than the purpose of the organisation. This is about the *legitimacy and social value of business*, in particular.

Sustainability is an area of huge complexity, yet leaders of the future will have to confront increasingly complex issues around the role and behaviour of business in society. Leaders who are rigid and dogmatic in their view of the world will not be able to contribute to this conversation and will have difficulty finding answers to increasingly complex problems. This is particularly true in the African context, where both social and environmental issues are often extreme.

Samuel Njenga's chapter in this book expands on the issue of sustainability, and provides several useful frameworks for leaders. Leaders of the future will require the flexibility and the ability to engage with others, to find innovative solutions to very complex problems. It should be noted that climate change is increasingly contributing to extreme weather events. For example, 2015/2016 saw the strongest hurricane ever recorded in the Pacific off the coast of Mexico, and the strongest storm ever to hit a land mass recorded off the coast of Fiji. Leaders are increasingly going to have to prepare for and deal with the results of extreme weather and other natural disasters – so-called black swan events.[16]

Globalisation

It goes without saying that the world is highly integrated and interdependent – the global financial crisis was a stark illustration of this. As a result, leaders need to be aware of events globally, and the potential impact such events will have locally.

Furthermore, Africa is increasingly in the cross-hairs of global organisations that see huge growth potential on the continent. The result is that local organisations will need to raise the bar if they are to compete in the global market. In addition, the focus on Africa has presented opportunities for African companies to expand on the continent and beyond. This is a challenge which many have exploited very successfully. I have, however, also worked with clients who believe they can take a business model that worked for them in their home country and transplant it into other African countries. They learned a very expensive lesson in the process.

Leadership in a global world needs to be highly sensitive to local cultures, markets and country risks. The importance of globalisation applies equally to public sector leadership. Many potential opportunities for economic and social change are being inhibited by a lack of leadership on the part of governments and politicians. For Africa to reach its potential, the flow of people and goods as well as the building of infrastructure is key. This will involve the establishment of public–private partnerships and the eradication of corruption. The latter aspect, in particular, will require significant courage and resilience from leaders.

Without such leadership, Africa has little hope of being a serious player in the global economy.

VUCA

VUCA stands for volatility, uncertainty, complexity and ambiguity.[17] The term, which characterises the world of leadership, has profound implications for the kind of leaders who will be successful in the 21st century.

How leaders behave is largely dependent on how they view the world – their mental models. These are the psychological lenses that leaders use to give meaning to the world and filter out that which is not perceived as relevant to their mental framework.

How they solve complex and systemic problems is a critical issue. Morné Mostert provides interesting insights into this subject in his chapter in the book.

In a VUCA world, the antithesis to effective leadership is rigidity. Instead, cognitive agility is a key attribute.

Table 5.1 proposes emerging leadership mental models that are likely to be relevant in a VUCA world, and indicates how they differ from traditional world views.

Table 5.1 Leadership mental models

Traditional mental model	Shift to VUCA-relevant mental model
Focuses on what and how – efficiency	Focuses on who and why – effectiveness
Simple univariate universe	Complex, multi-variable universe – systemic
Law abiding	Chaotic
Controllable	Uncertain, volatile
Fragmented, atomistic	Interdependent, systemic
Either/or	Both/and
Individualistic	Collaborative
Predictive planning – extrapolation	Multiple possible futures – scenarios
Values predictability	Thrives on uncertainty
Top-down leadership	Dispersed leadership

Traditional mental model	Shift to VUCA-relevant mental model
Truth defined as absolutes	Multiple interpretations – postmodern
Bureaucratic	Agile
Standardisation	Innovation
Replicates past successes	Entrepreneurial

How will organisations need to be designed to be effective in the modern world?

Organisations are designed by leaders to create the context for the behaviour of both employees and teams. *How organisations, through their leaders, talk about themselves will determine their people's behaviour.*

Traditionally, organisations have been defined by clear structures, job descriptions and processes. Ask most organisations what they look like, and they will most likely draw an organogramme. Such organisations create silos in which functions, divisions, teams and hierarchies define their constituent parts. The severe implications of silos are described in Gillian Tett's powerful book *The silo effect*.[18]

Modern organisations will increasingly be described as networks, which suggests that they revolve around relationships. Increasingly, organisations will consist of networks of teams. Not surprisingly, organisational design is now considered one of the most important leadership abilities.[19] This has significant implications for leaders: rather than focusing on teams, functions and divisions, the emphasis will need to be on organisational collaboration, energy flows and partnerships. I would argue that organisational collaboration will be the most important future leadership competency and will replace the traditional emphasis on team leadership. It should be noted that collaboration is not just about being "nice" to people: *it is about forging agreements that will benefit all the stakeholders involved.*

As organisational boundaries become increasingly porous, collaboration will need to extend to encompass a variety of stakeholders inside and outside the organisation. Collaboration will be greased by "social" technology, such as that used and offered by IBM,[20] which will enable people to connect with anyone, anytime, anywhere – see André Horak's chapter, which explores the impact of social technology on organisations. Such technology requires and will contribute to a culture of transparency and information sharing. It will facilitate innovation and knowledge creation.

Leaders in a connected world will need to embrace the values and processes that enable effectiveness in an "open system" organisation that is agile, innovative and entrepreneurial. These characteristics are only possible through collaboration that breaks organisational and even mental boundaries.

It is said that "culture eats strategy". No matter how an organisation is designed, the design must align the culture with the strategy, structure and other organisational design issues. A key role of leaders in the future will be to actively create and sustain an appropriate culture that supports the above leadership style. This focus on culture as a strategic business priority is illustrated in almost all of the corporate case studies in this book.

Building organisations in Africa that can compete effectively in a globally connected and disruptive world will require a new leadership framework, and "followers" will need to be empowered and educated to work in such an environment. Traditional mental models will need to be challenged by both leaders and "followers" – it is very convenient to follow rules and leave decision making to senior management, but such a perspective will increasingly be an impediment to success.

What will leadership be about in this connected world?

Traditionally, leaders have been depicted as the people at the apex of the hierarchical triangle, with responsibility for leading a team, be it a small operational/project team, a function or a division within the organisation. This is commonly represented in the following way:

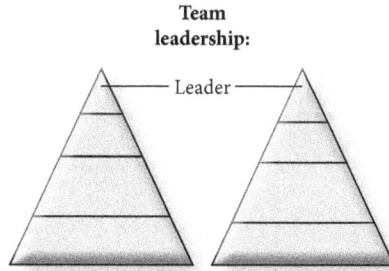

**Team
leadership:**

Leader

Figure 5.3   Team leadership hierarchy

By definition, this creates a context that reinforces silo behaviour. Reward and other systems reinforce the focus on team goals and objectives, often at the expense of the greater organisational "whole". Witness an Exco competing for funds at budget time! While team leadership is clearly important, in modern organisations, in a connected world, this approach can be counterproductive as team interests tend to supersede the interests of "the greater good" (i.e., the organisation as a whole).

In a connected world a stakeholder collaboration model of leadership is more relevant than a team leader model. In the former model the leader is the central cog in a network of stakeholders and is required to provide leadership to players well beyond his/her immediate team. The focus of such leadership is to achieve the aims and goals of "the organisational whole", rather than the team. It also requires different skills and a unique mental model.

The following is a representation of a stakeholder collaboration model of leadership:

Collaborative leadership

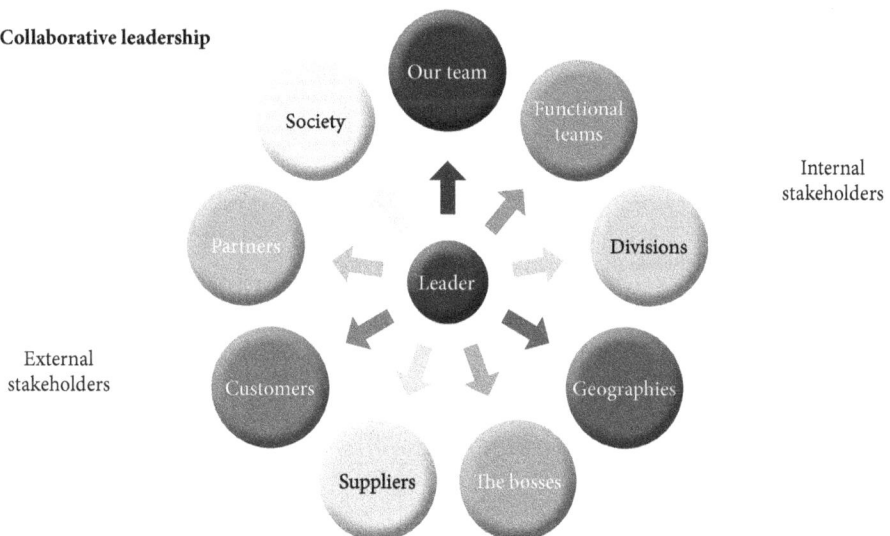

Our team

Society

Functional teams

Internal stakeholders

Partners

Divisions

Leader

External stakeholders

Customers

Geographies

Suppliers

The bosses

Figure 5.4   The stakeholder collaboration model of leadership

In Figure 5.4 the leader fulfils a leadership role to a variety of internal and external stakeholders. Of course the list of stakeholders will be much broader than the one provided here. Hence, leaders in a connected world need to pay attention to, and take control of, the effectiveness of their relationship with all stakeholders. Collaborative relationship building and managing "energy flow" are key requisite skills.

When running leadership development programmes I often ask participants to undertake a short exercise on understanding "energy flow". You are encouraged to try it. Draw a diagramme like the one above with, say, ten key stakeholders that are important to your success as a leader. They must be specific, so name them. Don't just choose only those you get on with, but also consider stakeholders outside the organisation. Colour the lines between yourself and each stakeholder using the following guide:

- Red – this relationship presents an obstacle; the communication "pipeline" is blocked, there is little flow of energy and innovation;
- Amber – there is an acceptable relationship and flow of energy; cooperation is the norm, as required; and
- Green – the relationship and energy flow are highly energised, resulting in ongoing innovation; it is the place you want to be.

Most relationships function at an amber level; powerful, high-performance relationships are green; red relationships are toxic. Clearly, for a highly effective collaborative leader the aim is to shift red relationships to at least amber, and from amber to green. Highly effective organisations have a predominance of green 'relationships', whereas average organisations are predominantly amber. In toxic organisations, the lines are predominantly red.

The key is that unless leaders can quantify or describe their relationships with multiple stakeholders, even if it is by "gut feel", it is difficult to manage those. In the end, managing relationships is a key role of collaborative leaders.

The power of purpose

In a networked organisation, the gravitational force that aligns and maintains connections is purpose: it qualifies an organisation's existence and defines the "greater good" towards which all functions, departments and teams need to direct their efforts. The power of purpose is well described by Simon Sinek,[21] with his concept of the golden circle. In this framework he outlines that people identify with "why" you do what you do, rather than "what" you do and "how" you do it. This is what differentiates great leaders and companies such as Apple from the rest. People identify far more strongly with the "idea" that a company represents, than simply with a product or service which can easily be replicated.

Many leading organisations are now paying attention to identifying their purpose and the social value of their purpose which engages employees, customers and other stakeholders. *Making money is generally the result of one's purpose, rather than the purpose itself.*

Great leaders make an impact because of the cause or purpose they represent, and this is reflected in their leadership brand. In a connected world it is this cause or purpose that will create a centre of gravity for what organisations and their constituent parts do – serve the greater good!

Leadership success factors

Finally, having considered the challenges facing leaders and the organisations they lead, a number of leadership success factors and capabilities are required in a connected world. Many differ from those practised by traditional team leaders.

To create organisations that will successfully deal with the challenges discussed earlier, leaders in a connected world require the following capabilities:

- **Collaboration** with multiple stakeholders, both inside their organisation and externally, to facilitate high energy flows and innovation;
- **Cognitive agility** and the ability to perceive important issues when they appear on the edge of the radar screen. This, in turn, requires that leaders are not confined to traditional mental models and filters;
- The **motivation to break down and transcend** functional, divisional, hierarchical, team and mental **silos,** and to make decisions aimed at achieving the objectives of the "greater organisational whole", rather than vested silo interests;
- The ability to **lead disruptive innovation**, including product/service, process and fundamental business model innovation through collaboration between often disparate functions and perspectives;
- An **entrepreneurial perspective** in which opportunities (and threats) are identified and exploited;
- The ability to **create an agile organisation** that can respond rapidly to opportunities and threats and, if necessary, reinvent itself in the light of a changing environment;
- The ability to identify opportunities to continuously **leverage new technology** aimed at disrupting processes and business models;
- The ability to **work in a VUCA environment** characterised by multiple (more than 50!) shades of grey;
- A commitment to **work with diversity** in organisations and leverage diversity to enhance innovation and different mental models; and
- The ability to **learn, unlearn and relearn**. This is not just about "content" that continues to change, but is largely about "rewiring the brain" to understand different mental models.

Growing tomorrow's leaders

What is it that organisations need to do to grow the leaders who will make a difference in the connected world of today and tomorrow? Traditional leadership development strategies will remain relevant, to varying degrees. Undoubtedly there will be a greater emphasis on online learning rather than classroom learning. It will be a case of learning on demand – anyone, anytime, anywhere, and in any language!

Business school programmes, training courses, coaching and mentoring and experiential learning will, however, remain key elements of learning strategies.

The most significant changes are likely to emerge from learning through connectivity. Such learning will find people connecting with other people, organisations and knowledge, both formally and informally. This will be facilitated by "social" technologies and will see leading organisations using internal and external collaboration to generate knowledge and facilitate innovation. This is something that new generations will do spontaneously – organisations simply have to provide direction and focus to add business value. Communities of practice and expertise (mostly virtual) will be a source of innovation and knowledge generation.

Organisations will, in the future, need to include conscious collaboration and networking strategies in their leadership development strategies.

Furthermore, increasing use will be made of global travel and global assignments, to take future leaders out of their comfort zone and provide stretch assignments aimed at building resilience and cognitive flexibility. This will facilitate the building of global networks of leaders who are effective when faced with diverse, complex problems in a variety of cultures and contexts.

All of the above will contribute to the ability of leaders to function effectively in a VUCA environment.

Conclusion

If the original proposition of this chapter is true, and there is indeed a global leadership crisis in society and organisations of all kinds, the development of leaders for the future must be an imperative, especially in organisations.

Leaders who were successful in taking their organisations to new heights in the past may not be the ones who will take them to the next level of growth and effectiveness.

Knowing who the future leaders are in any organisation and what capabilities they require to take the organisation to the next level of performance must be key priorities for current leaders. However, those leaders are advised not to appoint carbon copies of themselves for this task, but to think very carefully of the challenges and capabilities needed by the next generation of leaders.

Endnotes

1   'Creating shared value', *Harvard Business Review,* January–February 2011, retrieved 22 December 2015, <https://hbr.org/2011/01/the-big-idea-creating-shared-value>

2   J Naidoo, Chairman of Global Alliance of Improved Nutrition and founding General Secretary of COSATU, South Africa's largest trade union, AFLI | African Leadership Institute, 2005, retrieved 23 February 2016, <http://alinstitute.org/>

3   '18th Annual Global CEO Survey: PwC', 2009, retrieved 24 December 2015, <http://www.pwc.com/gx/en/ceo-survey/>

4   'The results of the 2015 Fortune 500 CEO survey are in …', 2015, retrieved 24 December 2015, <http://fortune.com/2015/06/04/fortune-500-ceo-survey/>

5   'How are CEOs addressing the issues they consider most …', 2015, retrieved 24 December 2015, <https://www.conference-board.org/ceo-challenge2015/>

6   'CEO Study | KPMG | US', 2014, retrieved 24 December 2015, <http://www.kpmg.com/us/en/topics/pages/ceo-study.aspx>

7   'M-Pesa – Wikipedia, the free encyclopedia', 2011, retrieved 22 February 2016, <https://en.wikipedia.org/wiki/M-Pesa>

8   'Agent of change: The future of technology disruption in …', 2013, retrieved 24 December 2015, <http://www.economistinsights.com/sites/default/files/downloads/EIU_Agent%20of%20change_WEB_FINAL.pdf>

9   'Amazon.com: Leading in a changing world: Lessons for …', 2015, retrieved 24 December 2015, <http://www.amazon.com/Leading-Changing-World-Lessons-leaders-ebook/dp/B00YNGI47I>

10   'The future of work | Fast Company | Business + Innovation', 2014, retrieved 24 December 2015, <http://www.fastcompany.com/section/the-future-of-work>

11   'The empty raincoat: Making sense of the future', 2012, retrieved 23 February 2016, <http://www.amazon.com/THE-EMPTY-RAINCOAT-MAKING-FUTURE/dp/0099301253>

12   'A middle ground between contract worker and employee …', 2015, retrieved 10 March 2016, <http://www.nytimes.com/2015/12/11/business/a-middle-ground-between-contract-worker-and-employee.html>

13   I Davies, 'The Evolution of the Employee' Learning, Education & Careers, retrieved 28 August 2016, https://image-store.slidesharecdn.com/8ccfd47a-253b-4e7a-bf27-2ac3e2b784d5-medium.png

14   'Sustainable living', Unilever global company website, 2012, retrieved 24 December 2015, <https://www.unilever.com/sustainable-living/>

15   Unless otherwise stipulated, all tables/figures were created by the author.

16   'About | Black swan events', 2011, retrieved 23 February 2016, <http://blackswanevents.org/?page_id=26>

17   N Bennett & GJ Lemoine, 'What VUCA really means for you', *Harvard Business Review*, January–February 2014, retrieved 24 December 2015, <https://hbr.org/2014/01/what-vuca-really-means-for-you>

18   'The silo effect, by Gillian Tett', *The New York Times*, 2015, 22 December 2015, <http://www.nytimes.com/2015/09/06/books/review/the-silo-effect-by-gillian-tett.html>

19   'Human capital trends 2016 | Deloitte US | Human capital', 2015, retrieved 10 March 2016, <http://www2.deloitte.com/us/en/pages/human-capital/articles/introduction-human-capital-trends.html>

20   'IBM social business', 2015, retrieved 24 December 2015, <http://www.ibm.com/social-business/us-en/>

21   S Sinek, 'How great leaders inspire action', TED talk, 2014, retrieved 15 April 2016, <https://www.ted.com/talks/simon_sinek_how_great_leaders_inspire_action?language=en

References

'18th Annual Global CEO Survey: PwC', 2009, retrieved 24 December 2015, <http://www.pwc.com/gx/en/ceo-survey/>

'A middle ground between contract worker and employee …', 2015, retrieved 10 March 2016, <http://www.nytimes.com/2015/12/11/business/a-middle-ground-between-contract-worker-and-employee.html>

'About | Black swan events', 2011, retrieved 23 February 2016, <http://blackswanevents.org/?page_id=26>

'Agent of change: The future of technology disruption in …', 2013, retrieved 24 December 2015, <http://www.economistinsights.com/sites/default/files/downloads/EIU_Agent%20of%20change_WEB_FINAL.pdf>

Bennett, N & Lemoine, GJ, 'What VUCA really means for you', *Harvard Business Review*, January–February 2014, retrieved 24 December 2015, <https://hbr.org/2014/01/what-vuca-really-means-for-you

'CEO study', KPMG U.S., 2014, retrieved 24 December 2015, <http://www.kpmg.com/us/en/topics/pages/ceo-study.aspx>

'How are CEOs addressing the issues they consider most …', 2015, retrieved 24 December 2015, <https://www.conference-board.org/ceo-challenge2015/>

'Human capital trends 2016', Deloitte U.S, 2015, retrieved 10 March 2016, <http://www2.deloitte.com/us/en/pages/human-capital/articles/introduction-human-capital-trends.html>

'IBM social business', 2015, retrieved 24 December 2015, <http://www.ibm.com/social-business/us-en/>

'Leading in a changing world: Lessons for …', 2015, Amazon.com, retrieved 24 December 2015, <http://www.amazon.com/Leading-Changing-World-Lessons-leaders-ebook/dp/B00YNGI47I>

'M-Pesa', Wikipedia, the free encyclopedia, 2011, retrieved 22 February 2016, <https://en.wikipedia.org/wiki/M-Pesa>

Naidoo, J, AFLI | African Leadership Institute, 2005, retrieved 23 February 2016, <http://alinstitute.org/>

Porter, ME, & Kramer, MR, 'Creating shared value', *Harvard Business Review*, January–February 2011, 2014, retrieved 22 December 2015, <https://hbr.org/2011/01/the-big-idea-creating-shared-value>

Sinek, S, 'How great leaders inspire action', TED talk, 2014, retrieved 15 April 2016, <https://www.ted.com/talks/simon_sinek_how_great_leaders_inspire_action?language=en>

'Sustainable living', Unilever global company website, 2012, retrieved 24 December 2015, <https://www.unilever.com/sustainable-living/>

'The empty raincoat: Making sense of the future', 2012, retrieved 23 February 2016, <http://www.amazon.com/THE-EMPTY-RAINCOAT-MAKING-FUTURE/dp/0099301253>

'The future of work', Fast Company, Business + Innovation', 2014, retrieved 24 December 2015, <http://www.fastcompany.com/section/the-future-of-work>

'The results of the 2015 Fortune 500 CEO survey are in …', 2015, retrieved 24 December 2015, <http://fortune.com/2015/06/04/fortune-500-ceo-survey/>

'The silo effect, by Gillian Tett', *The New York Times*, 2015, 22 December 2015, <http://www.nytimes.com/2015/09/06/books/review/the-silo-effect-by-gillian-tett.html>

PART 1

CHAPTER 6

TALENT DEVELOPMENT FOR SUSTAINABLE COMPETITIVENESS
Samuel Njenga

Sustainability is one of the most important strategic issues facing organisations and leaders around the world. Too often it is relegated to someone far from the corporate centre, who becomes responsible for philanthropic gestures and for arranging photo-shoots for executives, for inclusion in annual reports.

More importantly, the key relationship between talent management and sustainability is seldom recognised. In an increasing number of leading organisations, sustainability has become central to strategy.

In this chapter, Samuel Njenga demonstrates how leadership and talent development should be inextricably linked by sustainability as well as strategy. He highlights the development required at the board, executive and workforce levels. Each level needs to understand the sustainability framework, as the organisation applies it, and the concomitant responsibilities in formulating or executing the strategy.

Since Michael Porter embraced the term "social value" in preference to "shareholder value", the debate about the role of organisations in society has been fierce. It is my view that the conversation about sustainability needs to shift to one in which the role of business in society becomes central.

The value of this chapter lies in the practical and conceptual frameworks that are provided to assist organisations in positioning sustainability strategically. The argument made here, is to ensure that it forms an integral part of talent development. The challenge that the author poses to leaders and readers, is to adopt a strategic framework that is relevant to the organisation, and to ensure that role players (talent) at all levels understand the centrality of the framework to their business in a practical and operational way. This begins at board level, involves senior management and is operationalised by the workforce.

It is my wish that this chapter, in particular, will initiate conversations in individual businesses and business communities that will advance the conceptualisation of the subject to a higher level and embrace the role of business (and other organisations) in society. In Africa, as in many developing economies, it is a subject of critical importance to the leadership of all organisations. Their reputation will increasingly be determined by their role in society, given that expectations (in developing countries in particular) extend well beyond traditional, narrow notions of shareholder value.

Introduction

The chapter explores how to develop organisational leaders and managers in order to enhance organisational sustainability practices, by viewing them as sources of competitive advantage. For many organisations, the subject of sustainability is often viewed as a compliance or guilt payment or, at best, a philanthropic exercise that is disconnected from the core boardroom discussion. Even with greater attention to integrated reporting, there is growing evidence of a further disconnect between the glamour depicted in corporate reports and the actual reality on the ground. It is also well known that in many organisations, the management and reporting of sustainability practices reside outside of mainstream organisational talent development. Thus, issues around sustainability are not seen as critical boardroom discussions or strategic human development elements. Instead, sustainability practices are seen as cost centres that are dealt with for compliance purposes. For example, it is rare to hear of line managers in production processes being trained on sustainability principles and practices. Even where such training is offered, it tends to have a strong bias towards "green" issues, without any connection to the business strategy and practices as reflected in the value chain.

It can be argued that only companies that make sustainability their key goal, including rethinking their business models, products, technologies and processes, will achieve competitive advantage.[1] The authors argue that

> [s]ustainability is a mother lode of organizational and technological innovations that yield both bottom-line and top-line returns. Becoming environment-friendly lowers costs because companies end up reducing the inputs they use. In addition, the process generates additional revenues from better products or enables companies to create new businesses. In fact, because [growing the top and bottom lines] are the goals of corporate innovation, we find that smart companies now treat sustainability as innovation's new frontier.[2]

It is clear that building capacity through talent development enables an organisation to find innovative ways of making sustainability a key driver of performance and a source of competitive advantage.

Defining corporate sustainability

The starting point in developing talent for sustainable competitiveness must be a discussion about a more systemic definition of corporate sustainability. A wide range of definitions exist in mainstream literature, and this section will only focus on a few by highlighting and emphasising particularly helpful aspects thereof. The UN Global Compact Office defines corporate sustainability as "a company's delivery of long-term value in financial, social, environmental and ethical terms".[3] While this definition is helpful in broadening the discussion on sustainability beyond "green" issues, it also highlights one of the barriers to corporate sustainability, namely the long-term view. The global economic challenges of our era continue to place tremendous pressure on CEOs to focus on delivering shareholder value and returns. The time horizon for many organisations is thus the tenure of the CEO and the reporting cycle to shareholders, while for government agencies the tenure tends to be the election cycle. Such a short-term approach, which focuses on the incumbent's tenure in office to determine organisational success, undermines those efforts aimed at long-term value (as envisaged in the definition by the UN Global Compact Office). Currently, the emphasis in many organisations is on practices that will deliver value during a leader's time in office. There is a need to enable organisational leaders (including shareholders) to shift from a myopic way of measuring organisational success to one that recognises the need to invest in long-term value.

The *King report on corporate governance in South Africa* defines the sustainability of a company as "conducting operations in a manner that meets existing needs without compromising the ability of future generations to meet their needs".[4] It implies a regard for the impact that business operations have on the life of the community in which the organisation operates. Sustainability includes environmental, social and governance issues.[5] This definition is seminal in many ways, but particularly in highlighting governance as a core element of corporate sustainability. If governance is then seen as a core element, it brings to the fore the need to build capacity across all organisational (and particularly management and leadership) functions.

Talent development

Talent development for board members

Talent development for sustainable organisations needs to be seen as a vital and essential aspect of the identity, viability and performance of the firm. At the board level, talent development becomes about ensuring that the organisation has a systemic understanding of governance issues, including the conceptualisation and implementation of its core purpose. Sustainability at this level is also about ensuring shared value creation for all the organisation's stakeholders. Board members need to be equipped to position the organisation as a sustainability leader, not only in its practices but, importantly, in the way it defines itself. Board members need training on how to address issues such as the management of stakeholder relationships, enterprise risk, value creation and integrated thinking. The board needs to be enabled to engage with questions around what constitutes value for both shareholders and the wider stakeholder community. Sustainability at board level needs to be seen as the core strategic imperative of any enterprise. Sustainability then moves from the activities we perform, to the core of our identity. Some interesting case study examples within the South African business landscape include Woolworths, Unilever and Nedbank. These organisations have made great strides in going beyond selling products that are produced sustainably, to showcasing sustainability as core to who they are as organisations. What a number of similar organisations have shown, is that corporate sustainability can be a great source of competitive advantage.

Talent development for managers

At the organisational management level, the required capacity building includes aligning the organisational strategy and its operational practices with the principles of corporate sustainability. It is imperative that each operational practice be linked to a strategy that has sustainability at its heart. The common practice, though, is that while the organisation at the reporting level may be telling amazing stories of its advances in corporate sustainability, our experience is that line managers do not necessarily see the link between their activities and the company's sustainability goals. Even where the line managers practise elements of sustainability they do so in a fragmented way, mainly to save costs and without understanding the complete architecture of their organisational sustainability intent. Arguably, in such cases we are guilty of implementing corporate sustainability in unsustainable ways.

There is thus a need for a more cohesive and integrated approach to how organisations conceptualise and implement corporate sustainability. Such an approach would make it easier to identify training gaps for line managers, while offering a means for evaluating successes in the implementation of sustainability practices. Talent development at the managerial level needs to ensure that all the organisation's operations are aligned to the commitments on sustainability made at board level. Employees in, say, the finance or security department (or any other function within the organisation) need to be able to see the link between what they do and the organisation's goal of corporate sustainability. At the moment there is a disjuncture, even in organisations that claim to be leaders in corporate sustainability. With a better understanding of the imperative of corporate sustainability, this gap can be narrowed through existing talent development efforts.

Frameworks for talent development in corporate sustainability

In the past few years, a number of helpful models and frameworks have emerged, but our experience is that these remain unknown to many organisational leaders. Three such models will be considered as tools that can assist organisations not only in assessing their own sustainability practices, but also by providing frameworks around which their corporate strategies and operational practices can be developed, implemented and assessed. The models are: the Six Capitals Framework, the Triple Bottom Line and the Crane Matten, and Spence Model.

The Six Capitals Framework

While many organisations use the Six Capitals Framework in their sustainability reporting, our experience is that very few have gone further to align their corporate strategy to the framework. In such cases, where the framework is only used in the reporting phase, there is a disconnect between corporate strategy and sustainability reporting. An emphasis on integrated reporting has not necessarily led to integrated thinking. Herein lies a capacity-building gap for many organisations – that of enabling a more integrated approach to sustainability. The Six Capitals Framework can be a helpful tool not only for measuring and reporting on progress made around elements of sustainable practices, but more importantly for enabling a shared approach to an organisational strategy with sustainability at its heart. The elements of models such as the Six Capitals can be helpful in focusing the implementation of an organisational strategy on sustainability. So what does the Six Capitals Framework entail?

The background paper for integrated reporting refers to this framework as "any store of value that an organization can use in the production of goods or services".[6]

All organisations depend on various forms of capital for their success. These capitals are stores of value that, in one form or another, become inputs to the organisation's business model. They are also increased, decreased or transformed through the activities of the organisation in that they are enhanced, consumed, modified or otherwise affected by those activities.[7]

These capitals are listed as

- natural,
- human,
- social and relational,
- intellectual,
- manufactured and
- financial.

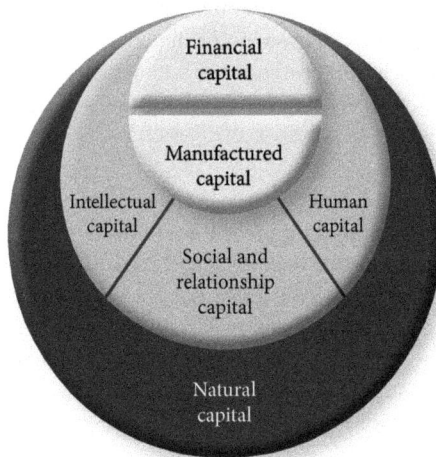

Figure 6.1   The Six Capitals Framework[8]

While not all organisations use all six capitals to the same extent, the framework is very helpful as a diagnostic tool not just for reporting on sustainability practices, but also for assessing an organisation's strategy. While many organisations are familiar with reporting on financial, manufactured and human capital, the other three capitals are not as well integrated into the measurement and reporting cycles. Thus, for example, an organisation may wish to assess what natural capital it requires for its operational practices, how it is sourcing and utilising the same, and where opportunities exist for finding more creative ways of using that capital. This approach could shift the focus from reporting to thinking. So, for example, an organisation may wish to engage with the question of how it can derive competitive advantage by shifting its thinking around its use of natural capital. A number of companies in the hospitality industry have found creative ways of recycling and using grey water. Others have invested in buildings that make better use of natural lighting and solar heating, and hence reduce the use of electricity and other sources of power.

The gap for talent development using the Six Capitals Framework may be in terms of how to train and equip all managers to understand the framework and, importantly, to align all operational practices to it. As a consequence, the emphasis will move from having a select group of people who use the framework to develop glossy reports, to a scenario where all operations are aligned to the framework. A similar approach can be followed for the other "capitals". One way of assessing the value of the other capitals is to think of the cost of replacement. For instance, what intellectual capital does the company need for its operations, and what would be the replacement cost involved?

It is important to note that there has been criticism of the limitations of using what is an economic model to assess and measure the complex and often nonlinear aspects of organisational life. However, the strength of the model lies not only at the point of measurement and reporting, but crucially at the point of strategy and talent development for sustainability. An organisation can use the framework as a way of ensuring that its strategy is more than merely a focus on financial numbers.

Triple Bottom Line

The Triple Bottom Line Model gained currency in the late 1990s, having first been articulated by John Elkington in his 1997 book *Cannibals with forks: The triple bottom line of 21st century business,*[9] which looks at sustainability in terms of three Ps: people, planet and profit. While the traditional approach to measuring organisational success mainly centred around financial achievement, the Triple Bottom Line introduced a more holistic way which also looked at the planet and people elements. Elkington, in his articulation of the term, calls for a more values-driven way of doing business, which sees corporates taking responsibility for their relationship with the earth and humanity as a whole. The use of the Triple Bottom Line as a way of measuring the impact and performance of an organisation saw the focus move from short-term financial measures to a more long-term focus that investigates the impact on the environment and society in general. This model calls on corporates to embrace a much deeper form of stakeholder capitalism that seeks value for the firm, while acting responsibly within the ecosystem in which it operates.

There has been criticism for the way this concept is understood and implemented, including the way people conceptualise the relationship between the three elements. Much of the literature depicts the relationship as three concentric circles that intersect, with sustainability happening at the point of their intersection (see Figure 6.2).

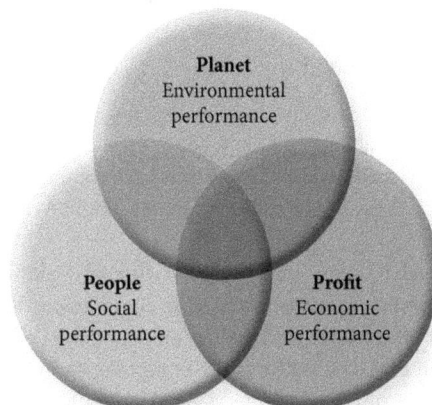

Figure 6.2   The Triple Bottom Line

Later thinking started questioning this understanding. The diagramme depicted sustainability as part of what the company does, which raises questions about what else the firm is doing that is *not* related to issues of sustainability. What resides in the other parts of the circles that fall outside of the points of intersection?

Recent thinking has focused on a different understanding of the relationship between the three circles. In Figure 6.3, the planet is depicted as the sphere that carries all matter (human and non-human), as well as all the social and economic activities we perform. Since economic activities fall within the social sphere, one could argue that a business cannot exist outside a social context, and that the social context cannot exist outside of an environmental context.

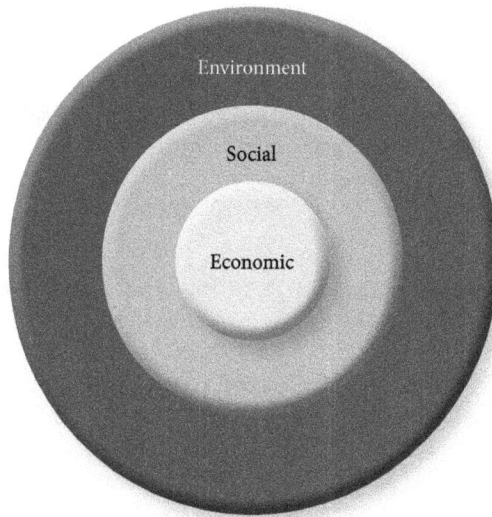

Figure 6.3   Triple Bottom Line Model

This model has seen the development of various tools that can be used to assist an organisation in developing its strategy, and ensuring that all three aspects are taken care of. Various other tools which are aligned to this model are available for measuring and reporting on an organisation's sustainability efforts.

The Triple Bottom Line Model is a useful tool in any organisation's managerial talent development process. Like the previous model, it can be used to assess the current activities of the organisation in each of three areas, and to set goals aimed at helping the organisation become more strategic in its sustainability efforts.

The Crane, Matten and Spence Framework

Crane Matten, and Spence view corporate sustainability as being at the centre of organisational strategy. Instead of strategy driving sustainability practices, sustainability informs and drives all aspects of organisational strategy, including its execution. These authors see corporate sustainability as encompassing four main areas: the marketplace, the workplace, the community and the environment.[10]

What does this mean in practice? If sustainability is at the core of organisational strategy, then it drives the organisation's engagement with the marketplace. Any commitment to corporate sustainability will then inform, for example, what products or services the company avails to the marketplace, along with its choice of packaging. It also means being sensitive to the impact the corporate's products and services have on the health and safety of the consumer community. The organisation's board needs to be guided by its commitment to corporate sustainability, as it seeks to provide the parameters within which the firm may operate in the marketplace.

Sustainability thus informs other aspects of the business, like partnerships, geographical location, etc. While these choices may come at a cost, they are useful indicators of the extent to which the firm is committed to its sustainability plan. A recent example within the South African business landscape is restaurants and fish markets that have chosen not to trade in endangered species of fish. The retailer, Woolworths, recently removed sweets from counters located next to the tills, as part of its commitment to the health of its customers.

The second element of the Crane Matten, and Spence understanding of corporate sustainability is that it needs to drive the firm's relationship with its internal workforce. A company that is committed to being a corporate citizen will prioritise any practices that enhance the welfare of its workforce. Such a company will commit to ensuring the best possible outcomes for its personnel/staff, which includes subscribing to fair practice in regard to staff remuneration, a healthy work-life balance and meaningful employment opportunities. Aspects like staff training and other human development activities are integrated and driven by its strategic focus on being a sustainable entity.

The third aspect of the Crane Matten, and Spence definition is one of community development. A company that has corporate sustainability at its core is also committed to ensuring that the community in which it operates is healthy. Participating in practices like community development, education, health-related or job-creation initiatives and other such projects becomes linked and is driven as part of the firm's strategy. In this respect, some organisations have explored creative ways in which to move away from philanthropic relationships with communities. Instead, they have found ways of building those communities as part of their value chain, allowing communities to become strategic business partners instead of passive recipients of donations. "Inclusive business practices" defines this attempt to build communities into the value chain of the organisation. In so doing, the firm converts such relationships with communities from a donor–recipient relationship to a strategic business partnership.

In the fourth instance, Crane Matten, and Spence argue that corporate sustainability drives the relationship of the firm with its natural environment. This entails reviewing its use of natural resources like water, as well as its waste disposal. If sustainability is the driving strategy, the organisation can and will find ways to shift to alternative energy sources as a strategic move which makes business sense. The firm is then able to make operational decisions, such as moving away from paper-based approaches to electronic processes. In this way, the company cuts down on the operational costs of material, while contributing to an improved and more efficient use of natural resources.

Conclusion

These three models have been presented as examples of frameworks that a company may use to structure its approach to corporate sustainability. Importantly, this chapter has sought to argue that companies need to see sustainabilty as a key strategic opportunity and imperative, hence the need to build it into their talent development agenda. Further, talent development for corporate sustainability must be availed to all levels of the organisation. At the board level, the emphasis would be on governance and organisational identity as a corporate citizen. At the management level, talent development should empower managers to centre and drive their organisational strategy off the bedrock of corporate sustainability. In other words, instead of strategy driving sustainability, the commitment to sustainability must determine the company's strategic choices. At the workforce level, the emphasis on talent development is on the execution of sustainability, across all the firm's operations and activities, and doing so in a focused manner.

Endnotes

1. R Nidumolu, CK Prahalad & MR Rangaswami, 'Why sustainability is now key driver of innovation', *Harvard Business Review*, vol. 87, no. 9, 2009, pp. 57-64.
2. Ibid.
3. United Nations Global Compact Office, 'Corporate sustainability blueprint', June 2010, retrieved 8 July 2016, <https://www.globalcompact.de/wAssets/docs/Reporting/blueprint_for_corporate_sustainability_leadership.pdf>.
4. Institute of Directors in Southern Africa, *The King report on corporate governance in South Africa*, Johannesburg, 2009.
5. Ibid, pp. 118, 128.
6. A Crane, D Matten & LJ Spence, 'Corporate social responsibility in global context', in *Corporate social responsibility: Readings and cases in global context*, Routledge, Abingdon, Oxon, UK, 2008, pp. 3–20, retrieved 8 July 2016, <http://ssrn.com/abstract=1667081>.
7. Ibid.
8. Integrated Reporting, 'Background paper for Integrated Reporting', retrieved 2013, <http://integratedreporting.org//wp-content/uploads/2013/03/IR-Background-Paper-Capitals.pdf>.
9. J Elkington, *Cannibals with forks: The triple bottom line of twenty-first century business*, Capstone, Oxford, 1997.
10. Crane, Matten & Spence, op. cit.

References

Crane, A, D Matten & LJ Spence, 'Corporate social responsibility in global context', in *Corporate social responsibility: Readings and cases in global context*, Routledge, Abingdon, Oxon, UK, 2008, pp. 3–20, retrieved 8 July 2016, <http://ssrn.com/abstract=1667081>.

Elkington, J, *Cannibals with forks: The triple bottom line of twenty-first century business*, Capstone, Oxford, 1997.

Institute of Directors in Southern Africa, *The King Report on corporate governance in South Africa*, Johannesburg, 2009.

Integrated Reporting, 'Background paper for Integrated Reporting', retrieved 2013, <http://integratedreporting.org//wp-content/uploads/2013/03/IR-Background-Paper-Capitals.pdf>

Nidumolu, R, CK Prahalad & MR Rangaswami, 'Why sustainability is now key driver of innovation', *Harvard Business Review*, vol. 87, no. 9, 2009, pp. 57-64.

United Nations Global Compact Office, 'Corporate sustainability blueprint', June 2010, retrieved 8 July 2016, <https://www.globalcompact.de/wAssets/docs/Reporting/blueprint_for_corporate_sustainability_leadership.pdf>.

PART 1

CHAPTER 7

DEVELOPING A COMPELLING EMPLOYER VALUE PROPOSITION TO ATTRACT AFRICA'S TOP TALENT
Jenali Skuse and Madeline Lass

I have always believed that there needs to be close alignment between a company's brand and the culture of the organisation. In fact, culture should be the internal representation of the promises and values of the external brand. This suggests that the expectations and values of employees at all levels need to be consistent with those of the culture and external brand. This approach supports the idea that committed employees contribute to loyal customers, who in turn positively impact financial value. Leading organisations understand this relationship.

This chapter demonstrates the importance of building a powerful employer value proposition (EVP) that will attract the kind of talent an organisation requires to support the organisational culture and external brand values. Having a strong, relevant EVP is essential not only for attracting talent from outside the organisation, but also for creating an identity that facilitates the deep engagement of current talent.

As with an external brand, an EVP needs to differentiate the organisation from those in similar sectors and should be compelling, rather than simply statements hanging against the walls in the company's reception area. That is one of the reasons why I believe employer branding is not the sole preserve of the HR function; it requires a collaborative partnership between marketing and HR specialists.

The great thing about this chapter is the evidence it produces in support of the arguments the authors make – particularly in the African context. Universum has a powerful research capability, and its history of research throughout Africa is clearly evident in, and adds great value and authenticity to, the chapter. It is professionally written and easy to read, with specific cases illustrating the competitive value of powerful EVPs.

This chapter is an essential read for anyone who wishes to take their organisation beyond the "normal". It will help organisations build an employer brand that is a significant differentiator in a competitive talent environment. The considerable amount of quantitative data on offer in the chapter is highly informative, particularly in the African context.

Introduction

A plethora of global studies and surveys, together with years of business experience, have demonstrated that an organisation's success is directly linked to its ability to attract and retain the right talent. The picture is no different in Africa. Indeed, the war for talent is likely to become increasingly fierce, owing to a number of unique challenges facing businesses operating on the continent. For this reason, it is doubly important for companies to focus on their employer branding activities.

Why is employer branding doubly important in Africa?

David Storey, EY Partner, People and Organisation, South Africa, commenting on EY's 2013/14 survey on sub-Saharan Africa (SSA) talent trends and practices, states:

> The survey results clearly indicate that whilst Sub-Saharan Africa is not a blank canvas upon which human capital practices can be imposed at will, there is still work to be done in preparing African workforces to support, participate in, and benefit from rapid economic development. Moreover a shotgun approach to human capital management practices on the continent is shortsighted; organisational and regional differences point to nuances that require differentiated and contextually appropriate responses. Success in Africa therefore requires a detailed understanding of the HR milieu, and an authentic commitment and investment in human capital.[1]

When EY was conducting its 2015 Africa Attractiveness Survey,[2] it found that some 70 per cent of African firms were recruiting to support their growth ambitions on the continent. Yet vacancies were taking longer to fill and employee turnover was high – this, despite the slow-down experienced by the region in recent years. Economic expansion was at its slowest in five years in 2015, mainly owing to lower commodity prices and the poor performance of the South African economy. EY[3] also found that investor sentiment had softened somewhat, and that foreign direct investment (FDI) projects were down for a second consecutive year in 2014.

SSA nevertheless remains more solid than many other developing and emerging regions of the world. The headwinds notwithstanding, growth in the region is set to beat the emerging market average, and will be outstripped only by a developing Asia. Ethiopia, Kenya, Tanzania, Mozambique, Zambia and Côte d'Ivoire are among 22 economies in the region that are expected to grow by more than five per cent in 2016. This makes Africa the second fastest-growing region in the world.[4]

It is important to remember, however, that the picture is mixed, reflecting the complexity of this great continent. EY nevertheless remains confident that the "Africa rising" narrative remains intact and sustainable.[5]

Unfortunately, the continent's continued growth has not always translated into progress in the fields of gender parity, social development and education. And this exacerbates the talent challenges facing local and international companies wishing to grow their businesses in Africa. The most critical of these are governance issues, as well as a shortage of scarce skills, soft skills and leadership material.

Globally, just one third of countries have achieved the measurable Education for All (EFA) goals set in 2000. None in SSA achieved them, and only seven countries in the region achieved even the most-watched goal of universal primary enrolment. Sixteen of the 20 lowest-ranked countries in terms of progress towards EFA are in the SSA region. An extra $22 billion a year is needed on top of already ambitious global government contributions to ensure that the new global education targets being set for 2030 are achieved.[6]

Unesco forecasts that Africa is likely to be home to half of the world's illiterate people in the coming years – a situation that will clearly limit the number of highly qualified employees available for hire by companies and other organisations.[7] EY's SSA Talent Trends and Practices Survey, 2013/14[8] had already established that this was the case. Add this to the fact that many companies conceded that they lacked the capacity to plan for and manage skills development. In the survey, which spanned 23 countries across SSA, the activities of developing and delivering technical and vocational skills, doing workforce planning,as well as career management and development, were rated lowest by 224 participants in respect of their capacity to perform and deliver.

This was confirmed by a new report on executive talent by Russell Reynolds Associates, which surveyed 230 senior leaders and recruiters in Africa.[9] The report shows that companies are eager to recruit great talent in the region, but are finding it difficult to fill positions where traditional management skills, such as the ability to drive change or build teams, are required.[10]

Considering the inability of staff within African-based HR departments to manage their talent attraction strategies adequately, as well as the paucity of companies in the region with "talent academies", it is clear that much work still needs to be done. Combine that with the continent's underinvestment in education and the shortage of good business schools, and the situation becomes even more critical.

To date, global firms have relied heavily on imported talent to fill local roles in Africa, but relocating people is costly and does not strengthen the local talent pipeline. Hiring expatriates is also becoming increasingly undesirable, for political and social reasons.

The EY SSA Talent Trends and Practices Survey[11] nevertheless shows that some companies are successful in developing their talent management skills. Those respondents who had found it easier to recruit during the period covered by the survey, cited the following reasons:

- Improvement in HR processes and, in particular, recruitment;
- A stronger employer brand;
- The use of capable agencies and HR service providers to undertake recruitment;
- High unemployment rates and the resultant availability of labour; and
- Recruitment focus on entry-level jobs.

Those who found it harder to recruit over the same period attributed this to a lack of talent with the right skills – particularly in the scarce skills categories. Specific concerns included the availability of skills, the quality of skills/levels of competence, and levels of experience.

Developing a differentiating employer brand

It is clear from the above that companies doing business in Africa need creative and innovative solutions to overcome the talent challenges they face. And, by extension, the place to start would be by improving HR processes and focusing on employer branding activities.

In this chapter we leave innovations around HR processes to those more qualified to discuss them. Instead, we focus on current thinking around brand building and EVP development, drawing heavily on research done by Universum.[12] Another source is *Employer brand management*, by Richard Mosley, VP of Strategy at Universum.[13]

What is the difference between an employer brand and an EVP?

'Employer brand' describes people's *perceptions* of an employer (good, bad, indifferent), whereas the EVP defines the qualities which a potential employer would like to be associated with, and consistently aspires to deliver through the employment experience. "Employer branding" describes the activities an organisation undertakes to communicate its employer brand image, while "employer brand management" describes the full spectrum of activities a company orchestrates to deliver both a consistent brand image and experience.

A good EVP affects revenue growth and profit margins. Recently, LinkedIn[14] surveyed 2 250 corporate recruiters in the United States to learn more about time to hire, cost per hire metrics and (most importantly) the impact of a strong employer brand. They discovered that companies with strong employer brands enjoy significant cost savings, with lower cost per hire and employee turnover rates.

- Companies with strong employer brands' reported cost per hire is less than half that of companies which are less popular; and
- Companies with stronger employer brands have 28 per cent lower employee turnover rates than those with weaker employer brands.

Why a strong employer brand matters

Employer branding is the process of generating appeal, creating an identity, communicating that identity and ensuring that the identity remains authentic and true. It is about ensuring that your organisation is known, respected and considered a great place to work. The "product" of your employer brand is your EVP, and your "customers" are current and prospective staff. Your EVP comprises both tangible and intangible benefits, such as salaries, bonuses, and the organisation's culture and values. It is these benefits that back up the employer's brand in the marketplace. Every organisation, without exception, has an employer brand (whether it is articulated or not), because both its internal and external audiences have an opinion about it as an employer. Such opinions will always be a mix of good and bad, and they will always exist. The art of employer branding is to take control of the brand and align it with the organisation's long-term business needs. In other words, the brand is designed to attract and retain the talent the company needs most; i.e., those who can help it innovate and improve its market share.

What is an EVP?

Richard Mosley[15] notes that EVPs typically include an overall core positioning statement supported by three to five additional attributes or pillars. He describes the role of the core positioning statement as defining the

- compelling essence or heart of your proposition;
- one thing you most want to be famous for as an employer; and
- quality or idea around which you build your employer brand story.

Mosley believes that the role of the pillars is to provide a consistent reference point and linking mechanism for

- building the employer brand image and reputation – the key qualities the organisation wishes to be associated with as an employer;
- defining the employment deal – the key benefits employees can expect from employment with the organisation, balanced with what is expected of them in return;
- determining the key employer brand communication themes; and
- shaping the employer brand experience – the key priorities for people management policies and practices.

Simon Riis-Hansen, Senior Vice-President of HR at the LEGO Group, has the following to say about their EVP:

> What our People Promise [EVP] has done is provide us with a compass that can guide us in multiple ways from our strategic direction to our everyday decision making and it is something you can see present all the way from our HR processes to the way we manage our value creation within the business to the way we communicate as leaders in the company every single day. You can find it has coloured everything we do as a company. It's been woven into the fabric of how we do things.[16]

What is the purpose of employer branding?

The purpose of employer branding is twofold: to retain and engage the right current employees and to manage the perception potential future employees have of you as an employer. Retaining the right employees has many benefits: chief among these is that it decreases staff turnover and hiring costs, and, second, it optimises engagement, which contributes positively to productivity. Being an attractive employer to the right external talent is equally important, primarily because it serves to increase the number of suitable individuals applying to the organisation in a spontaneous manner. A strong employer brand also helps ensure that the right candidates choose to accept an offer from your company when they have other offers on the table.

What is the relation between corporate brand and employer brand?

Organisations have a single corporate brand, which is the perception people have of the company or firm as a whole. Its employer brand, together with its product brands, is a facet of that overarching brand. For a company to be successful and profitable over time, every aspect of the brand must deliver on its promise. Three factors are common to all successful employer brands: they have buy-in from top management, a clear vision of what they want to achieve, and a realistic strategy for achieving their goals.

A guide to developing an effective employer brand

The strategic priorities of the business set the talent agenda

The ability of a business to grow its market share in Africa depends on its talent. Talent has therefore become a strategic priority for the majority of CEOs, which has changed the relationship between HR and the executive suite. CEOs work closely with HR in developing their goals and strategies.

Of course, the best employers have always cared about talent. General Electric has been grooming its top people in its corporate university in Crotonville for 50 years. Companies like Nestlé, P&G, McKinsey & Co and Unilever have been relentless in their pursuit of hiring and and training the best for decades, consistently falling back on hard numbers to inform talent-related decisions as well as making it a top management concern.

According to PWC's 18th Annual Global CEO Survey, which appeared on 19 January 2016,[17] the skills shortage has become a crisis-level priority for CEOs. The survey found that of the 1 300 CEOs polled, 73 per cent named the skills shortage as a threat to their business, compared to 46 per cent just six years ago.

The digital age has transformed a nagging worry into something far more challenging: 81 per cent of CEOs admit they are looking for a wider mix of skills than they did in the past. According to the report, businesses desperately need hi-tech innovators and "hybrid" workers who understand not only their own sector, but also complex digital technology.[18] Digital transformation is unstoppable; it affects every industry and business, and reaches far wider than just the internet of things [IoT]. CEOs are aware that they need to react rapidly to mitigate the risks involved in digital transformation.

KuppingerCole's principal analyst, Martin Kuppinger,[19] states that this means all organisations need to develop new business models: "Just think about smart manufacturing, smart wallets, smart vehicles, smart homes, smart grids, e-books, digital music, online retail and online payments." Such a new business model will, according to Kuppinger, include aspects such as business/IT integration (which goes beyond alignment); managing the connectedness of everything and everyone in the organisation; integrating safety and security to safeguard the organisation's digital transformation; and the ability to see that risks can sometimes be opportunities.[20] CEOs are dealing with "a boiling mix of opportunities and threats, driven by technology that's mining new markets but which is also transforming everything around them, from how their customers behave to what their people expect from work".[21] Clearly, this new way of thinking also demands a new way of thinking about talent: "Workers with the most in-demand-skills are creating a 'gig economy', where they're in control of where and when they work."[22]

Identify factualists vs. fatalists

Universum believes that "the most important divide in today's talent market runs between employers who prefer to stick with their gut feelings and trusted ways of working, oblivious to new challenges; and employers who view talent as a strategic and competitive asset".[23] The former are fatalists, leaving everything to chance, while the latter are factualists who make calculated, data-driven decisions. Fatalist organisations will find it difficult to deal with the changing economic and technological environment. Most importantly, they will not have the kind of talent that is capable of dealing with these changes. Factualist organisations will be equipped with the information they need to deal with market fluctuations and exponential technological change. Factualists know that the only sustainable way to maintain a competitive edge in the long term, is to simply be better than the rest. To do this they incorporate a number of approaches in their talent strategy:

- Redefine talent (what it is, where and how it can be found);
- Build talent rather than relying on education systems/other employers;
- Reskill and adjust the HR function to the new environment;
- Focus, above all, on organisational agility; and
- Tie together all efforts in the employer brand.

Assess your own employer brand

Factualists assess their employer brands by devoting time and attention to finding out where they stand, in the eyes of both their own employees and their target audience. A good place to start is to gather and review existing data and insights, through

- external reputation and attraction research;
- competitor analysis;
- new joiner surveys; and
- employee engagement surveys, exit surveys and focus groups.

Identify any gaps that need filling before progressing to proposition development. Universum's experience is that the biggest gap often involves qualitative research data. While engagement survey data may give an indication of relative strengths and weaknesses from a people management perspective, it seldom provides the necessary cultural insight required to build a distinctive EVP. In addition, it is valuable to benchmark yourself against your industry peers as well as top employers in adjacent industries in relevant geographies. By benchmarking your attractiveness and employer image against your chosen competitors, you can ascertain whether your messages are being communicated effectively, and portray a distinct brand.

It is surprising how little differentiation there can be between companies in a particular industry. Mosley[24] relates that he had the opportunity of working, at different times, with P&G, Unilever, L'Oreal and Pepsico. He was soon struck by the fact that the companies differed widely in respect of working practice and culture. It was to be expected that the American origins of P&G and Pepsico, the French L'Oreal and the Anglo-Dutch roots of Unilever would make them very different organisations to work for from a cultural point of view, yet in 2006 they described themselves to potential candidates in a remarkably similar manner:

- P&G: "Passionate about innovating and resolute about winning";
- Pepsico: "Constantly improving, innovating and driving new success";
- L'Oreal: "True entrepreneurs with creative flair and drive in a dynamic and passionate working environment"; and
- Unilever: "People with energy, creativity and commitment working together to fulfil ambitious goals".

Mosley points out that the main players in the market used the same words to describe the primary talent requirements within the fast-moving consumer goods (FMCG) sector: passion, innovation and performance. "What they hadn't focused on was what made them different from one another. What this example demonstrates is that 7–8 years ago the world's leading experts in differentiated product positioning had yet to fully apply the same thinking to their employer brands. Three years later the picture was very different."[25]

- PepsiCo decided to highlight its surprisingly varied range of career possibilities, which included a wide array of well-known companies and brands not usually associated with the company. They also made known the scale of their global presence, with close to 250 000 employees working across 200 countries;
- P&G's new brand positioning downplayed its size and smashed perceptions of it being process and systems-driven. Instead, the firm stressed the more personal and passionate side of the business: "We hire the person, not the position," located P&G as a people-oriented company with a high tolerance for (if not outright encouragement of) individual character;
- L'Oréal faced the challenge of being perceived as a suave and sophisticated company that had no difficulty attracting the brightest and best women and marketers. It therefore decided to reinforce its global business credentials, drive and global mindset to attract more scientists, engineers and commercial managers who previously may not have considered themselves right for L'Oréal;
- Unilever informed potential employees of its role in creating a better life for people in numerous small ways, every day, in virtually every country in the world. Since the days of Lord Leverhume's investment in making a better life for his workers at Port Sunlight, the social mission at Unilever has always been as strong as its business ambition. This seemed a unique way for Unilever to build on its historic roots, while reaching out – in a highly relevant way – to a new generation of more socially aware and committed graduates.

These examples represent four quite different ways of positioning each employer brand, which helped potential candidates better understand the companies' offerings. The examples illustrate why it is fundamental to be aware of how target group competitors present themselves.

Mosley's extensive experience extends to a recent employer brand development exercise he undertook in the oil and gas sector, alongside other major competitors for engineering talent where he found a very similar narrative pattern running through most of the companies' career sites:

- Committed people (Shell: Talent and tenacity; Exxon Mobil: Exceptional people; Chevron: People with the drive to keep moving; GE: Dedicated people; Rolls Royce: Committed to delivering; BMW: Passionate people)
- creating innovative solutions (Shell: More innovative solutions; Exxon Mobil: Take initiative and be innovative; Conoco Phillips: Innovation and excellence; GE: Dedicated to innovation; Rolls Royce: Relentless innovation; BMW: Innovative ideas)
- to big challenges (Chevron: Our team has the technology to take on big challenges; Schlumberger: Addressing the most challenging engineering problems on earth; GE: Taking on the world's toughest challenges)
- shaping the future (Shell: Shaping the future of energy; Chevron: Laying the groundwork for decades of progress: your energy shapes our future; BMW: No need to predict the future, you can create it); and
- realising their potential (Exxon: Unlocking your potential; Conoco Phillips: Realise your full potential; EDF: Fulfil your potential).

Once an organisation thoroughly understands the positioning landscape of its industry and other competitors, it will be able to create a positioning statement that differentiates it and clearly articulates its offering.

Understand what talent wants

Once you know what your talent needs are, you need to understand the preferences, opinions and expectations of target groups through extensive research to ensure that your employer branding strategies are appropriate for those groups. It enables employers to create messages for their marketing campaigns that clarify what they offer candidates as well as what they expect from them. Of importance will be understanding the preferences of the talent generations (Baby Boomers, Millennials and now Generation Z).

By 2030, many of the world's largest economies will have more jobs than skilled people to do those jobs. As a result, the talent market will be even more competitive than it is today. To prepare, Universum conducted the biggest Gen Z survey ever to help clients "visualise" their future workforce.[26] The over 40 000 Gen Z respondents came from 46 countries across the Americas, Europe, the Middle East, the Asia-Pacific and South Africa. The report's top findings include:

- Optimistic spirit: this generation believes anything is possible – 65 per cent are hopeful about the future;
- Values at work: nearly four in ten are afraid that they will not find a job that matches their personality. They have a strong desire to be themselves and express their personality at work – something employers must keep in mind;
- University alternatives: only 15 per cent accept that they may have to forego university outright, but 47 per cent say they would "maybe" consider the notion of joining the workforce, instead of pursuing tertiary studies. This means employers will have to invest more in training and development;
- Entrepreneurial mindset: interestingly, 55 per cent are interested in starting their own company. This figure is even higher in emerging markets, especially Africa. Some companies, such as Nestlé, are already positioning themselves as looking for talent with an entrepreneurial mindset;
- Gen Zs are greatly influenced by the economically challenging times they grew up in, which translates into a desire to volunteer or contribute to a higher purpose. As a result they are much more interested in charity work than the Millennials who came before them; over 25 per cent of today's older Gen Z members actively volunteer, and 60 per cent of them want their future career choices to change the world for good;
- Gen Z is also the most "plugged in" of any generation. Their five devices (on average) allow for greater ease of access to knowledge, and may in fact revolutionise, if not replace, the traditional college classroom style of learning.

In South Africa, Gen Zs use an average of 4.6 social media platforms, as opposed to the global average of 4.1. Facebook remains the most popular globally (77%), YouTube comes in second (59%); Instagram third (43%) and Twitter sixth (37%). While Facebook is the best medium for communicating with Gen Z, it is important to consider that, in South Africa, 38 per cent like receiving communications from potential employers on social media, while 68 per cent dislike it. The global picture is more balanced: 41 per cent likes vs. 59 per cent dislikes. This points to a shift in preferences and the fast-paced nature of their digital lives. It may, in some instances, mean employers and employer branding teams need to look at new social platforms such as Whisper and Snapchat to grab their attention.

As companies increasingly take up the opportunities offered by Africa's growth, the need arises to understand what future African employees expect from their employers. Universum's report, *Attracting talent in emerging markets: Focus on Africa*,[27] which reflects data from 1.2 million students and professionals across 50+ countries as its foundation, provides a number of interesting insights.

Africa's population is not homogenous, but the research indicates that young talent in Africa are self-starters who value entrepreneurialism and are looking for a challenge. On average, students in emerging markets rate work–life balance first. In African countries, however, being entrepreneurial is graduates' top career goal. There is more variation when it comes to professionals: in Kenya, for example, the top goal is being competitively or intellectually challenged; followed by work–life balance and then being entrepreneurial or creative/innovative. In Ghana, however, professionals cite the following goals in order of preference: being entrepreneurial or creative/innovative; being competitively or intellectually challenged; and being dedicated to a cause/feel they are serving a greater good.

What do students in emerging markets look for in future employers and roles?

- A creative and dynamic work environment is the most sought-after attribute of workplace culture among business and engineering students;
- Graduates find professional training and development very attractive job characteristics, more so than flexible working conditions or personal control over the number of hours worked; and
- Students in Africa prioritise the desire to feel they are contributing to serving the greater good.

These goals shift from year to year, and once again demonstrate how vital it is to keep abreast of the needs and attitudes of their talent target markets.

Your employer brand and corporate brand are interlinked

A company's employer brand should be intimately linked with its corporate brand values and purpose. It is extremely difficult to build an attractive employer brand when your corporate brand has serious issues. Companies with a great sense of purpose (they know why they are in business) and which can articulate it clearly, are more likely to attract great talent.

In *Start with why*,[28] Simon Sinek describes his "golden circle" theory, where the golden circle finds order and predictability in human behaviour: "Put simply, it helps us understand why we do what we do." Sinek points out that every company knows *what* it does. Organisations also tend to explain *how* something is different or better (their unique selling proposition [USP] or value proposition). But your *why* asks the question: What is your purpose, cause or belief? When most companies and people think, act or communicate, they do so from the outside in, from What to Why.

If Apple were like everyone else, they would say: "We make great computers. They are beautifully designed, simple to use and user-friendly. Want to buy one?" But Apple is not like everyone else because they say: "Everything we do, we believe in challenging the status quo. We believe in thinking differently. The way we challenge the status quo is by making our products beautifully designed, simple to use and user-friendly. And we happen to make great computers. Want to buy one?" Apple starts with its *why* – the company's purpose, cause and belief. It has nothing to do with *what* Apple does. What the company does – the products it makes – is not the reason to buy. Apple's products are the tangible representation of the company's purpose or cause. As Sinek keeps reminding us: people don't buy what you do, they buy why you do it. And Apple is surely one of the most remarkable organisations, driven by its guiding principles, which are not to be compromised for financial gain or short-term expediency.

There is a great danger in creating a set of values that are generic and meaningless: communication; respect; integrity; excellence. If every organisation articulates these, they must be true, right? But are they? It so happens that the above values were also Enron's. And we know how that ended. When values mean nothing, they create cynical and dispirited employees, alienate customers and undermine managerial credibility.

The opposite is also true. Southwest Airlines' values, for instance, clearly reflect the straight-talking influence of the company's founder, Herb Kelleher:

- Warrior spirit: work hard; desire to be the best; be courageous; display urgency; persevere; innovate;

- A servant's heart: follow the golden rule; adhere to the principles; treat others with respect; put others first; be egalitarian; demonstrate proactive customer service; embrace the SWA family;
- Fun-luvin' attitude: Have FUN; don't take yourself too seriously; maintain perspective; celebrate successes; enjoy your work; be a passionate team player.

Differentiation

The main focus of employer brand management over the past decade has largely been establishing consistency, but is increasingly shifting to differentiation. It is vital to position a company in terms of its distinctive qualities, which requires a clear statement of the quality you most want to be famous for as an employer.

There are eight common positioning territories: status, purpose, teamwork, autonomy, innovation, learning, career progression and performance. Because companies within the same market often gravitate towards the same core positioning territory, it is important to research the positioning territories of competitors.

Karl-Johan Hasselström, Global COO and MD EMEA at Universum, found several marvellous examples of positioning statements that fail to differentiate the company.

Opportunity:

- Bank of America: Welcome to a world of opportunities
- Careers at Citi: A world of opportunity
- HSBC: Gateway to a world of opportunities

DNA:

- Amazon: Innovation is in our DNA
- HP: Big ideas are in our DNA
- Atos: Innovation is in our DNA
- Samsung: Innovation is in our DNA

A competitive salary and benefits package is still necessary, but this is called a threshold offering. Millennials, for example, expect companies to paint a picture of what life would be like working for their organisation – the compensation and benefits packages are much less important than they were in the past.

Companies that are able to communicate a message that conveys what it would really be like to work there day-to-day, will stand out and attract the best talent. This is easier said than done, as is reflected in the results of Universum's Talent Attraction Barometer: more than half of companies surveyed listed "differentiation" as their top employer branding challenge. What makes differentiation difficult is that it requires time and patience to understand the intersection between what you have to offer and what your ideal employee wants. Marketing executives focus on this area by constantly conducting surveys and focus groups to determine why women buy a certain brand of wine, for instance. All their marketing decisions are made on the basis of their data. Unfortunately, talent managers are only now beginning to understand the importance of investing in research that defines the type of people they need to hire, and what messaging is necessary to spur them into action.

Many companies base their employer branding on the reams of big data that describe what motivates Millennials. Unfortunately, all these companies refer to the same data, which do not provide the kind of information needed to differentiate themselves. The result is that young talent cannot tell them apart either, nor do they have a good understanding of what it would be like to work at one organisation rather than another.

Case study: BP[29]

Founded over 100 years ago, in 1908, British Petroleum (BP) is one of the world's leading international oil and gas companies, with over 80 000 employees in around 80 countries. The company relies heavily on the availability of highly skilled people in a number of highly sought-after disciplines, particularly those requiring degrees in science, technology, engineering and maths (so-called STEM talent). The number of these graduates in developed economies has steadily declined over recent years, despite a significant increase in demand. BP sees this as an opportunity to establish itself as a truly global employer of choice, further extending the reach and appeal of its employer brand by marketing to emerging markets where the number of STEM graduates is much higher.

BP believes in a highly integrated approach to both brand and HR management. From a brand perspective, this means ensuring that every proposition – including the EVP – aligns clearly with the overall corporate brand; a commitment to building a stronger, more sustainable energy future; and a commitment to BP's core values: respect, one team, courage, excellence and safety. From a people management perspective, this means striving to be as joined-up as possible in engaging and developing people through the whole employee life cycle.

With this context in mind, and the need to reach out to a more diverse global talent audience and maintain a clear line of sight with the organisation's core purpose and values, the following EVP pillars were introduced to define BP's core deal with its employees and provide a new global platform for its employer brand marketing activities.

Committed today and tomorrow

BP takes a long-term view on your success and ours. We recognise that our commitment to deliver energy to the world is closely linked to our investment in the people who will make it possible.

This means providing people with continuous opportunities to evolve their skills and expertise, through world-class training and development, and the kind of career flexibility that enables people to explore their strengths and achieve their potential in whatever inspires them most.

This pillar underpins BP's corporate commitment "to make a real difference in providing the safe, secure and sustainable energy the world needs today and in the changing world of tomorrow", with a similar commitment to the long-term investment in its people. To give you a sense of the breadth and depth of this investment, BP currently has 19 Academies and Institutes providing technical learning and employee development including the Operations Academy set up in partnership with MIT and the Sales and Marketing Academy in partnership with Kellogg. BP also offers a wide range of leadership development programmes ranging from diversity training to the effective management of performance conversations. These programmes have been attended by 17 000 people in 74 countries and have been translated into ten different languages.

Good people to work with

BP works as one team, while respecting individual differences. We believe teams perform best when people are able to be themselves and given enough scope to bring a unique perspective to the challenges which shape our daily work.

We like to form long-lasting partnerships and people like to partner with us. Few people at BP think they have all the answers and nothing builds effective collaboration and strong relationships faster than trusting others, having honest discussions and taking on tough challenges together.

This pillar puts the typical profile and personality of BP people at the heart of the proposition, with the emphasis on two of BP's core values: respect and one team. While the majority of the companies in the oil and gas sector trumpet the exceptional abilities of their people, BP chose to strike a more grounded and personal note. BP's people are undoubtedly talented, but the most prominent theme that emerged from the many employee focus groups that informed the EVP was the warmth and sociability of the people who work for the company. This pillar also aligns closely with BP's diversity and inclusion agenda, demonstrating how the company values and recognises individual initiative and entrepreneurialism. Inclusion extends beyond BP's full-time employees to connect with the suppliers, contractors and joint venture partners recognising their important role in contributing towards the company's success.

Doing the right thing

BP strives to both do the right thing and do things right. We never compromise on our values or ethics, and safety is always our number one priority. This means having the courage to speak up and challenge ourselves to do the right thing.

In our quest for excellence, we embrace leading technologies as a way to deliver simple and effective solutions to complex problems. We put as much emphasis on consistent execution as continuous innovation. If your brain is in gear and your heart is in the right place, you'll find BP an excellent place to work.

'Doing the right thing' is a relatively common phrase, but it also reflected a common thread running through the employee focus groups and interviews with senior people. The pillar description reflects the courage required to speak up and challenge when employees feel that 'the right thing' is in danger of being overlooked. It also combines with the idea of 'doing things right'. BP recognises that a winning business needs to both get it right and get it done, simply, effectively and to the highest standards.

A step-by-step guide to developing your EVP

Drawing on the experience of leading around 50 different EVP development projects over the last ten years, Mosley recommends following a number of steps.[30]

Establish the right development team

The core development team (or steering group as it is sometimes called) should include representatives from HR, talent management and resourcing, marketing and communications, and where possible, line management. The process is usually led by HR with the support of the corporate brand team, marketing and communications, rather than the other way round.

In a global EVP development project, early regional representation is a critical factor in both getting to the right proposition and ensuring local management acceptance. In some cases it is worthwhile holding a number of different EVP development workshops in different markets and then bringing all of the findings together in one final global workshop.

Pepsico took this approach, running a workshop in Thailand with participants from its key emerging markets in India, China and Russia; a workshop in London, bringing together a number of key European managers; and then finally a workshop in the United States, to pull it all together.

Lafarge, the French building materials giant, adopted a similar approach, conducting development workshops in the key emerging markets of China, India and Egypt, before running a final global workshop with representation from a much wider range of markets in Paris.

Consult with executive management

Developing a successful EVP requires active commitment from the senior leadership team. Begin by clarifying the leadership's organisational development and talent agenda. If these have not yet been defined, the following questions need to be asked:

- What organisational capabilities are deemed critical to the company's future success? (These might relate to general operational effectiveness or potential areas of competitive differentiation);
- What, if any, organisational changes are being planned to reinforce and build these capabilities? (This might include global expansion, re-branding, restructuring, process reengineering and/or the adoption of transformative technologies); and
- What aspirations do the leadership team share in relation to the culture and reputation of the organisation? (This might include the shift towards a high-performance culture or the desire to be recognised as the leading employer of choice in your industry sector).

Consult with the HR leadership team

In addition to the above questions, it is important to establish the current HR priorities that have been set.

- What talent challenges currently or potentially stand in the way of realising desired organisational capabilities? (This might include attraction, engagement, development, succession planning, deployment and retention); and
- What changes or upgrades are being planned to HR policies and processes that need to be taken into consideration when developing the EVP? Of particular relevance are investments in HR technology, resourcing, onboarding, performance management, learning and development, total reward and talent management, as these may provide important additional benefits to current and potential employees, as well as potential opportunities for the employer brand team to embed new ways of thinking.

Universum conducted a survey between January and April 2016 among 2 500+ company representatives responsible for employer brand management at the global and local levels. The results provide interesting insights into what the most attractive employers are currently doing.

The survey sample included over 90 per cent of the World's Most Attractive Employers (WMAE), chosen by 240 000 students across 12 countries. These include 3M, ABInBev, ABB, Accenture, Adidas, Bank of America, Barclays, BASF, Bayer, BMW, BNP Paribas, Bosch, BAT, BP, Coca-Cola, Citi, Daimler, Danone, Dell, Deloitte, Deutsche Bank, Ericsson, Exxon Mobil, EY, Ferrero, Ford, GE, GM, Goldman Sachs, Google, Grant Thornton, GSK, Heineken, HP, HSBC, IBM, IKEA, Intel, J&J, JP Morgan, KPMG, Lenovo, L'Oreal, Mars, Michelin, Microsoft, Mondelez, Morgan Stanley, Nestle, Novartis, Oracle, Pepsico, Philip Morris, Philips, P&G, PWC, Samsung, SAP, Schlumberger, Schneider Electric, Shell, Siemens, Toyota, UBS, Unilever, VW, Volvo Cars and Volvo Group.

The study investigated to what degree these companies had defined their key target audiences.

Table 7.1   WMAEs' key target audiences

Procedure	WMAE %
We have developed one overall target profile that we apply to all potential candidates	44
We have developed target profiles for a number of our key talent segments	51
We have developed target 'personas' for a number of our key talent segments	13

Consult with the brand team

It is vital to ensure that the employer brand is effectively aligned with corporate and customer brands, which means that the employer brand development team must work closely with the organisation's brand managers. Ask the following questions:

- What is the current or planned customer brand proposition? Is it particularly important to identify the brand personality and service style?
- What are the most important points of differentiation (e.g., cost efficiency, speed, expertise, empathy, fun)?

Choose your agency support

It may be necessary to identify what kind of external support you need. The first question is, of course, whether you have the necessary budget allocation for external agency support. Most leading employers contemplating a major employer brand development exercise choose to invest in such support, for the following reasons:

- It provides specialist expertise and experience that may not currently exist within the organisation (helping to avoid dangerous pitfalls, draw on best practice, support and up-skill company managers involved in the project); and
- It helps provide the short-term boost internal resources often require to deliver an intensive project while maintaining "business as usual".

The second issue is to consider what kind of agency/agencies you need most. Marketing and communication managers who manage corporate and customer brands typically draw on a range of different agencies for support in relation to

- market research;
- product and service development;
- brand identity and design;
- advertising;
- PR;
- direct marketing;
- digital/'web' development; and
- internal marketing, communication and engagement.

Create a draft EVP

If you are attempting to develop a more integrated solution, it is a good idea to create a draft EVP first, to test what will work at the local level (including potential creative options as well as pillars). The Universum *Employer Brand Practice Survey* (January–April 2016), provides clear insight into best practice for EVP development. Among other things, respondents were asked which elements they had included in their EVP definition (Table 7.2), and key linkages to their EVPs (Table 7.3).

Table 7.2   Elements of an EVP definition

Elements	WMAE %
A short, single-minded statement or tagline capturing the essence of your proposition	65
A number of individually defined employer brands/pillars/attributes/themes	61
A short paragraph summing up all the key elements in your proposition	39
A description of what you expect of employees, alongside what they can expect from you	41

➡

Elements	WMAE %
A description of your employer brand personality	38
A list of proof points/reasons to believe	37
A definition of key differentiators/points of difference	36

Table 7.3   Key linkages to EVPs

Key linkages	WMAE %
Core values	81
Corporate vision/mission	78
HR/talent strategy	77
Business strategy	58
Corporate brand	58
Core competency framework(s)	36
Total reward policy	26
Customer brand	25

The survey revealed interesting results as regards the most common focus areas.

Table 7.4   Companies' incorporation of each attribute in their EVP (highlighting biggest differences)

Attribute	WMAE % (>10 000)		Small (<1000 employees) %	
Inspiring purpose	+16	30	14	
Commitment to diversity & inclusion	+16	23	7	
Professional training & development	+14	38	24	
Clear path for advancement	+13	25	12	
Innovation	+11	29	18	
Secure employment		4	13	+9
A friendly working environment		14	21	+7
Corporate social responsibility		13	20	+7
Attractive products & services		19	24	+5
Market success		12	17	+5
A creative & dynamic environment		24	28	+4
Flexible working conditions		13	17	+4

Host EVP development workshops

Universum's experience shows that EVP development benefits from specialist expertise and experience, but that it generally works best as a collective exercise. This is the case for two reasons: 1) strong EVPs need to balance a number of different perspectives, and this is more effectively accomplished when a diverse range of people are involved, than when a narrow functional perspective is adhered to; and 2) the ultimate success of the exercise relies on the understanding and commitment of a wide range of different stakeholders.

Hold an employer brand briefing

The employer brand briefing is designed to share the context, objectives and scope of both the overall brand development exercise and the workshop itself. It is also important to ensure that everyone understands the framework within which the company is working. This should include

- key terms of reference (e.g., the difference between employer brand reputation/how you are seen) and an EVP (promise/how you would like to be seen);
- clarity on the brand hierarchy (e.g., the relationship between the corporate, customer and employer brand, and if relevant, the relationship between the group employer brand and subsidiary company brands);
- the employer brand model (e.g., core positioning and pillars);
- employer brand activation (e.g., the scope of likely activity once the EVP has been defined, including creative development, validation, internal and external communication, and alignment of people management touch-points);
- the top-line results from the various avenues of research and analyses that have been pursued prior to the workshop; and
- potential EVP elements.

The most effective EVPs clarify not only what employees can expect from the employer, but also what is expected of employees in return. In other words, it is not just simply a one-way promise, but a "give-and-get" deal. This helps to ground the EVP in the reality of the business and working experience. If the major priorities for the organisation are quality, customer focus or enterprise-wide collaboration, then it is as important to reflect these desired capabilities in the EVP mix as it is to reflect the needs and aspirations of potential candidates.

It is crucial to use the research results to strike the right balance in this "give-and-get" deal. In addition, in cases where the supply of talent exceeds demand, it makes sense to up-weight the "get" side of the deal. But if the demand for talent outstrips supply, you will need to up-weight the organisational "give" to attract and retain the required people.

Once the EVP workshops have been completed, it is possible to refine your EVP draft, including a shortlist of four to six core pillars, each containing a cluster of more specific attribute claims and reasons to believe. It will probably not be perfect, but it nevertheless needs to be tested with a wider audience at this stage.

Finally, writing the EVP should not be attempted as a group exercise. "Writing by committee" wastes time, is frustrating and will produce something substandard.

The following example from the Italian multinational Ferrero[31] reflects the clear desire to clarify the key components of the employment offer, but also to capture the spirit and culture of the company.

Case study: Ferrero

Ferrero is the company behind some of the world's most iconic and best-loved chocolate and confectionary products, including Ferrero Rocher, Nutella, Kinder Surprise and TicTac. It was founded by the confectioner Pietro Ferrero in 1946, transformed into a global business by his son, Michele with the support of his wife Maria-Franca, and is currently headed by Pietro's grandson, CEO Giovanni Ferrero. With a desire to capture the distinctive essence of a company that is regularly named as the most desirable employer in Italy, and to communicate this more effectively around the world, Ferrero defined its EVP for the first time in 2013. Federico Giovannini, Chief Human Resources Officer, Ferrero Group, comments:

> When we embarked on our endeavour to develop the first global employer brand in the history of Ferrero, my first thought was that an employer brand, like any brand, should not simply be a descriptive representation of what the Company is as an employer. It should rather be a carrier of emotions, more than descriptions; of underlining motives, more than superficial peculiarities. It should rather be an icon of what we firmly commit to stand for as an employer, rather than simply promising a worthwhile career to future employees. In other words, it should be about the character and soul of the Company. We did not just aim at pleasing the audience, at being attractive at all costs. We did not intend to conform to what we knew the "Generation Y" expects from employers. Through our EVP, we wanted to broadcast a message to whoever had a fundamental individual affinity with Ferrero's character, in our deep belief that only a profound affinity between Company and individual's character provides the fertile soil on which a lifetime relationship can blossom. Which is precisely what Ferrero desires.

Table 7.5   The Ferrero proposition

Ferrero EVP core positioning: Intriguingly unconventional		
Summary proposition statement Ferrero is anything but ordinary. A family company with a truly progressive and global outlook. Driven and dynamic, yet always taking the long-term view. A highly successful business that puts its products and people first, combining skills that take a lifetime to perfect with leading-edge technology.		
Pillars		
Ferrero Forever	**Feeling Ferrero**	**Fast Forward**
Our products are iconic and enjoy long-term success, because we have the perseverance required for perfection. In the same way, we care for the long-term interests of our people. We strive to ensure people keep learning and growing as the company grows. Becoming Ferrero brings a quality to your life that stays with you forever	Ferrero puts people before process, because we believe striving for something special requires more collaboration than instruction. The distinctive values and strong sense of common purpose that define Ferrero also define the way we work together, with passion, with mutual respect, putting collective success before individual ambition	Our products are enjoyed all over the world and our organisation is becoming rapidly global as it welcomes an increasingly diverse range of talented new people into our extended family. Our continued growth in new markets presents exciting challenges for our people, alongside significant opportunities for career development and mobility

Develop a communication plan

The Universum *Employer Brand Practice Survey* (January–April 2016), asked companies what their communication objectives were. Their answers were insightful.

Table 7.6   Communication objectives

Objectives	Small %	Medium %	Large %	WMAE %
Improving general awareness of our employer brand	48	58	60	72
Communicating our EVP/key strengths more consistently	32	48	51	57
Improving brand awareness in key geographies or target groups	31	41	41	48
Differentiating our brand more effectively from key talent competitors	26	36	44	48
Promoting employee engagement	32	45	43	47
Translating our EVP more effectively to different target audiences	23	34	36	43
Establishing greater familiarity with our employment offer	32	38	34	38
Promoting active employee advocacy	20	23	21	30
Improving employee retention	24	28	29	30
Addressing poor perceptions of organisation as a potential employer	12	18	26	22
Addressing poor perceptions/low consideration of our industry sector	12	20	23	19

Once you are clear about your communication objectives and the EVP has been signed off, it is time to develop a communication plan by following three steps:

1. Decide how often you want to communicate. This will depend on how competitive the environment is, and how sought-after the target group is;
2. Allocate resources between the different channels; and
3. Evaluate and adjust the current messaging to ensure that targets are being reached and that recruitment needs are (and will be) fulfilled in accordance with the company's business plan.

The best way of deciding which channels to use, is to ask the audience. We now know that students, for example, use a broad range of media to fulfil different purposes. But you need a more nuanced picture to understand how the target group consumes different media and how you have influenced them in each. Possible questions include:

*   What channels are used to learn about potential employers?
*   Which recruitment competitors succeed best? (so that you can gain deeper insight into the competitive landscape)
*   In what way does your presence influence them: from building familiarity to actually applying and accepting a job offer?

- At what stage of the talent funnel does your target group find itself? (this is necessary to segment your communication plan appropriately)(see Figure 7.1).

Consider what effect you want the channel to have on the talent during the various stages of the talent funnel (see Figure 7.2). If there is a lack of awareness about the organisation, a mass campaign aimed at alerting the broader potential talent base about the organisation might be best. However, if the organisation is at the stage of the employer branding process where you are recognised as an employer of choice, but are struggling to get target groups to apply, an approach which allows for face-to-face interaction on a more personal level might be best.

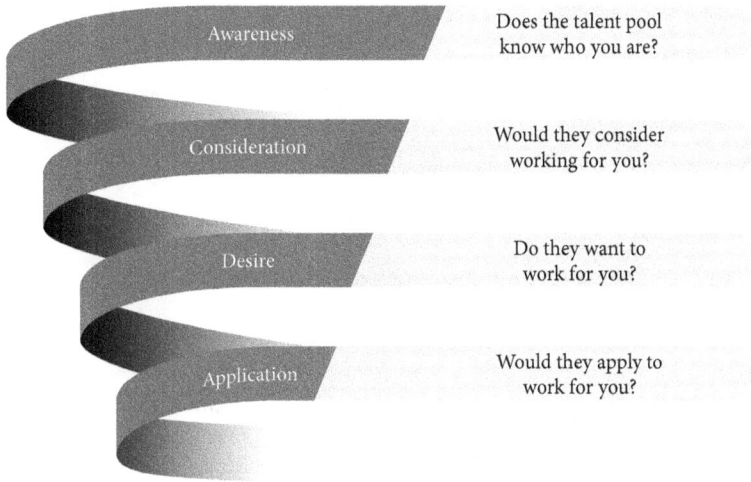

Awareness — Does the talent pool know who you are?

Consideration — Would they consider working for you?

Desire — Do they want to work for you?

Application — Would they apply to work for you?

Figure 7.1   The talent funnel

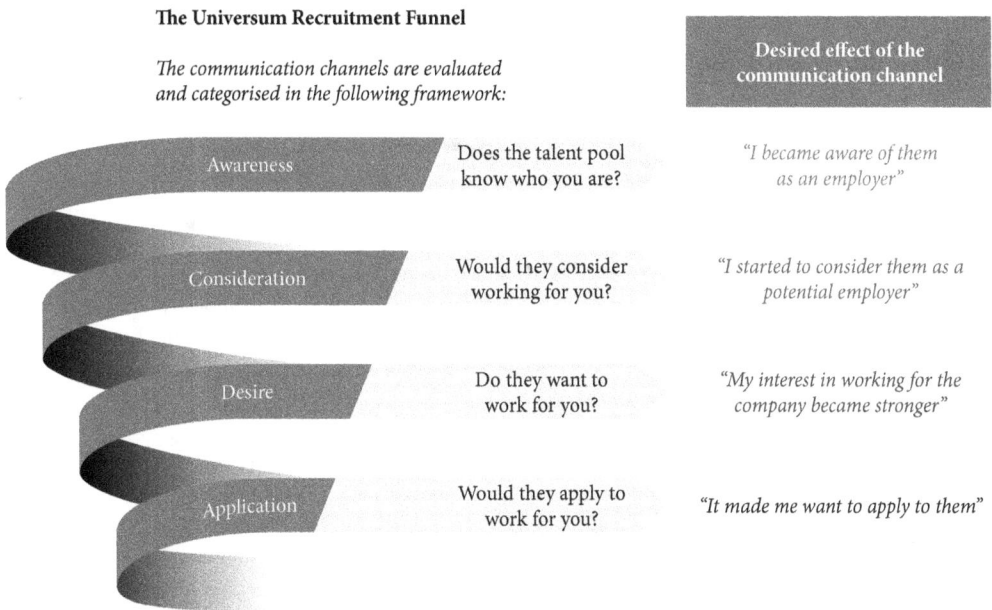

The Universum Recruitment Funnel

The communication channels are evaluated and categorised in the following framework:

Desired effect of the communication channel

Funnel stage	Question	Desired effect
Awareness	Does the talent pool know who you are?	*"I became aware of them as an employer"*
Consideration	Would they consider working for you?	*"I started to consider them as a potential employer"*
Desire	Do they want to work for you?	*"My interest in working for the company became stronger"*
Application	Would they apply to work for you?	*"It made me want to apply to them"*

Figure 7.2   The desired effect of the communication channel on the talent funnel

Different communication channels have different purposes

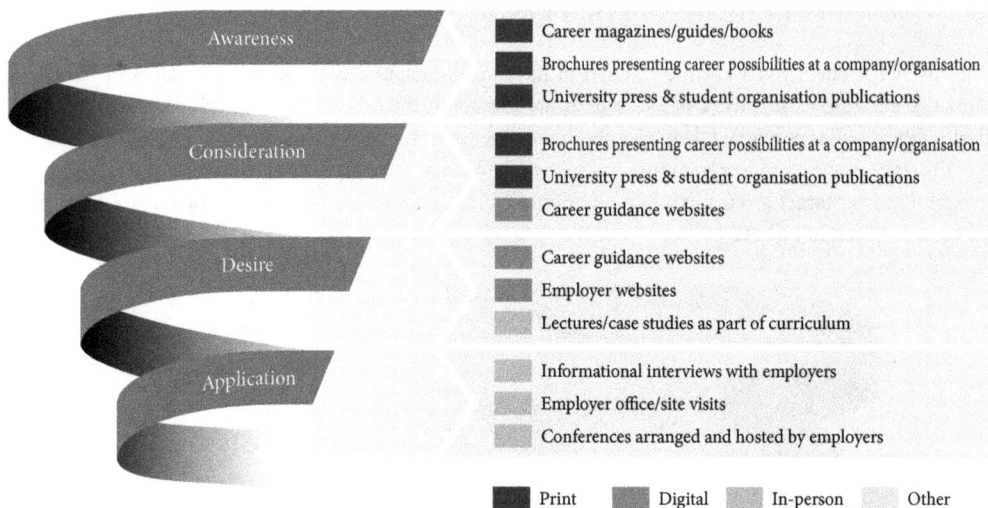

Figure 7.3   The most effective communication channels for different stages of the talent funnel

It is clear from Figure 7.3 that different channels have different purposes. Career guidance publications, university presses and student publications are best for stimulating awareness. Clearly, in-person communication events are most effective for inspiring a candidate to apply.

The research also confirmed the growing opportunities that social media present in engaging with current and potential employees. However, some employers are not yet fully engaged. Students' perception is that employers are less active on social media than they would like them to be. While social media remain the most popular sources of information for students, it is worth remembering that they use a variety of media to find out about employers. Research from Universum South Africa's 2015 student survey found that, on average, students use 9.1 different channels to source information about potential employers. Surprisingly, 71 per cent of students use print channels. The challenge is thus to maintain a balance between offline and online channels.

If you target students online, you will need to do it across devices and apps (computers, smartphones, tablets). An increasing number of students (29%) use apps to search for potential employers, but no doubt that figures will rise.

With regard to social media channels for internal audiences, many companies fear the effect that unmediated public conversations could have on their employer brands. But the truth is that employers cannot control social media. Employees will continue to use Facebook, Twitter and LinkedIn, whether employers like it or not. Therefore, the most productive thing to do would be to embrace it as something that will keep people updated on what is going on with your brand.

Because using social media is about building relationships, employers must begin to contribute to an authentic and transparent story about their brand. Social media offer multiple platforms for sharing insights into what makes an organisation a great place to work, and for helping people succeed. But the emphasis must remain on building relationships. Take the time to listen to what people are saying about your employer brand. Interacting on social media platforms is like attending a party: if you talk about yourself non-stop, people will stop listening, drift away and eventually avoid you. The same applies in the social media context: ask yourself what your audience wants to learn about your organisation. What interests them? Then contribute to the conversation. Understanding the intricacies of this aspect of the communications strategy will allow your company to optimise its selection of communication channels and will deliver the best possible return on investment (ROI).

Select key performance indicators and set objectives

The goal of any HR specialist is to help his/her company achieve its business goals by finding and hiring the right people, and then training and managing them in the right way and ensuring the consistency of the process. HR's goals and strategies may well have been clearly defined, but it is not always clear whether the HR department is on the right track. Is the HR strategy being executed effectively? Key performance indicators (KPIs) will help in this case, but only if applied according to certain rules. Deciding on which KPIs to use in measuring success is a matter of returning to both the business and HR strategic priorities.

When measuring the impact of the employer brand externally, many companies use the ABC model:

- A – attractiveness: the level of attractiveness in the selected target group;
- B – brand perception: the extent to which the brand is associated with the key attributes defined in the EVP;
- C – conversion: the ability to convert a general interest in the company as an employer into a desire to work in the company (employer of choice) and converting the desire into an application.

Universum's "talent attraction barometer" keeps a live barometer with benchmark results and key trends in the field of talent management and employer branding. The scope of the barometer entails cooperating with large, medium and small companies across global, regional and local perspectives. This project is already identifying new key trends in employer branding and talent attraction. In the first data cut, one of the questions touched on metrics: "Which KPIs are used in your organisation to evaluate its employer branding activities?" Participants could choose as many as applicable. What were the results? Here is a first cut from the data representing around 600 answers.

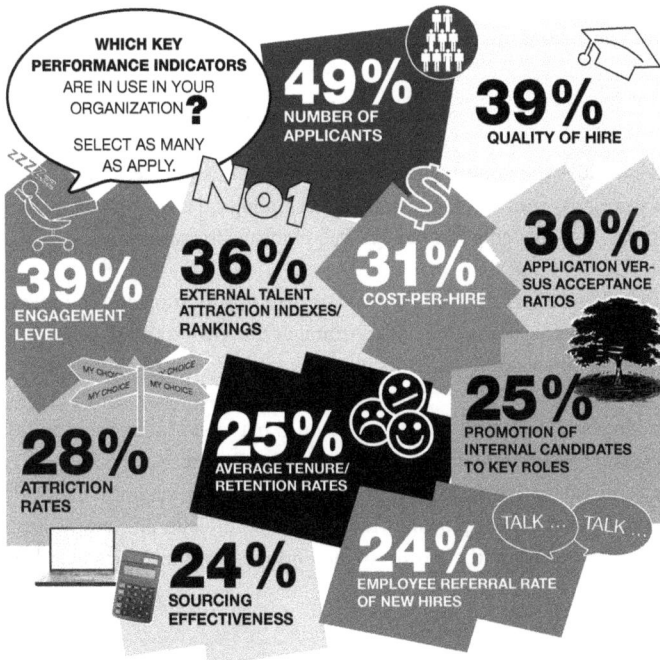

Figure 7.4   Talent attraction barometer, 2012

Create an annual plan

A large number of the components of your annual employer branding plan (business needs, target groups' definition and insights, EVP, communication mix, objectives, main strategies, KPIs) will be in place by this stage. The remaining component is the activities plan, that sets out which activities the company will implement, and when. But, as suggested earlier, employer branding activities are not the purview of the talent manager or employer branding manager alone. An annual plan encompasses all employer branding activities for the year and should include at least the following four people or departments:

- The CEO has the decision-making authority to ensure that the vision is included in the EVP and that the teams work together;
- The Corporate Communications Director is the custodian of the corporate brand and his/her department has the technical skills to align the messaging and manage the media creation and placement process. This is where the lion's share of the communications budget is spent;
- The HR Director/Regional HR Director has a full overview of the HR strategy in the company and understands the full scope of the workforce plan;
- The Employer Branding Director/Talent Attraction Director is responsible for the talent attraction strategy.

The details of the plan will depend on the goals set out in the workforce plan and will include both internal and external target groups. Once the plan and communication ideas are in place, execution begins. The key steps involved in monitoring and reviewing performance are:

- Conduct regular review meetings to determine if the strategy is achieving the desired results;
- Share results with stakeholders;
- Assess internal and external stakeholder perceptions by means of focus groups or further in-depth research;
- Where necessary, take action to ensure the objectives and goals outlined in the strategy are met and/ or adjust the strategy if necessary; and
- Provide feedback on actions taken.

Conclusion

It is a cliché to say the world is changing exponentially. It is nevertheless true, and this has a significant effect on talent attraction strategies. The changing social and technological environment, the emergence of a new generation of employees, and changing business models continue to create challenges for talent managers.

In Africa, the above challenges are amplified by shortcomings in education and training in many countries, mobility, and a particular shortage of scarce skills. Although the "Africa rising" trend is continuing, it has a tendency to mask the many inequalities and difficulties experienced on the continent.

Businesses in Africa understand that they cannot rely on expat talent indefinitely and that they will need to build development and training – a much-admired attribute in potential employers – into their offering. There can, however, be no doubt that building a strong brand based on an authentic EVP is one of the most effective ways of boosting their talent pipeline. This process is difficult and costly, but far outweighs the alternative – a lack of talent to ensure the growth of their business within African markets.

Endnotes

1   EY, 'Realising potential: 2013/14 Sub-Saharan Africa Talent Trends and Practices Survey', EY, Johannesburg, 2014, p. 3, retrieved 12 March 2016, <http://www.ey.com/Publication/vwLUAssets/EY_->

2   EY Emerging Markets Centre, 'EY's Attractiveness Survey Africa 2015: Making choices', EY, Johannesburg, 2015, p. 34.

3   Ibid, p. 2.

4   Ibid.

5   Ibid.

6   Unesco, 'Education for all, 2000–2015: Achievements and challenges', Unesco, Paris, 2015. This paper was produced by an independent team at Unesco which has tracked progress on these goals for the past 15 years and is based on the EFA *Global Monitoring Report* (GMR), retrieved 6 March 2016, <http://unesdoc.unesco.org/images/0023/002322/232205e.pdf>

7   Ibid.

8   EY, *'Sub-Saharan Africa Talent Trends and Practices Survey'*, op. cit.

9   Russell Reynolds Associates, '*Attracting and Retaining Executive Talent in Africa 2015, Survey findings*', 9 December 2015, retrieved 12 February 2016, <http://www.russellreynolds.com/insights/thought-leadership/Documents/Africa%20Leadership%20Survey%20v20151118.pdf>

10 Ibid, p. 6.

11 EY, *'Sub-Saharan Africa Talent Trends and Practices Survey'*, op. cit.

12 Universum is an international corporation that delivers surveys to millions of students and professionals and provides Ideal Employer™ research, full-service communication and strategic consulting services to more than 1 200 clients globally. Its global focus is reflected with teams in Stockholm, New York, Cologne, Stockholm, Singapore, Shanghai, etc., all working to connect employers to top talent in over 40 countries. Renowned media outlets such as CNN, Forbes, *BusinessWeek*, HBR, *Le Monde*, *The Economist*, *The Financial Times*, *Wirtschaftswoche*, *China Daily* and many others often cite and refer to Universum data and insights. Universum has granted the author permission to use its material.

13 R Mosley, *Employer brand management*. Extensive quotations reproduced with the kind permission of the author.

14 LinkedIn, Eda Gultekin, '*What's the value of your employment brand?*', retrieved 7 July 2016, <https://business.linkedin.com/talent-solutions/blog/2011/12/whats-the-value-of-your-employment-brand>

15 R Mosley, op. cit.

16 Ibid.

17 PWC, *18th Annual Global CEO Survey: The marketplace without boundaries 2015*, accessed 20 March 2016, <http://www.pwc.com/gx/en/ceo-agenda/ceosurvey/2015.html>.

18 Ibid.

19 M Kuppinger, 2015 European Identity & Cloud (EIC) conference, Munich, opening address, May 2015, reported by Warwick Ashford, ComputerWeekly.Com, 6 May 2015, retrieved 29 March 2016, <http://www.computerweekly.com/news/4500245737/Digital-transformation-affects-every-business-says-Martin-Kuppinger>

20 Ibid.

21 PWC, op. cit.

22 Ibid.

23 Universum, 'The Talent Agenda: Thriving in an Uncertain World #1 2014', Universum Global, Stockholm, 2014.

24 R Mosley, loc. cit., p. 110.

25 Ibid..

26 Universum, 'Generation Z – The next generation of talent'. The report defines Gen Z as youth aged 15–18 who can imagine obtaining a university or comparable degree. This entails high school students, and a small fraction of youth who have already started their studies or already have a job.

27 Skuse, *Attracting talent in emerging markets: Focus on `Africa*, Universum South Africa: Johannesburg, 2016.

28 S Sinek, *Start with why*, retrieved 4 April 2016, http://www.pearsonandassociates.co.uk/uploads/files/start-with-why-by-simon-sinek.pdf.

29 R Mosley, loc. cit., pp. 33–35.

30 Ibid, pp. 126–132.

31 Ibid, pp. 139–140.

References

EY, '*Realising potential: 2013/14 sub-Saharan Africa Talent Trends and Practices Survey*', Johannesburg, 2014, p. 3, retrieved 12 March 2016, <http://www.ey.com/Publication/vwLUAssets/EY_-_Realising_Potential/$FILE/131014%20 SSA%20Survey%20Report_Short-Version_v7_email.pdf>.

EY, Emerging Markets Centre, '*EY's Attractiveness Survey Africa 2015: Making Choices*', Johannesburg, 2015, p. 34.

Kuppinger, M, European Identity & Cloud (EIC) conference, Munich, opening address, May 2015, reported by Warwick Ashford, ComputerWeekly.Com, 6 May, retrieved 29 March 2016, <http://www.computerweekly.com/ news/4500245737/Digital-transformation-affects-every-business-says-Martin-Kuppinger>.

LinkedIn, Eda Gultekin, '*What's the value of your employment brand?*', retrieved 8 June 2016, https://business.linkedin. com/talent-solutions/blog/2011/12/whats-the-value-of-your-employment-brand.

Mosley, R, *Employer brand management: Practical lessons from the world's leading*, 2014, Wiley, West Sussex, United Kingdom.

PWC, '*18th Annual Global CEO Survey: The marketplace without boundaries 2015*', retrieved 20 March 2016, <http:// www.pwc.com/gx/en/ceo-agenda/ceosurvey/2015.html>.

Russell Reynolds Associates, '*Attracting and Retaining Executive Talent in Africa 2015: survey findings*', 9 December 2015, retrieved 12 February 2016, <http://www.russellreynolds.com/insights/thought-leadership/Documents/Africa%20 Leadership%20Survey%20v20151118.pdf>.

Sinek, S, *Start with why*, retrieved 8 June 2016, http://www.pearsonandassociates.co.uk/uploads/files/start-with-why-by-simon-sinek.pdf.

Skuse, J, *Attracting talent in emerging markets: focus on Africa*, : Universum South Africa, Johannesburg, 2016.

United Nations Educational, Scientific and Cultural Organisation (Unesco), *Education for all 2000–2015: Achievements and challenges*, Unesco, Paris, 2015, retrieved 6 March 2016, <http://unesdoc.unesco.org/images/0023/002322/232205e. pdf>.

Universum survey, 'Generation Z – The next generation of talent', Universum Global: Stockholm 2016.

Universum, 'The talent agenda: thriving in an uncertain world #1 2014', Universum Global: Stockholm, 2014.

PART 1

CHAPTER 8

EXECUTIVE TALENT IN AFRICA
Debbie Farnaby
Supported by the Heidrick & Struggles Johannesburg Partners
[Robyn Imray, Veronique Parkin, Johan Redelinghuys and Allen Shardelow]

If Africa is to realise its potential, there is a strong need for viable and sustainable organisations – whether in the private, public or development sector. Furthermore, it is generally accepted that start-up businesses driven by entrepreneurs will make the biggest contribution to employment and economic development on the continent.

For such organisations to grow and be sustainable they will need executives who have the ability to lead them in turbulent economic, social and political times. The traditional reliance on expatriate executives to lead the local or country operations of global companies is not sustainable and certainly not desirable.

There are many outstanding examples of truly capable African executives who have built and run highly successful local and multinational organisations. However, there is a significant need to expand the existing pool to help build and grow the very organisations that will take Africa into the future and enable the continent to compete in a volatile global economy. Such executives will need to be globally astute, while understanding the dynamics of the very diverse countries that make up the African continent. In a connected world, networks will be a key success factor for executives everywhere.

This chapter discusses the African context and the pipeline of executive talent which is available both on the continent and within the diaspora at large. It also examines the skills and capabilities that executives need to function in a VUCA world generally, and in Africa in particular. Finally, the authors pose the very intriguing question: In a connected world, can Africa become a major source of executive leadership? Their conclusion is that, as African economies continue to grow their talent, it undoubtedly can.

As a global leadership advisory firm, Heidrick & Struggles engages with clients across the globe in terms of leadership consulting, organisational culture and executive search, and is consequently well placed to author this important chapter.

Introduction

There is a preference among African states for "African solutions to African problems" – an oft-quoted adage used by Africans and non-Africans alike.

The pertinent questions addressed in this chapter are: Is there an African approach to developing and retaining executive talent that differs from the approaches taken in other regions of the world? Does African executive talent have an impact and a relevance that reach beyond the borders of Africa? Are there characteristics by which African executive talent can be uniquely defined?

To adequately answer these questions we first need to conceptualise what exactly 'Africa' entails. Of course Africa is understood to be the continent, but it comprises 55 nation-states, each at its own point in a developmental cycle that rises and falls as a consequence of economic, political and environmental factors. No two countries are at an identical point in this cycle, therefore Africa cannot be considered a singularity.

It is important to consider the factors at play in each individual nation and region on the continent. The most widespread Ebola epidemic in history, which began in 2013 and continued for over two years, resulted in a significant loss of life and caused social disruption across West Africa, with a material impact on the nation-states of Guinea, Liberia and Sierra Leone. The summer of 2015 witnessed the most devastating droughts in living memory in the southern nations of Africa – droughts which have materially affected the livelihoods of thousands of individuals in the region. The economic and social impact of Arab Spring uprisings across several North African nations has been both severe and lasting.

Each of these factors, amongst many others, has affected the people in a particular region of Africa, which in turn has impacted the nations in which those people live and transact on a daily basis. This has subsequently affected those nation-states with whom people in the region have economic and social ties. The knock-on effect defines, to a lesser or greater degree, the availability, capability and future pipeline of executive talent in Africa – in both a negative and a positive manner. We unpack these linkages in further detail as we consider the various issues.

In this chapter we identify those patterns and factors at play across multiple nation-states and regions that may be considered noteworthy and observable trends with respect to executive talent in Africa. To do this we look at the required capabilities and characteristics of 21st-century executive leadership, the inherent characteristics and challenges of Africa and how these may foster the development of contemporary leadership talent. We pose the question: Can Africa become a major source of global executive leadership talent?

As a global leadership advisory firm, Heidrick & Struggles engages with clients worldwide in terms of leadership consulting, organisational culture and executive search, and is consequently well placed to make these observations. Collectively, our Johannesburg office staff have over 100 years of experience in engaging with executive talent on the ground. We can therefore provide valuable examples and comments on observations which have emerged in our dealings on the African continent. Each observation made in this chapter is based on actual interactions with clients. While their identities remain protected for professional reasons, certain trends do emerge.

Characteristics of 21st-century leadership

Any reference to leading business media will quickly highlight that we are currently living in what is considered a VUCA world. This trendy acronym, initially borrowed from the military, stands for *volatility, uncertainty, complexity* and *ambiguity*. As it sums up the many and diverse challenges of the rapidly evolving global marketplace, the acronym encapsulates the rapid pace of change, driven by the so-called Fourth Industrial Revolution and the move to the Digital Age. VUCA refers to an environment where consumers have access to global platforms through social media and are able to challenge and invite discourse on a variety of issues. A VUCA world is further characterised by a marketplace where startups are disintermediating industries, and where new market players are asking us to think about traditional issues and business models from completely fresh points of view. A case in point – consider the impact Uber has had on vehicle ownership, public transport and the traditional taxi industry.

In a VUCA world, a new calibre of executive talent is required to lead those organisations that will drive the economy forward. The demand is for leaders who possess a combination of qualities and capabilities that are suited to an environment where uncertainty, ambiguity, complexity and volatility are the order of the day.

In the 2015 report entitled *Embracing the paradoxes of leadership and the power of doubt*,[1] in-depth interviews with 150 CEOs of companies around the world from a wide range of sectors indicated that business leaders need to be able to develop new skills to lead in an ever-changing world. Executives will be required "to lead at the intersection of adaptability, resilience and flexibility".[2]

The report reveals that 75 per cent[3] of the CEO respondents feel the job has changed significantly over the past decade, as new influences from outside the organisation compete with traditional accountabilities to boards, shareholders, employees and customers. Stakeholders are proliferating, and CEOs must navigate politics, geopolitical unrest, natural disasters, governments, regulators, competitors and a digitally empowered public: in the words of one CEO,[4] it is "coming out of everywhere. How do you manage transparency [so that] you have consistency, and at the same time realise that not everything has to be said, but everything that's important has to be said?"

The degree of transparency today, where every decision can be googled and analysed from multiple angles in real time, requires a different ability, awareness and skill set. Being adaptable, resilient, flexible and, above all, ready, is the new normal. "Every successful business model works until it doesn't," notes one CEO. "This strategy we're working on today is going to be supplanted by something else."[5]

The report also highlights that business leaders face new interpersonal challenges. Notably, most respondents spoke of the growing importance of being perceived as more approachable, engaged and caring – in other words, more "human" and connected. Nonetheless, they are still expected to be heroic leaders who "own the chair".[6] This creates organisational tension, as companies also recognise the benefits of involving more stakeholders in strategy, decision-making and execution.

These views are reinforced by other market commentators. The *PwC 2015 Annual CEO Survey – a marketplace without boundaries? Responding to disruption*[7] indicates that the dynamics of leadership have changed and what used to be referred to as soft skills have become essential to CEOs' success. In describing the characteristics of 21st-century leaders, the PwC report notes that respondents identified the need for vision, agility and flexibility in decision-making and highlighted the importance of being curious and analytical, as it gives a CEO the insight to separate fundamental changes from temporary hype, and act decisively on the former. In addition, the report states that

> above all, though, perhaps the quality CEOs most need to master is humility. *By being humble while leading, a CEO will be able to listen and learn from the team they have built around them; they'll be able to take maximum advantage of the diversity they are cultivating and they'll be receptive to the insights they gain from new collaborations.* Most important, this humility will give CEOs the confidence to pass on what they have learnt to the next generation of leaders.[8]

In the words of one CEO: "In today's world, which is becoming more global and multicultural, whether you like it or not, industries overlap and penetrate each other. If you don't know how to learn, you will not survive."[9]

Both the Heidrick & Struggles and the PwC reports reflect that leaders in a VUCA world will need to demonstrate a combination of skills, capabilities and potentials (potential, in this sense, is the ability to learn and adapt to a complex, changing environment). In essence, senior executive talent will need to be resilient, agile, curious, flexible, consistent, humble and adaptable. They will need to thrive amidst uncertainty and be stimulated by complexity. They must have the ability to build a broad network of relationships and should constantly scan and interpret the environment for information on trends and opportunities. They need to listen carefully and analyse continuously. And, if that were not enough, they need to engage emotionally at every level, both internal and external to the organisation.

However, each of us is the product of our environment. We learn skills and competencies not only in the formal domain (school, university, training courses), but also from our upbringing and situations we find ourselves in on a daily basis. Perhaps Darwin really did get it right – the skills we internalise and develop to the fullest are those we require to survive. Under what conditions can we thus best learn to be resilient, agile, curious, flexible, consistent, humble, adaptable, emotionally connected? Remember, it is from an environment that naturally fosters these skills that we will source a pool of relevant 21st-century executive talent.

Africa – a continent in flux

Africa is the world's second-largest and second-most-populous continent, accounting for 1.1 billion people or 15 per cent of world's population.[10] More importantly, Africa is home to the youngest population, with a median age of 19.7 compared to a worldwide median of 30.4.[11] According to the United Nations report *World population prospects: The 2015 revision, key findings and advance tables*,[12] more than half the world's population growth between 2015 and 2050 is expected to occur in Africa. Of the additional 2.4 billion people projected to be added to the global population, 1.3 billion will come from Africa, resulting in a population of approximately 2.4 billion inhabitants by 2050 – an estimated 25 per cent of the world's population.[13]

Add to this equation the cultural diversity inherent in Africa, not only linguistically where an estimated 2 000+ mother tongues are spoken, but also in the breadth and tradition of cultural practices.

Between 2000 and 2008, Africa's working-age population (15–64 years) grew from 443 million to 550 million – an increase of 25 per cent. This represents a growth of 13 million or 2.7 per cent per annum.[14] If this trend continues, the continent's labour force will be one billion strong by 2040, making it the largest in the world, surpassing both China and India.[15]

Africa's youth population is not only growing rapidly, it is also becoming better educated – albeit off a low base.

In the introduction to *Remapping Africa in the global space – propositions for change*,[16] African academic Oliver Masakure, Associate Professor in the Business Technology Management and Human Rights/Human Diversity programmes at Wilfrid Laurier University, Brantford, Canada, states that although not without its complex socio-political and economic challenges, present-day Africa is making significant positive strides. Even where there is evidence that the continent is faced with issues of political conflict, corruption, crime and much more, studies by the World Bank[17] as well as numerous scholars[18] indicate that economic policies on the continent have improved, and that in some countries where political stability exists, substantial resources have been allocated to education, while new technologies (especially in mobile communications) have boosted Africans' access to markets and information in a revolutionary way, thereby drawing Africa into the Fourth Industrial Revolution.

Masakure further notes that education being prioritised by African governments is a step in the right direction, as the continent is already, by its very nature, producing people who are resourceful, tenacious and resilient – traits needed for successful leadership in any environment, including business. This presents Africa with the potential to provide quality talent globally, particularly with Africa's population poised to overtake that of China and India in the near future.

A consistent and substantial investment in education is a significant factor in a country's ability to develop, attract and retain talent. It is only when the resources to support education are available on a sustainable basis that youth are given opportunities to achieve their potential. Disruptions in the form of political, social and environmental upheavals interrupt the schooling cycle and affect the talent pipeline into the future.

The African Economist July 2013[19] edition featured an article on literacy levels in Africa – only 37 of the 55 nation-states had literacy levels above 50 per cent, while only 13 countries had levels above 80 per cent indicating that significant gaps still exist in certain regions in respect of educational quality. These will need to be systemically addressed if Africa is to achieve its full potential. It comes as no surprise that the countries with the lowest levels of literacy – at around 20 per cent – are those which have seen the most disruption (socially and politically) for a sustained period of time.[20]

Many youngsters in Africa are growing up in an environment of flux and change. They live with uncertainty on a daily basis and are developing entrepreneurial skills and strategies to survive regardless. They engage and connect with one another by creating networks of resources to resolve issues. This has led to an explosion of innovation on the continent, driven by a combination of basic human need and very limited resources. The February 2014 issue of *Forbes Magazine* carried an article entitled 'Seven innovative products from Africa you should know about'.[21] The products described here range from Mubser (a navigational tool for the visually impaired) to the Cardiopad (which allows for ECGs to be performed in remote rural locations, with doctors elsewhere analysing the data) to the Saphonian zero blade wind convertor (that harnesses energy from wind through the use of a sail).

These trends – specifically a focus on improved education, together with increased levels of innovation and self-resilience, coupled with a steady growth in population – offer an unrivalled opportunity for Africa's economic and social development, if the talents of this fast-growing pool of human capital can be harnessed and directed 1) towards the productive sectors of the economy, both in Africa and outside of the continent, and 2) towards developing pipelines of future leaders.

Africa's executive talent pool

The nations from developed economies often observe developing markets with interest. They see growing populations as opportunities and markets for potential growth, and view political instability and market swings in terms of arbitrage. All too often we hear concerns voiced by well-established organisations regarding the "risk of doing business in Africa".

Africa has produced extraordinary leaders – Nelson Mandela and Kofi Annan spring to mind. It has also produced world-class entrepreneurs such as Strive Masiyiwa (founder of Econet Wireless), Mo Ibrahim (founder of Celtel), Aliko Dangote (of the Dangote Group) and Mike Adenuga (of the Globacom Group), each of whom has established an African conglomerate. This begs the question: Are these exceptions, or are the fundamentals in place for this to be the start of something sustainable?

In our interactions in Africa we have interviewed and engaged with a number of exceptional African leaders; individuals who have held executive roles in global organisations in some of the most challenging markets. In most cases these individuals experienced their primary schooling in their home nation in Africa, and their secondary schooling in a different country due to (in many cases) political or social upheaval. Their tertiary education has often been at some of the best universities and business schools across the globe, and they often hold multiple qualifications. These leaders display a thirst for knowledge beyond what we see in other markets. They are true global citizens, who are comfortable operating across the globe. Many of them display a vast number of the characteristics identified earlier as prerequisites for leaders of the 21st century.

We are frequently surprised at the number of individuals in the African diaspora approaching us wanting to return to Africa, where they see both opportunity for growth and development and the ability to make a greater impact than they would in developed economies. This longing to return is driven by a strong ethnic consciousness which has been sustained over years and is based on a common history, the transmission of a common culture and a religious heritage which urges them to return to Africa and "give back" in the form of skills transfer or the establishment of new economic endeavours.

Under the auspices of the Heidrick & Struggles global partnership with the World Economic Forum (WEF), the Johannesburg office is involved in reviewing the African nominations for the WEF Young Global Leader programme[22] on an annual basis. This detailed review of a range of profiles allows us to explore the achievements and impact each of these individuals has made in business, culture, academics, society or politics. These interactions expose us to remarkable young African leaders who will leave their mark on Africa – and in some cases, across the globe. They allow us to acknowledge the breadth of African talent. Often these young global African leaders display high levels of altruistic entrepreneurship as well as a rapid career trajectory, having overcome adversity and personal challenges as a result of complex socio-political and economic challenges in their region/country of origin.

In our early interactions in Africa, we engaged with large multinationals, predominantly in the consumer markets space. These organisations recognised the potential of cost savings from manufacturing and producing goods in low-cost markets. In most cases they brought expat executive talent into Africa, thanks to their know-how and specialised skills. Engineering and human resource skills were sourced to establish and manage plants and distribution centres, and to transition this knowledge over time to local executives. The role of the human resources team was to identify and develop a pipeline of talent for the future operation of the business. In most cases these businesses expanded considerably, and today are staffed by local talent from the shop floor through to executive level – Kenyans in Kenya, Ethiopians in Ethiopia, Nigerians in Nigeria. Our current mandate with these organisations is usually to search for an African national with at least five to seven years' experience in a global consumer products organisation, either gained elsewhere within Africa or offshore. We are often tasked with identifying talent in the diaspora and encouraging them to return.

The private equity market in Africa has witnessed considerable interest and activity over an extended period, given high economic growth rates and a rising middle class. We have been retained over the years by several major global as well as African private equity firms wanting to hire top-notch experienced and well-educated private equity professionals, to lead the origination and execution of investment transactions in Africa, with a focus on Kenya in East Africa and Nigeria in West Africa. Given the nature of operations in Africa, successful individuals tend to be those who can effectively deal with environments with limited access to financial information – people who understand and are sensitive to social, cultural and political impacts.

While previously a number of firms based their African operations outside the continent, more and more have recognised the need to have Africans based in Africa, to ensure success. Global firms see emerging markets as having potential for future growth, and recognise that professionals who are experienced in developed markets will not be appropriate to ensure this growth. Interestingly, experience in operating successfully in Africa is also a highly sought-after skill in other emerging markets such as Latin America and Asia.

An interesting trend is the willingness for individuals in various African countries to act as sources and link us into their local networks. We often find ourselves having conversations with individuals on a particular leadership role. They willingly identify a number of possible alternative candidates, before connecting us to a network of likeminded professionals who are, in turn, prepared to assist. Social networks are of vital importance to African executives, and business deals are mainly facilitated through networks of contacts. The following are examples of recent engagements:

> We were appointed on a leadership succession assignment for a leading financial services institution in West Africa. Our brief was to evaluate the existing senior leadership team and benchmark them against the best candidates available for this senior leadership role.

Governance procedures within the organisation were exemplary and internal candidates went head to head against the best candidates sourced globally. Our client was pleased to have achieved a rigorous, inclusive and world-class succession process.

In 2015 we entered into discussion with an African organisation that has a significant ownership of the terrestrial towers that power the mobile communications network across Africa. They have a clear sense of purpose and vision, and will emerge as a significant force in the global market. The calibre of the African leadership we engaged with, was world class.

We also engaged with a company which drives new initiatives in the education market in East Africa. This organisation leverages new technologies to provide educational support to children in remote areas, resulting in a 70 per cent improvement in the results of scholars who participated in the programme. All content and technology was developed within a single country in East Africa, and the company is now expanding into neighbouring countries.

In tandem with the changing demands of our clients, are the changing demands of the talent pool in Africa. Where previously many talented individuals were content to be employed in a role in their home country, a growing pool of youngsters are looking for employment in large multinationals, in the hope of being given an opportunity to develop and hone their skills in more sophisticated markets. These individuals are attracted by the opportunities for development and experience on offer in more sophisticated markets and stable environments. The desire to spread their wings is, however, often countered by pressure from local governments to remain at home and benefit the local economy. Conversely, many talented entrepreneurial individuals set their sights on establishing their own organisations.

One of the challenges facing developed countries (and, by extension, multinationals) is the economic conundrum of an aging population. In developed economies most executive positions are occupied by professionals in the mid-50–60s age group, whose institutional knowledge and practice are historically conservative and traditional. The availability of talent in the 35–44-year age group – traditionally used as a source of succession candidates for these roles – is shrinking as a result of population dynamics. As a consequence, businesses in developed economies are reaching beyond their home markets to compete for professionals who can help them sustain their operations.

One of the telling statistics which support this statement, is the rise in diaspora remittances to developing countries. In the 2014 World Bank *Migration and development brief*[23] it was noted that remittances to sub-Saharan Africa grew by 3.5 per cent to reach $32 billion in 2013, with flows forecast to rise to $41 billion in 2016. Such an increase reflects an outflow of talent from this region of Africa to external markets; a 'brain drain' of talent that would potentially have made a difference in the country of origin. Yet there is a positive side to this outflow of skills, as it reflects that professionals from developing countries have been proven to be both efficient and successful in the global environment. Interestingly, much of this outflow is used to fund the education of members of the extended family back home.

The development of Africa's executive talent pool

For Africa to capitalise on its potential to become a source of world-class talent, the nations of the continent will have to respond strategically, to take the lead and include different stakeholders who together can offer a range of expertise. These stakeholders include government regulators, educational institutions, business corporations and civil society. African nations will need to align their efforts towards re-branding the continent as the next best place where talent is developed, retained and/or exported. This does not need to be a coordinated effort across Africa; rather each nation state should focus on developing skills through a heightened emphasis on education, opportunities for broadening and diversifying the capabilities of talented individuals, and the provision of appropriate incentives to establish economic enterprises. These initiatives should be rolled out at a pace that is appropriate for the point at which each nation finds itself in the developmental cycle.

We are already seeing pockets of excellence across the continent – innovative solutions being applied by Africans using local talent. The more these proliferate, the greater the development opportunities for individuals. Multinationals have also come to the party. Global firms that previously relied on imported talent or expats to fill local roles have discovered that it is costly to move people, that expat appointments do not necessarily strengthen or support the local talent pipeline or yield significant results for the business. So, in the absence of traditional management training capabilities on the ground, companies such as Coca-Cola, Heineken and Diageo have developed their own programmes to nurture Africa-based leaders. In an article by Lindsay Gellman entitled 'Why nurturing talent is hard in Africa', James Newlands, who leads the Americas-Africa business centre at EY, was quoted as saying: "It's not a sustainable solution to run your business on expat management."[24]

Africa does not currently offer the range of business schools or academies required to meet the demand of individuals and organisations for talent development, but in true African style, solutions are being identified. In many cases, large multinationals are establishing training and development programmes for future talent based on identifying in-country talent and enrolling them in bespoke, international assignments where candidates spend six months to a year being exposed to organisational practices and best-in-breed delivery. In other cases, multinationals scour the top global universities looking for members of the African diaspora whom they then recruit into the organisation, allowing these individuals to prove their worth before placing them back in their home country.

The growth of online business and management programmes from reputable business schools across the globe is also allowing individuals to take control of their own development programmes. Many global institutions now offer modular programmes where coursework can be completed after-hours, and intense on-campus sessions are offered for two to three-week periods which can be accommodated by leave periods. The Graduate Institute for Business Science of the University of Pretoria (GIBS) now offers programmes specifically tailored to emerging markets with a focus on Africa.

Recently, Harvard Business School (HBS), which offers executive education programmes across the globe, introduced a programme to be offered from South Africa. HBS is working in conjunction with GIBS to offer a new three-module Senior Executive Program Africa qualification,[25] designed to examine the experiences of executives from Africa and around the world, to illustrate leadership best practices. The programme is designed to prepare executives to seize Africa's growth opportunities and build insights into local, regional and global markets, by exploring the approaches of successful leaders. HBS hopes that local, multinational and pan-African businesses, non-profit organisations and government agencies will be represented on the course. When questioned why HBS had taken this approach, Prof Das Narayandas, Senior Associate Dean and Chair of Executive Education and Harvard Business Publishing commented that

> Africa's expanding population and dynamic markets create a unique set of challenges and growth opportunities. This course teaches executives to design and execute effective strategies, nurture high-performance teams, and establish a network of peers that will help them generate short-term and long-term success in their organisations.[26]

The question that remains unanswered is how this future talent will be identified. In our conversations with organisations we still see that a focus on entrepreneurial behaviour and a willingness to continually seek innovative solutions remain vital in identifying so-called "high-flyers". In many cases it is the resilience to keep looking for solutions to issues in the face of failure that sets future leaders apart from their peers.

In an article co-authored with Rick Kirkland, Aliko Dangote is quoted as saying:

> Africa, as a whole, has been growing by 5.5 percent a year for the past 12 years, and it has been sustainable. This growth, when you look at it, really is without power. With power, we could have double-digit growth. In addition, there has been a lot of political transformation. Various governments in Africa are making life easier, much easier than before. Our government used to change the rules of the game almost on a monthly basis, or even on a daily basis. That's not happening right now. So investors can actually see what they will get over the next ten years. Things have changed dramatically. My advice is that you better invest now, before it's too late. The train is about to leave the station. Africa should develop its leaders, what really matters is human capital: hiring people who are smarter than you. Because what we need to do is make sure that this company outlives us. We are trying to leave something for posterity. We've done quite a lot in terms of hiring and we have a plan for succession, so I have a very, very robust team. Without the right team, I would not be able to deliver the results that we've been delivering all these years. So the credit goes to Dangote's management. We pay more attention to business development today. We develop companies and then we establish them. And now we take them to the market. So the most important thing for me is the development of the company, in terms of processes and people.[27]

In summary, Dangote believes "Africa should lead by example, begin to invest on the continent first and foremost, cultivate talent to be the best contributor to the world economy and not look to the outside to rescue this continent".[28]

Conclusion

In the introduction we posed the following questions: Is there an African approach to developing and retaining executive talent that differs from the approaches taken in other regions of the world? Does African executive talent have an impact and relevance that reaches beyond the borders of Africa? Are there characteristics by which African executive talent can be uniquely defined?

To answer these questions we looked at the capabilities and characteristics of 21st-century executive leadership, as required to lead in a VUCA world. We identified that, in essence, executive talent needs to be resilient, agile, curious, flexible, consistent, humble and adaptable. It needs to thrive amidst uncertainty and must be stimulated by complexity. It requires the ability to build a broad network of relationships and must constantly scan and interpret the environment for information on trends and opportunities. It needs to listen carefully, analyse continuously, and connect and engage emotionally at every level, both internal and external to the organisation.

We discussed some of the inherent characteristics and challenges facing Africa, including political, social and environmental flux, together with significant and sustained population growth and linguistic and cultural diversity, and asked how this environment might foster the development of 21st-century leadership talent. We discussed the fact that the youth of Africa have to make plans to survive, innovate and meet their basic human needs, with minimal resources at their disposal.

We noted our observations regarding executive talent in Africa – that most of the talent we engage with have lived in more than one country, have been educated in more than one country, speak multiple languages, are culturally sensitive by necessity, are connected within a community and have networks extending across various and diverse interest groups. They have a strong focus on education and on developing a career through exposure to opportunities in global markets. We raised the issue of diaspora remittances, and how many Africans in the diaspora return to their homeland. We observed that our clients are seeking Africans for leadership positions in Africa, that expat assignments no longer yield the desired benefits.

In our view, Africa could indeed become a major source of global executive leadership talent, provided that issues related to literacy and the variable quality of education are addressed in a systemic and strategic way, by each African nation.

Returning to the words of Oliver Masakure:

> … economic governance and political institutions have improved …; democracy and electoral competition have become the norm across the continent. It is to be recognised that in Africa, democratic governments have been successful, while authoritarian governments have largely failed. Over the last two decades the prevalence of war has diminished, reducing the number of civil war casualties in recent years to historic lows for the region. While improving democracy and sustaining peace have traditionally been a challenge in some parts of Africa, the rise of a new generation of political leaders has brought new ideas and attitudes to the fore. In most of the continent, leaders are taking initiatives to tackle ethno nationalism and its corollaries of xenophobia, inter-communal mistrust and social divisions. Newly democratic regimes have been more eager to embrace new information technologies that can improve the efficiency of markets and facilitate the formation of grassroots political and civic organisations.[29]

In other words: things are changing for the better.

Surely with many of the fundamentals in place, now is Africa's time to shine; to nurture generations of leaders who are able to lead their organisations and countries through the turbulence of a VUCA world and to demonstrate that out of the uncertainty and complexity, ambiguity and volatility of Africa, innovative, curious, resilient, agile, humble, flexible, consistent and adaptable, connected leaders can emerge.

In a recent conversation with a young black African CEO, he made the following comment: "Africans lead with relationship and intuition, Africans feel before they think or strategise … the difference between an African and Western leader is the reliance on tribe, family and relationship above all else. That's what makes us unique globally."[30]

It is Africa's environment that fosters a different kind of leader and a different approach to the development of executive talent. The kind of leader developed within Africa has relevance beyond the borders of this continent, and has the potential to positively impact the globe.

Endnotes

1   Heidrick & Struggles in partnership with the Saïd Business School, University of Oxford, 'Embracing the paradoxes of leadership and the power of doubt', 2015, retrieved 1 August 2016, <http://www.heidrick.com/~/media/Publications%20and%20Reports/The-CEO-Report-v2.pdf>.

2   Ibid., p. 5.

3   Ibid., p. 4.

4   Ibid.

5   Ibid., p. 5.

6   Ibid.

7   PWC, 'PwC 2015 Annual CEO Survey – a marketplace without boundaries? Responding to disruption', retrieved 1 August 2016, <https://www.pwc.com/gx/en/ceo-survey/2015/assets/pwc-18th-annual-global-ceo-survey-jan-2015.pdf>.

8   Ibid., p. 35.

9   Ibid., p. 34.

10   Population Reference Bureau, '2013 World population data sheet', p. 6, retrieved 18 August 2015, <www.prb.org>.

11   United Nations, 'World population prospects: The 2015 revision, key findings and advance tables', 2015, p. 2, retrieved 1 August 2016, <https://esa.un.org/unpd/wpp/publications/files/key_findings_wpp_2015.pdf>.

12   Ibid.

13   '2013 World population data sheet', op. cit.

14   *African Economic Outlook*, 'Special edition on youth employment', Chapter 6, p. 99, retrieved 15 January 2016, <http://www.cpahq.org/cpahq/cpadocs/Promoting%20Youth%20Employment>.

15   Ibid.

16   O Masakure, 'Introduction', in E Shiza (ed), *Remapping Africa in the global space – propositions for change*, Sense Publishers, Rotterdam, Boston and Taipei, 2014, p. vii.

17   Ibid., p. vii.

18   Ibid.

19   *The African Economist*, 6 July 2013, retrieved 15 January 2016, <http://theafricaneconomist.com/ranking-of-african-countries-by-literacy-rate-zimbabwe-no-1/#.V58dSut951s>.

20   Ibid.

21   *Forbes Magazine*, 'Seven innovative products from Africa you should know about', February 2014, retrieved 15 January 2016, <http://www.forbes.com/sites/mfonobongnsehe/2014/02/13/seven-innovative-products-from-africa-you-should-know/#6200dde0107b>.

22   Heidrick & Struggles and the World Economic Forum (WEF), 'WEF Young Global Leader programme', retrieved 30 July 2016, <https://www.weforum.org/communities/forum-young-global-leaders/>.

23   World Bank, 'Migration and development brief', 11 April 2014, p. 6, retrieved 1 August 2016, <https://siteresources.worldbank.org/INTPROSPECTS/Resources/334934-1288990760745/MigrationandDevelopmentBrief22.pdf>.

24   L Gellman, 'Why nurturing talent is hard in Africa', *Business Day*, December 2015, retrieved 30 July 2016, <http://www.bdlive.co.za/business/management/2015/12/09/why-nurturing-talent-is-hard-in-africa>.

25   'GIBS Executive Education Programmes', retrieved 30 July 2016, <https://www.gibs.co.za/programmes/open-programmes/pages/harvard-business-school-senior-executive-program.aspx>.

26   D Narayandas, 'Harvard Business School launches senior executive program in Africa', retrieved 31 July 2016, <http://www.prnewswire.com/news-releases/harvard-business-school-launches-senior-executive-program-in-africa-300235759.html>.

27   R Kirkland & A Dangote, 'Dangote Group on the Africa opportunity', McKinsey online publication, retrieved 30 July 2016, <http://www.mckinsey.com/global-themes/leadership/dangote-group-on-the-africa-opportunity>.

28   Ibid.

29   O Masakure, op. cit.

30   Private conversation, name withheld to protect candidate's anonymity.

References

African Economic Outlook, 'Special edition on youth employment', Chapter 6, p. 99, retrieved 15 January 2016, <http://www.cpahq.org/cpahq/cpadocs/Promoting%20Youth%20Employment>.

Forbes Magazine, 'Seven innovative products from Africa you should know about', February 2014, retrieved 15 January 2016, <http://www.forbes.com/sites/mfonobongnsehe/2014/02/13/seven-innovative-products-from-africa-you-should-know/#6200dde0107b>.

Gellman, L, 'Why nurturing talent is hard in Africa', *Business Day*, December 2015, retrieved 30 July 2016, <http://www.bdlive.co.za/business/management/2015/12/09/why-nurturing-talent-is-hard-in-africa>.

'GIBS Executive Education Programmes', retrieved 30 July 2016, <https://www.gibs.co.za/programmes/open-programmes/pages/harvard-business-school-senior-executive-program.aspx>.

Heidrick & Struggles and the Saïd Business School, University of Oxford, 'Embracing the paradoxes of leadership and the power of doubt', 2015, retrieved 1 August 2016, <http://www.heidrick.com/~/media/Publications%20and%20Reports/The-CEO-Report-v2.pdf>.

Heidrick & Struggles and the World Economic Forum (WEF), 'WEF Young Global Leader programme', retrieved 30 July 2016, <https://www.weforum.org/communities/forum-young-global-leaders/>.

Kirkland R & Dangote A, 'Dangote Group on the Africa opportunity', McKinsey online publication, retrieved 30 July 2016, <http://www.mckinsey.com/global-themes/leadership/dangote-group-on-the-africa-opportunity>.

Masakure, O, 'Introduction', in E Shiza (ed), *Remapping Africa in the global space – propositions for change*, Sense Publishers, Rotterdam, Boston and Taipei, 2014, p. vii.

Narayandas, D, 'Harvard Business School launches senior executive program in Africa', retrieved 31 July 2016, <http://www.prnewswire.com/news-releases/harvard-business-school-launches-senior-executive-program-in-africa-300235759.html>.

Population Reference Bureau, '2013 World population data sheet', p. 6, retrieved 18 August 2015, <www.prb.org>.

PWC, 'PwC 2015 Annual CEO Survey – a marketplace without boundaries? Responding to disruption', retrieved 1 August 2016, <https://www.pwc.com/gx/en/ceo-survey/2015/assets/pwc-18th-annual-global-ceo-survey-jan-2015.pdf>.

The African Economist, 'Ranking of African countries by literacy rate', 6 July 2013, retrieved 15 January 2016, <http://theafricaneconomist.com/ranking-of-african-countries-by-literacy-rate-zimbabwe-no-1/#.V58dSut951s>.

United Nations, Department of Economic and Social Affairs, Population Division, 'World population prospects: The 2015 revision, key findings and advance tables', 2015, p. 2, retrieved 1 August 2016, <https://esa.un.org/unpd/wpp/publications/files/key_findings_wpp_2015.pdf>.

World Bank, 'Migration and development brief', 11 April 2014, p. 6, retrieved 1 August 2016, <https://siteresources.worldbank.org/INTPROSPECTS/Resources/334934-1288990760745/MigrationandDevelopmentBrief22.pdf>.

CHAPTER 9

A COMPREHENSIVE TALENT MANAGEMENT FRAMEWORK IN ACTION
Johan Ludike

This is a wonderful chapter to close the first section of the book – Shaping the strategic landscape.

Johan has extensive experience in a variety of leading organisations which are major players throughout Africa and the Middle East. He is thus eminently capable of bringing to the table a deep theoretical knowledge of his field, supplemented by practical examples taken from the companies he has worked in.

When I consult to companies on talent management I advise that the first thing they do is to create the executive and management structures that will provide governance of the system. In this chapter, Johan provides detailed insight into the functioning of such a governance structure. He also demonstrates the importance of the relationship between an organisation's talent strategy, and the business strategy and drivers that shape the strategy, to ensure that the talent strategy remains strategic and relevant.

Leading companies understand the importance of transition management. They adopt processes that ensure effective transition from one level to another, so that talent is set up for success. Johan provides some very important guidelines for managing such transitions. The framework that he provides and the insights which he has taken from a rigorous knowledge of theory and extensive practical experience make this a powerful chapter for leaders and HR professionals who need to implement a comprehensive talent system and strategy.

Introduction

> An organization's ability to learn, and translate that learning into action rapidly, is the ultimate competitive advantage – Jack Welch[1]

It is increasingly becoming apparent that talent is being recognised as both a strategic leadership imperative and a competitive reality in today's hypercompetitive global marketplace. Given the recent plethora of research literature relating to talent management, it could well be argued that a renewed focus on talent could signal a paradigm shift for both organisations and human resources, in that we have entered the age of strategic talent.

Aguirre et al.[2] maintain that organisations, their CEOs and HR practitioners alike can ill afford to cling to, or remain trapped in, talent management models or talent paradigms which are reminiscent of the 20th century. They urgently need to reframe, innovate and reposition talent management strategically, to ensure that organisations become talent-powered[3] and talent-driven.[4]

Ashton and Morton[5] compellingly argue that there is not a single consistent or concise definition of strategic talent management, as they believe that current or historic cultural attributes play a part in defining talent, as do an organisation's business models (given that talent is increasingly aligned with business strategy or its operational parameters of strategy execution). In the start-up phase of a business, for example, the talent emphasis will be different from the innovative or creative talent needed to bring new products to market. Similarly, in a turnaround business context the talent needs will be significantly different, hence any definition needs to be fluid – as business drivers change, so arguably the definition will change as strategic priorities change.

Much has been written on talent management. For the purposes of this chapter, strategic talent management can now be more accurately and dynamically defined as an integrated set of processes, programmes and cultural norms in an organisation which are designed and implemented to attract, develop, deploy, engage, as well as retain and leverage talent, to achieve strategic objectives and meet future business needs.[6]

To illustrate (and in many ways breathe life into) the aforementioned definition, the objective of this chapter is to suggest a comprehensive, coherent and integrative talent management framework. It is essential to appreciate that this framework is not just well researched, systemic and holistically integrative in nature, but has effectively been implemented in multinational diversified financial services, telecommunications and hospitality industries, both in well-developed (UK, Europe) and emerging economies (Africa, Middle East, Asia).

As per the title, an attempt will be made to illustrate some of said components with actual case study examples to clarify the notion of what was done and how the framework was put into action and/or operationalised. The comprehensive talent management framework will highlight the need, as emphasised by Aguirre et al.,[7] for the robust strategic governance, interpretation and integration of a range of currently dynamic, globally complex, and in many ways unprecedented, business drivers. It will further elaborate on the need to anticipate the inherent risk management dimensions of talent accounting, demand-planning and the advancement of high-potential leadership and other more pivotal talent potential. The objective of the framework will be to ensure that strategic talent management not only provides for current business outcomes, but also for the specific future talent needs which could ensure sustainable growth and competitive differentiation.[8] Talent management, according to Aguirre et al.,[9] needs to be strategically innovative to unlock the inherent value of a new array of talent segments within the 21st-century workforce.

As Gubman and Green[10] further suggest, the strategic management and leveraging of talent entails more than a series of HR programmes, processes and/or fragmented deliverables. Talent management frameworks and their implementation need to be monitored to evolve through what Silzer and Dowell[11] refer to as five stages of talent management integration: journeying from reactive and programmatic to more comprehensive, aligned and strategic. In many ways the proposed talent management framework needs to evolve to a stage where it is embedded as talent management architecture within the overall organisation culture. This is evident in how a company's talent significantly differentiates the organisation in terms of innovative strategy formulation, execution and proven operational excellence.

The underlying rationale, associated components/elements, practices and processes of a comprehensive talent management framework are elaborated on in Figure 9.1. Where relevant, real-world in-action examples are provided.

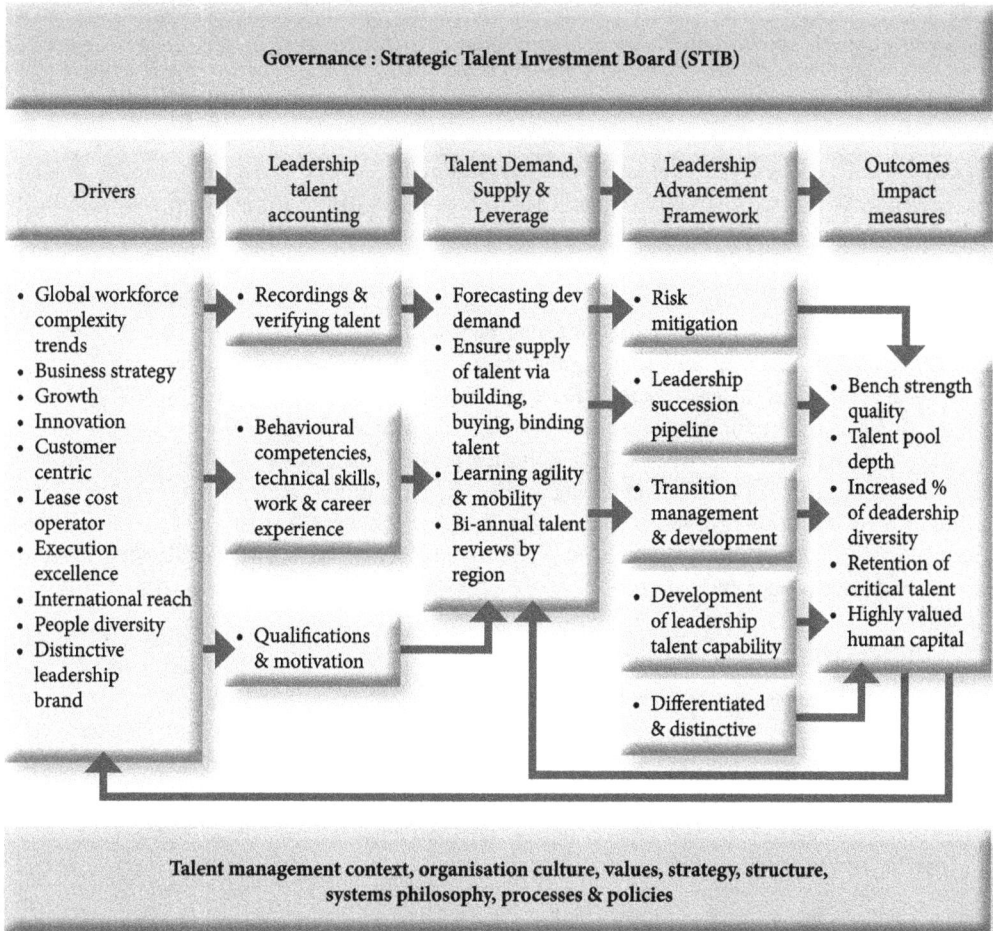

		Governance : Strategic Talent Investment Board (STIB)		
Drivers	Leadership talent accounting	Talent Demand, Supply & Leverage	Leadership Advancement Framework	Outcomes Impact measures

- Global workforce complexity trends
- Business strategy
- Growth
- Innovation
- Customer centric
- Lease cost operator
- Execution excellence
- International reach
- People diversity
- Distinctive leadership brand

- Recordings & verifying talent
- Behavioural competencies, technical skills, work & career experience
- Qualifications & motivation

- Forecasting dev demand
- Ensure supply of talent via building, buying, binding talent
- Learning agility & mobility
- Bi-annual talent reviews by region

- Risk mitigation
- Leadership succession pipeline
- Transition management & development
- Development of leadership talent capability
- Differentiated & distinctive

- Bench strength quality
- Talent pool depth
- Increased % of deadership diversity
- Retention of critical talent
- Highly valued human capital

Talent management context, organisation culture, values, strategy, structure, systems philosophy, processes & policies

Figure 9.1   Integrated talent management framework[12]

Governance

Ashton and Morgan[13] as well as Silzer and Dowell[14] argue that strategic talent management should be

- driven by business strategy;
- integrated with other processes;
- managed as a core business process; and
- ingrained as a talent mindset.

Yet a large percentage of interviewed CEOs, business unit leaders and HR executives continue to think that a lack of collaboration across the organisation prevents talent management from having the necessary degree of impact and/or from delivering tangible business value.[15] Given this state of affairs, as well as the fact that corporate leaders have traditionally tended to merely relinquish the organisation's talent strategy to either market forces (conveniently termed 'business drivers') and/or to their HR departments, they have copied and perfectly imitated, via "causal benchmarking",[16] the famous best practices of high-profile global brands. The caveat is that the proper governance, oversight and indeed innovation of these practices and processes are required. Prudent strategic governance needs to ensure that it (1) aligns and fits with the requisite, distinctive talent requirements which drive the execution of the organisation's strategy, culture and values, and (2) optimally leverages the collective skills, abilities and expertise that enable a particular company to consistently out-execute and outperform the competition.

Charan,[17] in describing how the boards of companies are changing to become more progressive, states that such boards look to the company's long-range success, beyond the term of any given CEO, "market opportunity" or "product cycle". They exercise active governance, evaluate strategy and management, and take hiring and firing the CEO very seriously. He further argues that board meetings will increasingly become more cooperative and lively, and will pursue more productive relations with the CEO, as boards are expected to add value and competitive advantage without wasting management's time.

It is for these reasons that two large telecommunications companies (one African, one Middle Eastern) considered the establishment and promulgation of an influential, progressive governance body and mechanism as the principal departure point for any strategic talent management framework. They deemed it essential for their talent management strategy to be legitimised, driven and galvanised across multiple countries in Africa, the Middle East and Asia. It further provided the necessary impetus to their strategic talent management efforts, in addition to being useful to overall position such a body as a strategic review and/or investment board. The principal purpose of the latter was to, inter alia, ensure that pivotal leadership potential was identified, assessed, developed, engaged, retained and leveraged, so as to mitigate talent supply, demand and sustainability risks.

The Corporate Leadership Council[18] defines a number of risks:

- *Vacancy risk*: no mission-critical positions are left vacant;
- *Readiness risk*: no promotions into positions without the requisite capabilities and/or development;
- *Transition risk*: poor assimilation of talent and knowledge transfer across the organisation;
- *Portfolio risk*: the inappropriate placement of individuals does not occur; and
- *Legal risk*: where relevant, an organisation is able to fulfil its localisation and regulatory labour transformation requirements.

The mitigation of the aforementioned risks, as well the realisation of a wide range of talent management value-based benefits, was achieved via the creation of a governance body and board, convened as follows:

- Twice-annually, for two full days, to strategically review and consider requisite business capabilities, giving comprehensive consideration to alignment with the complexity and diversity of the global talent pool;
- To reflect on the impact and alignment of the business capability review, with matching requisite strategic pivotal, scarce and critical as well as leadership talent management requirements from an entire organisation's talent pool;
- To strategically consolidate, align, integrate and focus decision-making on key talent moves through focused business-led talent reviews and structures on an operational and/or a geographic basis in South, Central, West and East Africa as well as the Middle East and Asia;
- To review, reflect on and approve pivotal leadership talent management engagement and retention strategies, tactics and plans from a risk management perspective;
- To evaluate internal resourcing and career mobility effectiveness, e.g., how many external vs. internal candidates were reported on, using metrics on a regular basis;
- To develop a willingness within the organisation to share key pivotal talent across businesses, enabling a climate of trust and a "one-enterprise culture" which result in high strategic talent agility;
- To use specific and uniform collective people intelligence and talent profile information to clearly identify developmental roles/positions across divisions within the organisation, to enable the flow of talent via the use of, inter alia, talent investment matrix-like (performance x potential) mechanisms;

- To ensure the retention and development of key individuals;
- To evaluate how many mission-critical roles are filled by top performers;
- To determine the bench-depth for each mission-critical role;
- To determine and evaluate how retention rates for top and pivotal talent compare with those of competitors;
- To evaluate how close the organisation is to 100 per cent compliance with agreed-upon standards and processes for setting goals, evaluating performance and developing talent;
- To review, where appropriate, (secondment/expatriate) strategies, tactics and plans by size of business and market share growth, size and demand for headcount growth, FTE turnover, planned retirement, etc.;
- To develop deepened insight into critical roles and the risks of filling these;
- To review, reflect on and approve external buy (recruitment, resourcing) strategies, tactics and plans for CEO and C-suite candidates (normally those reporting directly to the CEO's office, such as the CFO and COO);
- To ensure prudent maintenance of high people management standards across the organisation;
- To review the succession readiness of nominated individual talent pool participants, using relevant talent profile information at hand to support and verify their continued eligibility;
- To review, reflect on and approve leadership talent management international deployment strategies, tactics and plans;
- To accelerate the implementation of realistic and practical career and development plans;
- To review and approve budgets and funds for pivotal and leadership talent development, engagement, rotation and deployment purposes;
- To consider a wide range of appropriate pivotal talent and leadership talent management deployment and development recommendations, both in the short and long term;
- To compare costs and time to fill vacancies with external buy recruitment options; and
- To review the supply of the right calibre, type and quantity of leaders for future success.

The above elements were captured in the actual agenda of the governance body, variously referred to as a Strategic Talent Investment Board or a People Capability Review Board. Its agenda continually evolved to ensure that it addressed and developed foresight from its current as well as its anticipated competitive landscape and labour market context, much of which was encapsulated in reference to a range of volatile, complex and ubiquitous business drivers. Again, it is important to emphasise that many talent management efforts go astray and/or lack the necessary strategic impact as a result of the actual business and requisite talent needs not being integrated, aligned and (more critically) implemented, from a governance and risk management perspective.

For both telecommunications companies it was strongly recommended that the governance body be chaired by the Group Chief Executive, proactively facilitated by the organisation's most senior HR executive (preferably someone represented on the main board to ensure a high degree of legitimacy and credibility, and to safeguard the integrity of strategic talent management). It was further considered essential that the remaining members of this governance and strategic review board(s) be executive-level officials, representative (as appropriate) across all operating functions, companies and/or geographic territories. These executives were invited, when and as required, across functions from within the group. Membership changed in accordance with the changing strategic business needs and capabilities of the organisation, and the need to proactively align strategic leadership talent management requirements. For this reason, the Strategic Executive Review Board committed to meet at least twice a year, either face to face or via video/teleconferencing.

The positioning of this governance body essentially ensures that talent management is top of mind for the organisation. This greatly compliments and galvanises Ashton and Morton's[19] systemic view of talent management, by ensuring that it is driven strategically from the top of the organisation. It further enables the commitment of senior managers, supporting the view of Lawler[20] and Michaels et al.[21] of clear advocacy for a higher degree of involvement, responsibility and accountability for talent management on the part of boards of directors.

Business drivers

In order for talent management to be a strategic differentiator, it needs to be fully driven and integrated with the business strategy.[22, 23] A range of options will now be explored. Keep in mind that these business drivers, needs and associated business strategies will mostly be nation-, industry-, organisation- or labour market context-specific.

The following serve as examples from within previously referred to financial services and telecommunication industry companies across multiple countries in Africa, the Middle East and Asia. They are representative of the type of business drivers which were mostly anticipated, integrated and aligned with their respective talent management strategies. Their intention is to ensure a culture and talent management mindset. Many of these business strategies and drivers could have an impact on other systemic elements (e.g., talent accounting/ planning, supply/demand options) of the talent management framework. Responsive, innovative as well as specific matching and aligned talent management practices, processes and activities need to be designed and leveraged to provide for a distinctive talent architecture. Such a configuration would be uniquely tailored to each organisation and, as such, could provide for superior performance and act as a source of competitive advantage.[24]

- *Globalisation* is increasingly reshaping the competitive landscape and will continue to do so for the foreseeable future, given organisations' appetite for expansion and growth offshore. Today's global interconnected economy has created a more complex and dynamic environment in which most companies must learn to compete effectively to achieve sustainable growth. Moving into new markets provides many opportunities but also multiple challenges, and the concept of a larger, more globally mobile, diverse and highly-educated global workforce is becoming all the vogue,[25] requiring organisations to ensure global consistency in their talent management practices;
- *Workforce demographics* closely related to globalisation indicate that there are dramatic shifts in the composition of the labour pool in both developed and emerging economies. Meister and Willyerd[26] believe that age, gender and ethnicity will challenge employers, given that an anticipated five generations will soon collaborate in the workplace, as many more mature workers delay their retirement. For the first time in human history, there will be more old people than children on the planet. The manner in which worker expectations are evolving is proving to be both dynamic and characterised by uncertainty. However, in emerging economies there will be numerous highly educated young people, with the likes of China and India each graduating well over 400 000 scientists and engineers a year – a significant percentage of whom will be highly mobile. The bottom line is that multiple generations will be working together; increasing numbers of women will enter the workforce; and there will be a greater diversity of ethnic, socio-economic, religious and national backgrounds. Relocating work to locations with a good supply of willing and able talent is being accelerated by quantum-leap advances in technology;
- *Strategies:* a wide array of these are formulated by organisations and the majority – if Treacy and Wiersema[27] and Porter[28] are to be believed – centre around operational excellence, innovation, customer-centricity or intimacy, product leadership, cost, differentiation, value and then (invariably) either internal organic growth strategies or (more ambitiously) growth via mergers and acquisitions. The business landscape increasingly demands a frequent revision of these strategies, business models and value drivers, as boards and financial markets cry out for double-digit growth and earnings. These factors are increasingly more evident and rampant within the financial services, telecoms, retail and hospitality industries;

- The *transformation* of organisations and workplaces is considered an integral priority aimed at providing greater and more equitable representation, both to accelerate redress and ensure a higher degree of economic advancement for people and communities which were previously socially and economically disadvantaged;
- *Employee expectations* or "peculiarities"[29] refer to the ever-evolving demands and beliefs of a new army of highly skilled and internationally mobile knowledge workers who, amongst a range of other idiosyncrasies, are less accommodating of traditional structures and authority, more focused on work-life balance and more prepared to take ownership of their own careers and development.

Organisations and HR practitioners alike will need to continuously anticipate and collaborate with a broad range of stakeholders to scrutinise these business drivers and jointly evaluate their impact on the next components of an integrated talent management framework. The objective is to ensure the more coherent integration of talent management strategy and processes directly into, and aligned with, the business strategy.

The companies in the industries referred to earlier considered it necessary to comprehensively account for their existing talent demand, and the need to match and align their requisite talent, while meeting their current business goals and reflecting on future needs. These will be expanded on next.

Talent accounting and the talent supply–demand equation

The organisations in question made use of a range of expertly facilitated workshops to essentially address a series of burning questions, prompted by the aforementioned challenges of a globally competitive talent landscape. These questions were all courageously confronted to gain advanced insights into what talent and potential types of talent they currently had on board. More importantly, they wanted to find out what talent was required in order to meet their current business objectives as well as the future growth aspirations of their stakeholders, and customers and shareholders in particular.[30]

Questions from these strategic talent accounting workshops included the following:

- What insight (people intelligence) do we as an organisation have into the skills, knowledge, competencies, abilities and experiences of our current talent?
- To what extent do our talent have the skills, knowledge, competencies, abilities and experiences required for competitive advantage?
- Do we have the right talent in terms of skill and capability for the future?
- Where is our existing talent?
- To what extent have we identified a pivotal game-changing role, i.e., what pivotal job families/roles are most critical to executing the business strategy?
- Where relevant, how can we find the right people to deploy or recruit in the high-growth, hot markets of China, Dubai, Germany, Eastern Europe, Russia and/or South America?
- How can the organisation not only source but also attract, engage and retain the so-called new generation of innovative knowledge workers in science, engineering, technology, etc., over the next five years?
- Where are our high-potential employees and future leaders who are currently not in sight?
- What criteria (e.g., science, technology, engineering, mathematics or "knowledge-rich") should we use to define either critical skills and/or pivotal roles?
- How are critical, scarce skills and/or pivotal roles defined?
- Do we have differentiated talent pools for our managerial leadership, professional, technical or functional requirements?
- How will we differentiate talent strategies/investments accordingly?
- To what extent do any of these talent pools contain scarce and/or critical skills?
- Have we identified our high-potential employees from these talent pool segments?

- How do we intend managing and investing in their development and deployment?
- Have we determined and/or ensured that, where appropriate, these differentiated talent pools contain a high degree of learning, agile and mobile employees?
- Do we know the retention risk of each person considered high-potential (thanks to scarce and critical skills), who is currently in a strategically pivotal role or is earmarked for such a future role?
- To what extent have we identified successors and do we have a development plan for them?
- How robust is our existing leadership pipeline, and where are the risks?
- What leadership competencies/attributes are required to drive our business strategy and lead the evolution of an innovation culture?
- What is the extent of the organisation's gap between current talent and what is required for the future?
- What are our future talent requirements and can they be met?
- Have possible successors for C-suite-level talent been identified and assessed?
- To what extent is "promotability" and/or readiness to move being managed, i.e., does the organisation know who is ready for promotion and who can transition to the next level?
- What competencies, technical skills and/or experiences within our talent pools are most likely to differentiate us from our competitors?
- Technically and professionally, what expectations do our customers and/or suppliers have of the proficiencies of our workforce? How are these changing?
- Are appropriate and relevant on-boarding and transition development plans in place for these individuals, to reduce the risk of derailment or failure at the next level?
- Do these plans enable and prepare potential successors to master the realities of new multicultural organisations or a fast and complex organisational change context?

In exploring and searching for answers, it became obvious that innovative future-focused practitioners will have to develop comprehensive and reliable processes, mechanisms and techniques to obtain relevant people intelligence. These insights will, in many ways, ensure alignment with challenges related to the internal demand and external supply of the requisite talent.

To fill individual and organisational gaps, Ulrich[31] advances the notion that organisations could consider investing differentially in talent through the following strategies (another phase of the aforementioned strategic talent workshop(s)):

- *Buy*: recruiting, sourcing, securing new talent for the organisation, including involving customers/suppliers to source, interview and orient new talent;
- *Build*: helping people grow through learning and development or on-the-job/life experiences, e.g., creating exchanges where employees take assignments in customer or supplier organisations; involving customers/investors in the design and delivery of development programmes; designing stretching cross-functional and multinational assignments;
- *Borrow*: bringing knowledge into the organisation through advisors or partners, e.g., innovatively sourcing knowledge and expertise from contractors, vendors, consultants or others outside the organisation and/or creating web-based social networks to find ways of doing work;
- *Bounce*: removing poor performers from their jobs and/or the organisation; considering the use of customer criteria as part of the alternate deployment and/or rightsizing process; outplacing employees into supplier/customer networks;
- *Bind*: retaining top talent and remaining flexible as to re-hiring talented employees who have left; using the employee referral programmes of future employees as a way to retain the best.

In addition to the above strategies, Cappelli[32] advances the notion of "talent on demand" as a means to reduce the effects of uncertainty about the nature and type of talent which the organisation will require, through the use of talent pools/portfolios. Similarly, it is important to keep in mind that potential, performance and readiness are not the same thing. Many organisations and practitioners understand the idea of a high-potential pool or group of people who receive more focused developmental attention. However, it is imperative that from a strategic talent and leveraging perspective, the differences between potential, performance and readiness are better understood and appreciated. Many organisations, in their quest for acceleration, confuse "quick and dirty", and/or use large-scale fanfare-driven events to hide the fact that they now, more than ever, need high-potential talent with an openness, a willingness to learn and the flexibility to execute complex strategies. Talent-powered organisations require potential leaders who are curious about the world, willing to learn and experience new things, and have high ambiguity tolerance, good people skills, vision and are innovative. "Learning agility" has been used to describe individuals who possess such skills, and is currently viewed as a key indicator of potential.[33] Taking a leader from potential to readiness is an enduring process: it takes, on average, ten years for a high-potential leader to advance into a senior position. Along the way, that individual requires mentoring, stretch cross-functional and (where relevant) multinational assignments, personalised yet flexible career development plans, and customised as well as synchronised development activities to build key skills. Most importantly, such potential talent requires significant learning agility and an inherent drive for results.[34]

Essentially, the above takes account of organisations' current supply of high-potential talent vs. their requisite supply for the future, be it categorised and/or segmented as professional, technical functional or leadership potential. It is advisable to be clear about what the HR practitioner and the organisation are looking for. Experience as well as a host of research[35] suggests that it is useful to generate a comprehensive talent success profile consisting of the following:

- *Competencies:* the behavioral attributes which drive performance;
- *Experience:* the evidence-based application of knowledge and skill obtained through exposure which is consistently associated with high performance;
- *Technical skill:* what is known and can be applied and is associated with successful performance; and
- *Mobility:* personal dispositions and motivations that relate to learning, adaptation, satisfaction, success or possible failure and derailment in a job, either at the next level or two up and/or in a multicultural, expatriate foreign assignment.

These talent success profiles, by any definition, are not to be confused with role profiles and/or static job descriptions, as they represent more accurate and detailed definitions of what is required for exceptional performance in a given role/job or even a significant career transition (e.g., from managing yourself to managing others), function or enterprise[36] or significant organisation change context (e.g., start-up, turnaround or realignment).[37]

A comprehensive talent accounting exercise (talent balance-sheet) across the entire enterprise was used and conducted against these key talent success profiles which were, given their comprehensive nature, reflective of current as well as future business contexts. Any gaps in requisite talent thus identified were used to inform talent strategies (e.g., develop, deploy, buy, build, etc.).

In summary, then, the key to supplying talent in addition to addressing the range of earlier questions, is to meet the following challenges:

- *Increased business competition* and the attraction of highly skilled talent remain key challenges, therefore the retention of high-potential scarce, critical and pivotal skills in science, engineering, technology and mathematically rich roles, will be a key differentiator;
- *Managing the economic downturn* remains a key priority to sustain performance through people;
- *Technological changes* bring new skill requirements, e.g., remote and virtual working, supply chains, etc.;
- *Industry diversification* trends affect talent supply and demand;
- *Talent poaching* requires new and innovative approaches to talent management;

- *Innovation and new product development* can assist in creating barriers to entry for competitors (so that the organisation is first to market); and
- *Disciplined execution* of stated business goals and strategies is important for sustainable success.

Although outside the scope of this discussion, it would be remiss not to mention that in order to leverage and accelerate the deployment of the integrated talent management framework, it was highly beneficial (and hence advisable) to automate all talent information, from a technological perspective. Comprehensive people-intelligence requirements were captured and leveraged via a specialist talent management system. Some of the criteria used at the time to deploy such technology across 34-odd countries, deemed truly enabling and differentiating from an automated talent management viewpoint, meant it had to be web-enabled, self-service and social-networking centered. This approach ensured a high degree of adoption of mobile technology by a broad range of stakeholders. Apart from obvious employees and line managers, it also provided for input by having customers and suppliers drive key talent specifications and/or evaluations (e.g., via 360° feedback).

Charan,[38] Goldsmith[39] and others consider filling the leadership pipeline and planning for succession as ranking high on every company's priority list, especially since CEOs' length of tenure is declining, and internal candidates are becoming the main source of talent. Thus, following from the demand and supply equation of talent, the grooming of leaders throughout an organisation is absolutely critical for international competitiveness. As such, the advancement of leadership talent within the context of global succession management (inclusive of identification, assessment and development of an expatriate management pool) will be explored further as per the integrated strategic talent management framework.

Leadership Talent Advancement Framework

This section serves to illustrate that the various components, practices and processes inherent to an overall framework need to be closely aligned and integrated with the overall business strategy, in a systemic way. Depending on the aforementioned sequence of business drivers, talent accounting and supply, as well as demand for talent, this section could just as well be dedicated to the techniques, methodologies, activities and measures associated with high-potential professional, functional or technical talent. The aim is to mitigate the risk of the organisation not having the requisite talent to execute its strategy. It will, however, focus on leadership talent management strategy: in many instances, leadership is not merely viewed as a critical enabler of the organisation's specific vision and growth ambitions, but is also considered imperative as a source of competitive differentiation.

The quality of its leadership[40] assists in ensuring that the organisation has a distinctive leadership brand, which makes it not merely a leading employer of choice in the territories, markets and countries where it chooses to operate, but also provides investors with a high degree of confidence, which allays fears associated with the risk of sustainability. Identifying, assessing and developing appropriate high-potential leadership talent to ensure a pipeline of leaders for the future will go a long way in answering the question which many organisations' CEOs lose sleep over: "Do we have the necessary leadership bench strength to execute our strategy and, most of all, when will those identified for these critical leadership positions be ready?" Berke,[41] who insists that succession management is intended to be more than mere replacement planning, refers to it as an organisation's processes for identifying, assessing, selecting and managing talent to build bench-strength and ensure the readiness of talent to move immediately into key positions, when necessary. Such movements can occur when a position becomes vacant as a result of a resignation or dismissal, or when a position is newly created to meet a business need. It is the proactive effort by an organisation to encourage individual advancement and ensure a continuity of talent which is ready to assume key positions, be these local, regional or even international. As such, leadership talent management succession entails specifically delving deeper into robust and customised processes which include

- identifying leadership potential specifically;
- assessing succession readiness via performance and competency assessments, particularly as they relate to working at one or two levels up and managing transitions[42] and/or working in a new organisational context;[43]
- determining strategies to develop and close any gaps;
- providing opportunities for employees to pursue career paths and express career interests; and
- verifying mobility by determining suitability for international assignments.

A primary outcome of succession management is the accelerated development of high-potential and high-performing leadership talent. To ensure such an implementation, many organisations robustly manage leadership pipelines. Succession management represents the deliberate and planned development and preparation of identified successors, therefore regular executive talent reviews with the CEO and board to consider assessment results and plan developmental moves for these next-generation leaders (see discussion on governance) are essential for ensuring the quality of the leadership talent bench. To facilitate such reviews, the famous nine-box "Performance x Potential" matrix, popularised by General Electric, is frequently used.

Many approaches to leadership talent development tend to place the emphasis and focus on building a narrow set of either functional or behavioural competencies and a fairly generic and non-differentiating set of aptitudes for leadership talent.

In both industries and for all three companies referred to earlier, it was important to ensure that the leadership talent management journey helped create a distinctive leadership brand. Hence, a more holistically integrative framework for leadership advancement (see Table 9.1) was jointly developed via consultation and involvement with a wide range of stakeholders and accordingly adopted in differing formats. It attempts to combine leadership competencies (targeted to the individual) with differentiated experiences and exposure which aligns with capabilities that spell success for a particular organisation (e.g., capabilities in enhancing the customer experience, or acquiring and integrating new businesses or achieving operational excellence in rolling out infrastructure development). Leadership talent development is therefore not merely a set of activities, deliverables or high-profile events. It is an essential enabler of the business strategy and reflects the diversity of the company's customer and employee base.

Such an approach to deepening an organisation's leadership bench-strength over time becomes a sustainable organisational capability, not simply a way of growing a few individual leaders. It is reminiscent of global organisations such as IBM, Proctor and Gamble, Unilever, etc., which have achieved legendary status and, as part of their signature, provide frequent challenging and stretching cross-functional and international assignments to advance multinational and global leadership talent potential.

Following this argument, then, talent (or more precisely leadership potential) can be viewed as the ability to learn from experience. Identified successors, however, do not always have access to those experiences that would best develop their executive abilities, therefore organisations need some mechanism or process that determines who has what experience. This framework-within-a-framework provides an example of how the process was approached.

Table 9.1   Case study example of Leadership Talent Advancement Framework inclusive of transition challenges, competencies and learning experience context

Leadership transition phase	Key transition challenges	Competencies	International global factors	Exposure and experiences to be provided/ obtained
Transition from Group Leadership to Enterprise Leadership *(Where individuals are responsible for more than one business)* Themes: Multinational Domain + Organisational Domain	Understanding trade-offs – success or failure is based on three or four high-impact decisions a year – stakes are significantly higher Managing a broad range of external constituencies proactively Letting go of primarily focusing on individual pieces and focusing on the whole Reinventing oneself as an enterprise manager	Dealing with ambiguity Intellectual rigor Learning agility Dealing with paradox Perspective Drive for results Managing vision and purpose Political savvy	Global business knowledge Cross-cultural resourcefulness Cross-cultural agility Org positioning from remote locations Humility Cross-cultural sensitivity Assignment-hardiness	Start up a business in international market Turn around a business in local or international market
Transition from Business Leadership to Group Leadership *(Where people are accountable for the results of a business)* Themes: Multinational Domain + Organisational Domain	Going from running own show to running a number of shows Valuing the success of other people – can be difficult for results-oriented people Ability to take difficult decisions Shifting thinking from a functional perspective to profit generation	Business acumen Drive for results Standing alone Strategic agility Managing vision and purpose Perspective Priority setting Influence and work across organisation, division and /or functions	Global business knowledge Cross-cultural resourcefulness Cross-cultural agility Org positioning from remote locations Humility Cross-cultural sensitivity Assignment-hardiness	Develop, design and implement a strategy for increasing customer intimacy Design, develop and implement as well as evaluate a strategy to increase market share in new local markets

➡

Leadership transition phase	Key transition challenges	Competencies	International global factors	Exposure and experiences to be provided/ obtained
Transition from Functional Leadership to Business Leadership (*Leadership of an operating unit with Profit and Loss*) Theme: Organisational Domain	Communicating through two levels of management Learning about and valuing aspects of the business that are not within their direct experience Monumental shift in thinking – longer timeframes, different trade-offs have to be made Emotional fortitude and personal authenticity become as important as business skills and knowledge	Business acumen Delegation Innovation management Organisational agility Perspective Priority setting Strategic thinking and agility Building effective teams	Global business knowledge Cross-cultural resourcefulness Cross-cultural agility Org positioning from remote locations Humility Cross-cultural sensitivity Assignment-hardiness Remote and virtual working via use of appropriate technology	Fix up division Undertake multinational assignment Design a strategy for a business in a developing economy Develop and implement a strategy for a business impacted by high convergence of technologies Develop either comprehensive change management and/or risk management strategy for sizeable project
Transition from People Leadership to Functional Leadership (*Leadership of a Functional Area*) Theme: Operational Domain + Organisational Domain	Creating time for less tangible activities (e.g., coaching/ mentoring) Managing through other managers rather than directly Communicating and influencing with a wider circle of stakeholders Broader knowledge of the organisation and how to get things done	Directing others Informing Managing and measuring Motivating others Developing direct reports Fairness to team Interpersonal savvy Sizing people up Building effective teams	Global business knowledge Cross-cultural resourcefulness Cross-cultural agility Org positioning from remote locations Humility Cross-cultural sensitivity Assignment-hardiness	Develop and implement a strategy that requires significantly new/ different skills Develop and implement comprehensive change management approach to ensure service, quality and/ or process improvement inclusive of business case and evaluation of impact of change

➡

Leadership transition phase	Key transition challenges	Competencies	International global factors	Exposure and experiences to be provided/ obtained
Transition from Self Leadership (*Self-Management + Self-Awareness*) **to People Leadership** (*Leading others and managers*)	Letting go of work which defined previous successes Effectively managing the performance of others Focusing on the team rather than individual agenda Putting trust in others to deliver results	Action oriented Customer focus Functional/ technical skills Perseverance Problem solving Technical learning Business acumen Service quality Interpersonal skills	Integrity Open-mindedness Learning agility	Review and develop comprehensive process improvement plan as it relates to service and/or quality dimensions of your function, division or organisation

The Leadership Advancement Framework is based on research by McCall[44] as well as Lombardo and Eichinger[45] who advance the notion of using both competencies and experiences, not only as a means to integrate various talent management sub-processes, but more specifically to answer strategic questions relevant to organisations' industry-specific challenges and strategies:

- What challenges will future (next generation) leaders face?
- What kind of job experiences would best prepare the next generation of leaders for these challenges?
- At what stage of their careers and during which transition stage should they be exposed to planned and deliberate cross-functional assignments and/or projects?
- How and during which career transition stage is it best to expose these future leaders to multinational, global assignments?
- How do we best assess the learning agility and mobility of these leaders to determine who is most suitable, with the least risk of failure and/or career derailment?
- How do we implement a leadership advancement framework to ensure that skills and capabilities gained on assignment are utilised and developed further in subsequent assignments?
- How do we best facilitate career development which ensures that, where relevant, international movement results in positive career advancement, i.e., so that individual mobility is rewarded?
- How do we integrate, where relevant, this framework to create a talent-rich culture that values international mobility and diversity?
- How do we ensure the adequate preparation, tracking and integration of these development competency and experienced-based learning objectives in individual development plans before, during and after assignments, rotations, etc.?
- To what extent does such an integrated leadership talent advancement approach accelerate the (leadership) succession readiness to lead?

The Leadership Talent Advancement Framework demonstrates how succession management – and more specifically, how planning the improvement of leadership readiness – is no longer just a matter of identifying individuals and populating a spreadsheet with names of suitable candidates. Neither is creating and/or arbitrarily designating a group as a "top leadership talent pool" likely to do much to meet an organisation's future strategic leadership needs. Practitioners who merely schedule and/or populate development plans with endless structured formal training events which offer little rich and/or multifunctional and global experiential-based learning, at best put their organisations at risk and do very little to leverage its inherent leadership potential.[46]

Evaluating the impact and outcome of integrated strategic talent management

Practitioners and organisations alike are under close scrutiny from a broad range of stakeholders (including society) to demonstrate that both their general business strategies and their specific talent management strategies significantly distinguish them from a competitiveness point of view, while advancing the interests of the greater community. Parochial approaches which advocate "best in class" and "most admired company to work for", or even represent a "compelling place to work" are unlikely to sustain the 21st-century organisation.

For this reason, amongst others (see business drivers), a measurement of outcome and impact component is essentially included in the Integrated Talent Management Framework, to systemically validate its comprehensiveness.

Effron and Ort[47] compellingly argue, though, that there is a need, in integrating talent management strategically, for practitioners to start with science in mind: they must simultaneously eliminate complexity and create transparency, as well as a strong sense of accountability. Practitioners are urged to work in partnership with stakeholders to nail down a few simple metrics and/or measures to determine what to measure in processes inherent in the framework, and also what the framework should achieve.

Examples of such metrics, which proved valuable in operationalising and cultivating said frameworks within the companies under study (which employ in excess of 35 000 people), include the following:

- Bench strength gives the number (no.) or percentage of headcount of those ready for promotion, and indicates the quality of those identified for said promotion;
- Talent pool depth indicates the no. of successors per key or critical/pivotal role – normally, having two to three successors per role is considered progressive;
- Talent pool diversity, again in no. and percentage terms, e.g., what percentage of identified successors is female?
- Retention rate of critical or key pivotal talent, e.g., what is the no. and percentage of critical positions which have been filled with high-quality internal candidates during the talent period under review?
- The percentage and no. of rotational assignments completed;
- The no. and percentage of identified high-potential successors willing to be globally mobile; and
- The no. and percentage of staff with development plans.

Note that identifying the criteria by which success is to be measured and defining relevant metrics are unique to each organisation's specific strategy, industry and, most of all, its aligned talent management strategy.

Conclusion

Many of the most pressing competitive challenges confronting 21st-century organisations are directly related to talent – be it attracting, selecting, developing or engaging (if not leveraging) potential talent to its optimum. Organisations and practitioners dedicate huge amounts of energy to ensuring that they urgently address this with as much strategic foresight as possible.

In this chapter an attempt was made to position the business drivers relating to talent management as comprehensively as possible. In doing so, the deployment of a proven in-action Integrated Talent

Management Framework was proposed to strategically govern talent, and cater for the accounting, supply and demand of anticipated talent. As an example a real leadership advancement framework to address the management of leadership talent succession in particular was presented to demonstrate the application of the framework. Finally, the chapter explored the need to develop relevant and meaningful outcomes measures in the process of talent management.

By designing, developing and adopting an integrated talent management framework organisations can ensure that their related efforts are continually driven and renewed by their business strategy. The result, as is evident from the case studies, is that talent which is unique to an organisation can be leveraged as a core business capability, thus demonstrating a differentiating talent mindset which is truly representative of the liberating nature of human potential.

Endnotes

1   J Welch, Speech delivered to General Electric Annual Meeting. Charlotte, North Carolina, 23 April 1997.
2   D Aguirre, SA Hewlett & L Post, *Global talent innovation: Strategies for breakthrough performance*, Booz and Co, USA, 2009.
3   P Cheese, RJ Thomas & E Craig, *The talent powered organization: Strategies for globalization, talent management and high performance*, Kogan Page, London, 2007.
4   P Adler, *Leveraging the talent driven organization*, Aspen Institute, Houghton Lab Lane, Queenstown, 2010.
5   C Ashton & L Morton, 'Managing talent for competitive advantage', *Strategic Human Resources Review*, vol. 4, no. 5, 2005, pp. 28–31.
6   R Silzer & B Dowell, *Strategy driven talent management: A leadership imperative*, Jossey-Bass, San Francisco, 2009.
7   Aguirre, op. cit.
8   J Boudreau & PM Ramstad, *Beyond HR: The new science of human capital*, John W Harvard Business School Publishing Corporation, Boston, 2007.
9   Aguirre, op. cit.
10 EL Gubman and S Green, *Strategy-driven talent management: A leadership imperative*, Jossey Bass, San Francisco, 2007.
11 Silzer & Dowell, op. cit.
12 Adapted from Ashton & Morton, op. cit.
13 Ibid.
14 Silzer & Dowell, op. cit.
15 M Guthridge, AB Komm & E Lawson, 'The people problem in talent management', *McKinsey Quarterly*, 2006, no. 2, p. 6.
16 J Pfeffer & RI Sutton, *Hard facts, dangerous half-truths and total nonsense: Profiting from evidence-based management*, Harvard Business School Press, Boston, 2006.
17 R Charan, *Boards that deliver*, Jossey Bass, San Francisco, 2005.
18 K Lamoureux, M Campbell & R Smith, 'High impact succession management', Center for Creative Leadership, April 2009, retrieved 20 July 2016, <http://www.ccl.org/leadership/pdf/research/HighImpactSuccession Management.pdf>.
19 Ashton & Morton, op. cit.
20 EE Lawler III, *Talent: Making people your competitive advantage*, Jossey Bass, San Francisco, 2008.
21 E Michaels, H Handfield-Jones & B Axelrod, *The war for talent*, Harvard Business School Press, Boston, 2001.
22 Lawler, op. cit.
23 Silzer & Dowell, op. cit.
24 Aguirre, op. cit.
25 DR Briscoe, RS Schuler and LM Claus, 2009, *International human resource management: policies and practices for multinational enterprises*, Routledge: London & New York.
26 JC Meister & K Willyerd, *The 2020 workplace: How innovative companies attract, develop, and keep tomorrow's employees today*, Harper Collins Publishers, New York, 2010.
27 M Treacy & F Wiersema, 'The discipline of market leaders: Choose your customers narrow your focus', *dominate your market*, Addison-Wesley, Reading, MA, 1997.
28 ME Porter, *On competition*, Harvard Business School Press, Boston, 2008.
29 Guthridge, et al., op. cit.

30   D Ulrich & N Smallwood, *Leadership brand: Developing customer focused leaders to drive performance and build lasting value*, Harvard Business Press, Boston, 2007.

31   D Ulrich, *Human resource champions: The next agenda for adding value and delivering results*, Harvard Business Press, Boston, 1997.

32   P Cappelli, *Managing talent on demand: Talent in an age of uncertainty*, Harvard Business Press, Boston, 2008.

33   RW Eichinger & MM Lombardo, 'Learning agility as a prime indicator of potential', in *Human resource planning*, 27, no. 4, 2004.

34   M Lombardo & R Eichinger, 'High potentials as high learners', *Human Resource Management Journal*, vol. 39, no 4, 2000, pp. 321–330.

35   MW McCall, & MM Lombardo, 1988, *The lessons of experience: How successful executives develop on the job*, Free Press. New York.

36   R Charan & S Drotter, *The leadership pipeline: How to build the leadership powered company*, Jossey Bass, San Francisco, 2001.

37   M Watkins, *The first 90 days: Critical success strategies for new leaders at all levels*. Harvard Business School Press, Boston, 2003.

38   R Charan, *Leaders at all levels: Deepening your talent pool to solve the succession crisis*, John Wiley and Sons, Hoboken, NJ, 2007.

39   M Goldsmith, *Succession: Are you ready?*, Harvard Business Press, Boston, 2009.

40   Ulrich & Smallwood, op. cit.

41   D Berke, *Succession planning and management: A guide to organizational systems and practices*, Centre for Creative Leadership, Johannesburg, 2005.

42   Charan and Drotter, op. cit.

43   Watkins, op. cit.

44   MW McCall, *High flyers: Developing the next generation of leaders*, Harvard Business School Press, Boston, 1998.

45   Lombardo & Eichinger, op. cit.

46   L Bossidy & C Charan, *Execution: The discipline of getting things done*, Crown Business, New York, 2002.

47   M Effron & M Ort, *One page talent management: Eliminating complexity, adding value*, Harvard Business School Publishing, Boston, 2010.

References

Adler, P, *Leveraging the talent-driven organization*, Aspen Institute, Washington, DC, 2010.

Aguirre, D, SA Hewlett & L Post, *Global talent innovation: Strategies for breakthrough performance*, Booz and Co, USA, 2009.

Ashton, C & L Morton, 'Managing talent for competitive advantage', *Strategic Human Resources Review*, vol. 4, no. 5, 2005, pp. 28–31.

Berke, D, *Succession planning and management: A guide to organizational systems and practices*, Centre for Creative Leadership, Johannesburg, 2005.

Bossidy, L & C Charan, *Execution: The discipline of getting things done*, Crown Business, New York, 2002.

Boudreau, J and PM Ramstad, *Beyond HR: The new science of human capital*, John W Harvard Business School Publishing Corporation, Boston, 2007.

Briscoe DR, RS Schuler & LM Claus, *International human resource management: policies and practices for multinational enterprises*, London, Routledge: New York: . 2009.

Cappelli, P, *Managing talent on demand: Talent in an age of uncertainty*, Harvard Business Press, Boston, 2008.

Charan, R & S Drotter, *The leadership pipeline: How to build the leadership powered company*, Jossey Bass, San Francisco, 2001.

Charan, R, *Boards that deliver*, Jossey Bass, San Francisco, 2005.

Charan, R, *Leaders at all levels: Deepening your talent pool to solve the succession crisis*, John Wiley and Sons, Hoboken, NJ, 2007.

Cheese, P, RJ Thomas & E Craig, *The talent powered organization: Strategies for globalization, talent management and high performance*, Kogan Page, London, 2007.

Effron, M & M Ort, *One page talent management: Eliminating complexity, adding value*, Harvard Business School Publishing, Boston, 2010.

Eichinger, RW & MM Lombardo, 'Learning agility as a prime indicator of potential', in *Human resource planning*, vol. 27, no. 4, 2004.

Goldsmith, M, *Succession: Are you ready?*, Harvard Business Press, Boston, 2009.

Gubman, EL, & S, Green, 2007, *Strategy-Driven Talent Management: A Leadership Imperative* ; San Francisco, Jossey Bass.

Guthridge, M, AB Komm & E Lawson, 'The people problem in talent management', *McKinsey Quarterly*, 2006, no. 2, p. 6, retrieved 12 July 2016, <https://supplyxiii.wikispaces.com/file/view/McKinsey_People_in_Talent_Management.pdf>

Lamoureux, K, Campbell, M & Smith R, 'High impact succession management', Center for Creative Leadership, April 2009, Retrieved 20 July 2016, <http://www.ccl.org/leadership/pdf/research/HighImpactSuccessionManagement.pdf>.

Lawler III, EE, *Talent: Making people your competitive advantage*, Jossey Bass, San Francisco, 2008.

Lombardo, M & R Eichinger, 'High potentials as high learners', *Human Resource Management Journal*, vol. 39, no 4, 2000, pp. 321–330.

McCall, MW & MM Lombardo, *The lessons of experience: How successful executives develop on the job*, Free Press, New York, 1988.

McCall, MW, *High flyers: Developing the next generation of leaders*, Harvard Business School Press, Boston, 1998.

Meister, JC & K Willyerd, *The 2020 workplace: How innovative companies attract, develop, and keep tomorrow's employees today*, Harper Collins, New York, 2010.

Michaels, E, H Handfield-Jones & B Axelrod, *The war for talent*, Harvard Business School Press, Boston, 2001.

Pfeffer, J & RI Sutton, *Hard facts, dangerous half-truths and total nonsense: Profiting from evidence-based management*, Harvard Business School Press, Boston, 2006.

Porter, ME, *On competition*, Harvard Business School Press, Boston, 2008.

Silzer, R, & B Dowell, *Strategy driven talent management: A leadership imperative*, Jossey-Bass, San Francisco, 2009.

Treacy, M & F Wiersema, *The discipline of market leaders: Choose your customers, narrow your focus, dominate your market.* Addison-Wesley, Reading, MA, 1997.

Ulrich, D & N Smallwood, *Leadership brand: Developing customer focused leaders to drive performance and build lasting value,* Harvard Business Press, Boston, 2007.

Ulrich, D, *Human resource champions: The next agenda for adding value and delivering results*, Harvard Business Press, Boston, 1997.

Watkins, M, *The first 90 days: Critical success strategies for new leaders at all levels,* Harvard Business School Press, Boston, 2003.

Welch J, Speech delivered to General Electric Annual Meeting, Charlotte, North Carolina. 23 April 1997.

PART 2

CHAPTER 10

"FEELING THE MAGIC": WOOLWORTHS CAREER PATHS PROJECT
Chantal Butler

My mission to have a chapter on Woolworths started when I went to buy a few pairs of jeans. I began at a well-known competitor where options were non-existent (for those of us who need jeans with either wider waists or shorter legs) and where I was completely ignored. Then I went next door to Woolies and got what I needed with the aid of some really helpful assistants.

I was left wondering how it is that whenever you go to Woolies, the service is always friendly and authentic. Surely HR must have a role in fostering the competencies and positive attitudes of staff, that are so consistent across all stores.

Many years ago I used a case study in teaching about the turnaround at Sears Roebuck, the motherhood-and-apple-pie of American retailers. As part of a major turnaround strategy, they qualified the following formula:

> X% increase in staff satisfaction led to Y% increase in customer satisfaction which led to Z% financial impact.

It was an impressive case study on how this formula turned the company around at the time. The relationship between these factors was again made clear to me by one of South Africa's top HR executives, when she said that if HR cannot show their impact on the (ultimate) customer experience, it is missing something.

This case study touches on all of these things. It demonstrates the importance of a comprehensive organisational diagnostic approach and the provision of holistic solutions to a business problem. It demonstrates how a silo-free approach to the problem by HR and the business can have a profound impact on the implementation of an organisation's business strategy. Further, it shows that HR can earn its place at the table by looking at problems and opportunities through a business rather than an HR lens. Finally, it shows that organisational transformation and business strategy execution are parallel journeys that never end.

Next time you enter a Woolies store and experience the great and authentic service that come standard (especially relative to many of their retail competitors!), remember how the culture that drives the EVP (and ultimately the customer value proposition [CVP]) was shaped in that company. This is an insightful case study about what talent management is, and the potential benefits it has for all levels of an organisation.

Always think customer

Retailers live or die by their service. How customers are treated by the employees they meet in-store, is at the core of how they feel about a brand. If products capture the mind, service captures the heart.

While all retailers would say that excellent service is vital, the majority of Woolworths' customers would probably agree that service is, indeed, a genuine differentiator for the brand and that that difference comes from its staff. Since Woolworths opened the doors of its first store in Adderley Street in 1931, the service value – "always think customer" – has been a mantra and, for a long time, a very effective one.

However, while its focus on service value over the past eight decades has been absolutely consistent, Woolworths as a business has changed significantly – especially in recent years. Between June 2005 and December 2015, Woolworths opened over 500 new stores, taking its total number across South Africa and Africa to 676, with a staff complement of nearly 30 000. Over this period, the business widened in scope and increased in complexity – factors which are attributable to the following, amongst others:

- Building a BIG food business, powered by both food stand-alone stores and "SuperWoolies" – the supermarket format;
- Launching concept stores and brands;
- Using increasingly sophisticated systems and processes;
- Building a new, world-class distribution centre in Gauteng;
- Actively expanding into Africa;
- Developing a vision of becoming the "largest and most sustainable southern hemisphere retailer"; and
- Using strategies like the Good Business Journey and Good Food Journey.

All of these factors combined to create a very different staff environment. By 2012 Woolworths realised that, in every sense, it had come a long way from Adderley Street in the 30s.

Obviously, the driving force behind this expansion and development was the desire to give Woolworths customers even more of what they wanted, to continue to improve the customer value proposition (CVP). However, what Woolworths realised was that if it wanted to continue capturing hearts and building the life-long relationships with customers which it aspired to, something more had to be put in place. The employees whom management were depending on to deliver the CVP had to be the right people, with the right skills. In addition, those who were being asked to make this rapidly evolving business work, needed a better sense of how it was working for them – the right environment, the right opportunities, the right rewards. In other words, the *employee* value proposition (EVP) had to keep up, if the CVP was to be delivered successfully.

> The business had grown faster than our HR infrastructure. There were discrepancies – both real and perceived – with remuneration and there was no consistent structure to how people progressed through the organisation. Some employees were unhappy and staff turnover was a concern. We knew things needed to improve if we were going to attract the right people, keep them and create real Woolworths brand ambassadors who could take us to the places we wanted to go. It might be a cliché, but we knew that to create the magic, our staff had to first feel it.[1]

What were the challenges?

Attempts to improve the EVP started soon after the expansion process began. However, if Woolworths wished to enhance its employment brand and move from being a "preferred employer" to "an employer of choice", important issues needed to be addressed.

Remuneration and flexibility of the workforce

- As a result of new employee categories being introduced over time, pay guidelines were vague, and there were many anomalies and variances in the way people were remunerated;
- There was one broad remuneration band for store staff, which was now totally inadequate for the much wider range of roles the business required and the much higher numbers of staff it employed.

Organisational development

- There was no clear, communicated career paths framework;
- Performance management was not implemented consistently, nor was it clearly integrated with development and remuneration;
- Job naming conventions were not clear, causing confusion.

Learning and development

- There was no clearly understood link between training and development and career paths;
- Criteria for progression were unclear, with no ongoing assessment of competence relative to the job and career progression.

Recruitment

- There was limited assessment during recruitment processes.

Communication and engagement

- Communication and engagement practices in stores were inconsistent, and not the enablers they should have been. This became very evident during a month-long strike in September 2008.

Legislation

- While there was no doubt that things needed to change for the sake of the business, there was also the impending (2013 and 2104) legislation contained in the *Basic Conditions of Employment Act* (BCEA) and the *Labour Relations Act* (LRA). Particularly relevant here were the "equal work for equal pay" provisions which state that employees doing the same type of work must be remunerated the same, irrespective of employment type.

With inconsistencies in terms of both roles and remuneration in Woolworths, it was difficult to answer the question: What is equal work? In short, people were not completely happy with where they were career-wise, especially in relation to others; they had no clear idea of where their careers were going (or could go), nor did they have any real understanding of how they might get there.

> I applied for a vacancy but was told I didn't have the right training. So I couldn't go any further. I didn't know I needed that training for that job. I wanted to know what training was available earlier, so that I could be ready if a job came up.[2]

> I had four people who reported to me. I knew someone in the stockroom who didn't manage anyone but she earned about the same. People that put in more effort and have more responsibility should earn more.[3]

Case study – part 1

Tami Baloyi was a Till Operator in Eastgate. She'd been there for two years, but was thinking about leaving as she didn't feel she was progressing in her career. Plus, when she first arrived, she'd heard you needed to be friends with management to get ahead. She wasn't and she couldn't see much point in staying on. She had started to apply for other jobs when she and her colleagues were told about the Career Paths Project in one of their "Let's Talk" meetings.

Meeting those challenges: The Woolworths Career Paths Project

Phase One

The first phase of the Woolworths Career Paths project, which was rolled out between July and November 2012, focused on two crucial issues: lack of structure in career progression (which included confusion around role definition) and perceived (and actual) inequalities in terms of remuneration.

The Career Paths Framework (CPF)

The first task the HR team had to tackle was to come up with ways of redesigning, simplifying and streamlining the many roles staff were performing. In the first half of 2012, the organisational development team, in partnership with the business-facing HR team in retail operations, and representatives from staff and management, reviewed the organisation design for all staff roles in stores. The aim was to produce clear job descriptions and competency requirements for each role.

Based on those competencies, each role was then placed in one of five categories – creating 5 CS (corporate stores) levels, each with a "core competency cluster" characterising the kind of skills needed. There were also job families within those CS levels: for instance, CS Level 5 roles were split into "operations" and "supervisory", CS Level 3 into "products" and "services" (depending on the exact nature of the job). There was also a clear view of the development required to move between roles or to progress up the career ladder.

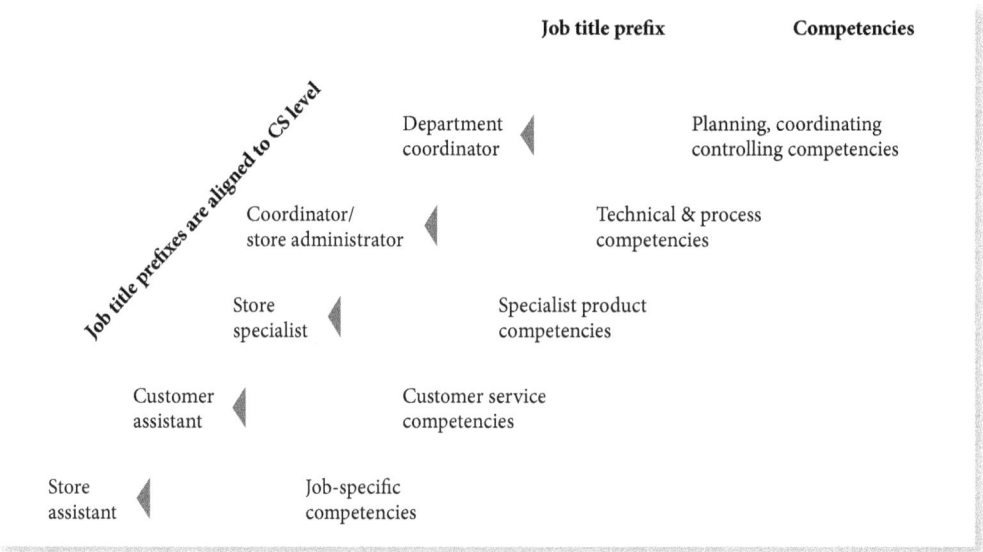

	Job title prefix	Competencies
Department coordinator		Planning, coordinating controlling competencies
Coordinator/ store administrator		Technical & process competencies
Store specialist		Specialist product competencies
Customer assistant		Customer service competencies
Store assistant		Job-specific competencies

Job title prefixes are aligned to CS level

Figure 10.1   The Career Paths Framework[4]

Five career streams were created, which corresponded with the main areas of the business – "clothing and general merchandise", "food", "administration and finance", "operations" and "other".

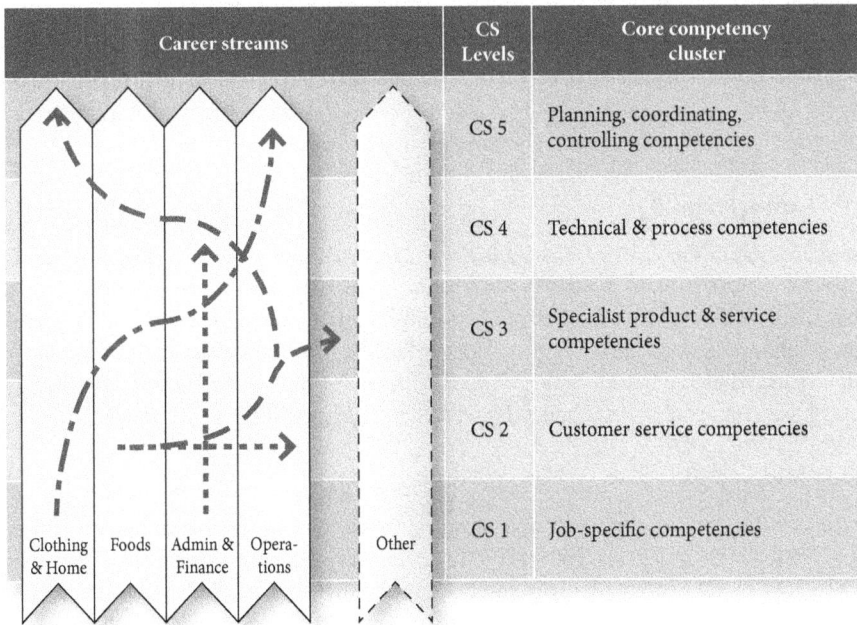

Career streams					CS Levels	Core competency cluster
					CS 5	Planning, coordinating, controlling competencies
					CS 4	Technical & process competencies
					CS 3	Specialist product & service competencies
					CS 2	Customer service competencies
Clothing & Home	Foods	Admin & Finance	Operations	Other	CS 1	Job-specific competencies

Figure 10.2   Career streams

The aim was to ensure that every staff member had a clear idea of where their role fit into the framework, how it was characterised, and (most importantly) what competencies they might need to acquire in order to develop further.

While the framework clarified matters, it was also flexible. Staff could progress within a stream or move across streams (from clothing to food, for instance) but still have a clear idea of the kind of roles they could fulfil. They could even skip a CS level, depending on the training they had received. The main idea was that, whatever option they chose, they could do so knowing where they had come from, where they were going and what they needed in order to achieve their career goals.

It was also made clear that staff were not *required* to move around at all if they did not want to. The business knew it had "progressive" (ambitious) and "non-progressive" staff members (the stable core and vast majority) and this system was designed to accommodate both groups. As long as people were performing in their jobs, they would not be pressurised to move up the scale – growth was the key message. Those who were happy in their roles could remain there – but at least they knew where "there" was.

Alongside the Career Paths Framework, the teams launched a comprehensive learning offering which outlined the training available to each job.

Remuneration to fit the role

Once the framework had been created, the next priority was to develop a pay structure aligned to it. With all jobs clearly categorised, like could be compared with like. It thus became much easier to build on such a structure – in which "equal work for equal pay" was not only possible, but would become the norm.

Five salary bands were aligned to the five CS levels – which staff now clearly understood – and salary levels were corrected and adjusted throughout the workforce. Comprehensive plans were put in place to navigate the transition from the many different employment categories to just one type, known as "Flexitimers". By the end of the first phase of the Career Paths Project, all corporate stores staff were on Flexi 8, 28 or 40-hour permanent employment contracts. This meant that rather than fixed hours, staff were guaranteed the number of hours per week stipulated in their contracts, but this could be "flexed up". This created optimum flexibility for Woolworths when it came to having the right people in the right place at the right time to realise their vision for the business, but it also meant transparency and consistency for the staff.

Getting the message across

The implementation of the Career Paths Project was supported by a comprehensive, integrated change plan. When it came to communicating with staff, the focus was on making the best use of existing (already successful) channels. Information about the Career Paths Framework, remuneration and the Career Paths Project in general was sent out to stores via a variety of media – DVDs, leaflets, information in *Shop Talk* (internal staff magazine) and roadshows – or disseminated via the weekly "Let's Talk" meetings. Store management teams were fully briefed and well prepared to champion and lead the project.

And the response was?

The HR teams – if they had given totally honest answers at the time – were not completely sure what the response to Phase 1 of the project was going to be. Any change can cause disruption, even if it is implemented with the best possible motives and using absolute best practice. But if the project were to succeed, it was vital for the team to understand what kinds of reaction these changes might elicit.

Woolworths conducts an annual "Let's Ask" survey which tests levels of staff satisfaction with all aspects of their employment. The designated team ensured that they investigated reactions to the Career Development Framework and the remuneration changes in the subsequent survey. What they found was that morale had not been affected negatively by the changes: in fact, if anything, the opposite was true – people were happier. The team ascribed this to several factors.

First of all, the communications and change management around the project seemed to have been handled well enough that everyone – staff and management alike – felt properly informed and understood what was happening. But it was more than that: the changes had immediately started to make staff feel more comfortable. Employees now had a clear definition of their roles and where those roles fit into the framework. They knew what job opportunities were available, and what training and skills they needed in order to progress – if they chose to do so. There were transparent and equitable pay bands that meant the removal of any sense of unfairness when it came to how they – and their colleagues – were rewarded.

Furthermore, managers referred to the framework to lead their teams and manage their people processes in respect of recruitment, development, performance and career planning. Individual members understood where they fit in and what was expected of them. Using the framework, managers could assess their staff's current performance fairly, while helping them to set goals and start to realise their potential in the business.

At the same time, the business introduced study leave for staff members who opted to attend training courses to acquire news skills. Woolworths also began an incentive scheme which meant employees could earn cash bonuses based on store performance.

> When we first started hearing about [the Career Paths Framework], I thought it's 'just another management thing'. But at the first "Let's Talk" meeting, my DM said "we know

things aren't right at the moment" and "maybe you feel like no one really has a plan for you and what you want to do" – and I'd felt both those things in the past. Then he listed some of the changes and for all of them I thought – "yes, that's what we need". It took a bit of time to understand exactly what the new categories meant but … it's really made a difference to how it feels, coming into the store every day.[5]

The virtuous – "sustainable" – circle

What all these innovations added up to was happier, more engaged employees. Staff turnover decreased. This, in turn, meant a more stable workforce, with people being around long enough to undergo training, develop new skills and progress through the system. It subsequently translated into employees having a greater affinity with, and a deeper understanding of, the brand, resulting in a better experience for the customer – i.e., better service.

Furthermore, the savings from reduced staff turnover were redirected into staff development and progression. Thus, while the project had begun its life focused on the "service" value, it now was feeding directly into another core Woolies' value, sustainability.

Overall, the goal of the project was being realised. The EVP was starting to do a better job of enabling the CVP. The project had created a virtuous circle: *improved staff morale and development led to enhanced customer experience which drove business performance.* This, in turn, fed back into a positive staff environment and rewards.

The magic makers were beginning to feel the magic:

> Somehow the energy that people had been putting into worrying about their place in the company or being angry about other people's progress and rewards as compared with their own, now seemed to be being channelled back into the business. This is when we could see this wasn't just about something being bolted on from the outside. It was an intrinsic change to the way our staff were relating to us as their employer, to Woolworths as a brand and, because of that, ultimately to our customers – which meant better service, a stronger business, more reward and development for staff – and we have an upward spiral.[6]

Phase Two: "Let's Grow"

Phase Two of the Career Paths Project was rolled out between February and July 2013. The aim was to build on Phase One, particularly when it came to embedding people's understanding of the skills they needed to do their jobs and, crucially, what skills they should acquire if they wanted to progress along the career paths they could now see mapped out before them.

Phase One of the Career Paths Framework had included a "menu of learning options". Now it was a question of working with staff to consider these options and help them plan ahead – i.e., to introduce a "learning" framework to support the Career Paths Framework.

The right assessments

The learning framework was integrated with the Individual Performance Management (IPM) process – something that had also been improved and enhanced in the course of Phase One. This meant that, as managers sat down to discuss performance with their staff, they could much more easily discuss their individual goals and the training needed to achieve those goals, draw up action plans and set quantifiable objectives, because they had a framework to support them.

"Do I have what I need for what I do now?"

Once staff began to understand the framework and the idea of a set of "competencies" attached to each role, many asked for a means of establishing that they were, in fact, competent in their current roles – partly for their own satisfaction and partly so that they could prove this to, say, a new line manager.

To do this, the HR team introduced a job competency evaluation process. The evaluation, which assessed employees' skills in their current positions, consisted of a "knowledge" quiz that was completed online, preceded by an "observed" component, where a line manager watched the staff member performing their role. Together, the manager and employee would decide when the staff member was ready to take the test – usually when all the necessary training had been completed or when s/he had been performing well in their job for some time.

Competency evaluations were available for nearly every position by the end of Phase Two (September 2013). Almost a year later (from July 2014), the evaluations were sufficiently entrenched in the business that any staff member who wanted to progress had to have completed a competency evaluation for their current job, prior to being recruited to a higher position.

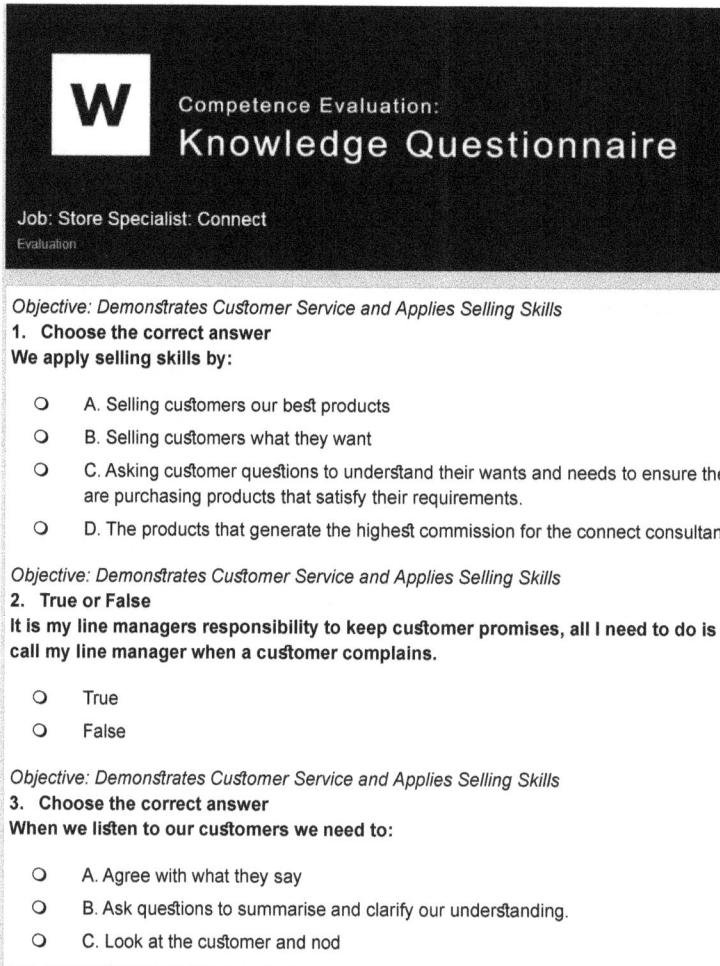

Figure 10.3   Competence evaluation: Knowledge questionnaire

The target the team set themselves was for 25 per cent of staff to have completed an evaluation by July 2014.

The team drove the process by having "change champions" at all management levels – store managers, HR business partners, line managers and trainers. Managers were encouraged to congratulate staff publicly when they received certificates, to actively urge staff to go through the evaluation process and to make sure their own management teams understood their role in the process and fulfilled their end of the bargain – for instance, by carrying out proper observations.

By August 2014, in fact, around 60 per cent of staff had completed competency evaluations.

Case study – part 2

Tami's line manager, Mary Ndlovu, set up a performance and career discussion with her to find out where she saw herself in the future. Tami said she was really interested in becoming a Pay Point Controller (PPC) and felt she could do the job even though it was at a CS Level 4, while her current position was at a CS Level 2. Mary showed Tami what training courses she would have to complete to learn the skills she needed to perform at a higher level. She also suggested that Tami undergo a competence evaluation to show that she could effectively perform in her current job. They ended up setting out Tami's career goals and outlining what she needed to do to achieve them. Tami left the meeting feeling excited about her future – which she saw as being with Woolies.

Recruitment focus

In any organisation, it is not only vital to make the most of the potential of your current staff, it is obviously very important to attract (and appoint) the right calibre of new people. Phase One of the project had mainly focused on existing employees. Phase Two now gave the HR teams a chance to apply the clarity and focus they had achieved in the preceding six months, to the recruitment process.

Well-defined roles and precise lists of competencies significantly increased their chances of being able to identify and recruit the right people for the job, to make sure that recruitment criteria were consistent across the business, that the process was fair, that vacancies were filled more quickly and, because there was a greater likelihood of finding (and retaining) the right people, it meant a much more efficient use of resources – further reinforcing the project's focus on sustainability.

WOOLWORTHSPEOPLE **W**

JOB PROFILE

BUSINESS UNIT	Corporate Stores
JOB TITLE	Customer Assistant: Tills
JOB LEVEL	CS2
REPORTING TO	Department Manager: Foods/Clothing & GM
DATE	February 2014

MAIN PURPOSE
To deliver exceptional customer service at the till points, thereby creating a positive, lasting impression as the customer leaves the store.

KEY OUTCOMES
Demonstrates customer service
• Greet, smile and acknowledge customers
• Thank card customers by name to ensure exceptional customer service

Applies selling skills
• Demonstrates an understanding of World of Difference by offering non-Woolworths card customers the Woolworths loyalty card
• Offers the customers available services (e.g. utility bill payments and airtime)

Processes till transactions effectively
• Processes till transactions efficiently and effectively in line with till policies and procedures e.g. checks scanned price against SKU ticket (product price in FSA stores)
• Scans and packs efficiently at till points and check all payments for irregularities
• Understands and promotes the different methods of payment or transactions (e.g. Gift cards, World of difference cards)

Demonstrates product knowledge and standards
• Knows what special events are being promoted in the store (e.g. Christmas, Mother's Day, Valentines Day)

Figure 10.4   Extract from job profile - Customer Assistant: Tills

Phase Three: whereto next?

The 12 months of the Career Paths Project launch and implementation was a time of rapid change and innovation. The teams achieved an enormous amount over a relatively short period, so once Phase Two was being implemented, the main task was to let both phases bed down and run their course. However, from the outset, the emphasis had been on sustainability – and that meant not just one intervention but an ongoing, evolving initiative that grew (and continues to grow) with the people it seeks to benefit.

Phase Three, just as with Phase Two, was largely shaped by what had come before.

Infrastructure for training

Now that the Career Paths Project was becoming properly integrated and staff were able to focus on the training they required to achieve their goals, the business realised that it had to provide people with the facilities in which that learning could be delivered, in terms of actual desks, chairs, computers, square metres of space and learning resources in general. To facilitate that, Phase Three began with considerable investment in, and the upgrade and expansion of, existing facilities. To this day, Woolworths is continuing its research and development into new ways of delivering training via, for instance, e-learning.

Figure 10.5   ROG Business strategy

Multiskilling

Another innovation of Phase Three was the idea of "multiskilling" – i.e., recognising situations where employees spend time working in a higher CS level job than their current position, for instance when filling a vacant role or covering for another employee who is on extended leave. With the Career Paths Framework in place, it was much easier to quantify this kind of "acting up" and to assess it in terms of additional remuneration and other types of recognition. In the first instance, the framework allowed the business to assess whether it could afford to systematically increase remuneration for acting beyond the bounds of an existing role. Woolworths still regards multiskilling as a significant growth opportunity. At the moment it happens mainly in smaller stores, rather than across the business. Work on how best to implement it for the benefit of both staff and the business, without incurring high costs or disrupting career paths planning, is ongoing.

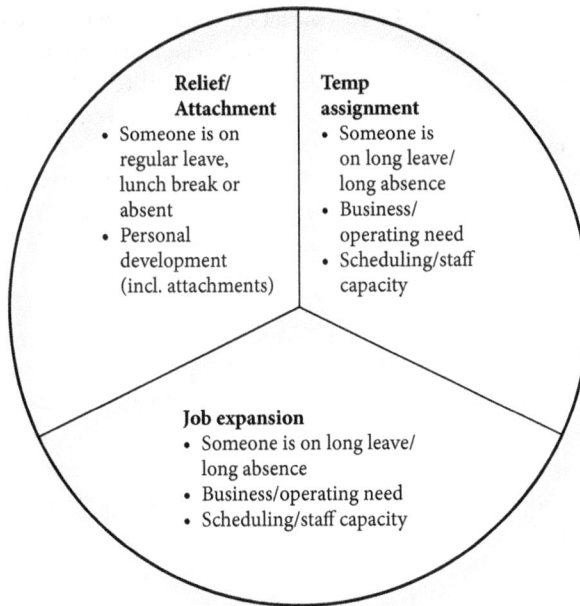

Figure 10.6   *Multiskilling opportunities*

Case study – part 3

Tami completed all the training she needed as well as her competence evaluation. When a vacancy was advertised for a PPC job, she applied. Tami was invited to an interview where she wrote a recruitment assessment and was asked questions to test whether she had the competencies required for the higher-level job. She was successful and now works as PPC. She's already looking to the future and wants to work towards becoming a Departmental Coordinator and later a Departmental Manager in Foods.

Year(s) of the DM

With the dual focus of the Career Paths Programme (delivery of an unrivalled customer experience and a sustainable approach) firmly in mind, the beginning of 2015 saw the launch of the Year of the Departmental Manager (DM) – the men and women who manage the teams on the store floors and make sure everyone is "thinking customer".

Of course, the DMs (like all other employees) were very much part of the overall Career Paths Framework. However, Woolworths recognised that this vast team of first-tier managers (in 2015 there were around 1 400 across South Africa) are not only the pool from which their more senior management will emerge, they also have the most direct impact on the experience customers have in stores on a daily basis. When it comes to making the magic, these really are the wizards-in-chief.

This called for a significant and particular investment in the development of Woolworths' DMs. The team began by speaking to the DMs themselves, and finding out what support they actually needed. Based on that research, some of the changes Woolworths implemented in the first year of the initiative were:

- Formalised DM forums and created a DM newsletter to improve communication and share knowledge;
- Developed the DM Career Paths Framework and progression principles so that the way forward was clearer;

- Put together a blended, modular DM Development Programme (DMDP) to enhance leadership and management skills, so as to help DMs motivate their teams more successfully;
- Clearly defined the core competencies that DMs need to be effective in their jobs;
- Refreshed the job profiles so that they were more consistent, and more accurately reflected what a DM does on a day-to-day basis;
- Improved the DM recruitment processes to make sure the right people were in place; and
- Identified issues affecting DM morale and performance in the "Fix the Basics" work stream. This addressed aspects such as alarm call-out fees, transport expenses, and awareness of and education on key benefits such as medical aid.

> I've been with Woolies for nine years. I started as a Paypoint Controller and worked hard to get on. I was so excited when I finally made it to DM in womenswear. I'd always had that as a goal. But for a while, it seemed like we were carrying a lot but we weren't seen as much different from other store staff. And it was difficult to see where things might lead. The Year of the DM has made such a difference. Just having a kind of DM network really helps and now I do feel that the business recognises there's something extra in the work I do.[7]

Never a last phase

Phase Three of the Career Paths Project is ongoing and, in some ways, is an initiative which will never really come to an end. As the business evolves, so must the environment in which its staff operate. While the name of the project might change, Woolworths has realised that close attention to the EVP must be ongoing and consistent.

Who made this happen?

The feeling of shared ownership of the "people agenda" between HR, line leadership and management – particularly in retail operations and in stores – contributed hugely to the success of this project. Within the HR function, the partnership between the HR centres of excellence and business-facing HR in Retail Operations was key. The main groups involved and their roles were as follows:

- Employee Relations Team – key to supporting and guiding the transition to a flexible workforce in Phase One;
- Remuneration (REM) Team – developing the revised fixed pay model aligned to the Career Paths Framework, guiding stores through a complex annual salary review process and playing an ongoing governance support role;
- Organisational Development (OD) Team – the glue of the project: designing and delivering the Career Paths Framework and Competency Framework, guiding the business towards finding solutions to complex challenges such as multiskilling;
- Learning and Development (L&D) Team – partnering with the technical and functional learning team in Retail Operations to produce the learning offer; and
- Recruitment Team – partnering with OD, employees and line management to develop in-house assessment tools aligned to the competencies required for the respective roles.

Where did the path lead?

Achievements from the period in which the Career Paths Project was implemented and integrated into the business, are reflected in Table 10.1.

Table 10.1   *The Career Paths Project in numbers*

Variable	2008/9	2013/14
Labour turnover	38.97%	26.40%
New hire labour turnover (staff leaving within one year of being employed)	59.64%	42.39%
Culture and Climate Survey score	62.30%	74.60%

The Career Paths Project has been key to changing the essence of our employment brand. This inclusive, systematic and consistently driven initiative has made the essential difference that we needed for the business to move forward. The most important thing now, of course, is that we keep that momentum, keep evolving it, keep up the energy. Because our staff need that, they need to know that amongst the challenges of this fast-changing, expanding Woolworths environment, this framework is there as their support and their key to moving forward with the business.[8]

The Career Paths Project marked a profound change in the Woolworths staff experience. A company that grows from one store and one man's vision to a multifaceted, multinational retailer will invariably hit crisis points along the way – points at which something significant has to happen to allow it to progress, or which might mark the beginning of the end, if they are not handled correctly.

In this case, the HR function correctly identified and analysed issues that were eroding the Woolworths EVP. They subsequently crafted a solution to those issues that helped create a flexible, resilient, motivated, well-rewarded staff contingent who understood completely where they fit in the business, where they wanted to go career-wise and how to get there. Furthermore, they delivered a solution that was genuinely – and therefore sustainably – integrated into the fabric of the organisation. Woolworths has its own career path, its own goal – that of becoming "the largest and most sustainable southern hemisphere retailer". The Career Paths Project laid the foundation and established the momentum that will get it there.

Endnotes

1   Chantal Butler, Woolworths: Head of HR.
2   Brendan, Sales Assistant, Randburg.
3   Numsa, Stockroom Controller, Somerset West.
4   Unless otherwise stipulated, all data, graphs and images are taken from Woolworths internal documents.
5   Dumisani, Sales Assistant, Menlo Park.
6   Andrew Sonnenburg, Woolworths: Head of HR: Retail Operations.
7   Busi, DM Childrenswear, Kimberley.
8   Andrew Sonnenberg, Woolworths: Head of HR: Retail Operations.

PART 2

CHAPTER 11

THE ROLE OF ORGANISATIONAL CULTURE IN THE ATTRACTION AND RETENTION OF TALENT – THE NEDBANK STORY
Abe Thebyane

I have said on several occasions that the talent management strategies in many organisations are missing a key point. Their focus is on attracting and developing individual talent, while ignoring or relegating culture to the OD silo of HR.

Yet any type of talent can be bought, albeit at a cost. It is therefore not in itself a differentiating factor that creates competitive advantage. A good illustration would be the four major South African banks. They all have, for the most part, equal levels of talent and skill – if they did not, they would not be players in the financial services industry.

What this chapter illustrates is that the differentiator is the organisational culture which contributes to attracting the right people and creating the chemistry that enables talented people to be engaged and perform at a superior level.

This is an important chapter, on many levels, for numerous reasons:

- It illustrates the importance of a proactive approach to building the right organisational culture;
- It outlines the power of culture in an organisational turnaround strategy;
- It emphasises the importance of leadership commitment to the emergence of culture; and
- It sketches the role of HR in contributing to the strategy of the organisation through effective partnering with leaders in the business.

In my view, this is a world-class case study in how talent management has to work at both an organisational and an individual level. Furthermore, as organisations progress along their growth path, the kind of culture and leadership strengths required will change, thus an understanding of, and response to, those changes are key factors in ensuring sustainability.

In this chapter Abe demonstrates how a deep understanding of organisational behaviour and transformation is essential for driving the strategic agenda, by proactively creating a culture that is unique, difficult to replicate, and thereby provides a competitive advantage in a highly competitive environment.

Introduction

I was somewhat surprised by the reaction of delegates who attended my presentation at the IPM conference[1] in November 2014 – a presentation not made during the plenary session, but as part of the breakaway sessions. The reaction that surprised me was not the immediate feedback following the presentation – no, the surprise came a few days post-conference, when I received numerous enquiries about job opportunities at Nedbank, from some of the delegates. It was clear that based on what I had shared with the delegates about the state of HR in Nedbank, many of them wanted to leave their jobs and join our organisation! I found this reaction surprising, because the last thing on my mind was to "advertise" for Nedbank in my presentation. My objective, really, had been to demonstrate to other professionals how HR as a profession can add genuine value to a business and make a meaningful impact. In fact, the title of the presentation, 'HR that enables high performance: Building cultural capital through an integrated strategy and leadership effectiveness' captures this intention very well. The idea was to show HR professionals what they can do – in practical terms – to be at the centre of organisational performance.

But what was in this presentation that elicited such a reaction? The presentation was about the turnaround story of Nedbank, starting in 2003/2004 under the former CEO, Tom Boardman, and the role of organisational culture and leadership in driving Nedbank's turnaround during those difficult years.

The reaction of many of the IPM conference delegates to this presentation confirmed the importance of organisational culture in attracting, retaining and enabling the performance of top talent. To paraphrase Bill Clinton: 'It is all about culture, stupid',[2] and this is the story of the present chapter – the important role organisational culture plays in attracting and retaining top talent.

Cultural capital – the new frontier of competitive advantage

My presentation started with an attempt to demonstrate the importance of organisational culture in enabling competitive advantage. The purpose was to show HR professionals that one way of adding value and contributing to the success of their organisation, was by sharpening their knowledge of how culture drives competitiveness sustainably. This would allow them to become custodians and stewards of the culture in their organisations. Naturally, some organisations consider culture to be a "fluffy, pie-in-the-sky" topic, yet it is imperative that HR professionals be convinced that it is not, so that they, in turn, can convince those hard-nosed business types about how culture contributes to organisational success.

Fortunately there is plenty of credible research that shows exactly this – that culture is the new frontier of competitive advantage, and I cited extensively from such research for the benefit of my audience.

In the seminal book, *Conscious capitalism*, Raj Sisodia and John Mackey write extensively on the role culture plays in the success of the organisation: 'A company's culture can be a severe constraint on its success or a source of strength and sustained competitive advantage'.[3]

The idea that culture can enable or neutralise good strategies is well known, based on Peter Drucker's assertion that "culture eats strategy for lunch".[4] This means that if you have a brilliant organisational strategy that calls for fundamentally different behaviours from the organisation, without any direct intervention to change "how we do things around here", the organisation will simply default to the way things have always been done, thus neutralising the strategy.

Put differently, a good strategy requires a supportive, enabling culture to succeed. Ferran Adria reduces this topic to hard financial numbers that will surely appeal to those hard-nosed business types: "High performing companies tend to be known for among other things their strong cultures, and companies with a strong culture have a 61% more likelihood of having above medium EBITDA than those with not so strong cultures." [5] This is a clear indicator of the contribution culture makes to the financial performance of the organisation.

To quote CEO John Mackey:

> The culture of a company is the place where people are front and center, where richness and complexity of human beings reside, where your humanity shines through. As such it is the most powerful part of business. When it is consciously affirmed, nurtured and developed over time, it becomes both a true differentiator and the ultimate competitive weapon.[6]

In the book Mackey co-authored with Sisodia, he explains in detail the culture that he helped build in Whole Foods Market – a culture that differentiates this company from competitors: in his view, culture both differentiates and is a mighty weapon in the hands of any organisation.

James Heskett, of Harvard Business School, states that "a strong culture can help or hurt performance. Culture can account for up to half of the difference in operating profit between two organizations in the same business. Shaping culture is one of a leader's most important jobs; it can be ignored, but only for so long and at one's peril." [7] Jim Collins and Jerry Poras state simply that "long lasting companies have a vision-guided, values-driven culture that gives guidance to all employees". [8]

I concluded this part of my presentation by asking two questions:

1. If culture is the only source of sustainable competitive advantage, what are we doing as HR professionals in the area of culture?
2. What, then, is the role of culture in talent attraction and retention?

The role of culture in Nedbank's turnaround story

In 2003, Nedbank found itself in a difficult, dark place. Following a number of serious strategic mistakes, the bank's performance and reputation were completely destroyed. In fact, the very survival of the organisation was at stake. Headline earnings, the measure of profitability based on the JSE, had plunged 98 per cent to R55 million.[9] Return on equity, being the returns that shareholders receive on their investment, was at a paltry 0.4 per cent.[10] Nedbank's market capitalisation was at an all-time low, at R17 billion – the desperately needed recapitalisation and a R5.2 billion rights issue was embarked upon.[11] Old Mutual, the parent company, had to inject R2 billion in secondary capital.[12]

So negative was market sentiment about the appointment of Tom Boardman as new CEO, that the share price dropped by six per cent on the announcement.[13] Newspaper headlines at the time captured these sentiments very well (see Figure 11.1).

When he took over the reins, Boardman instituted a turnaround strategy to improve Nedbank's performance by focusing on corporate strategy and operations, corporate culture and leadership. The top 500 leaders of the bank were invited to attend strategy, values and brand (SVB) workshops to brainstorm the new strategic direction of the bank, its corporate aspirations, key focus areas and core values.

After many iterations the workshop outputs were summarised in a single document, known as the Dagwood (see Figure 11.2) that outlined the group strategy, values and brand.

Nedbank 2003   The Dark Days

Figure 11.1   Market sentiment towards Nedcor, as reflected in various newspaper clippings from 2003

Figure 11.2   The Dagwood[14]

Global research has shown that highly successful companies often use a single concept to focus all organisational efforts. Such powerful single concepts are built on three pillars: what the organisation is passionate about, what sets the organisation apart from competitors, and what drives the organisation's economic engine. For Nedbank, the heart of the Dagwood meant "listening, understanding clients' needs and delivering"[15] on those needs.

In an effort to be more client-centered and remove the silo mentality, the business model was reviewed and client-focused business units were created. To encourage unity, the corporate values of the parent company, Old Mutual, were adopted, i.e., accountability, integrity, respect, pushing beyond boundaries. In addition to these values, staff were invited to select a fifth value that would be unique to Nedbank.

People-centeredness was chosen by the majority of employees. To create a high-performing culture, it was critical that these values be adopted and lived by all employees and be seen to exist within the top leadership team. Another key concept arising from the SVB workshops was "Deep Green", an idea about a corporate culture which encompasses the vision, and is driven by a depth of aspirations, values and focus areas, built around Nedbank's brand image. "Deep Green" came to represent the totality of what Nedbank stood for as an organisation. It represented the feeling which the senior leadership team at the time felt accurately summarised the Nedbank they envisaged and wanted to work towards.

To enable "Deep Green", the Leading for Deep Green programme was instituted in partnership with the Centre for Conscious Leadership. Based on pure psychological tests, the focus of this programme was to enable Nedbank leaders to obtain personal mastery by being self-aware with regard to their personality, leadership style, and impact and influence on others. The programme also covered team effectiveness.

At the same time, the Barrett Culture Survey[16] was introduced as an instrument to measure the culture of Nedbank, by evaluating employees' personal value against current and desired organisational values. The fundamental principle of the Barrett methodology is that when there is a match between employees' personal values and the current values of the organisation, then employees fit well into the culture and are therefore able to bring themselves fully to work. The Barrett Culture Survey also measures entropy, or the level of dysfunction in an organisation: a low entropy score is good, as it is evidence of minimal dysfunction. In 2005 Nedbank's entropy was a high 25 per cent, perhaps the clearest indication of employee sentiment about those dark days.

The Nedbank Staff Survey[17] was also introduced to measure organisational climate by focusing on dimensions such as vision, strategic alignment, management style, transformation, ethics, conditions of service and communication, amongst others. Part of this survey was the Hewitt Engagement Survey,[18] which compared Nedbank to global financial services and global best employers in terms of employee engagement.

Based on the above, it should be clear to anyone that culture, leadership effectiveness and a focus on employee engagement and organisational climate were integral components of Nedbank's turnaround story.

If one fast-forwards to 2016, Nedbank is a financially performing organisation with headline earnings above R10 billion, and a return on equity of 17 per cent.[19] The organisation's entropy score is at 11 per cent,[20] the Nedbank survey score is at a high of 75 per cent[21] and employee engagement is far above the global financial services industry and within the best employer range.[22] Nedbank's culture is people centered and renowned for being the best in the banking industry. In short, the turnaround was successful. Nedbank really is a great place to work for.

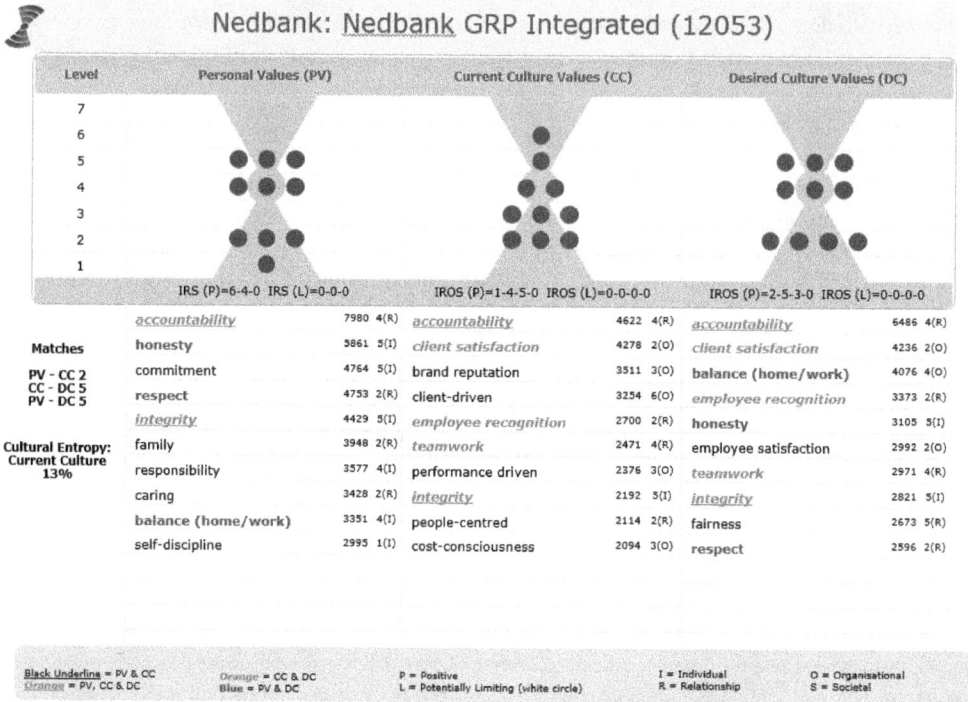

Figure 11.3   Summary of results from the Barrett survey[23]

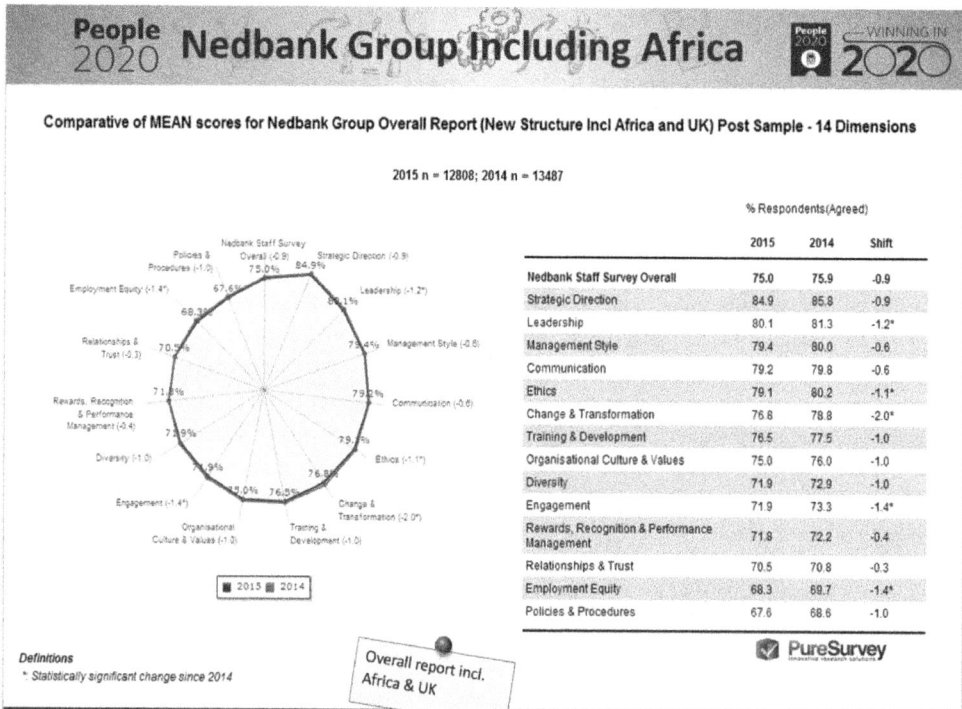

Hewitt Engagement Model

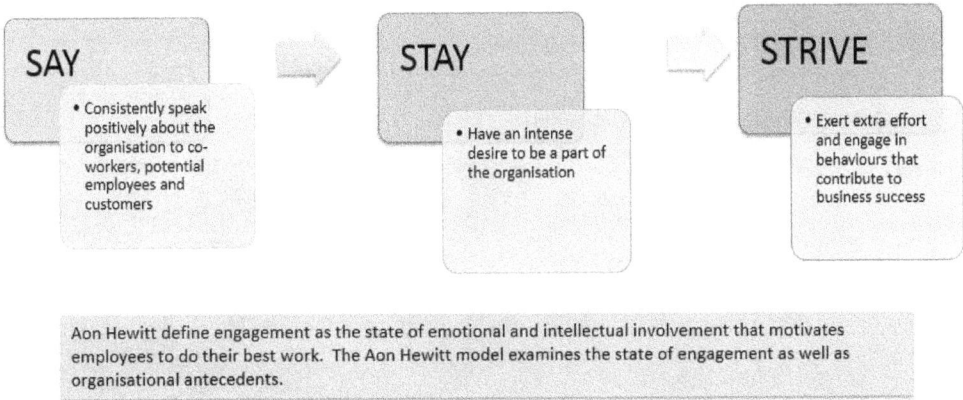

SAY
- Consistently speak positively about the organisation to co-workers, potential employees and customers

STAY
- Have an intense desire to be a part of the organisation

STRIVE
- Exert extra effort and engage in behaviours that contribute to business success

Aon Hewitt define engagement as the state of emotional and intellectual involvement that motivates employees to do their best work. The Aon Hewitt model examines the state of engagement as well as organisational antecedents.

Figure 11.4   Summary of results from the Nedbank Staff Survey[24]

Based on the above measures (financial, cultural and engagement score), Nedbank is a truly transformed organisation. In my view, this transformation can be attributed to the change framework used as a model of organisational change. This model is underpinned by a fundamental principle that Richard Barrett taught Nedbank, which is that "organizations don't transform, people do".[25] The next principle of change is that "organizational transformation starts with the personal transformation of the leaders of the organization".[26]

The Culture Change Framework...

Overarching Conceptual Framework that continues to shape our journey...

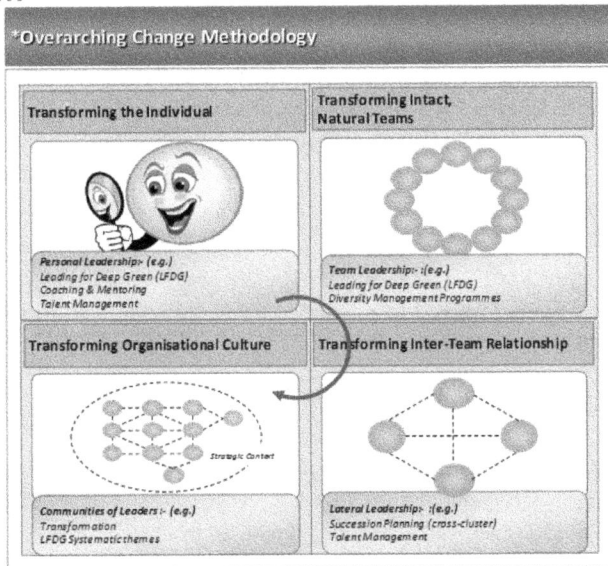

The lessons that we have learnt along the way guide our approach...

•Cultural change needs to be supported by various levers. From an HR perspective, all initiatives are geared to enhance our culture journey

•The transformation of 2000 leaders through LFDG has proved to be a tipping point for a major change

•This programme is being cascaded to the next +/- 7000 in the next 3-5 years, this can only strengthen our gains

•Measurement still matters- 'what we can measure we can manage'. Next step is to measure behaviours linked to our values and leadership philosophy

•Cultural capital is the outcome of everything that we do and continue to be accelerated through 3 levers:
    •Values-based leadership, strategy and transformation

Overarching Change Methodology

Transforming the Individual

Personal Leadership:- (e.g.)
Leading for Deep Green (LFDG)
Coaching & Mentoring
Talent Management

Transforming Intact, Natural Teams

Team Leadership:- :(e.g.)
Leading for Deep Green (LFDG)
Diversity Management Programmes

Transforming Organisational Culture

Communities of Leaders :- (e.g.)
Transformation
LFDG Systematic themes

Transforming Inter-Team Relationship

Lateral Leadership:- :(e.g.)
Succession Planning (cross-cluster)
Talent Management

Figure 11.5   The Culture Change Framework[27]

Nedbank's transformation can be said to have reached a tipping point when about 2 000 of its leaders underwent a leadership personal change journey through the Leading for Deep Green programme. As leadership is a critical ingredient in shaping culture, transforming leaders would automatically transform the organisation's culture. To sustain this leadership transformation and align it closely to Nedbank's business requirements, a leadership framework was developed.

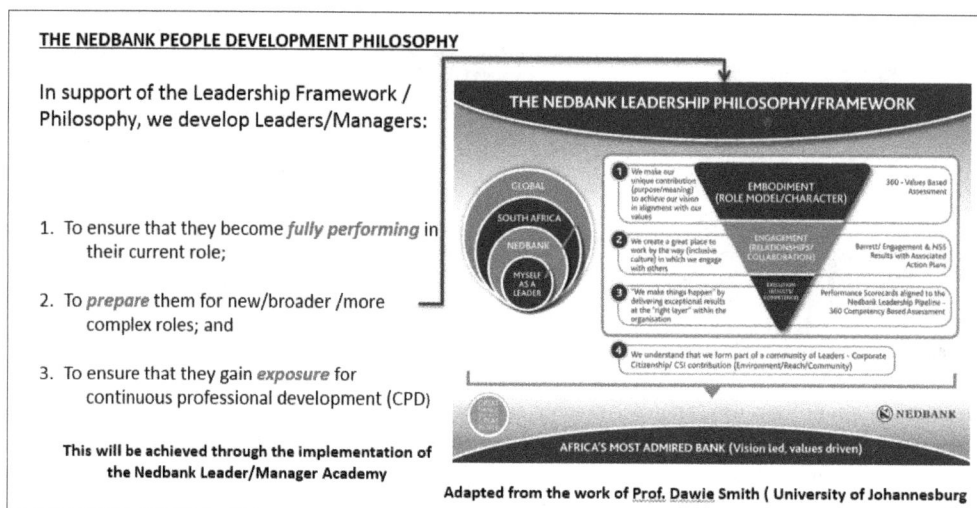

THE NEDBANK PEOPLE DEVELOPMENT PHILOSOPHY

In support of the Leadership Framework / Philosophy, we develop Leaders/Managers:

1. To ensure that they become *fully performing* in their current role;

2. To *prepare* them for new/broader /more complex roles; and

3. To ensure that they gain *exposure* for continuous professional development (CPD)

This will be achieved through the implementation of the Nedbank Leader/Manager Academy

THE NEDBANK LEADERSHIP PHILOSOPHY/FRAMEWORK

AFRICA'S MOST ADMIRED BANK (Vision led, values driven)

Adapted from the work of Prof. Dawie Smith (University of Johannesburg)

Figure 11.6   The Nedbank Leadership Philosophy Framework[28]

Based on this framework, leaders in Nedbank have to deliver outcomes in four areas of organisational life:

1. Embody the values of the organisation and create meaning and purpose for their employees in line with the vision of the organisation;
2. Drive employee engagement by the inclusive culture they create through engagement;
3. Deliver business results by executing business strategies and priorities flawlessly; and
4. Be effective community leaders and stewards of the environment.

The Nedbank of today is a magnet for talent that is inspired by a great culture and great place to work. The bank's attrition rate has been hovering at a low eight to nine per cent[29] for many years. Nedbank is attracting more people than it is losing to other financial services organisations; it is attracting more staff from direct competitors than it is losing to them, including at senior management levels.[30] There are various instances of staff leaving Nedbank, only to return, citing organisational culture as the reason.[31]

Where is Nedbank today and what is the plan for the future?

Nedbank's turnaround, which aimed to address the problems of the past and improve performance, came to an end as a project in round 2013.

In 2014/15, the bank's leadership team put on the table the aspiration of "Winning in 2020" as a theme for driving business planning. The HR team developed the "People 2020", a "strategy to enable Nedbank to win through its People in 2020". This was approved by the Executive Committee and launched formally in the Top 200 leadership forum held in June 2015. "People 2020" aims to pull three levers to enable Nedbank to win in 2020 through its people: culture, leadership and talent. On the issue of culture, the question HR had to assist the organisation in answering was: What culture would Nedbank require to enable "Winning in

2020"? This has to be a kind of culture that will directly and specifically support and enable "Winning in 2020", rather than just a people-centred culture which is conducive to a great place to work. To illustrate, the current culture of the bank enables employees to bring themselves fully to work and to be engaged, thereby going the extra mile for the organisation, to have a propensity to stay with the organisation while being advocates of the organisation to their family and friends. All these cultural outcomes drive organisational performance. However, in 2015 the issue related to culture was how to make it directly supportive of "Winning in 2020" strategies. The HR team subsequently sourced the Competing Values Framework. Before discussing this framework, it is important to consider why the Barrett Culture Survey could not assist in defining the culture required for "Winning in 2020".

Applying ADDITIONAL Models of Thinking for Organizational Culture
- Towards a "both-and" view of culture

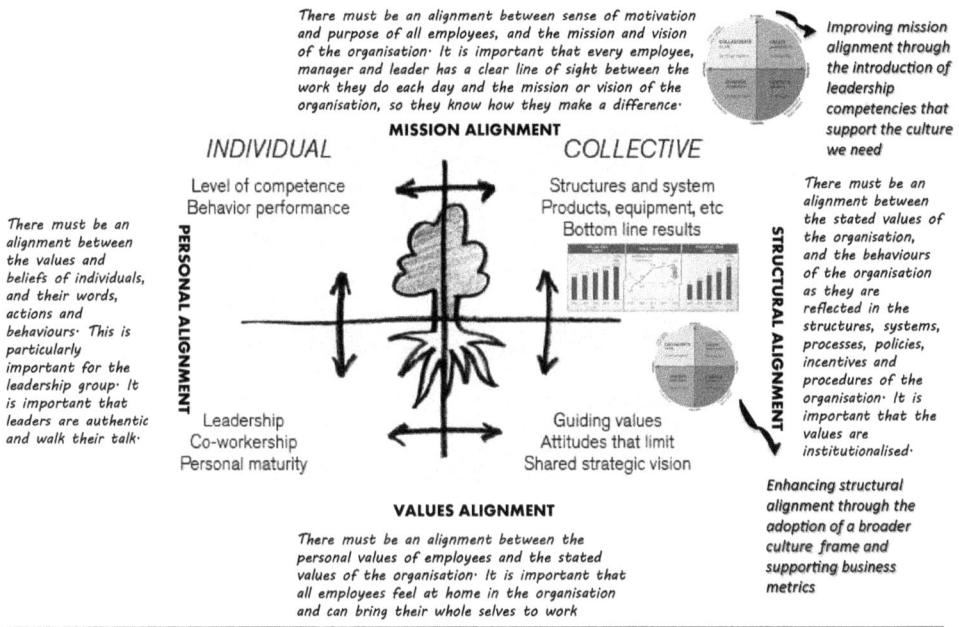

There must be an alignment between sense of motivation and purpose of all employees, and the mission and vision of the organisation· It is important that every employee, manager and leader has a clear line of sight between the work they do each day and the mission or vision of the organisation, so they know how they make a difference·

MISSION ALIGNMENT

INDIVIDUAL

Level of competence
Behavior performance

COLLECTIVE

Structures and system
Products, equipment, etc
Bottom line results

PERSONAL ALIGNMENT

There must be an alignment between the values and beliefs of individuals, and their words, actions and behaviours· This is particularly important for the leadership group· It is important that leaders are authentic and walk their talk·

Leadership
Co-workership
Personal maturity

Guiding values
Attitudes that limit
Shared strategic vision

STRUCTURAL ALIGNMENT

Improving mission alignment through the introduction of leadership competencies that support the culture we need

There must be an alignment between the stated values of the organisation, and the behaviours of the organisation as they are reflected in the structures, systems, processes, policies, incentives and procedures of the organisation· It is important that the values are institutionalised·

Enhancing structural alignment through the adoption of a broader culture frame and supporting business metrics

VALUES ALIGNMENT

There must be an alignment between the personal values of employees and the stated values of the organisation· It is important that all employees feel at home in the organisation and can bring their whole selves to work

Figure 11.7   Additional models of thinking related to organisational culture[32]

What the Barrett survey did for Nedbank was to align the organisation around a set of values (values alignment). In addition, the methodology created an environment where employees could align their own personal values with those of the organisation (personal alignment). What Barrett could not do was to enable mission and structural alignment. The Competing Values Framework closed this gap for Nedbank by enabling it to define the specific organisational culture which would support "Winning in 2020".

Using this framework, Nedbank defined the requisite culture as one that is more innovative and creative (adhocracy) and competitive (compete). The hierarchy/control aspects were to be reduced somewhat from their levels at the time, while clan elements needed to be maintained at the same level.

After the "Winning in 2020" culture had been defined, the next step was to define the leadership behaviours that would build and sustain this culture. To do this, the HR team organised a leadership lekgotla that was attended by the Top 400 leaders in the bank. This group was tasked with defining leadership requirements in the context of "Winning in 2020" strategies, the winning culture, and Nedbank's new brand essence.

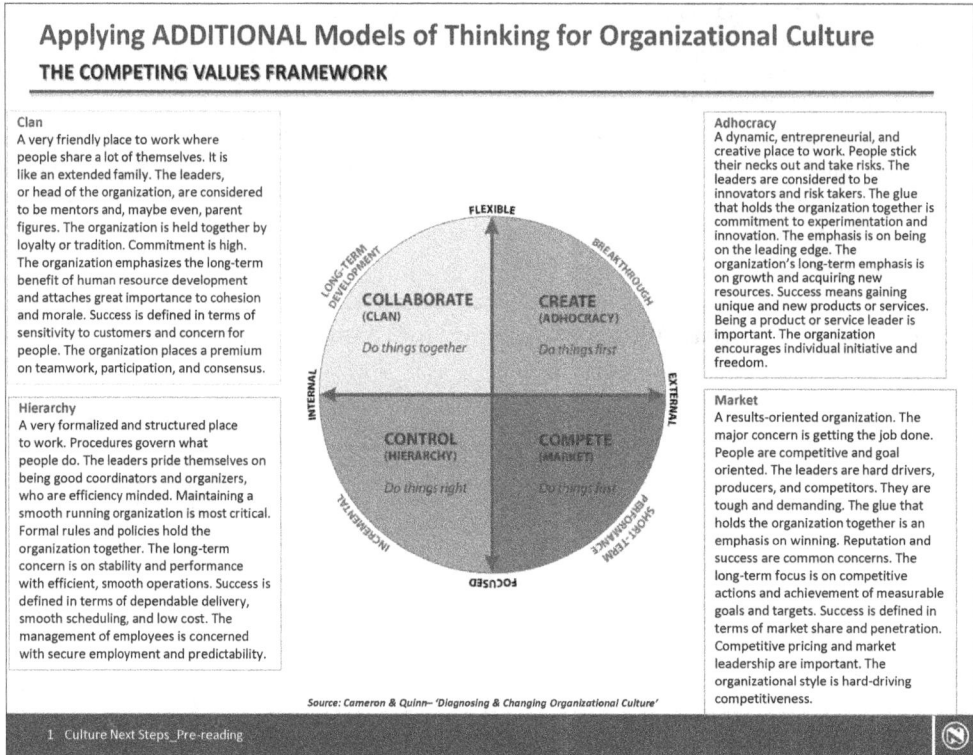

Figure 11.8   *The Competing Values Framework*[33]

The lekgotla attendees deliberated and agreed on a new leadership persona for Nedbank, which consists of the following ten sub-types:

- The strategist
- The commercially savvy innovator
- The enterprise citizen
- The client-centric advocate
- The culture carrier
- The brand ambassador
- The change leader
- The high-performance enabler
- The CEO

Figure 11.9 illustrates how the leadership persona of the bank will contribute towards creating the required culture.

The fact that the leadership persona sub-types are concentrated in the adhocracy and competition quadrants, is an indication that the leadership persona will shift Nedbank's culture to make it more adhocracy and competition based.

The below narrative highlights a number of salient points. Just as cultural transformation (and concomitantly leadership transformation) were critical in the Nedbank turnaround, so culture and leadership are key to Nedbank "Winning in 2020". The bank's leadership persona is the starting point in defining its talent requirements. Talent management processes are currently being reviewed, to ensure that they deliver the requisite capabilities for innovation, client-centricity, excellence in execution, leading change and great leadership.

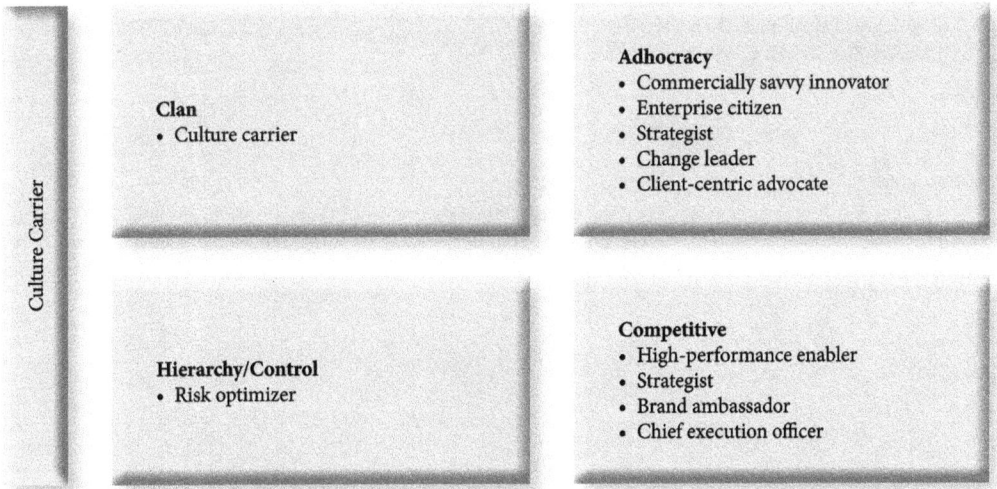

Figure 11.9   The quadrants of the Completing Values Framework[34]

In addition, the talent that will be attracted to Nedbank will be the kind that highly values innovativeness and competitiveness. Knowing this will make our talent attraction efforts more effective, in that we will target the right candidates. Nedbank will thus draw talent that not only fit into the bank's culture, but also thrive in this environment.

Conclusion

Organisational culture is a magnet for talent. Understanding the capabilities required to build a strong, adaptive culture translates into understanding the talent required to drive performance, and thrive in the environment. Culture should therefore be the starting point in both talent attraction and retention.

Having reviewed the above narrative, I finally understood the reactions of those HR professionals who had come to listen to my presentation at Sun City. They were attracted to Nedbank after receiving confirmation that is a great place to work for, with a great culture.

Endnotes

1. A Thebyane, 'HR that enables high performance: Building cultural capital through an integrated strategy and leadership effectiveness', IPM conference, Sun City, November 2014.
2. Bill Clinton actually said: 'It's the economy, stupid.'
3. J Mackey & R Sisodia, *Conscious capitalism: Liberating the heroic spirit of business*, Business Review Press, Harvard, Boston, 2013, p. 217.
4. Ibid.
5. F Adria, *Business Strategy Review*. No further details available.
6. J Mackey & R Sisodia, op. cit., p. 216.
7. J Heskett, cited in *Conscious capitalism*, op. cit., p. 217.
8. J Collins & JI Porras, *Built to last: Successful habits of visionary companies*, Harper Business Essentials, USA, 1994.
9. Nedbank, 'The role of strategy, culture and leadership in the Nedbank turnaround – the Tom Boardman story', retrieved 2 August 2016, <https://www.valuescentre.com/sites/default/files/case-studies/NedbankTurnaround CaseStudy.pdf>.
10. Ibid.
11. Ibid.
12. Ibid.
13. Ibid.
14. Ibid.
15. Ibid, p. 11.
16. Ibid, p. 5.
17. Ibid, p. 12.
18. Nedbank Group, 'Sustainability review', 2015, retrieved 2 August 2016, <https://www.nedbank.co.za/content/ dam/nedbank/site-assets/AboutUs/Information%20Hub/Integrated%20Report/2015/2015_Nedbank_Group_ Sustainability_Review.pdf>, p. 32.
19. Nedbank Group, 'Integrated report', 31 December 2014, retrieved 2 August 2016, <https://www.nedbank.co.za/ content/dam/nedbank/site-assets/AboutUs/Investor%20Centre/Latest%20Financial%20Results/Integrated%20 Report/2014_Nedbank_Group_Integrated_Report.pdf>, pp. 7, 11. Report not available to the public.
20. Ibid, p. 61.
21. BusinessTech, 'Here are the best and worst banks in South Africa', 6 April 2016, retrieved 2 August 2016, <http:// businesstech.co.za/news/banking/119227/here-are-the-best-and-worst-banks-in-south-africa/>.
22. 'The role of strategy … ', op. cit., p. 12.
23. 'Integrated report', op. cit.
24. 'The role of strategy … ', loc. cit.
25. R Barrett, *Liberating the corporate soul: Building a visionary organisation*, Routledge, Oxford, 1998, p. xxi.
26. Ibid.
27. Centre for Conscious Leadership, 'Leading for Deep Green', September 2013, retrieved 2 August 2016, <http://ccls. co.za/wordpress/wp-content/uploads/2013/09/nlfdg_casestudy.pdf.pdf>, p. 11.
28. Adapted from the work of Prof. Dawie Smith (University of Johannesburg). The Nedbank Leadership Philosophy Framework. No further details available.
29. 'Integrated report', op cit., p. 49.
30. Ibid.
31. Ibid.
32. KS Cameron & RE Quinn, *Diagnosing and changing organisational culture: Based on the Competing Values Framework*, Jossey-Bass, San Francisco, CA, retrieved 2 August 2016, <https://www.researchgate.net/file. PostFileLoader.html?id=559077c25e9d9768f68b4570&assetKey=AS%3A271750183489537%401441801700739>.
33. Ibid.
34. Ibid.

References

Barrett, R, *Liberating the corporate soul: Building a visionary organisation*, Routledge, Oxford, 1998, retrieved 30 July 2016, <www.valuescentre.com/resources/book>.

BusinessTech, 'Here are the best and worst banks in South Africa', 6 April 2016, retrieved 2 August 2016, <http:// businesstech.co.za/news/banking/119227/here-are-the-best-and-worst-banks-in-south-africa/>.

Cameron, KS & RE Quinn, *Diagnosing and changing organisational culture: Based on the Competing Values Framework.*, 2006, Jossey-Bass, San Francisco, CA, retrieved 2 August 2016, <https://www.researchgate.net/file.PostFileLoader. html?id=559077c25e9d9768f68b4570&assetKey=AS%3A271750183489537%401441801700739>.

Centre for Conscious Leadership, 'Leading for Deep Green', September 2013, retrieved 2 August 2016, <http://ccls.co.za/wordpress/wp-content/uploads/2013/09/nlfdg_casestudy.pdf.pdf>.

Collins, J & JI Porras, *Built to last: Successful habits of visionary companies*, Harper Business Essentials, USA, 1994.

Mackey, J & R Sisodia, *Conscious capitalism: Liberating the heroic spirit of business*, Business Review Press, Harvard, Boston, 2013.

Nedbank Group, 'Sustainability review', 2015, retrieved 2 August 2016, <https://www.nedbank.co.za/content/dam/nedbank/site-assets/AboutUs/Information%20Hub/Integrated%20Report/2015/2015_Nedbank_Group_Sustainability_Review.pdf>.

Nedbank Group, 'Integrated report', 31 December 2014, retrieved 2 August 2016, <https://www.nedbank.co.za/content/dam/nedbank/site-assets/AboutUs/Investor%20Centre/Latest%20Financial%20Results/Integrated%20Report/2014_Nedbank_Group_Integrated_Report.pdf>.

Nedbank, 'The role of strategy, culture and leadership in the Nedbank turnaround – the Tom Boardman Story', retrieved 2 August 2016, <https://www.valuescentre.com/sites/default/files/case-studies/NedbankTurnaroundCaseStudy.pdf>.

Thebyane, A, 'HR that enables high performance: Building cultural capital through an integrated strategy and leadership effectiveness', IPM conference, Sun City, November 2014.

PART 2

CHAPTER 12

DISCOVERY'S INFORMAL AND INNOVATIVE TALENT MANAGEMENT APPROACH
Terence Okeke Taylor

Discovery is becoming known as a great global company. In particular, it is recognised for its innovation and industry disruption.

To be successful in the modern economy, a culture of innovation, entrepreneurship and agility is essential, and those qualities need to be reflected in the organisation's leadership. This chapter illustrates the importance of a holistic approach to creating a culture of innovation, and the essential role of an effective talent and leadership development strategy in creating such a culture. Hence it provides critical insights for organisations that wish to play in a disruptive strategic space.

Despite this being a relatively short chapter, it also illustrates the power of focusing on the few strategies and practices that make a significant impact on the company's culture.

Another crucial lesson from this chapter is the importance of leadership in building a leadership culture and ensuring that an organisation has the leaders it requires as it progresses along its growth path. Discovery is well known for the quality of its leaders, being admirably led by CEO Adrian Gore. I had the privilege of teaching a module on one of its leadership programmes at team leader level. Discovery is one of the few organisations I have come across where leaders at all levels are able to provide a consistent answer to the question: What does leadership mean in this organisation?

This reinforces the importance of a common understanding of leadership, whether through a framework or charter, or some other mechanism.

The five practices shared here provide an integrated approach to creating a culture of innovation through the Discovery People (DP) strategy. Most importantly, this is not a typically boring HR strategy, but projects the message that Discovery is a fun place to work for, while committing to excellence in all spheres of the business. This vibrant and innovative culture will be particularly attractive to younger employees.

Discovery has significant strategic ambitions as a player on the global stage. In his final remarks, Terrence Okeke Taylor poses questions about what the next phase of Discovery's talent management strategy will be, as it scales up to achieve those ambitions.

This chapter is yet another illustration of the importance of culture as a fundamental aspect of talent management and the need for a holistic approach to ensure that an organisation has the right people – especially leaders – to drive the culture. It also illustrates once again how HR can have a powerful impact on the business through partnerships with leaders in an organisation.

Introduction

At Discovery, our core purpose is to make people healthier and to enhance and protect their lives. To achieve this, we create a powerful platform to liberate the best in great people and empower them to build extraordinary legacies. The pillars of this platform are entrepreneurial values; powerful leadership principles; and innovative, integrated and comprehensive talent and leadership practices that springboard our company and people towards becoming the best insurance organisation in the world, and a powerful force for social good.

Discovery has a multifaceted and integrated talent management approach that has been informal, innovative and highly effective so far, but may now be at a crossroads. This approach is based on a set of embedded practices that guide how Discovery builds disruptive and entrepreneurial institutions. Yet as Discovery pursues its ambition to become the best insurance organisation in the world and a powerful force for social good by 2018, the need has deepened to grow the bandwidth of executive talent and strengthen its culture.

To support Discovery's ambition and noble core purpose, Discovery People (DP) is transforming into the most thoughtful, innovative and value-adding HR community in the world. Over the past few years, DP's strategy has focused on strengthening Discovery's TLC (Talent, Leadership and Culture) and fostering dialogue among its leaders and people. DP revamped the organisation's Core Induction and launched Leadership Game Changers to create dialogue about topics that enhance the organisation's character and culture.

In this brief case study, we review five key practices that inform Discovery's talent management and highlight emerging challenges as the company seeks to scale talent management to attract its next 10 000 employees and fulfill its 2018 ambition.

The Discovery case study

Practice 1: Attracting, amplifying and liberating talent

Attracting, amplifying and liberating talent has been core to building Discovery. From inception, founder and Group CEO, Adrian Gore, has invested in attracting key leaders. These include the vast majority of current key executives such as Barry Swartzberg (recruit number 1 and current CEO of Discovery Partner Markets), John Robertson (recruit number 2 and Group CIO), Herschel Mayers (CEO of Vitality Life), Alan Pollard (CEO of the Vitality Group) and Hylton Kallner (CEO of Discovery Life), to name a few. In the early years, Adrian mentored and groomed key executives such as Hylton Kallner, who worked as his Executive Associate.

Barry Swartzberg
CEO of Discovery Partner
Markets

John Robertson
Group CIO

Herschal Mayers
CEO of Vitality Life

Alan Pollard
CEO of the Vitality Group

Hylton Kallner
CEO of Discovery Life

Dr. Shrey Viranna
CEO of Discovery Vitality

Dr. Ryan Noach
Deputy CEO of Discovery
Health

Dinesh Govender
Chief Marketing Officer for
Discovery

Anton Ossip
CEO of Discovery Insure

Yet, as Discovery continues to build several large institutions from the ground up (Discovery Health, Vitality, Discovery Life, Discovery Invest, Vitality Group, Discovery Insure), Adrian's time and focus are increasingly directed to growing Discovery into a global financial services company. Coincidentally, some recent senior appointments have come from outside, including Dr. Shrey Viranna (CEO of Discovery Vitality), Dr. Ryan Noach (Deputy CEO of Discovery Health), Dinesh Govender (Chief Marketing Officer for Discovery) and Anton Ossip (CEO of Discovery Insure). Discovery is clearly able to attract key external talent. Yet the current model of exporting Discovery's IP through Discovery partner markets to assist large, well-established insurers (like AIA in Asia, Ping An in China, Generali in Europe and John Hancock in the US) in using Vitality to benefit from dynamic underwriting, calls for the grooming and exporting of ambassadors. They must be steeped in an understanding of Discovery's shared value business model, product portfolio and culture – in other words, Discovery's global growth requires more homegrown executive talent.

AIA Vitality   **GENERALI** Vitality   中国平安 PINGAN   John Hancock | Vitality

In response to the need for homegrown talent, Dr. Penny Tlhabi (Head of Discovery People and Sustainability) has made talent management and leadership development key focus areas. Since 2013, she and the talent management and Leadership and Learning (L&L) team have worked with Exco to create and develop talent pools for strategic, executive roles, to ensure that Discovery can deepen a bench of homegrown talent to drive local and global opportunities.

Practice 2: Setting a dynamic rhythm to drive innovation

Discovery is a disruptive innovator that has built a dynamic pace through 90-day challenges, bi-annual product launches that significantly improve the value of products for members and an annual Inspiring Excellence process (see Adrian Gore's recent contribution to *McKinsey Quarterly* about Inspiring Excellence)[1] that focuses and channels the entrepreneurial energy of over 1 200 Discovery leaders across all sectors, on the innovative improvements and initiatives that refresh and revitalise Discovery's businesses and products. The combined impact of these practices and programmes is a dynamic rhythm of rituals that inspire people to unleash their innovation and optimism, so as to dazzle our clients.

The rituals that underpin Discovery's dynamic rhythm of innovation build competence and confidence in the organisation's people. For example, several Inspiring Excellence innovations have resulted in product innovations which become enhancements for bi-annual product launches. A case in point is Active Rewards, which came from an innovation suggested by one of the Inspiring Excellence finalist teams. In addition, during 90-day challenges, each business sets stretch goals that focus the energy and attention of all its people and departments.

Yet an opportunity exists for Discovery to further catalyse innovation. While Inspiring Excellence taps into the ideas of over 1 200 Discovery leaders, broadening it to all DPs would bring ideas and potential innovations from close to 10 000 or almost ten times as many individuals. Such a move would increase the volume of ideas, but may not necessarily improve the quality of those ideas. To generate higher-quality ideas, all Discovery's people would need deeper insight into the organisation's shared value business model and products. The L&L function seeks to provide exactly such insights through practices 3 and 4 (see below).

Practice 3: Supporting inspirational leaders who never stop learning

Discovery supports inspirational leaders to learn on demand how to better lead their innovative businesses and people. L&L invests in innovative initiatives that provide these leaders with demand-driven learning anytime, anywhere, on any device. L&L recently launched Learning as a Service to give Discovery leaders the technological tools to control and own their learning. Some of these tools include a Leadership App, Discovery GetAbstract, OverDrive (a service that allows Discovery's people to electronically borrow, read and return books), Discovery YouLab and a Discovery YouTube channel.

Practice 4: Developing outstanding, distinctive and inspirational leaders who achieve extraordinary things for Discovery and the world

Learning as a Service is a crucial part of an integrated approach to leadership development, designed to build generations of outstanding and distinctive leaders for both the organisation and the world – leaders who are skilled and inspired to perform at their peak. This approach supports building a base of team leaders to divisional managers and deepening a bench of Deputy General Managers as well as General Managers (see Figure 12.1).

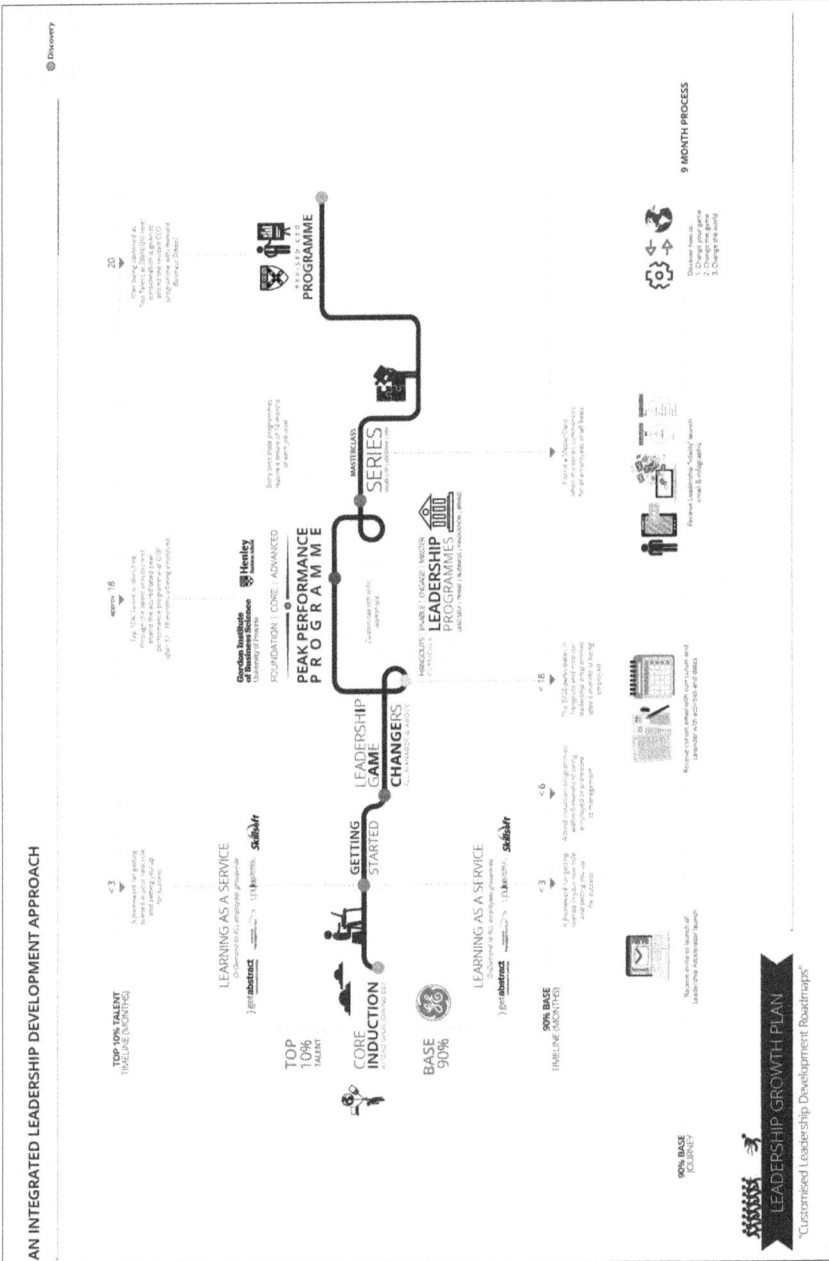

Figure 12.1   An intergrated leadership development approach

One of the key elements is Discovery's portfolio of Leadership Development Programmes (LDPs), the Peak Performance Programmes and the CEO Programme, which have been developed to build leaders who are competent and confident about contributing towards achieving Ambition 2018. The Peak Performance and CEO Programme are designed with top local and international business schools, and are highly customised to skill leaders at all levels (from staff to senior executives) to contribute distinctively to meeting Discovery's bold ambition and massive agenda. DP also provides tools such as a development calendar, which enables businesses and leaders to plan for the time required to attend these programmes.

To strengthen its entrepreneurial culture, Discovery uses its leaders (especially executives) as faculty in onboarding programmes and master classes, to inspire new recruits and incumbents to be purpose-driven, principled and values-based leaders. For instance, Discovery runs a Core Induction programme every month for all newcomers (currently 100–120 people). It runs a leadership induction programme, Leadership Game Changers, to re-inspire and reconnect our leadership team to the nobility of our purpose, as well as our conviction that inspirational leadership unleashes entrepreneurial energy and strengthens mindfulness, wellness and wisdom.

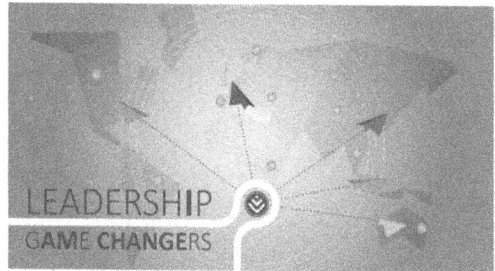

Practice 5: Recognising and rewarding excellence

Discovery not only inspires but also incentivises and rewards excellence. Its group-wide and business-specific programmes recognise people for living entrepreneurial values, and making measurable and meaningful contributions towards achieving the core purpose. Programmes include Inspiring Excellence and Star Awards.

Perhaps one of the most powerful stories of Discovery recognising and rewarding excellence, is Themba Baloyi's journey as founder of Discovery Insure. Themba's story is well documented and shared broadly within the organisation. He approached Adrian after the latter had invited attendees at 'A conversation with Adrian' at the Sandton Convention Centre, to speak to him about their entrepreneurial business ideas. As Themba was walking back to Discovery's offices (which are around the corner from the centre) he noticed that Adrian was also walking back. Themba struck up a conversation about his business idea to contribute to making our roads safer and reducing the annual road carnage. At the time, Discovery was not involved in short-term insurance. Adrian invited Themba to pitch his idea. Between that pitch and the launch of Discovery Insure there was a eight-year journey filled with ups and downs, twists and thrills. Ultimately, Discovery made Themba's idea a new and growing line of business. Themba has been and continues to be recognised and rewarded for his role as Founding Executive of Discovery Insure.

The way forward

After 23 years of informal and innovative talent management, Discovery now faces the challenge of scaling its talent management practices to find its next 10 000 staff, as it pursues global growth.

Endnotes

1   A Gore, 'How Discovery keeps innovating', *McKinsey Quarterly*, May 2015, retrieved 1 August 2016, <http://www.mckinsey.com/industries/healthcare-systems-and-services/our-insights/how-discovery-keeps-innovating>.

References

Gore, A, 'How Discovery keeps innovating', *McKinsey Quarterly*, May 2015, retrieved 1 August 2016, <http://www.mckinsey.com/industries/healthcare-systems-and-services/our-insights/how-discovery-keeps-innovating>.

PART 2

CHAPTER 13

HOME-GROWN AFRICAN BOTTLER SHOWS WINNING SPIRIT AND CULTURE: THE COCA-COLA STORY
Tracy Potgieter

It is such a pleasure to read the story of how a company that started as a relatively small bottler in Port Elizabeth has grown into a respected force in the industry in a number of African and Asian countries, and is now without doubt a major force in the industry across emerging markets.

The lessons in this chapter reinforce my view that talent management is not just about attracting and retaining the right talent, it is also about creating a culture which is attractive to talent and in which talent can thrive. The whole is truly greater than the sum of its parts.

There are many important lessons to be learnt from this chapter, but perhaps the most crucial is the role of leadership and values in creating a great culture. It illustrates the point that "soft is the new hard", as there is a direct correlation between culture and organisational performance.

It also demonstrates the importance of family and family values in driving culture – something I have observed in a number of family-dominated organisations.

Tracy Potgieter has done a superb job in describing both the company's journey and the power of values and leadership in steering that journey. She did this while the organisation was involved in a major merger – a true demonstration of the "can do, willing to do" culture!

This chapter provides a number of very practical interventions based on a sound leadership philosophy that will be of interest and benefit to any organisation embarking on a talent journey.

Introduction

The link between organisational culture and leadership is a fascinating subject which is told through this study of a local Port Elizabeth-based South African organisation with a proud heritage and big dreams. This is the story of Coca-Cola Sabco (CCS) (Pty)Ltd and the central role which organisational culture has played in the success of the organisation.

In my account, I acknowledge the many organisations that have their own "culture" story to tell. Hopefully, this narrative will expand the interest of others in sharing how they have balanced the need to achieve profitability, while at the same time creating a workplace where people find purpose and meaning in a positive environment and can contribute to the best of their potential.

Culture is a powerful dynamic force which plays a central role in employee engagement and performance results. It is a critical factor and competitive advantage for the business success of CCS. The unique Sabco culture currently attracts some of the continent's best talent, as the organisation continues to build its footprint across Africa.

The Sabco culture story starts with the founding family, the Gutsches, who own the majority share in CCS, with a member of the second generation leading the business as chairman, and family members serving on the board. The role of the family in establishing the founding principles of Sabco and the unique family culture for which it is so well known and loved among CCS stakeholders, continues to this day. It is not unusual to see Gutsche family members in the corridors, chatting to employees by name or conducting market visits in countries in which Sabco operates. This passionate love for the brand, as well as the people of the organisation, had its genesis in the family and now permeates the organisation, from the vision "To be the best bottler in the world" through to the operating practices and principles which put customers and people first.[1]

Various Sabco leaders and CEOs have weaved the organisation's culture into its DNA and operating framework. In 1999, under the leadership of Martin Jansen, Sabco's culture was clearly articulated through the organisation and its various development interventions, including a workshop held with all employees titled: "I am the values".[2] The culture story gained momentum at this critical stage, as Sabco expanded outside South Africa's borders into Africa and Asia. Culture became the glue that held all employees together during the company's organisational transformation and growth. This allowed leaders in new territories to be on-boarded effectively and efficiently, thanks to the rapid deployment of various organisational practices, including a unique "Sabco distributor model".[3] This eventually played a role in positioning the organisation as an emerging market specialist in the Coca-Cola system on a global level.

The Sabco story started in Port Elizabeth, South Africa, expanding from there into nine African and Asian countries. Sabco leveraged the experience gained working across these vastly different cultures (Ethiopia, Vietnam, Uganda and Nepal, to name a few) to build cultural fluency and agility, and shape a strong appreciation for diversity as a competitive advantage. Exposure to the challenging social, economic and political factors operating in emerging markets (e.g., a tsunami in Sri Lanka; a Maoist uprising in Nepal; droughts in Africa; floods in Mozambique; political unrest in Kenya) built the resilience and adaptability of its leaders and employees, enabling them to deal effectively with extreme challenges. This meant that leaders had to be able to respond effectively "in the moment" with few resources, yet remain highly accountable to achieve results despite external forces. In doing so, Sabco became known as a "can do, willing to do"[4] business whose leaders felt empowered to take action.

People development was established as a core value early in the articulation of the culture, and this commitment to development was reinforced by each successive CEO. This led to the significant development of a talent pipeline which supported rapid growth at the specific time when it was crucial to business success. CCS's people-centric culture subsequently expanded into the community, empowering over 100 000 women through business development and integration into the business value chain, through the 5x20 programme.[5]

As the organisation matured in terms of its values and culture, so leaders' skills were built through intense leadership development and coaching, to enable them to continue to drive and shape culture.

The executive committee, led by Doug Jackson, decided to further buttress the organisational culture in the hearts and minds of all employees in order to deal with the economic volatility and uncertainty of 2014/15. This specific organisation-wide OD process was to become known as Vuca! (volatility, uncertainty, complexity, ambiguity) amongst employees (more about this later).

Coca-Cola Sabco has been measuring employee engagement levels since 2006, and year on year there has been a consistent and significant growth in organisational performance and employee engagement levels. The numbers continue to beat all expectations, despite changes in leadership, competitor activity, currency devaluations and other market forces which could have had a negative impact on performance.

The CCS winning culture

The executive leadership of CCS identified the importance of fortressing the organisational culture as a critical success factor, since employees needed to navigate new business priorities in the ever-changing world around them and the resulting changes within the business. Soon Sabco's culture became known within the world-wide Coca-Cola system as a highly desirable factor for doing business with the company.

The entrepreneurial culture of CCS enables the growth strategy of the organisation through reinforcing the following elements:

- **Innovation and risk taking:** creativity, experimentation and renewal are encouraged;
- **Outcome orientation:** management focuses on results or outcomes, rather than techniques and processes;
- **People focus:** employees are highly valued; and
- **Team approach:** activities are organised around teams rather than individuals, and teams are empowered to manage themselves.

In contrast, the following dimensions receive little reinforcement in the CCS culture:

- **Aggressiveness:** employees who are aggressive and competitive, rather than supportive;
- **Stability:** where the status quo is maintained, rather than encouraging renewal, growth and change; and
- **Lack of attention to detail:** accuracy, analysis and perfection are required and encouraged.

With this in mind, qualitative interviews with a 360° sample consisting of board members, members of the executive committee, managers and employees, shareholders, external service providers and suppliers, resulted in the reframing of the culture statement into six elements:

- Family
- Love Coke
- Humility
- Hard on results
- Teamwork
- Soft on people

Ensuring that employees master these elements was deemed key to future stability and success in a Vuca! world.

Figure 13.1 The six elements of SSC's culture[6]

171

Implementing the winning culture

After articulating the CCS culture, senior leaders were surprised during the AGM meeting with a "flash-mob" session during which they were recruited into creating a dance video representing each of the cultural elements. The video went "viral" amongst employees who appreciated management's willingness to be "real", authentic and have fun – all for the common good.

This was followed by a full roll-out of Winning Culture workshops across the entire organisation during the ensuing months. The aim of these sessions was to entrench a 'winning spirit' within the group. The training added great value as it made delegates more aware of the external forces at play in terms of changing markets, and consumer trends and behaviour. More than ever, creativity, flexibility and agility were needed to ensure customer loyalty.

Operating in a Vuca world means doing things with greater efficiency and effectiveness. A greater awareness of the cost to serve, which includes consciously minimising costs and a mindfulness of the impact on the world around us, was also highlighted. The essence of the CCS working culture was brought home to delegates during a three-hour session of DVDs, discussions, role-playing and storyboard exercises. Some participant comments appear below.

> The trainer was knowledgeable, group presentations were great and brought out a lot of hidden talent from many of the delegates, and the duration of the training was perfect. I personally appreciated having attended that course and mastering the six cultural elements of Sabco. Thank you very much.

> One big thing which I learnt was all about teamwork – the success of any business or family will only be there when we work as a team because everyone needs support from the other to make the business or family survive or continue improving.

> It showed us how the world is changing and to live in a Vuca world we need to be prepared for new challenges using our winning spirit.

> It was great. It was a short, high-energy, captivating exercise that we had lots of fun doing. It made us all realise the need to trust those that lead us. It also made me feel like CCSM, while it is hard on results, is a fun place to work at and that we have a part to play in achieving those results and making it the best working environment.

> The following were my key learnings: Our six cultural elements are suited to make myself, CBC and Sabco win in this Vuca world all the time and every time. To remain competitive, our vision, alignment (with all the stakeholders), clarity and agility will be the key drivers.

The role of the founding family

An organisation's initial culture sprouts from its founder's thinking and business philosophy. If the founder is driven by achievement and success, an achievement culture is likely to develop. If the business is initially managed along rigid rules and guidelines, chances are that it will develop into a very hierarchical and bureaucratic organisation with a rigid culture.

SSC's success of over 75 years is built on the entrepreneurial flair of the Gutsche family, the major shareholders of this private company. Starting from humble beginnings in Port Elizabeth, which is still the location of its headquarters, the organisation has kept the vision of being "The best bottler in the world" clearly in its sights by working towards doubling its business volume by 2020, while operating within a highly competitive and fast-changing environment.

CCS is known both internally and externally as a family-based organisation. A family culture is characterised by personal, face-to-face relationships with the leadership team based on benevolence, where people are taken good care of and strong relationships are forged based on mutual trust and respect.

The organisation is currently led by Philipp H. Gutsche, Executive Chairman and Jacques Vermeulen, CEO. Both leaders have a personable, authentic and humble leadership presence. Mr Gutsche regularly addresses the organisation with his "recipe for business success", with insights which are indicative of the general "can do, willing to do" attitude of the employees, that reinforces the following messages:

In the marketplace

- "Do your best and forget the rest"
- "Turn your mistakes into an advantage"
- "Make things happen"
- "Make sure the product is ice cold, within arm's reach"
- "Be conscious in growing our market share"
- "Be assertive in reaching for growth and new territories"
- "Have total dedication".

Employees and family

- "Trust people and be prepared to let them do their job"
- "Employ people more competent than yourself"
- "Give people clear latitude and a clear job description"
- "Create the best, world-class learning and development programmes – induction is critical".

The product and stakeholders

- "Your #1 relationship is with our product – Coca-Cola"
- "Build goodwill"
- "Do not tolerate arrogance".

Faith, ethics and passion

- "Believe in miracles"
- "Always do what is right"
- "Inculcate and carry on our traditions of family and fun!"

Vision, mission and values

CCS is no stranger to transformation, having reframed itself from a small bottler operating locally to a multinational employing over 9 600 employees. A lesson to be learned from CCS is not to leave culture to chance. At CCS, leaders consciously shape the culture through visible leadership actions and the deployment of the organisation's systems, processes, policies, KPIs and talent management practices.

The vision, mission and values of the organisation have remained unchanged for decades:

Mission statement

Our vision

"We will be the best Coca-Cola bottler in the world."

- The best: in sales volume and in return on capital employed;
- Coca-Cola bottler: a consumer-driven, customer-oriented, manufacturer, sales and distribution company that markets the products and brands of the Coca-Cola Company;
- In the world: we measure ourselves against the best Coca-Cola bottlers in the world.

Our purpose

To create value for everyone touched by our business by providing, with passion and focus, the right refreshment, at the right price, in the right place.

Our values

We will create an environment where our people are passionate about performance. This will be based on the following:

- Integrity: be honest, open and sincere;
- Individual initiative: take pro-active steps to drive performance;
- Customer value: exceed customer expectations and add value to customers' businesses;
- Teamwork: work with and support colleagues to raise overall performance;
- People development: realise employee potential through training and development;
- Mutual trust and respect: treat each other with respect, dignity and earn trust; and
- Commitment: be accountable and do as you say.

CCS's organisational culture is a very powerful guide to its leaders and employees, because it has created a corporate identity that distinguishes it from other bottlers, while staying aligned to the overall values of the Coca-Cola Company. As a result, it gives employees an identity and a strong commitment to organisational goals and objectives. The values of the organisation provide a compass to employees in terms of acceptable behaviours and attitudes, especially when they have to make decisions and solve problems. The family-based, people-centric culture provides emotional security and a clear yardstick for evaluating and correcting deviant behaviours and rewarding desired behaviours.

The role of Asian acquisitions in CCS's cultural fluency and appreciation of diversity

CCs' 2005 acquisition of bottlers in Vietnam, Cambodia, Laos, Nepal, Bangladesh and Sri Lanka changed the way we saw ourselves. We were no longer only the anchor bottler for Africa – we were now a multinational with operations on more than one continent.

According to Talent and Learning Manager (Asia), Melanie Forlee, Asia was, for many within the organisation, a totally different world, and as CCS we needed to learn about the people and culture, both organisationally and nationally, very quickly. "The way things work around here" had to be quickly understood and adapted to by the CCS team who were supporting the Asia territories. The unspoken carries significant weight in Asian culture, and as South Africans we needed to be aware of how to clearly communicate the message without giving offence. This allowed us to provide encouragement and support where required, to ensure the success of our organisation in these territories.

Even within the region an awareness of diversity was critical for success – Indochina responds to different cues and messaging styles than Indian subcontinent cultures do. The Vietnamese are seen as abrupt, while the Sri Lankans convey more openness. The truth of the matter is that neither of these generalisations could be taken at face value: we needed to understand the broader culture of the region, to grasp subtle differences.

What did this mean? It meant that we needed to be willing to listen and adapt our style of communication to each culture we interacted with. For some, we needed to be expansive, while for others, being brief, concise and to the point was key. It was imperative to always keep in mind the cultural norms and cues which, if understood, would facilitate working with the teams, but which would, if ignored, make interaction that much more challenging.

The Asia operations brought significant diversity to CCS, and for those of us who worked and interacted with the teams on a daily basis, it opened our eyes and minds to a myriad new and different opportunities, and allowed us to be more adaptable and flexible to cultural differences. Forlee believes this has made us stronger, more adept to change, and has built resilience within all of us.

Role of leadership in articulating and shaping culture

The organisation's vision is to be the best Coca-Cola bottler in the world, working towards the goal of doubling business volume by 2020, while operating within a highly competitive and fast-changing environment.

To reach such targets, CCS requires authentic leaders who can guide staff to high levels of employee engagement and innovation. For this reason, Ashridge Business School in the United Kingdom developed the Coca-Cola Sabco Breakthrough Leadership Programme, based on the concept that "great leadership starts with the self".[7] Delivered over four days, the aim of the programme is to develop inspirational leadership role models across CCS, who deeply understand their individual drivers and values, and how they interact with others. The programme was designed to reinforce a values-driven leadership culture in which leadership is "owned" by the team.

This was followed up with an intense qualitative 360° leadership evaluation against the Leadership 2020 competencies for all senior leaders, developed and conducted with an external consultancy, Heidrick & Struggles.[8]

The organisation's envisaged leadership culture has become a reality thanks to the programme, resulting in individuals striving to stretch themselves and their boundaries. Levels of motivation, focus and performance have increased since the programme was introduced; stronger team connections have been built; leaders have re-engaged with their personal purpose; and personal breakthroughs relating to health and well-being have been seen.

Cathy Albertyn, HR Director at Coca-Cola Sabco

The power of the programme lies in being able to

spend time with team members in a manner conducive to reflection and growth. As a result, a deeper understanding both of individual strengths as well as team dynamics has been gained, which has translated to a more positive team spirit and higher levels of performance at work. The sporting connection also assisted in bringing alive some strong messages for participants.

Ian Garnett, CFO at Coca-Cola Sabco

This set of leadership development programmes has assisted in taking CCS one step closer to achieving its 2020 goal.

Performance and employee engagement results

Year on year, CCS delivered results which are significantly higher than market trends in non-alcoholic ready-to-drink beverages (NARTD). The current CEO, Jacques Vermeulen, continues to drive stellar performance across the business without compromising the values of the organisation. He entrenches the need to continue to develop people through a "coaching culture".

Jacques Vermeulen, CEO of Coca-Cola Sabco

Employee engagement scores for the organisation (see Figure 13.5) have grown by 3.2 per cent per annum, on average, since 2007, from an average of 64 to 83 per cent. Ethiopia moved from 69 per cent in 2011, steadily increasing to the highest level of engagement in the organisation in 2015 with a score of 92 per cent.

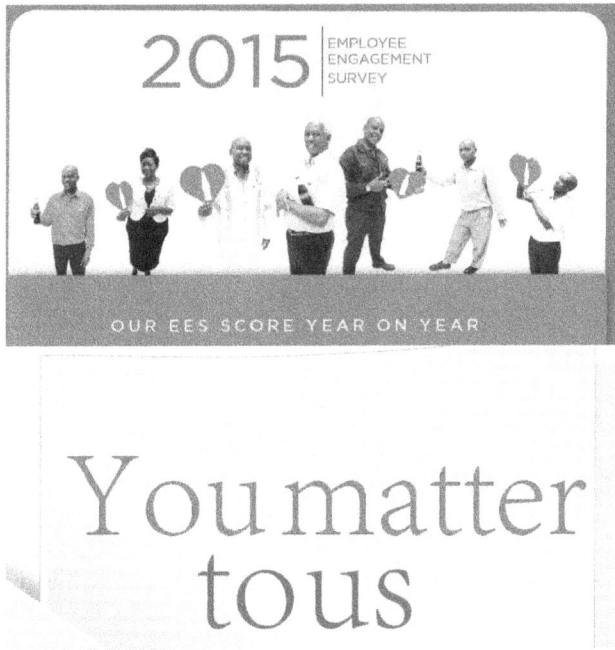

Figure 13.2 Employee engagement survey

Using the capability wheel as a framework (see Figure 13.3), the specific practical actions taken in Ethiopia provide an explanation for the significant improvement in both business results and employee engagement scores. It is the simple and practical things that make a difference.

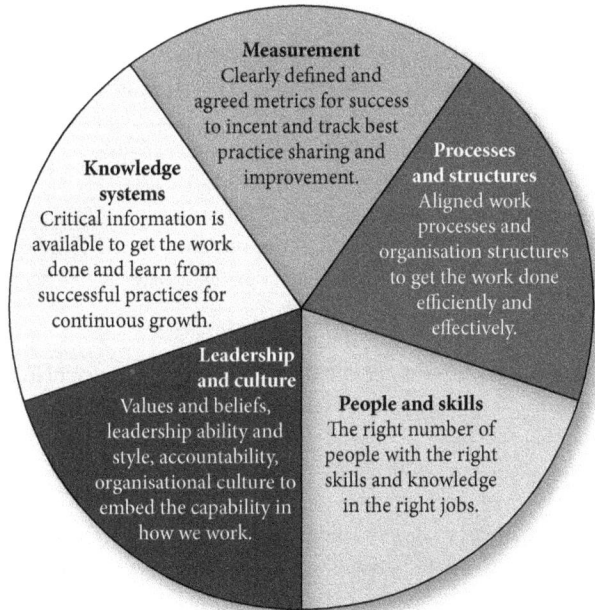

Figure 13.3 The capability wheel

Conclusion

Culture is shaped by the founding members of an organisation and reinforced by senior leadership. Culture is enduring. For Sabco, culture is a truly valuable asset or competitive advantage which facilitates the growth and expansion of the business.

The **commitment of senior leadership to the organisational culture** is evident in how effectively they take responsibility for the culture, and also communicate it in clear terms to all employees. More importantly, how they model these values, attitudes and behaviours in their day-to-day functioning will continue to strengthen the culture. Leaders who do not "live the values" will inevitably find that they cannot work against the prevailing culture – they will therefore need to either align to the culture or leave the system.

Orientation and immersion training programmes with both ideological (culture) and practical content teach values, norms, history and tradition, and are valuable tools in on-boarding senior leaders and employees. The learning and development function can be utilised to teach technical skills, while at the same time importing important values and lessons.

On-boarding by peers and immediate supervisors is one of the best ways to introduce new employees to the organisational culture, and explain what is expected of them through the socialisation process. Supervisors and key employees should be trained to share relevant and correct information. Mentors can also exert a powerful influence on the personal experiences of employees and/or leaders.

Rigorous policies of up-through-the-ranks promotion reinforce organisational culture. Only those employees who have demonstrated that their attitudes and behaviours are congruent with the desired organisational culture, should qualify. If innovation, collaboration and ethics are the core values of the organisation, only employees who make a valuable contribution to innovation, demonstrate superior networking and cooperative behaviours, and act ethically should be considered for promotion.

Exposure to legendary stories of 'heroic deeds' and corporate exemplars includes having the board and senior leaders interacting with employees during fireside conversations and face-to-face meetings. Such opportunities expose employees to accounts of exceptional achievement on the part of their colleagues, and remind them of the heritage of the organisation and the CCS family culture.

A unique language and terminology reinforce a specific mindset and create a sense of belonging to a special collective. In CCS, phrases/terms such as "Can do, willing to do"; "Hard on results; soft on people"; "Roughly right, not precisely wrong"; and "Vuca!" encapsulate the values of entrepreneurship, family and people-centrism.

Corporate songs, cheers, affirmations or pledges that reinforce psychological commitment to organisational values also help to create a spirit of fun.

Celebrations serve to reinforce successes, belonging and the idea of being special.

Tight screening processes mean that during selection, applicants are not only matched with the requirements of the job, but their compatibility with the organisational culture is given serious consideration. Culture fit is of critical importance when selecting the most senior leaders in the organisation.

Investments (both monetary and in the form of time) create 'buy-in'. Successful organisations spend money on campaigns, change programmes, training and reward schemes to gain support from managers and employees for the organisational culture, its espoused values and appropriate behaviours.

Constant verbal and written emphasis on corporate values, heritage and the sense of being part of something special reinforces the corporate culture. Management should continuously articulate the vision and values of the organisation in speeches, communications and documentation.

Summary

In summary, then, CCS's leadership cohort utilise a number of key mechanisms to proactively shape the culture of the organisation, to support and drive successful results. This is not an exhaustive list, but it highlights some of the mechanisms used on the CCS journey.

In good times and bad, CCS employees and leaders use the company's culture and values both to "anchor" and provide a "north star" to guide their behaviour. The value of culture is so strong that executive management consider it an asset that needs to be protected and strengthened as a key business driver of success.

Yes, there are times when the culture seems threatened by leaders who "go off course" or by situations that seem so "out of control" that they threaten the very survival of the organisation's culture. But survive it does, every time, bouncing back to reconfirm employees' faith in the letter and spirit of Sabco's code of conduct.

The CCS culture is a source of pride amongst all employees who drive exceptionally high levels of engagement and productivity, despite the challenges of "emerging market" volatility. I personally consider myself lucky to have stumbled into such an energetic working culture – most importantly, one which shows great integrity and does not let "the end justify the means".

Thank you for listening to our story – I hope it will inspire you to learn more about Sabco and the exceptional leaders and employees who bring the culture to life. As CCS continues its journey to maintaining world-class standards and becoming "the best bottler in the world", the organisation's unique leadership and culture are critical core capabilities which will help it reach its ambitious goal.

Endnotes

1   Coca-Cola Sabco, 'Mission statement: "We will be the Best Coca-Cola bottler in the world"', retrieved 1 August 2016, <http://www.cocacolasabco.com/company/our-company>.
2   Ibid., 'The mid-2000s: The achievements continue', 2006,
3   Ibid.
4   Ibid.
5   B Jenkins, K Valikai & P Baptista, 'The Coca-Cola Company's 5x20 Initiative: Empowering women entrepreneurs across the value chain', Harvard Kennedy School, 2013, retrieved 1 August 2016, <https://www.hks.harvard.edu/m-rcbg/CSRI/CSRI_BusinessFightsPoverty_5by20Report_September2013.pdf>.
6   Unless otherwise stipulated, all data, images and graphics were taken from Coca-Cola's unpublished in-house documents.
7   Ashridge Business School, UK, Coca-Cola Sabco Breakthrough Leadership Programme, see <http://tools.ashridge.org.uk/Website/Content.nsf/FileLibrary/F7B34BA58CA4949280257CE50030CFD4/$file/Exec%20Leaders%20in%20Africa%20Prog%20brochure_V2.pdf>.
8   Heidrick & Struggles, Leadership 2020 competencies for senior leaders, see <http//www.heidrick.com/Knowledge-Center>.

References

Ashridge Business School, UK, Coca-Cola Sabco Breakthrough Leadership Programme, see <http://tools.ashridge.org.uk/Website/Content.nsf/FileLibrary/F7B34BA58CA4949280257CE50030CFD4/$file/Exec%20Leaders%20in%20Africa%20Prog%20brochure_V2.pdf>.

Coca-Cola Sabco, 'Mission statement: "We will be the Best Coca-Cola bottler in the world"', retrieved 1 August 2016, <http://www.cocacolasabco.com/company/our-company>.

Heidrick & Struggles, Leadership 2020 competencies for senior leaders, see <http//www.heidrick.com/Knowledge-Center>.

Jenkins, B, Valikai, K & Baptista, P, 'The Coca-Cola Company's 5x20 Initiative: Empowering women entrepreneurs across the value chain', 2013, Harvard Kennedy School, retrieved 1 August 2016, <https://www.hks.harvard.edu/m-rcbg/CSRI/CSRI_BusinessFightsPoverty_5by20Report_September2013.pdf>.

CHAPTER 14

THE ROLE OF BUSINESS SCHOOLS IN GROWING AFRICA'S TALENT
Terry Meyer

I have been associated with a variety of top South African business schools for more than 20 years and have overseen or lectured on programmes from Master's level to executive education courses for all levels of management. I have also had the privilege of engaging with top global business schools while leading international study groups.

Business schools play an important role in developing talent and leaders on the continent and globally. Yet, like all enterprises, change is in the wind and they, like their clients, need to be responsive to such changes.

This chapter discusses the future role of business schools in the economy and society, and takes a look at the challenges they will have to overcome if they are to remain relevant in a fast-evolving business environment.

It also discusses how organisations and programme participants can get the best possible return on their considerable investment in business school education. This needs to be done through a partnership between the organisation, the business school and the learner, where each plays an important role in the success of learning and organisational performance.

In researching this chapter I had the privilege of meeting with Prof Nicola Kleyn, Dean of the Gordon Institute of Business Science (Gibs), Prof Steve Bluen, Director of Wits Business School and Prof Howard Thomas, former dean of a number of top global business schools and currently affiliated to the University of Singapore as an expert in business education. The time and insights these academics provided, are greatly valued.

The heads of business schools play a significant role in the provision of future leaders and talent in both their own countries and on the continent. There is no doubt that management education (in this country at least) is in the hands of leaders who are truly worthy of the responsibilities they hold.

What is essential in converting education into individual and organisational performance is improved quality in the collaboration between all players involved – business schools, organisations and learners.

Introduction

This chapter examines the role of business schools in building Africa's talent. In most surveys covering human capital challenges in Africa and globally, leadership is almost always amongst the top five priorities of executives or HR professionals. The Bersin[1] by Deloitte *Human capital trends* is one of the most comprehensive surveys available.[2]

In examining the role of business schools in building talent, a number of questions need to be addressed:

- What is the overall role of business schools in society and the economy?
- What kind of programmes do business schools offer and what are their benefits?
- How should organisations, business schools and learners partner to ensure learning has the required impact on organisational performance?
- What are some of the challenges facing traditional business school methodologies?
- What is the role of technology as a game changer in how business schools operate?
- What are some of the systemic issues that management education faces, moving towards the next decade?
- What will leading business schools look like in 2025?

These questions speak to the overarching role of business schools in building future leaders in Africa, as well as a number of specific issues that need to be addressed to improve the contribution of their programmes in enhancing individual and organisational performance. It also brings to the fore issues arising from the emerging landscape of business and organisations, and the changes that business schools need to make to remain relevant in this environment in the future.

The role of business schools in society and the economy

> Questions have been raised from outside and within management academia not only about whether and how business schools truly fulfil their promise to develop leaders, but also about what kind of leaders their graduates become and on whose behalf – with whose interests at heart – they lead.[3]

Following the 2008 global financial crisis as well as many examples of questionable ethical behaviour on the part of local and global companies, questions are increasingly being asked about the kind of management education that leaders in business and elsewhere are receiving, and to what extent business schools are (at least partially) complicit in shaping such behaviour. This issue goes to the heart of what leadership should mean in the 21st century. Is business leadership purely about deriving maximum profit for shareholders through the exploitation of resources, or is the role of business and business leadership much wider than that? Should the training of business leaders be restricted to the largely traditional subjects of marketing, finance, strategy, organisational behaviour, IT and project management, or should there be a shift to include, as core subjects, the key issues of effective corporate governance, ethical decision making, social and environmental sustainability, innovation, entrepreneurship, personal insight, systemic problem solving and other similar imperatives that are increasingly the concern of business and society as a whole?

It is not only subject matter that impacts the learning that takes place at business schools; they have a powerful socialising role that can shape the thinking and behaviour of those who attend programmes for a considerable time to come. As an INSEAD professor who researches the role of business schools observes:

> Elite business schools are known for the powerful socialization that takes place inside the walls; indeed it's one of the things that makes them attractive to those of us who sought a business degree […] [At business school], managers revisit their identities and aspirations. Strive to align what they can do with who they want to be. Refine their view of what it means to lead and whom they are meant to serve. Join communities that pressure, guide and support them long after classes break.[4]

Globally (and especially in Africa) the expectations stakeholders have of leaders and managers are changing. Organisations are more frequently reviewing the kinds of leaders they will need to take their organisation forward in an increasingly complex and fast-changing world. Business schools across the continent need to have similar conversations to ensure that their programmes and the broader experience they provide to learners reflect the changing needs of organisations and society.

In addition to questions about the kind of leaders business schools help shape, it is important to ask whether such schools should take a stand – or at least facilitate debates – on economic, social, political and environmental issues occurring in the countries in which they operate.

In my view, business schools, like the businesses they serve, should know and articulate what they stand for and this should guide their broader role and advocacy positions in society. In my experience, few (if any) are prepared to take leadership positions and prefer, at best, to simply facilitate debates on key national issues of the day. Healthy debate is important, but I would suggest that business schools and academics alike need to be proactive in communicating what they stand for and why, without sacrificing their need to remain stakeholder-neutral. It suggests they need to publicly take principled positions on key issues, especially where these affect business.

Prof Nicola Kleyn, Dean of Gibs (which is attached to the University of Pretoria) referred to the convening power of business schools and their faculty: this is largely due to their stakeholder neutrality, which provides a safe space for sensitive discussions. She pointed out that while academic freedom needs to be respected, it brings with it the responsibility to lead important discourse which is bound in scholarship.[5]

By taking a public stand on fundamental issues of principle, such as corporate governance and ethics, business schools begin to play a role in educating the greater business community and society as a whole through the signals that such advocacy sends.

Another role that business schools are well positioned to play is to contribute to the resolution of key social and economic issues – significant challenges for most African countries. It is my contention that business schools, thanks to the considerable intellectual resources at their disposal, could, through participation in relevant forums, research or the development of position papers, contribute to resolving numerous issues of importance. They are in a unique position to remain stakeholder-neutral while facilitating dialogue.

Prof Steve Bluen, Head of Wits Business School, noted that each school has its own "flavour" and positions itself uniquely.[6] Wits, for example, places considerable emphasis on students understanding the "context" of business and society. Themes such as the importance of creating social value permeate their programmes.

As academic institutions, business schools are involved in research. There are two questions that need to be asked in this respect:

- To what extent do research reports by doctoral and Master's students have an impact (beyond providing academic papers for academics) and how many are relegated to a database of research reports, never to be looked at again? My experience suggests that there is plenty of opportunity to leverage learner research reports so that they have a much broader impact; and
- To what extent do business schools attract funding for research into important issues through partnerships with business and research funding organisations? In many traditional academic faculties (e.g., medicine), research funding by funding organisations is key to their relevant research output. Globally, many leading companies have research contracts with business schools and other faculties (e.g., engineering) for important, relevant research.

The role of relevant research at business schools on key economic, business and social issues is a debate worth having across the continent and, in fact, on a global scale. I would argue that in the same way that businesses and all other organisations need to adopt different mental models in a fast-changing business environment, business schools need to re-examine their mental models about research and its role in impacting organisations and the economy. The opportunities for innovative disruption in the very traditional world of academic research are considerable.

Prof Howard Thomas, Director of Academic Strategy and Management Education at Singapore Management University makes the point that as long as academics are remunerated and receive tenure based primarily on their research contribution to high-level academic journals, problems around the relevance of research will remain.[7]

Encouragingly, Gibs is considering various research options, one of which is to create a school research agenda which will facilitate relevant research. It will also contribute to "cluster" research, where literature, methodology and other collaborations can result in a "body" of pertinent, research-based knowledge.[8]

Wits is focusing on academic excellence and draws excellent faculty from many African countries to support this goal.[9] Interestingly, the university allows four options for MBA research recognition: a traditional research report; a proposal for a new venture; a report related to social entrepreneurship and a consulting intervention supported with an appropriate theoretical base. At Wits, an additional focus of research derives from a number of Master's of Management (MM) programmes that the school offers, and that require more in-depth research. This is fine for MBAs and academic programmes aimed at individual development, but in the field of customised executive education, which is the fastest-growing sector of most business schools, organisations are looking for more than just courses – they want *solutions* to organisational issues and capability building that will assist in the implementation of strategy. In my experience, too many business schools provide clients with what are often standard courses, repackaged to include some relevance to a sector, and little else.

A good example was given to me by the HR director of a large global mining organisation. The request to all the top business schools in South Africa was for a programme to help their executives rethink the global mining business model to ensure sustainability – a key issue for mining companies around the world. The response from almost all business schools merely entailed repackaged, standard courses. This, in my opinion, illustrates the substantial shift that business schools need to make in programme design, namely a *solutions*-based rather than a *programme*-based approach. Prof Kleyn pointed out that while it is unlikely that business schools will take on a consulting role, there is often a need for an in-depth diagnostic phase at the start of client engagement, which results in the co-creation of programmes and solutions with the client concerned. This significant shift for traditional business school approaches requires different skills – it obviously does not apply to clients who simply want general capacity building.[10]

While the above issues concerning the roles of business schools are important, as things are, the products of business schools are programmes and the learners who sacrifice their time and energy to benefit from those programmes.

For organisations it is important to gain an overview of the kind of programmes that business schools typically offer, and their relevance to specific identified needs.

Business school programmes

Most business schools offer three types of programme:

- Academic programmes (e.g., an MBA or specialist MM) which result in a qualification;

- Open executive education programmes (e.g., a Management Development Programme [MDP], New Managers Programmes [NMPs] and Executive Development Programmes [EDPs]). Such programmes typically draw people from a variety of organisations and follow a standard curriculum; and
- Customised executive education programmes which are designed specifically for an organisation.

There are many advocates and detractors of MBAs in particular. I believe an MBA has the following benefits:

- Participants, most of whom come from a specific functional discipline such as accounting or engineering, are exposed to all other major functional disciplines;
    - they learn how to work under considerable pressure;
    - how to analyse problems, understand the dilemmas associated with complex problems and apply processes to resolve them; and
    - how to work in teams.
- From a potential employer's perspective, some degree of pre-selection has occurred, as leading business schools have stringent selection criteria.

Executive education programmes are typically non-degree programmes which are a major source of revenue for business schools.

The advantage of open programmes is that participants are able to engage with their peers from different companies and sectors. This challenges them to think beyond their sectoral, organisational or functional paradigm. The programmes are particularly useful for individual development, but the disadvantage is that there is limited organisational impact, since generally only the participant has been through the experience. However, some organisations send a number of managers simultaneously (or over time) to attend the same programme. This builds a critical mass of knowledge and contributes towards a common language and understanding of management issues.

Customised or "in-house" programmes are designed and run for a specific organisation and are aimed at building capacity in the organisation, for a particular purpose. Such programmes, which can be customised for the particular organisation and sector, are very powerful in building a common understanding and approach to key organisational issues and challenges. They also facilitate networking in the organisation and the breaking down of functional, geographical and divisional barriers. One potential disadvantage is the possibility of dominant paradigms remaining unchallenged despite the best efforts of faculty. The second potential challenge is the danger that although participants learn new and important things organisational systems may not change, thereby creating considerable frustration within the organisation. A related problem occurs when courses are run for lower and middle management, but are not attended by senior and executive management – the experience is therefore not vertically integrated into the organisation. Such practices lower the return on investment considerably and can, in fact, cause frustration.

Customised programmes need to be considered organisational change processes, rather than competency-building processes.

Increasing the impact of business school programmes: Organisation, business school, learner partnerships

Business school programmes are expensive, with some companies spending hundreds of thousands or millions of dollars on them. For companies to get the return they expect there are at least three key players who have to fulfil their expected roles.

Organisations

The ultimate aim of a business school intervention is the improved performance of individuals and, ultimately, the organisation itself. A business school programme on its own is unlikely to have optimal impact. To obtain the required returns, organisations need to do certain things before, during and after the programme.

Before the programme: critically important is the selection of the participants and courses. If an organisation does not have a talent management system that identifies potential and the specific development needs of individuals, it is quite likely that the wrong people will attend the courses. Programme directors and faculty are often faced with this problem, both on open and customised executive education courses, whereas academic programmes tend to have more rigorous selection criteria.

The result is either that participants do not know why they are on a programme or do not have the experience/capability to succeed at the level of the programme. They may have been better off on a lower-level programme that can prepare them for higher-level programmes over time. The result is that they fail the course (or standards are expediently dropped) and that has significant personal and career implications which could have been avoided with proper selection and talent management.

It is essential that in the "needs identification" process required for building customised programmes, executives are involved in determining the strategic needs of the organisation. Often the HR function manages the interface with the business school, but does not fully understand the business issues that the various programmes are designed to address.

HR departments need to ensure that people are earmarked for programmes which are at the appropriate level and meet the individual's specific learning needs.

There is some debate about the role business schools should play in assisting organisations with this process, but the reality is they are good at running programmes, not consulting. They do not provide holistic talent management solutions.

During the programme: in this phase, organisations need to legitimise the attendance of each programme participant, so that their immediate managers understand the challenges they are facing. They should be willing (if not required) to provide some space for learners to meet the (often very onerous) requirements of their course.

Leading organisations frequently engage and support learners on business school programmes (be it an MBA or executive education programme), and ensure that their immediate line manager is aligned with the process.

After the programme: another role of organisations concerns their actions after a participant (or group) has attended a programme.

When I was teaching on a leading MBA programme it was common for participants (all high potential) to change jobs. The reason was that they were exposed to cutting-edge thinking and motivated to try it in their organisations, but at that point they felt stifled – there was no opportunity to apply what they had learnt, so they moved to an organisation that would enable them to do so.

Leading organisations not only create a climate where participants are encouraged to apply their learning, they are actually required to share their learning and implement changes.

If the behaviour of the individual or organisation (and hence performance) does not change, for whatever reason, there is no return on investment!

In the longer term, leading organisations create communities of leaders who have attended business school programmes and encourage engagement well after the programme is concluded. They ensure that participants participate in projects that stretch them to apply their learning.

Business schools

The key role of business schools is to provide stimulating and impactful programmes, and facilitate the socialisation process referred to earlier. While recognising the academic nature of such schools, it is important that faculty are engaged with, and understand, the changing business environment. This creates a tension in many business schools between the need for faculty to teach, publish research and consult to business.

Most leading business schools incorporate self-assessment and personal insight in their programmes. They also include action learning projects which enable participants to apply what they have learnt to a real business problem. Action learning projects are very powerful at creating an integrated learning experience.

Learners

Business school programmes are hard work, and many sacrifices often have to be made. Divorces are not uncommon amongst MBA candidates. It is up to learners to "contract" with their companies – and especially their families – so that they understand the pressure they will be under and the time demands they will face. For married participants, this is a family project!

Another key requirement for learners is a willingness to learn. This may sound obvious, but participants who enter a programme with a closed mind and preconceived ideas that they refuse to relinquish, will not benefit from such an opportunity.

Most business school participants find their programmes a life-changing experience – as it should be. For those who are not prepared to experience personal change, the value they derive from such a programme will be limited at best, and destructive at worst. In fact, when I worked in a corporate role, one of the prime motivations for sending managers on business school courses (myself included) was the value of having current mental models challenged. The value derived from participating in a business school programme, like all courses, is largely dependent on the effort learners put into the experience.

Learning methodologies: Their relevance in a connected world

There are a number of ways in which business school learning methodologies will need to adapt if they are to remain relevant in a rapidly changing, connected world.

Silos

> ... times have changed [...] As organizations have become flatter, those running them are looking for leaders who can see opportunities and address problems that cut across functional boundaries.[11]

One of the effects of a connected world is the increased breaking down of silos, in whatever form. This includes organisational as well as mental silos (i.e., the way we classify things). In *The silo effect*,[12] Gillian Tett, a highly rated financial journalist for the *Financial Times* with a PhD in Anthropology, points out that

> [m]any of the really important patterns we use to classify the world ... are inherited from our culture. They exist at the borders of conscious thought and instinct. They seem natural to us, in the same way our culture appears 'normal.' So much so, that we rarely even notice them at all.[13]

What the book illustrates, through the use of a number of business case studies, is the material impact that our assumptions about how things should be classified have on how we organise organisations, work and knowledge. In business schools these assumptions are largely about how we classify knowledge into disciplines.

Aligned with this challenge to the traditional classification mode is the concept of Mode-2 knowledge, which differs from Mode-1 knowledge in that it is cross-disciplinary in nature rather than encompassing traditional, academic, discipline-specific knowledge streams. It also emphasises the combination of specialities and specialists into groups to work on complex problems. "Transdisciplinarity methods will need to be utilized in order to open the endless ways of thinking that is Mode-2".[14] In a connected and fast-changing world where innovation and entrepreneurship are key capabilities, its importance is obvious.

The relevance to business schools is that there is a long-held traditional set of assumptions about how management should be broken into silos and subsequently taught. Hence, typical programmes involve lectures by experts in finance, marketing, organisational behaviour, operations and similar subjects. These are covered independently by the lecturer concerned, with little alignment let alone integration.

In business, problems seldom conveniently fall into these time-honoured categories, although most organisations still structure themselves accordingly. Problems are increasingly systemic and multifunctional. In a connected world it will not be appropriate to apply these classifications independently, neither within organisations nor in programmes. When an organisation has to respond to a disruptive change in the environment or implement a change in strategy, such responses need to be cross-disciplinary. The question that then arises is how business schools can teach traditional subjects in a cross-disciplinary manner. This is very much "work in progress", and I do not have a tested solution.

Prof Bluen points out that Wits has a well-developed case centre and this, along with global business visits, guest lectures by business leaders and research options encourages a holistic approach to business problems.[15]

Prof Kleyn makes the important point that in the modern world of work, meta-skills that are not content specific are arguably more important than traditional content knowledge (the shelf-life of which is reducing significantly). At Gibs various approaches are being applied to deal with the problem of "silo knowledge/ teaching".[16]

Some schools will argue that group projects provide a basis for integrating knowledge. In my view, entirely new ways of dealing with knowledge generation and learning are required in the modern business school. The same applies to research – many practitioners would rather seek knowledge from articles and the findings of large consulting firms than traditional and academic business schools, because of the narrow nature of academic research.

This shift will, however, require major psychological adaptation by academics and institutions alike.

Technology

> Successfully managing technology to provide the greatest value to any organization is a challenge, but the competitive environment of business schools to distinguish and reinvent themselves adds to the complexity of obtaining the highest return from technology innovations at the lowest cost.[17]

The use of online learning as a supplement to traditional teaching is still "work in progress" at most business schools, especially in South Africa. New models will certainly continue to emerge. There is no evidence that simply taking existing material and making it available "online" will add value or reduce costs, and as pointed out by Prof Bluen, quality assurance becomes a key issue.[18]

Amongst the new models are massive open online courses (MOOCs) and similar platforms which are potential game changers in the field of management education. Again, the operational and financial models are still being constructed. Whichever model a particular business school adopts, what is clear is that having delegates sitting in a classroom for days at a time is expensive. The use of technology will enable learners to access knowledge and information from anywhere, at any time, anyhow. This then raises questions about the future of the classroom and face-to-face engagement.

Ultimately, learners will be required to spend far more time doing online "research" and preparation, so that when they engage with faculty and fellow students in the classroom the rich conversation will be about the application of their knowledge, rather than listening to lectures on subject content. This implies a significant change in the role of faculty, from distributor of content to facilitator of thinking, and the application of knowledge based on structured preparation. One of the prerequisites for such learning is that learners be willing and able to prepare for classroom engagement. For many there will be an expectation of being "taught", and the ability to find and consolidate information on the internet and elsewhere may prove difficult. The time and discipline needed to prepare for classroom-based work may be lacking. This will provide challenges for business schools and the design of such a blended model.

It is unlikely that pure online learning will replace some form of classroom interaction, even if such interaction is "virtual". One of the huge benefits of business school programmes is that they are not simply about content – in most good programmes it is a total learning experience, where the whole is greater than the sum of the (content) parts.

As I write this I am preparing to lecture on the Master of Business Leadership (MBL) programme offered by Unisa's School of Business Leadership. This is a distance learning model in which lectures play a small part in the learning experience, and participants are located around the world. In this model technology has a potentially huge role to play.

The area where there is the greatest scope for a revolutionary reinvention of learning through technology is probably in the "social" space. In many large companies (e.g., IBM), technology (and culture) facilitates connectivity amongst employees (in the case of IBM, around 450 000) globally. Hence, collaborative problem solving becomes a key strength. Connecting people with people and ideas probably presents the greatest opportunity for game-changing technology in business schools. The formal or spontaneous emergence of communities of knowledge, both relating to specific programmes and across the entire alumni, presents important opportunities for a new model of learning to supplement programmes. Gibs is exploring various options in this space.[19]

Case studies

> The case method packs more experience into each hour of learning than any other instructional approach. It stimulates students' thinking and encourages discussion. Not only is it the most relevant and practical way to learn managerial skills, it's exciting and fun.[20]

Research suggests that most top business schools use case studies as a key learning methodology – Harvard is world renowned for the development and use of such studies. In South Africa, Wits Business School has a similar case centre which generates African cases for use in business school programmes.

Case studies are a very powerful method of getting participants (normally in teams) to analyse complex "problems", debate the dilemmas that these present, and propose possible solutions. The role of the faculty is to facilitate the discussion and ensure that participants are challenged and develop a deep understanding of decision-making processes based on real-life situations. Case studies train managers to take decisions where issues are complex and key information is often missing. (To watch a Harvard professor teaching a case is to observe art in the making!)

However, the nature of case studies may change. Prof Kenneth W Freeman, Dean of Boston School of Management, points out that

> instead of static management cases, frozen in time and context, teachers will be able to offer data-rich and immersive materials and experiences, enabling students to engage in real-time problem-solving.[21]

Unfortunately, case studies still tend to be discipline specific and to focus on the discipline that the sponsoring faculty specialises in. I have always thought that the use of a case study by multiple faculty, covering different disciplines, would be a good way of illustrating the need for discipline and functional alignment in resolving strategic problems.

Experiential learning

Most business schools place considerable emphasis on experiential learning. This includes action learning projects which are very powerful in assisting learners to work effectively in teams, apply complex problem-solving processes, gather and analyse information, and persuasively present solutions to a panel of actual senior managers or executives.

Other forms of experiential learning include projects in environments with which learners are typically not familiar – many business schools design corporate social investment (CSI) projects that have community benefits, but also require learners to solve problems without the corporate resources they would normally have at their disposal.

A number of top business schools include an international study tour as a compulsory subject in their MBA programme, and many have exchange programmes with business schools globally, where learners visit the partner business school for a semester and attend classes.

Systemic issues

In my very fruitful discussions with Prof Thomas,[22] a number of systemic issues arose. There is insufficient space to address them in depth, but I highlight the following:

- The standards associated with tenure and hence remuneration are currently based on research output in academic journals. This needs to be reviewed if research and teaching are to be relevant to clients;
- In many South African business schools the challenge to employ and retain good academics is inhibited by remuneration issues. This applies particularly in South Africa to black academics. In my view, an entirely new remuneration model needs to be developed in which consulting is a means of earning considerable additional remuneration, with the added benefit of gaining relevant experience for the academic and branding the business school;
- The emphasis on the scientific and quantitative approach in management education and research needs to be tempered with strategic and systemic thinking and processes;

- In Africa specifically, business schools cannot be seen in isolation. They are part of an education system. Prof Thomas believes that the undergraduate pipeline needs to be addressed, to ensure that those entering postgraduate studies have the necessary meta-skills to succeed.

Business schools: 2025

IMAGINE THAT IT'S MAY 2025, and a new crop of business school graduates is entering the workforce. What kinds of experiences will these graduates need to find jobs in their fields? What skills will employers value most? And how will their careers be different from those of graduates today?[23]

Based on their conclusions from interviewing key thinkers in the field, *Bized Magazine* identified four attributes that will ensure business schools remain relevant in the future.

Training

This refers to the need for workers to stay up to date in a fast-changing world. It means that

the growing demand for just-in-time, brief, and highly focused learning opportunities represents "a huge opportunity for providers [...] [Wilyard] sees the possibility for more subscription-based models of learning, which would allow practitioners to access webinars and in-person discussions throughout the year to catch up on their industries.[24]

Time

As referred to previously, workers of the future will demand time-efficient ways of learning. Many different options will be available for those looking for just-in-time" learning rather than (or in addition to) lengthy, formal programmes. This suggests that knowledge can be accessed from a variety of resources (e.g., MOOCs, YouTube videos), with leading organisations providing such access.

The challenge then becomes one of accreditation and ensuring that the "whole" learning experience is greater than the sum of the parts.

In a few years, I see half of all executive education programs going out of business, unless business schools tap into the demand for shorter-term and more consumer-oriented online training options.[25]

Technology

Managers of the future will need to keep up with rapidly changing and often disruptive technology. There will be an increasing need to help organisations bridge the technological skills gap.

Team-based collaboration

Increasingly, organisations are employing a variety of matrix and other organisational designs that result in teams requiring collaboration across countries and cultures, time zones, disciplines and even organisations. The ability to work in fluid, diverse teams will be a key skill in the future. Business schools therefore need to ensure that their learners develop these skills, thus it will have to become a "core" feature of their programmes.

In a recent *Wall Street Journal* article, Kenneth W Freeman, Dean of Boston University School of Management, identified two ways in which business schools will improve in the future:[26]

1. They will be closing of the gap between industry and academia and "together we will find new ways to integrate education with the practical demands of employers";[27].

2. By increasing the impact of business school research, as discussed previously: "As with the curriculum, we will work more closely with industry leaders, routinely seeking their input and ideas as we set directions for research and engaging them directly as thought partners in projects of real relevance".[28]

Shift from content to application

Because of rapid changes in the world of business, successful employees and managers of the future will need to learn to learn, unlearn and relearn to keep up. Again, this suggests that in addition to content, cognitive capability and problem-solving processes will be key elements of any business school curriculum (see chapter in this book by Morné Mostert).

Not only will managers need to learn quickly and "rewire their brains", they will need to present logical and persuasive arguments to a variety of stakeholders. My experience is that this is currently a serious deficit amongst many programme participants.

Emotional and spiritual intelligence, which contribute to resilience, as well as belief systems aligned to the organisation, are currently valued and will increasingly be valued. What these examples illustrate, is that while content is important it is the other factors (cognitive, personal effectiveness and communications skills) that will take on greater importance in a world where content is freely available and accessible.

Neurolinguistic and other research into learning and communicating will be increasingly incorporated into business school programmes.

Conclusion

There is no doubt that business schools will continue to play a significant role in shaping Africa's talent. But business schools are expensive to run and not all their activities are income generating. It is probable, and certainly desirable, that collaboration will become an important feature of the business school landscape throughout Africa. This means partnerships between top business schools will emerge, to ensure that scarce intellectual capital and academic capability are best utilised to build the skills required by the continent.[27] The business schools that thrive will be those of significant size, resulting in economies of scale. Furthermore, for businesses to succeed in Africa, their relationship with government is a key factor. Business schools will have an important role to play in facilitating that relationship.

Business school education is in a changing space. For such schools to remain relevant and perpetuate their important roles, they will need to continually reinvent themselves in the same way that their clients do. Academia is a tough ship to turn, but leading business schools must continuously adapt to fresh needs and opportunities on the continent.

Endnotes

1   Karen O'Leonard & J Krider, *Leadership development factbook 2014: Benchmarks and trends in US leadership development*, Bersin by Deloitte, 2014, retrived 1 August 2016, <http://marketing.bersin.com/leadership-development-factbook-2014.html>.

2   Deloitte, 'Introduction', *Human capital trends 2015*, retrieved 16 February 2016, <http://www2.deloitte.com/us/en/pages/human-capital/articles/introduction-human-capital-trends.html>.

3   Academy of Management, 'How can business schools develop leaders?', 2013, retrieved 16 February 2016, <http://aom.org/DevelopLeaders/>.

4   G Petriglieri, 'The important role business schools can play in framing ...', 2013, retrieved 16 February 2016, <http://www.huffingtonpost.com/judith-samuelson/post_5639_b_3921422.html>.

5   Interview with Prof Nicola Kleyn at Gibs, 2 March 2016.

6   Interview with Prof Steve Bluen, 9 March 2016.

7   Interview with Prof Howard Thomas, 14 March 2016.

8   Kleyn, op. cit.

9   Bluen, op. cit.

10   Kleyn, op. cit.

11   J Podolny, 'Harvard Business School discusses future of the MBA', 2015, retrieved 20 February 2016, <http://hbswk.hbs.edu/item/harvard-business-school-discusses-future-of-the-mba>.

12   *The New York Times*, review of 'The silo effect' by Gillian Tett, 2015, retrieved 19 February 2016, <http://www.nytimes.com/2015/09/06/books/review/the-silo-effect-by-gillian-tett.html>.

13   Ibid.

14   Schmidty, 'Mode-2 and Mode-1 knowledge', Redbubble, 2007, retrieved 19 February 2016, <http://www.redbubble.com/people/schmidty/journal/240669-mode-2-and-mode-1-knowledge>.

15   Bluen, op. cit.

16   Kleyn, op. cit.

17   'TBSr - Technology in Business Schools Roundtable – Home', 2004, retrieved 19 February 2016, <http://www.tbsroundtable.org/>.

18   Bluen, op. cit.

19   Kleyn, op. cit.

20   'Case method teaching – Harvard Business School Press', 2015, retrieved 20 February 2016, <https://cb.hbsp.harvard.edu/cbmp/pages/content/casemethodteaching>.

21   'What business schools will look like in the future...', 2015, retrieved 20 February 2016, <http://blogs.wsj.com/experts/2015/05/01/what-business-schools-will-look-like-in-the-future/>.

22   Thomas, op. cit.

23   *Bized Magazine*, 'Are business schools ready for the future of work?', 2016, retrieved 20 February 2016, <http://www.bizedmagazine.com/archives/2016/1/features/focus-on-the-future-are-business-schools-ready-for-future-work>.

24   Ibid.

25   Ibid.

26   'What business schools will look like in the future', op. cit.

27   Bluen, op. cit.

References

Academy of Management, 'How can business schools develop leaders?', 2013, retrieved 16 February 2016, <http://aom.org/DevelopLeaders/>.

Bized Magazine, 'Are business schools ready for the future of work?', 2016, retrieved 20 February 2016, <http://www.bizedmagazine.com/archives/2016/1/features/focus-on-the-future-are-business-schools-ready-for-future-work>.

'Case method teaching – Harvard Business School Press', 2015, retrieved 20 February 2016, <https://cb.hbsp.harvard.edu/cbmp/pages/content/casemethodteaching>.

Deloitte, 'Introduction', *Human capital trends 2015*, retrieved 16 February 2016, <http://www2.deloitte.com/us/en/pages/human-capital/articles/introduction-human-capital-trends.html>.

Interview with Prof Nicola Kleyn, Dean of the Gordon Institute of Business Science, at Gibs, Johannesburg, 2 March 2016.

Interview with Prof Steve Bluen, Director of Wits Business School, Johannesburg, 9 March 2016.

Interview with Prof Howard Thomas, Director of Academic Strategy and Management Education at Singapore Management University, 14 March 2016.

O'Leonard K. & Krider, J. *Leadership development factbook 2014: Benchmarks and trends in US leadership development*, Bersin by Deloitte, 2014, retrieved 1 August 2016 <http://marketing.bersin.com/leadership-development-factbook-2014.html>.

Petriglieri, G, 'The important role business schools can play in framing ...', 2013, retrieved 16 February 2016, <http://www.huffingtonpost.com/judith-samuelson/post_5639_b_3921422.html>.

Podolny, J, 'Harvard Business School discusses future of the MBA', 2015, retrieved 20 February 2016, <http://hbswk.hbs.edu/item/harvard-business-school-discusses-future-of-the-mba>.

Schmidty, 'Mode-2 and Mode-1 knowledge', Redbubble, 2007, retrieved 19 February 2016, <http://www.redbubble.com/people/schmidty/journal/240669-mode-2-and-mode-1-knowledge>.

'TBSr - Technology in Business Schools Roundtable – Home', 2004, retrieved 19 February 2016, <http://www.tbsroundtable.org/>.

The New York Times, 'The silo effect' by Gillian Tett, 2015, retrieved 19 February 2016, <http://www.nytimes.com/2015/09/06/books/review/the-silo-effect-by-gillian-tett.html>.

'What business schools will look like in the future...', 2015, retrieved 20 February 2016, <http://blogs.wsj.com/experts/2015/05/01/what-business-schools-will-look-like-in-the-future/>.

CHAPTER 15

BUILDING AFRICA'S TECHNICAL AND VOCATIONAL SKILLS
Nazrene Mannie

This is one of the most important talent issues for Africa, and Nazrene masterfully shares frameworks and research into the subject of technical and vocational skills development. It is hence one of the most important chapters in the book!

One of the greatest challenges facing Africa is the need to establish a pool of technical and vocational skills, so that countries and organisations are not dependent on expensive expatriates for such skills. By sharing extensive research on the subject and case studies from south and central Africa, Nazrene demonstrates the success factors involved in such skills development, whether in large manufacturing organisations or small-scale agricultural communities.

One crucial factor is the partnership between the many stakeholders involved in technical and vocational training. If such skills development is to be sustainable, the entire system must be designed to be collaborative and aligned so that each role player fulfils a particular role. It demonstrates that governments are critical in providing an overarching framework for effective skills development, but that private or public colleges, employers, learners and other stakeholders are equally essential if the system as a whole is to succeed.

A major challenge facing the development of such a system is funding. As global and national economies stagnate or contract, financing for skills development often dries up. Few organisations recognise that skills development needs to be counter-cyclical to the economy. It is gratifying to see that funding agencies are able to assist in certain projects. However, employers, large and small, need to take a long-term view of needs, and ensure that programmes and projects are sustainable over time and not subject to the volatility of short-term economic variances. Skills development is a long-term process which has a history, in commodity-dependent economies, of inconsistent funding resulting in a counter-cyclical supply of skilled people – training is reduced or stopped during the "bad times", leading to skills shortages when the cycle turns.

Nazrene contributes extensive experience in research, national and sectoral policy development and the implementation of technical and vocational skills development in organisations. This experience, as the chapter demonstrates, offers great value to organisations and policy-making structures at national and sectoral levels. The chapter is essential reading for all stakeholders involved in technical and vocational skills development.

Introduction

The African continent faces numerous challenges and critical inequalities in terms of investment, job creation and poverty alleviation. There is a continent-wide need to develop proficient technical skills, as they form the backbone of thriving societies. Approaches to technical and vocational skills development have varied over the past 40-odd years, in line with a particularly severe drop in investment and a shift in focus in the 1980s as a result of economic pressures in many countries.[1] There is, however, international consensus on the value of a "holistic, integrated, inter-sectoral approach to education",[2] which includes a focus on technical and vocational education and training. Such an approach is currently reflected in multiple international organisations, including the World Bank, the International Labour Organisation (ILO) and the United Nations Educational, Scientific and Cultural Organisation (Unesco).

In South Africa, there is a clear recognition that the Technical, Vocational and Education Training (TVET) sector will be a key role player in addressing educational and skills levels in this country, as these currently create a major barrier to the attainment of the five to six per cent p.a. economic growth commonly deemed necessary to impact on unemployment. Several policies – including the National Development Plan (NDP), the Industrial Policy Action Plan (IPAP) and the New Growth Path – refer to the fact that technical skills development must be addressed as a priority.

The role of business and business leadership is key to the continent's future and can provide crucial leverage and support to address challenges related to skills development. The competitive context of business is shaped by the standards of education, productivity and skills levels of the broader society, while poverty and instability threaten profitability and productivity.

With specific reference to jobs and skills, business leaders can help shape the policy environment and corporate and education systems strategies by reaching out and influencing government at senior levels, their business peers, company and plant-level operations, and other sectors of society (e.g., communities, civil society organisations, education and training providers). In a country like South Africa, which has a very structured skills development system, the role of entities such as the South African Qualifications Authority (Saqa), the Sector Education and Training Authorities (Setas) and the Quality Council for Trades and Occupations (QCTO), amongst others, also have a pivotal role to play in the development and implementation of an integrated, multi-sectoral TVET system.

Such a commitment has been evident in technical training in recent years, where close collaboration between the private and public sectors is helping to shape curricula, lecturer development and quality delivery within the TVET environment. This involvement in shaping technical skills development is aimed at ensuring that the needs of the labour market are taken into consideration, with the added benefit of enhancing the employability of learners.

The OECD skills outlook 2015: Youth, skills and employability[3] highlights the fact that in situations where the education system and the labour market co-exist as two separate worlds, young people face a number of challenges when transitioning from one to the other. The research has found that the best way to integrate young people into the world of work is through flexible education systems which are responsive to the needs of the labour market as well the important role of engaged employers. The latter have the critical task of both designing and providing education programmes. The system must also support the need for access to high-quality career guidance and further education that can help the youth match their skills to prospective jobs, especially when institutionalised obstacles to entering the labour market (even for those with the right skills) are removed.

This chapter will attempt to highlight key elements of projects that test the hypothesis that collaboration between the public and private sectors can positively impact on technical skills development.

Case studies: South Africa

The two case studies using examples from the South African context view the TVET college system as central to the success of technical training, particularly in terms of the transfer of theoretical knowledge to learners. The TVET system is positioned within the post-school education and training environment, which is intended to address the needs of both adolescent school leavers and adult learners.

Two key policy documents have been developed: the *Green Paper for Post-School Education and Training* (2012) and the subsequent White Paper (2013), both of which take a long-term view of the public training system. The research shows that the post-school system and related institutions remain weak, with relatively poor results in a changing policy and process environment.[4]

Despite these issues, the Department of Higher Education and Training (DHET) remains committed to the TVET/FET college system. This is due to the fact that the system is a key area which can potentially arrest the challenges facing the almost four million young people who are NEETs (not in education, employment or training), by offering this increasingly marginalised section of the population options for further skills development, aligned to the needs of the labour market. NEETs are a global problem and this chapter aims to highlight possible solutions which can cut across countries and sectors. Figure 15.1 illustrates some of the issues related to NEETs.[5]

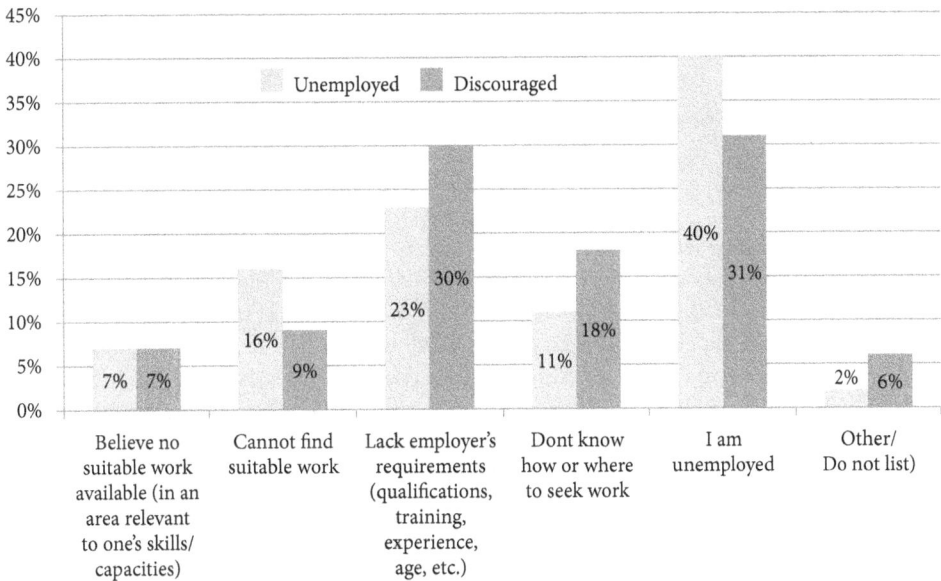

Figure 15.1   Unemployed versus NEET: Self-reported reasons for not working[6]

The Green Paper further positions the role of the sector in terms of its relationship to industry – a critical aspect of successful technical training which is aligned and responsive to the needs of the labour market:

> They [colleges] must develop close ties to workplaces in the public and private sectors, becoming responsive to the needs of the employers in their surrounding communities, and offering tailor-made programmes where possible in addition to their core programmes. In line with NSDS III, colleges must develop close ties to SETAs, which will play an increasingly important role in linking colleges with employers.[7]

The case for a business partnership in strengthening the TVET sector

Based on this commitment, the National Business Initiative (NBI), an organisation focused on maximising the relationship between business, government and society so as to grow prosperity in South Africa,[8] has pursued a number of TVET college–industry partnership initiatives within the construction and manufacturing engineering sectors, as well as lecturer development efforts within the travel and tourism environment.

Acknowledging the fact that the TVET colleges play a crucial role in developing mid-level skills with a resultant impact on the employability of college learners,[9] the findings of the NBI confirm the following:

- The success of initiatives in the TVET space are underpinned by the active participation of companies as well as commitment from the college sector and government, specifically DHET;
- On-going research and studies confirm that the profile of TVET college lecturers indicate a combination of staff who have industry experience but lack teaching qualifications, and vice versa; and
- Given national policies such as the NDP, IPAP and New Growth Path, revised curricula are required to address to the needs of emerging sectors such as the Green Economy, and to create more competitive and relevant construction and manufacturing sectors.

The projects are all at various stages of delivery. A number of solutions have, however, been generated and models exist which can be replicated in technical, vocational and skills development systems in other sectors and countries. These include:

- **Curriculum design**
  Working closely with industry experts who can influence the design and development of sound and sustainable curricula which align with the needs of industry, both theoretically and practically. The intention is to ensure that the curriculum is not strictly academic in nature, but is created with the intention that learners gain the ability to apply theoretical knowledge situationally, once they are in the workplace.
- **Strengthening college lecturers and academic support staff**
  The college must always maintain an appropriate level of skilled staff who can offer a combination of the relevant theory and practice in all vocations in which qualifications are offered. This was achieved by highlighting the findings of 2011 research which addressed college lecturers' profiles and any gaps identified during the study.[10] As the research was commissioned by the DHET, there was a commitment to address the findings. Positive outcomes include formal TVET college lecturer programmes being developed and offered in a number of universities and universities of technology.
- **Strengthening practical training in college workshops**
  The success of this element is largely based on the close cooperation between the colleges and partner companies, where support is offered in the form of equipment, the practical training of lecturers in using the equipment, as well as the presence of industry specialists who contribute their time and expertise in practical workshops as part-time lecturers.
- **Lecturer training and workplace exposure**
  The work of the NBI has highlighted the need for close and ongoing engagement with lecturers, who are the principal partners in the delivery of content within the college environment. As such, their personal continued training and development are key to increasing their competence and will result in an improvement in the knowledge base of learners. Lecturer support is two-fold: it includes a combination of placing lecturers on the same training as their industry counterparts (industry partners offer lecturers places on internal company training) and bringing lecturers into the industry environment in order to observe, first-hand, the latest techniques, equipment used and practices employed.

- **Workplace exposure for learners**

  The evidence shows that learners who have been exposed to the practical world of work, in their field of study, exponentially increase their chances of employment by up to 80 per cent.[11] This means that it is imperative for TVET learners to be exposed and orientated to the workplace in the course of their studies. All NBI projects include an element of workplace learning as a central component of project success.

How business shapes demand-led technical skills training. A case study of the Scaw Metals group

The Scaw Metals group is a leading producer of steel and steel products, with manufacturing and distribution facilities in South Africa and Australia. The company, which also has a presence in Ghana, Zambia and Namibia, produces a wide range of steel-based products that include grinding media and rolled, cast and wire rod products. These are supplied to diverse sectors in the construction, railway, power generation, mining, marine engineering and agricultural markets.

As a result of its commitment to world-class, globally recognised products, Scaw Metals has established a School of Production Excellence and launched a pilot Production Professional Development Programme. The concepts of a "Production Professional" and an accompanying "Production Professional Career Path" are intended to function as enablers in the development of a skilled and qualified workforce, which will be the foundation for building sustainable competitiveness in the manufacturing sector.[12]

The August 2015 issue of *SEIFSA News* focused on the critical value of manufacturing to the national economy. Industrialised countries across the world have realised that a vibrant manufacturing sector is a critical and essential part of their economies. Keeping manufacturing local retains revenue, creates employment and is essential to the social fabric of the economy.[13]

A fundamental competent of a vibrant manufacturing sector is a skilled labour force and Scaw has decided to focus on the professionalisation of production professionals, both from a skills perspective and the creation of a career pathway which allows for progression through ongoing learning and development. The emphasis on production employees is particularly important, as Scaw recognises that in this job category there is potential for expanded job creation, given the ratio of ten production workers to one artisan in the manufacturing sector.

Scaw Metals' School of Production Excellence was established to address the needs of the steel and engineering manufacturing sector at large, in addition to the company's own skills needs. The key focus of the school includes

- tackling the skills and career development of Scaw Metals' internal workforce – in particular, shop-floor production employees;
- sharing this facility with other industry players so as to develop and provide customised training for production employees in the steel manufacturing and fabrication sector;
- acquiring the relevant accreditation which enables it to deliver sought-after qualifications for production employees in the sector;
- promoting job-creation opportunities, promotion and the creation of small business entrepreneurship opportunities; and
- actively pursuing fabrication opportunities; i.e., to identify products which will generate a road to market and facilitate import substitution, localisation and entrepreneurship.

Key elements of the programme are the following:

- Preparing candidates to become highly skilled production professionals who can progresses from shop floor operators to production operations managers in Scaw and in the broader steel fabrication and manufacturing sector;

- Working closely with the wider sector to develop a steady talent pool of young learners who will be appropriately trained, developed and prepared to have a production fabrication and manufacturing-related career in the sector; and
- Ensuring the output of production professional workers who are key to building a sustainable steel manufacturing capability.

The programme on offer is based on a combination of 12–15 months of theoretical and practical training and assessments in the production school, as well as workplace-based experiential learning and assessments. Thereafter, learners are certified as competent to be appointed in permanent production positions on the shop-floor in Scaw Metal's plants.

A strong point of the programme is the selection of suitable candidates who demonstrate ability against an ideal competency and career interest profile. Learners who are selected enter a focused work readiness and personal mastery programme.

Only once the former have been addressed, can learners move into a technical production skills training programme, based at the production school. The programme covers all relevant modules in production operations, quality, safety and legal compliance, which must be successfully completed prior to moving into a plant for practical, on-the-job training.

The programme is unique in that it bridges fundamental skills, including English, mathematics, computer literacy, work readiness, self-leadership mastery and vocational theory and simulations. This combination is intended to thoroughly prepare learners to seamlessly enter the workplace for the work experience component of their learnership. It is advised that any company interested in rolling out similar programmes, should ensure that it offers a suitable combination of life skills along with the requisite technical skills embedded in the learning.

Another feature of the Scaw Metals programme is the customised curriculum which is rooted in the learners' industry environment. This has worked for Scaw learners, as they develop a sound understanding of industry processes and products upfront. In turn, this immersion helps them understand and master their specific role in the production manufacturing process.

The framework for the learnerships is illustrated in the schematic below:[14]

Production Training School Programme Strategy		
Production School Knowledge/theory in classroom	**Production School** Practical on training machines	Production on-the-job training. Work experience
On-the-job assessment		
National Certificate: Production Technology NQF Level 2–4. SAQA & MerSETA Accredited		

Figure 15.2   Framework for learnerships

A great deal of effort went into designing and developing a career path for production professionals. The pathway, which has multiple entry and exit points, is built on practical and theoretical knowledge progression.

The pilot programme, which is currently being rolled out, is monitored and evaluated at all stages of design and delivery. It is intended that the lessons learnt will be used to shape and improve the implementation of the programme in years to come. It is further anticipated that the programme can be replicated by other companies and industries as a model for technical skills training, with the key output being well-prepared, work-ready learners.

Building and sustaining a smallholder agri-business – a case study of initiatives in Central and West Africa

The Sustainable Smallholder Agri-Business Programme is implemented by German International Cooperation (GIZ) in Nigeria, Cameroon, Côte d'Ivoire, Ghana and Togo. The project is commissioned by the German Federal Ministry for Economic Cooperation and Development (BMZ), with financial support from the European Union and the agency NIRSAL of the Central Bank of Nigeria. It is aimed that the programme will run for four years, from 2014–2018.

The goal of the programme is to support 350 000 cocoa-producing smallholders, mainly in the cocoa-producing areas of the partner regions, to sustainably improve their income generation and food supply from diversified production.[15]

The projects focus on agricultural smallholders, as research indicates that the more than three million smallholdings in these countries produce at least 75 per cent of the world's cocoa supply. Additional agricultural income is derived mainly from food products.

The programme aims to address a number of key issues that negatively impact the optimal production of cocoa and other crops in the partner regions. The challenges span a range of issues:

- Lack of technical knowledge and skills on good agricultural practice to increase the agricultural yields of cocoa and food products;
- Lack of entrepreneurial skills which impact the ability to operate an effective and profitable business – in particular, financial management, investments with own capital, and access to both finance and new markets;
- Poverty in the region, where research indicates that the average income is just 1.50 USD per person per day; and
- The challenges relating to poverty and the lack of a diversified crop as a source of income have resulted in impoverishment, malnutrition and social problems such as child labour.[16]

The cost-effective, competitive production of quality cocoa and food commodities remains a significant priority in the national sector and economic development strategies of all the countries involved in the programme. Key themes and outcomes of the programme include the following:

- A strong element of partnership, where over 50 public and civil society organisations and companies are currently involved in terms of support and implementation;
- The development of the Farmer Business School (FBS) approach, which helps agricultural smallholders develop and apply their practical business skills;
- The establishment of Business Service Centres (BSCs) which offer technical advice, market information, financial advice and assistance; and
- Developing training aimed at improving the cost effectiveness of food production.

According to the lead implementer, the Deutsche Gesellschaft für Internationale Zusammenarbeit (GiZ GmbH), there are already a number of significant results to report on:

- Over 302 000 cocoa smallholders (27% women) have been directly trained in FBS. Training certificates, which verify their achievements, are used to access loans;
- 61 per cent of FBS graduates opened savings accounts;
- 27 per cent received loans for cocoa or food production;
- 32 000 smallholders, of whom 20 per cent are women, have sourced quality inputs from 11 BSCs;
- Cocoa yields increased between 33 and 50 per cent, and maize yields between 50 and 100 per cent;
- Annual net income from non-cocoa products increased to between €630 and 830 (baseline: €54–165 per household, depending on country);
- The FBS curriculum has been adapted and introduced by other development programmes for cotton, rice, coffee and cashew producers in eight other African countries.[17]

Table 15.1 FBS projects[17]

Overview on Farmer Business School projects and farmers trained				
Project	**Countries**	**Lead products**	**Secondary products**	**Farmers trained**
SSAB	Ghana, Nigeria, Côte d'Ivoire, Cameroon	Cocoa, rice, cotton, tomato	Maize, cassava, cowpea, egusi, maize, soy bean	266 056
COMPACI	Malawi, Zambia, Mozambique, Benin, Côte d'Ivoire, Burkina Faso, Ghana, Cameroon	Cotton	Maize, ground nuts	90 917
ProDRA	Togo	Coffee, cocoa, cashew, cotton	Maize, cassave, soy bean, cowpea	3 204
ProAGRI	Benin	Cotton, rice, cashew	Soy bean, maize	13 593
AISP	Zimbabwe	Potatoes, sesame, groundnuts, horticultural products	Maize, ground nuts	15 000
CARI	Nigeria, Burkina Faso, Ghana, Tanzania	Rice	Cowpea, egusi	1 740
MOAP	Ghana	Cocoa, oil palm, mango	Chilli, maize cassava	4 000
PDA	Burkina Faso	Rice	Tomato, onion	340
			Total	393 874

SSAB: Sustainable Smallholder Agri-Business Programme; **COMPACI:** Competitive African Cotton Initiative; **ProDRA:** Programme pour le Développement Rural et l'Agriculture; **ProAGRI:** Programme Promotion de l'Agriculture; **AISP:** Agricultural Input Supply Programme; **CARI:** Competitive African Rice Initiative; **MOAP:** Market-Oriented Agriculture Programme; **PDA:** Programme du Développement de l'Agriculture

The results to date indicate the significant impact of the project, where initial outcomes are already showing positive returns in terms of crop yield, an increase in household incomes, and the adoption and application of new technical and entrepreneurial skills.

Conclusion

A recent McKinsey report[19] on the growth outlook for South Africa has identified several specific steps in relational to vocational education and technical education, many of which have been confirmed by the South African case studies as well as the SSAB programme in Central and West Africa, namely to

- strengthen career guidance and TVET advocacy;
- deepen involvement by industry;
- strengthen young people's readiness for work; and
- develop human capital and quality assurance.

The findings reflected in the case studies highlighted here, appear to align with OECD strategies[20] aimed at tackling issues of skills development and youth unemployment.

Strategies to deal with the youth unemployment crisis aim to

- tackle weak aggregate demand and boost job creation;
- provide adequate income support to unemployed youth until labour market conditions improve, but subject to strict mutual obligations;
- maintain, and where possible expand, cost-effective active labour market measures;
- tackle demand-side barriers to the employment of low-skilled youth; and
- encourage employers to continue or expand quality apprenticeship and internship programmes.

Strategies to improve the youth's long-term employment prospects aim to

- strengthen the education system and prepare all young people for the world of work;
- strengthen the role and effectiveness of vocational education and training;
- assist with the transition to the world of work; and
- reshape labour market policy and institutions to facilitate access to employment and tackle social exclusion.

DHET's Strategic Plan, 2015/16–2019/2020[21], identifies a number of key drivers that will support the development of a sound and responsive post-school education plan which aims to

- improve the capacity of the system through infrastructure development for technical and vocational education and training;
- maintain good stakeholder relations in support of an effectual post-school education and training system; and
- ensure good corporate governance including effectual resource management within the department and its entities.

It light of these findings and the emerging policy landscape, there is a clear case for continued technical skills development which is delivered in line with national policy and industry priorities. Technical, vocational education and training that is coordinated, quality assured and built on both theory and practice, must be enhanced in order to address the critical need for sustainable economic growth across the African continent.

Endnotes

1   African Economic Outlook, 'Developing technical vocational skills in Africa', retrieved 10 July 2016, <http://www.africaneconomicoutlook.org/en/theme/developing-technical-vocational-skills-in-africa/the-rationale-for-technical-and-vocational-skills-development/brief-history-of-the-evolution-of-technical-and-vocational-skills-in-national-and-international-agendas/>.

2   Ibid.

3   Organisation for Economic Cooperation and Development (OECD), 'OECD skills outlook 2015: Youth, skills and employability', 27 May 2015, retrieved 12 July 2016, <http://dx.doi.org/10.1787/9789264234178-en>.

4   Council on Higher Education and Training, *DHET Green Paper for Post-School Education and Training*, January 2012, retrieved 10 July 2016, <http://www.che.ac.za/media_and_publications/draft-legislation/dhet-green-paper-post-school-education-and-training>.

5   African Economic Outlook, 'Youth employment', retrieved 10 July 2016, <http://www.africaneconomicoutlook.org/en/theme/youth_employment/youth-in-african-labour-markets/who-are-the-unemployed-discouraged-inactive-youth-in-africa/>.

6   Author's calculations based on Gallup World Poll, 2010, 10 July 2016.

7   *Green Paper for Post-School Education and Training*, op. cit.

8   National Business Initiative (NBI), 'About us', 2015, retrieved 2 August 2016, <http://www.nbi.org.za/about.html>.

9   National Business Initiative, 'Lecturers and the world of work', August 2015, retrieved 2 August 2016, <http://www.nbi.org.za/about.html>.

10 National Business Initiative, 'Lecturer supply, utilisation and development in the Further Education and Training College Subsystem', 2011, retrieved 2 August 2016, <http://www.nbi.org.za/about.html>.

11 National Business Initiative, 'Choices and chances 2010: FET colleges and the transition from school to work', 2011, retrieved 2 August 2016, <http://www.nbi.org.za/about.html>.

12 P Chetty, 'Case study: A unique and pioneering skills & career development initiative to build sustainable competitiveness in the steel industry and manufacturing sector, as a whole', Scaw Metals Group, October 2015, retrieved 2 August 2016, <http://www.scaw.co.za/Shared%20Documents/Releases/2013/Coverage%20Report%202013-10.pdf>.

13 *SEIFSA News*, June 2015, p. 16, retrived 10 July 2016, <http://www.scaw.co.za/Shared%20Documents/Releases/2015/Coverage%20Report%202015-06.pdf>.

14 P Chetty, op. cit.

15 GIZ, 'Sustainable smallholder agribusiness in Western and Central Africa', retrieved 10 August 2016, <https://www.giz.de/en/worldwide/16002.html>.

16 Ibid.

17 Ibid.

18 Ibid.

19 A Leke, D Fine, R Dobbs, N, Magwentshu, S Lund, C Wu & P Jacobson, *South Africa's big five: Bold priorities for inclusive growth*, McKinsey Global Institute, August 2015, accessed 10 August 2016, <http://www.mckinsey.com/global-themes/middle-east-and-africa/south-africas-bold-priorities-for-inclusive-growth>.

20 OECD, 'The OECD action plan for youth: Giving youth a better start in the labour market', 2013, retrieved 11 August 2016, <www.oecd.org/employment/Action-plan-youth.pdf and www.oecd.org/employment/action-plan-youth.htm>.

21 DHET, 'Strategic plans, 2015–2019', retrieved 10 July 2016, <http://www.dhet.gov.za/Strategic%20Plans/Strategic%20Plans/Department%20of%20Higher%20Education%20and%20Training%20Strategic%20Plan%202015-16%20-%202019-20.pdf>.

References

African Economic Outlook, 'Developing technical vocational skills in Africa', retrieved 10 July 2016, <http://www.africaneconomicoutlook.org/en/theme/developing-technical-vocational-skills-in-africa/the-rationale-for-technical-and-vocational-skills-development/brief-history-of-the-evolution-of-technical-and-vocational-skills-in-national-and-international-agendas/>.

African Economic Outlook, 'Youth employment', retrieved 10 July 2016, <http://www.africaneconomicoutlook.org/en/theme/youth_employment/youth-in-african-labour-markets/who-are-the-unemployed-discouraged-inactive-youth-in-africa/>.

Chetty, P, 'Case study: A unique and pioneering skills & career development initiative to build sustainable competitiveness in the steel industry and manufacturing sector, as a whole', Scaw Metals Group, October 2015, retrieved 2 August 2016, <http://www.scaw.co.za/Shared%20Documents/Releases/2013/Coverage%20Report%202013-10.pdf>.

Council on Higher Education and Training, *DHET Green Paper for Post-School Education and Training*, January 2012, retrieved 10 July 2016, <http://www.che.ac.za/media_and_publications/draft-legislation/dhet-green-paper-post-school-education-and-training>.

Department of Higher Education and Training (DHET), 'Strategic plans, 2015–2019', retrieved 10 July 2016, <http://www.dhet.gov.za/Strategic%20Plans/Strategic%20Plans/Department%20of%20Higher%20Education%20and%20Training%20Strategic%20Plan%202015-16%20-%202019-20.pdf

Gallup World Poll, 2010, retrieved 10 July 2016, < http://www.gallup.com/poll/145487/gallup-global-employment-tracking.aspx>.

Deutsche Gesellschaft fur Internationale Suzammenarbeit, 'Sustainable smallholder agribusiness in Western and Central Africa', retrieved 10 August 2016, <https://www.giz.de/en/worldwide/16002.html>.

Leke, A, Fine, D, Dobbs, R, Magwentshu, N, Lund, S, Wu, C & Jacobson, P, *South Africa's big five: Bold priorities for inclusive growth*, Mckinsey Global Institute, August 2015, accessed 10 August 2016, <http://www.mckinsey.com/global-themes/middle-east-and-africa/south-africas-bold-priorities-for-inclusive-growth>.

National Business Initiative, 'Choices and chances 2010: FET colleges and the transition from school to work', 2011, retrieved 2 August 2016, <http://www.nbi.org.za/about.html>.

National Business Initiative, 'Lecturer supply, utilisation and development in the Further Education and Training College Subsystem', 2011, retrieved 2 August 2016, <http://www.nbi.org.za/about.html>.

National Business Initiative (NBI), 'About us', 2015, retrieved 2 August 2016, <http://www.nbi.org.za/about.html>.

National Business Initiative, 'Lecturers and the world of work', August 2015, retrieved 2 August 2016, <http://www.nbi.org.za/about.html>.

Organisation for Economic Cooperation and Development, 'The OECD Action Plan for Youth: Giving youth a better start in the labour market', 2013, retrieved 11 August 2016, <www.oecd.org/employment/Action-plan-youth.pdf and www.oecd.org/employment/action-plan-youth.htm>.

Organisation for Economic Cooperation and Development, 'OECD skills outlook 2015: Youth, skills and employability', 27 May 2015, retrieved 12 July 2016, <http://dx.doi.org/10.1787/9789264234178-en>.

SEIFSA News, June 2015, p. 16, retrieved 11 August 2016, <http://www.scaw.co.za/Shared%20Documents/Releases/2015/Coverage%20Report%202015-06.pdf>.

PART 3

CHAPTER 16

LEADING TALENT PROCESS: DESIGNING AND IMPLEMENTING A GRADUATE DEVELOPMENT PROGRAMME
James Hu
with contributions from Seryosha Padayachee

In most leading organisations, graduate development programmes are the nursery for future executives. As such, they play a key role in socialising future talent into the world of business and into the organisation, while providing a platform on which to build functional and leadership skills.

I have been involved in designing a number of graduate development programmes and shaping the extraordinary people who join them. It is a very rewarding experience. To be successful, however, it is essential that all participants – including leaders – be committed to the process, and that a culture of graduate development permeate the organisation.

When it comes to graduate development programmes, Unilever is known globally as being amongst the best of the best. This chapter therefore makes an important contribution to the development of Africa's future talent. Unilever is one of the world's oldest companies and has the ambitious strategy to double its business by 2020. Graduate development is thus essential to providing the future leadership needed to achieve and maintain that growth. What is important, is the emphasis Unilever places on sustainability as a core component of its strategy and hence its leadership values.

When discussing graduate programmes, the issue of millennials requires attention. This chapter provides useful insights into developing them as the next generation of leaders. As with any development of leaders, a holistic approach is essential and this chapter highlights the various strategies that need to be incorporated in such a programme – from attracting the best talent, to the role of line leaders in shaping and developing them. As a company, Unilever offers a wonderful value proposition to graduates, which encompasses the purpose, strategy and values of a great organisation:

> *At Unilever, you can realise your ambition to build a bright future for yourself and the wider world. You will work with outstanding brands and outstanding people to drive sustainable business growth. Together, we'll achieve our vision to double the size of our company, reduce our environmental impact and increase our positive social impact.*

That says it all!

Introduction

The increasing digitisation and interconnectivity of the modern world has had a profound impact on the business environment. With 89 per cent of Fortune 500 companies from 1955 no longer on the list in 2014, major corporations around the world have had to adapt to increasingly agile competitors in order to remain relevant.[1] While it is a well-used term within the business world, the Vuca (volatile, uncertain, complex and ambiguous) context remains a fundamental challenge for most businesses. The rise of software as a service (SaaS), the extraordinary successes of start-ups leveraging new technologies to disrupt traditional industries and ever-changing consumer behaviour have meant that large corporates are experiencing an unprecedented, exponential rate of change. Many organisations have begun to realise that a fundamental re-thinking of their businesses may be required in order to ensure their long-term survival.

While the impact of technology – especially that of global connectivity – may be the most significant for many organisations, it has arguably become the best understood. The smart phone revolution has provided a platform for people (and by extension employees) to gain full appreciation for the impact that mobile connectivity can have on their lives, which has translated into significant opportunities for businesses. As organisations become increasingly adept at scaling to the technological challenges of the modern business environment, their attention is turning to the challenge of scaling the organisation in a way that maximises the potential of its human capital.[2] For many organisations, graduate development programmes are attractive investments, as they provide a secure, comparatively low-cost, talent pipeline for young talent who can ultimately ensure the growth of the company in both the present and the future. For Africa, as the continent with the youngest population in the world – with over 200 million individuals between the ages of 15 and 24, that is set to double by 2045 – leveraging this young talent pipeline could form a significant competitive advantage globally.[3]

As a company that has been in existence since the late 1800s, Unilever has had a remarkably simple recipe for success by focusing on building great brands and emphasising their initiatives on people development. In 1887, Unilever was the first foreign manufacturing firm to be established in South Africa with the Sunlight brand, followed by the construction of the first Unilever factory in Africa in 1911.[4] It was the beginning of Unilever's long history of investment across the continent, which continues today, following the completion of a R4.5 million manufacturing investment programme in South Africa.[5]

In its modern incarnation, Unilever serves over two billion consumers daily with its products in one out of every two households in the world.[6] With a $130 billion market capitalisation and products in over 190 countries that serve the foods, personal care, homecare and refreshments (ice creams and teas) categories, Unilever has become one of the largest fast-moving consumer goods companies in the world.[7] One of the main reasons for Unilever's continued success is its history of marketing and product innovations – from being one of the first major television advertisers to developing the first food-product website in 1995.[8] Ranked as one of the world's largest spenders on advertising by Advertising Age, Unilever's investment in its brands has been built on the foundation of its "Crafting Brands for Life" marketing strategy.[9] In order for its marketing to be effective, Unilever believes that the brands need to achieve three things: put people first, build brand love and unlock the magic.[10]

In recent years, Unilever has begun to pivot to a new business model that leverages sustainability as the growth engine for the business. By integrating sustainability into the heart of its brands, operations and people, Unilever believes it is possible to grow the business, while decoupling its environmental footprint from growth and increasing its positive social impact. To achieve such an ambitious vision, Unilever views its management trainee pipelines as central to its future success. Young talent has always played a critical role in driving continuous innovation within the Unilever business, and the company's ability to grow sustainably is dependent on driving innovations across both the product lines and the business itself.

While the DNA of Unilever has always included young talent identification and development, as the company embarked on its new sustainability-driven business model, there was the realisation that a new way of approaching graduate development programmes was required. The need for a new approach to talent sourcing coincided with the generational transition from Gen X to Gen Y (also known as the millennial generation), which brings its own unique set of talent challenges. All of this provided the ideal platform for the development of the Unilever Future Leaders Programme (UFLP) – a global graduate development programme designed for a new generation of young leaders, adaptable to any local context, and one that fully leverages Unilever's world-class talent management capabilities.

This chapter explores the topic of designing and implementing graduate development programmes through the lens of the UFLP. While Unilever's Crafting Brands for Life is primarily a marketing strategy, it serves as an ideal framework for exploring the complexities of graduate development programmes. In "Putting people first", the following section focuses on the importance of understanding your target market and designing a graduate development programme that meet the needs of the millennial workforce. In "Building brand love", we look at the design of the UFLP and in "Unlocking the magic" we explore the factors that have made the UFLP one of Africa's premier graduate development programmes.

Putting people first

Unilever is a purpose-driven organisation. From its inception, the organisation has understood that its brands have the opportunity to deliver more than just the functional benefits of its products. Just as the first Sunlight soap was designed to improve people's livelihoods by providing a low-cost method to improve hygiene,[11] Unilever believes that a deep understanding of its consumers is the key enabler to achieving its purpose of helping people feel good, look good and get more out of life.[12] For its brands, Unilever leverages a tool known as People Immersions[13] to gain the deep understanding required. People Immersions provides organisations with the opportunity to connect at a deeper human level with the people they serve. The benefit lies in obtaining broad insights into the hopes, aspirations, fears and tensions that people may hold – not just a narrow subset of consumer behaviour. In designing the UFLP, a similar approach was taken with a focus on the consumer – in this instance, young millennials. In putting "consumers" first, the UFLP was consciously designed to meet the ever-changing needs of a new generation of employees. While generational buzzwords are often associated with hyperbolic generalisations, there are broad trends which millennials consider as important, and which have significant implications for the design of a graduate development programme.

Millennials tend to have higher levels of expectation when it comes to remuneration and career advancement than other generations[14] – they expect to progress through the ranks faster, and to be compensated better. These expectations have a significant impact when it comes to balancing the attraction and development elements of a graduate development programme. Over-exaggerating idealised career paths as part of the talent attraction element will have a detrimental effect on the retention of your young talent, as they can easily become disillusioned with the gap between reality and expectation. It is also important that managers – especially those with millennials in their team – provide candid and continuous feedback on their performance and potential, in order to manage a realistic expectation of the pace of career progression.

Studies have also shown that millennials use technology at work far more than other generations, although, interestingly, they are not more likely to be early adopters of new technologies.[15] The implication is that organisations need to consider whether they are adequately leveraging technological innovations across the attraction, selection and development areas of the graduate recruitment process. The increased use of technology has the potential to bring about significant cost-savings, and to increase the consistency and efficacy of graduate development programmes. Millennials can also provide invaluable feedback within the organisation on the effectiveness of its technology platforms. These insights can be very useful for senior leaders involved in reverse mentoring programmes in that it enhances the relationship between them and young talent. There is thus significant potential to improve the buy-in of leadership in a graduate development programme. Furthermore, for many millennials, increased technology use in the workplace means that they are able to achieve a more effective work–life balance – a significant differentiator for retention.

One of the unfortunate negative stereotypes around millennials is that they are seen as "job-hoppers", i.e., moving most frequently between jobs. The challenge of this stereotype is that it makes many organisations understandably reluctant to invest in talent that may easily exit the business. While aspects of this stereotype are true – compared to other generations, millennials are more likely to accept new job offers[16] – there is a fundamental misunderstanding of why they are more likely to leave. The reality is that they place a high premium on obtaining diverse experience. Many organisations, despite having the capability to provide these experiences, do not actively do so because they are not aware of the importance of this opportunity. In addition, there is the importance which millennials place on professional skills and personal development opportunities – a lack thereof increases the likelihood of them leaving organisations.[17] Thus, organisations that are actively able to provide a diverse range of job experiences and couple these with proactive skills development interventions, will have a far greater success rate in retaining their millennial talent.

While many broader millennial trends are universally applicable, some nuances are specific to the South African context. In a research study conducted in 2015, Student Village found millennials in South Africa to be risk aversive and, when deciding on a prospective employer, it is the organisation's reputation that is the primary consideration, rather than other attributes.[18] Furthermore, there is a strong desire amongst this group to travel internationally with their employer: they view international experience as an important part of their career development and a differentiator in their future marketability.

Building brand love

The UFLP is a globally standardised accelerated development programme for graduates entering the workplace. At Unilever, future leaders are expected to be high-potential employees who can ultimately form part of the talent pipeline into senior leadership roles. By ensuring standardisation across the world, the UFLP enables greater talent mobility within the business. As future leaders are selected and developed based on the same guidelines, it is expected that graduates will be able to perform on a similar level, regardless of their country of origin. This allows them to be deployed into any key role around the world.

Five talent principles underpin the UFLP,[19] the first of which is centred on diversity and inclusion. For a global organisation like Unilever, a culture of inclusivity is critical to its success. Inclusion allows employees to bring their whole selves to work, which enables them to share their insights and experiences without worrying about potential conflicts or prejudices. These insights allow organisations to serve their consumers better. An important aspect of leadership at Unilever is the ability to foster an inclusive culture, and this is a skill that needs to be instilled in the future leaders from the beginning.

Second, as all graduates are considered to be high-potential employees, assessing their work performance can be difficult. Given that future leaders are expected to move from a position where they have no prior work experience, to being management-ready (all within three years), this exponential development curve needs to be accompanied by a continuous and holistic approach to measuring performance and potential. Future leaders are therefore measured against both standard employees and their graduate peers, to ensure that they deliver on their current role and future potential.

The third principle requires that Unilever take an enterprise-wide view of talent, so that the strongest talent is always in a position to make the biggest impact on the business. A key element of managing young talent is enabling their performance and development by entrusting them with major roles. This, while cognizant of the fact that they are unlikely to have prior experience in delivering on the job, and may lack the requisite skill to achieve delivery immediately. Given their high-potential status, organisations have to trust that future leaders are able to learn rapidly on the job, and to problem-solve effectively to achieve the desired results. Giving graduates important roles and responsibilities, ensures that they are able to develop at the required accelerated pace and deliver the biggest possible business impact.

Unilever follows the principle that it takes leaders to build leaders. As a fourth principle, it is important for line managers and the senior management team to be authentic and to demonstrate the Unilever attributes of leadership consistently and effectively. Since graduates do not necessarily have prior work experience, their leadership styles are often modelled on their experiences of Unilever leaders. This is one of the great benefits of hiring graduates – they provide a blank canvas which allows organisations to drive the right behaviours from the very beginning. If graduates learn how to be effective leaders by modelling on the best leaders the organisation has to offer, they will reinforce these behaviours and cultures when they are in leadership roles. Of course, this means that the converse is equally applicable: expose graduates to negative behaviour early on, and it can be carried over once they have been promoted.

The final talent principle recognises that while they are on a standardised programme, the organisation cannot expect to treat all graduates in the same way. All future leaders come with their own inherent strengths and weaknesses, and it is the responsibility of the organisation to develop them to be the best they can be. This diversity and the successful development of these differences will be the differentiating factors of any successful organisation.

Attracting the right talent

In the South African context, students who are candidates for graduate development programmes are more likely to receive multiple employment offers.[20] There is significant competition in the graduate talent space, as businesses from different industries are all competing for the same pool of candidates. As an example, at a mid-career recruitment level, Unilever's talent competitors are often other fast-moving consumer goods companies such as P&G, Nestlé and L'Oréal, as the candidates' work experiences play a large role in the hiring decision. At a graduate level, as all candidates have very little work experience, the hiring decision is almost entirely centred on potential. For many companies, the discipline/area of study is not a factor for consideration – they simply set a specific academic average and a bachelor's degree as the requirement. As a result, at a graduate level, Unilever's talent competitors cover the full spectrum of the business world – from financial services firms to telecoms companies and more. Given the intensity of the competition, organisations need to ensure that they run effective attraction campaigns that will deliver a good return on investment.

The starting point of a talent attraction campaign is the proposition that is on offer for potential employees. Designing your proposition is a combination of understanding what your organisation is able to offer, and combining it with research insights on what is attractive to your target audience. One of Unilever's core value propositions has always been the opportunity for employees to make a positive impact on the lives of people around the world.[21] This is particularly relevant today, and is something that resonates strongly with young talent. This proposition is at the heart of Unilever's "bright future made by you"[22] messaging, that forms part of the global attraction campaign.

The Unilever employee value proposition

> At Unilever, you can realise your ambition to build a bright future for yourself and the wider world. You will work with outstanding brands and outstanding people to drive sustainable business growth. Together, we'll achieve our vision to double the size of our company, reduce our environmental impact and increase our positive social impact.[23]

Given the millennial target demographic, the UFLP is designed to support and enhance the core EVP with a number of elements that are specific to the graduate programme. As millennials are always connected online and adept at leveraging technology in a work environment, companies can gain significant advantage by fully utilising technology in the attraction process. An example of this is the Unilever Africa Idea Trophy – a student business case competition designed to provide a feeder pipeline into the UFLP.

Case study – Business Game Competition as an attraction tool for graduate recruitment

The Unilever Africa Idea Trophy is a case study competition designed to improve youth employability across Africa by providing students with the resources and experiences necessary to prepare them for the working world. The competition is built on a digital platform designed specifically to be mobile-first. The platform is optimised for slower network speeds and can be accessed through any mobile device – from feature phones all the way through to tablets and laptops. Thus, students from across Africa are able to access Unilever case studies and tools for free, on their own devices, even with an unreliable internet connection. This means that any student can access Unilever's resources upfront, prior to entering the competition, and use them to improve their employability – this is one of the significant differentiating factors of the Unilever Africa Idea Trophy, as other business case study competitions tend to provide these resources only in the latter stages of competition and thus reach fewer people.

The case studies provide students with examples of sustainable business initiatives that Unilever has launched across Africa and serve as a way to expose them to the opportunities that exist to deliver sustainable and inclusive business growth. The resources then provide them with tools as well as basic guides to topics such as marketing, consumer insights and digital execution. With all these assets at their disposal, the students are encouraged to submit their own sustainable business ideas, with the strongest ideas shortlisted for the next round. Students who progress to the next round compete at a country level before progressing through to the Africa finals.

The Unilever Africa Idea Trophy provides a good channel for attracting graduates to the Unilever Future Leaders Program as it offers students an opportunity to explore the company. The digital platform provides an effective avenue to reach a large number of students, in a way that is comfortable, easy and fast for millennials. The focus on sustainability also ensures that students are able to assess their fit with Unilever and the level of attractiveness of the Unilever employee value proposition.

Millennials' expectations of rapid career progression mean that an accelerated graduate development programme can be an attractive proposition. In the case of Unilever, the programme is designed to accelerate the development of graduates through multiple roles, so that they are ready for a management role within three years. This is a strong selling point for potential millennial candidates, because it provides them with clarity regarding their career paths, as well as the accelerated progression. Furthermore, the rotation of graduates through multiple roles not only provides them with a broad range of development opportunities, but also fulfils millennials' desire for new and diverse experiences. By building in an international assignment as part of the rotation plans, it caps off the development of future leaders as a global resource and provides a significant differentiator to other competitors – particularly those without an international presence. Thus, by leveraging Unilever's global resources and combining them with strong millennial insight, the rotation element of the UFLP becomes a critical asset from both an attraction *and* a retention perspective.

When it comes to the channel strategy for graduate recruitment, it often involves a combination of online media and targeted campus activations. While "digital" is often deemed a comparatively inexpensive method to reach a large audience, the reality is that a comprehensive digital strategy can become very costly, very quickly. Given the algorithm changes to Facebook, Instagram, Twitter and other major social channels, paid media are necessary to reach a meaningful portion of the target demographic. One method by which organisations can reduce their media spend is by ensuring that they target their audiences effectively. By being sharp and smart with targeting parameters, organisations can effect increased return on media investments or greater cost savings.

The challenging aspect of employer branding and talent attraction on campus is that the work has to begin afresh every year, as a new cohort of students enters university. This means that consistency is critical for building and maintaining the employer brand. Part of ensuring a consistent presence on campus is to build a strong partnership with each targeted university – either through careers offices, academic staff or student organisations. These relationships are important, as they offer valuable insights into the effectiveness of campaigns and whether an organisation's messaging and proposition resonate effectively with students.

When it comes to employer brand, there are always more channels than there is budget available – from career fairs to print publications, each channel has a different strength that is relevant to different organisations. By supporting an attractive EVP with the right marketing channels, this offers the necessary reach and student applications to enable an organisation to move onto the selection stage.

Selecting the right talent

UFLP's global selection process is based on a standardised profile and uniform selection criteria. The process assesses graduates' potential based on the Unilever Standards of Leadership model[24] – which looks at five leadership attributes that are applied globally: bias for action, accountability and responsibility, consumer and customer mind-set, growth mind-set and their ability to build teams and talent.

* *Bias for action*

  Unilever emphasises "bias for action", which is considered a predictor of action-driven leadership. For graduates to succeed in the corporate environment, they need to be able to make decisions quickly and effectively. A concern with millennials in South Africa is around their aversion to risk, as well as their fear of failure.[25] By assessing a graduate's bias for action, Unilever is able to predict whether s/he is likely to display analysis paralysis or whether they can confidently make a decision after considering all the options. Furthermore, "bias for action" assesses whether graduates are able to substantiate their view confidently when challenged on their thinking and decision. If they are able to display this trait successfully, it suggests they are likely to be able to overcome team resistance and be effective in influencing others once they are in a leadership role. The ability to simplify a complex problem, carefully make the right decision and give priority where needed, is key to succeeding in the modern corporate environment.

* *Accountability and responsibility*

  For our UFLP management trainees, the ability to hold both themselves and others accountable is an important predictor of success in the Unilever environment. One of the main challenges for young graduates at Unilever is that they are constantly expected to demonstrate an ability to effectively lead people, even without the formal authority to so. In many instances, graduates work as project leads with people who are older or more experienced – albeit at the same management level – and their ability to manage these relationships is critical to their success. If they are able to break down complexity, articulate tasks and expectations clearly, and ensure that there is a clear plan to deliver the work for both themselves and the rest of the team, this is a positive indicator that they have the potential to succeed within the business.

- *Consumer and customer focus*

As a company that serves the needs of over two billion consumers daily, Unilever's leaders are expected to be passionate advocates for improving the lives of their consumers. If a graduate can demonstrate a strong ability to listen to others and then articulate their needs in a way that shows an understanding of what is required, this suggests a potential for "bringing the voice of the consumer" into everything Unilever does. It is also an important attribute for driving innovation within the business, as graduates need to be able to find the human truths and insights which are at the heart of many of Unilever's product innovations.

Omo: Dirt is good

The consumer insight at the core of Omo is an understanding that there is an inherent tension for every parent between their controlling instincts (vis-à-vis dirt) and their desire for their children to be free to play, grow and discover the world for themselves. Omo's insight allowed the brand to approach "dirt" – normally seen as the enemy by parents – as an ally for children's development. By allowing children to play freely and grow by interacting with nature, parents can focus on the important moments with their children, rather than be consumed with worrying about the challenges of removing stains from the playing activity. This understanding of the consumer is the differentiator for Omo. The expectation for all Unilever future leaders is that they are able advocates and enable their consumers to lead better lives through these insights.

- *Growth mindset*

Ultimately, business leaders must demonstrate the ability to deliver growth, as well as return value to the shareholders. Future leaders need to show an ability to innovate and challenge the status quo in order to enable business growth. By proactively seeking opportunities to drive sustainability in their business areas, future leaders have the opportunity to create a brighter future for all, as shown in the Unilever Ola Ice Cream example.

Ola Ice Cream

As an "impulse" purchase, ice cream is a product category that needs to be readily available for consumers, which makes its distribution network critical to its success. Faced with the mammoth challenge of ensuring a sufficient supply, the Ola team saw this as an opportunity to tackle the increasing rate of unemployment in South Africa. Through the Ola bicycle vendor, a micro-entrepreneur initiative, Unilever was able to enable entrepreneurs to build their own ice-cream businesses by providing the necessary training, equipment and resources to get them started. The result of this was the creation of 2 200 new jobs in South Africa that simultaneously contributed towards the growth of Ola Ice Cream. This demonstrates the growth mindset that all Future Leaders need to display, for Unilever to succeed in bringing about sustainable growth.

- **Building talent and teams**

As future leaders of the Unilever business, it is important that graduates are able to demonstrate a strong ability to build talent and teams around them. Their ability to collaborate effectively with others to share ideas and expertise is a good indicator of their future leadership style. In an environment where there is never sufficient time, the importance that future leaders place on listening and learning from the experience of others will greatly aid in their success.

For organisations looking to recruit graduate talent, it is critical to understand the attributes that made them successful as a business. By understanding these success attributes, organisations can build a clear view of the ideal graduate profile that will then ensure the right level of consistency and organisational fit in the selection process. All selection processes must be tailored to meet the needs of the organisation sufficiently. For Unilever, this process involves a combination of psychometric assessments, job simulations, interviews and assessments. The graduate selection process can be time and resource intensive; however, given that graduate programmes are a significant long-term investment, this process must be completed correctly, to ensure that organisations deliver a return on graduate investment.

Unlocking the magic

Developing talent the Unilever way

Unilever's leadership development principle is rooted in the idea that it takes strong leaders to build leaders. By developing leaders who are resilient, values-led and purpose-driven, they ensure that the right culture and performance permeate the business. This belief and a commitment to build strong leaders form the bedrock of Unilever's culture and success as one of the world's most admired companies. To build leadership capability, Unilever has developed a suite of internal courses that focus on building leadership and coaching capability at all management levels. As employees progress to the next management level, this is reinforced and further developed. The impact on the graduate development programme is that young talent entering the business are exposed to a wide network of strong coaches and mentors who are committed to their development and success.

Thuli Sigasa – Unilever HR future leader

As someone who didn't have the luxury of her parents being able to afford her university fees, I know what it is like to have to make a plan. I was fortunate enough to get the opportunity eventually to get a university education through hard work and perseverance. Looking back, the struggles to get my degree were worth the sacrifices – I know now that it is something I would do again without hesitation. It also means that my job, and the opportunity to be on a graduate programme, is more than just a job – it is a lifeline that allows me to take care of those who made endless sacrifices so that I could be here today.

Unilever's learning and talent development philosophy is based on the 70/20/10 principle that sees on-the-job learning as the most critical element of development. With around 70 per cent of learning taking place on the job, future leaders' development needs should be planned around the specific roles that will best provide them with the opportunity to grasp those skills fully. The remaining 30 per cent of the learning is then split, with 20 per cent coming through coaching relationships with subject matter experts and ten per cent through formal learning interventions (training courses, e-learning activities). Only when future leaders can demonstrate that they have fully mastered their job – by displaying the right behaviours and delivering on the required business results – can those specific development areas be considered closed off. It is this learning philosophy which informs the job-rotation roadmap that is at the core of the UFLP.

Engineering future leader roadmap

The engineering unilever future leader begins his/her journey in the business with an initial three-month role in the Customer Development team. The latter provides graduates with an important grounding of the Unilever business through sales channels, which also allows them to expand their knowledge of Unilever products. This experience allows future leaders to gain real operational understanding in the field and to grasp the challenges of translating strategy into execution. By spending time in stores and interacting with both the consumer and the customer (i.e. retailers), future leaders are able to gain valuable insights into how consumers interact with Unilever products, and to develop insight into competitor products.

The business knowledge provided by the Customer Development rotation serves as a compass to orient future leaders in their home function roles. One of the biggest challenges that graduates face when entering the workplace is their limited understanding of how all the functional areas/departments operate together to deliver business results. Without a broad business perspective of how the interdependencies work, graduates can easily begin working in departmental silos. Teams that operate in their own silos can be productive in delivering their own KPIs, but counter-productive in delivering the overall business objective.

The first home rotation for an engineering Unilever future leader is designed to build professional skills and an understanding of supply chain basics. A good example of a first role is that of a Process Engineer – a well-defined job with a clear set of responsibilities. The role provides a comprehensive overview of the end-to-end process within a manufacturing plant, and has a strong tie-in with the rest of the business, as it is responsible for delivering product innovations. There is strong support from both the engineering and operational teams to provide future leaders with guidance and coaching. Thus, this is an ideal first role to immerse the graduate within the supply chain and engineering spaces.

As future leaders master the supply chain basics, their next role should provide them with an opportunity to build their professional or technical skills. In the instance of engineering future leaders, an ideal second role is that of Project Engineer. The role requires them to build their technical competencies, and to deliver on a tangible engineering project. The requirements of the role mean that future leaders develop project management as well as leadership skills if they act as project leads. Ultimately, the completion of this role should be accompanied by the full delivery of the project, which would demonstrate mastery of the technical and leadership skills required to move on to the next assignment.

Following the completion of the first three roles, the engineering future leader should have developed a good business understanding, as well as sound technical abilities and should be fully operational in their functional space. At this point, the future leader should be sent on an international assignment, as they are now equipped to succeed in an overseas role. International assignments should be selected based on the right development fit – e.g., a graduate might have a specific interest in working in the food sector, and an international assignment can develop them into an engineering expert in that specific category. The role should allow them, again, to deliver on a specific project objective that will prove their capability in a specific professional/technical area.

On their return to their home country, future leaders should be placed in a final role which will determine their readiness for management. For Engineering future leaders, their final role should be that of Assistant Engineer, where they are required to lead bigger teams. This role ensures the final development of their leadership capabilities and focuses on driving broader business performance. It also provides the senior leadership team with tangible/measurable proof of the development of the future leader, while allowing for an assessment of the best-fit management role for the graduate to take on post completion of the UFLP.

The condensed and accelerated nature of role rotations means it can be challenging for graduates to settle into their roles, as they are constantly building new relationships and adapting to new team dynamics. Furthermore, there is immense pressure on them – both self-inflicted and exterted by the organisation – to "hit the ground running" and succeed immediately. Research has shown that the younger an employee is and the shorter their length of service, the higher the risk of them leaving the organisation. To mitigate this risk and provide adequate support to future leaders in their role, Unilever provides a robust on-boarding programme aimed at ensuring that graduates are able to settle fully into the organisation.

A comprehensive on-boarding initiative provides a number of benefits. Driving employee engagement with future leaders right from the beginning of their careers can build graduates into brand ambassadors for the organisation. As graduates are often influential within their peer group, they can become highly effective tools in building the organisation's employer brand. Effective on-boarding also guarantees that the information shared with graduates remains consistent – it avoids the confusion and uncertainty that come with relying on disparate sources of information. By providing the business, functional and job-specific information necessary for graduates to be effective in their roles as quickly as possible, organisations can ensure that graduates start their development journey earlier. Throughout the development cycle of the future leaders, they will receive continuous developmental support from their line managers, mentors, HR business partners, as well as their peers in other functional areas of the business (this is an often-forgotten resource that organisations can leverage further).

Finally...

Graduate programmes are designed to be challenging. Young graduates are not only transitioning from university into the working world, but are also adapting to managing adult responsibilities and often adjusting to life in a new city – without their established social support networks. Added to this dynamic are their accountabilities at work and the gruelling demands of building their technical and leadership capabilities simultaneously. This is why it is imperative that companies are diligent in managing the end-to-end process of graduate recruitment effectively – any shortcoming in such an overwhelming environment can lead to problems for the organisation. However, companies that get this right can realise a significant long-term return on their graduate investment. For Unilever, its long history of graduate recruitment has meant that it has been able to benefit from a strong pipeline of young talent, many of whom have moved on to senior roles within the business. This talent pipeline has enabled Unilever's sustained period of growth and will be continue to play a major role as the company looks to realise its ambition of doubling the size of its business by 2020. By putting people first, building a graduate brand that people love and unlocking the magic of young talent, Unilever serves as a testament to the value that graduate development programmes can bring to businesses around the world.

Endnotes

1   S Ismail, MS Malone, & Y Van Geest, 2014
2   Ibid.
3   African Economic Outlook, 2015
4   Unilever, 'A brighter future: A better business', retrieved 1 August 2016, <https://www.unilever.co.za/> More detailed information is derived from internal documents which are not available to the public.
5   Ibid.
6   Ibid.
7   Ibid.
8   Ibid.
9   Ibid.
10 *Marketing Magazine*, 'Unilever CMO's vision for the future of marketing', 23 June 2014, retrieved 2 August 2016, <http://www.marketingmag.ca/news/cannes2014/unilever-cmos-vision-for-the-future-of-marketing-115967>
11 Ibid.

12   Ibid.
13   Ibid.
14   CEB Corporate Leadership Council, *The millennial myth*, CEB Corporate Leadership Council, Arlington, VA, 2014.
15   Ibid.
16   Ibid.
17   Ibid.
18   Student Village, Afrillennials™: SA's future leaders, Student Marketing, 2015, retrieved 10 July 2016, <http://www.studentmarketing.co.za/afrillennials-sas-future-leaders/>.
19   Unilever, op. cit.
20   South African Graduate Employers Association (SAGEA), *The SAGEA candidate insights 2015*, High Fliers Research, Cape Town, 2015.
21   Unilever, op. cit.
22   Ibid.
23   Ibid.
24   Ibid.
25   Student Village, op. cit.

References

African Economic Outlook, 'Promoting youth employment in Africa', retrieved 28 May 2015, ,<http://www.africaneconomicoutlook.org/en/theme/youth_employment/>.

CEB Corporate Leadership Council, *The millennial myth*, CEB Corporate Leadership Council, Arlington, VA, 2014.

Ismail, S, MS Malone & Y Van Geest, *Exponential organizations*, Diversion Books, New York, 2014.

Student Village, 'Afrillennials™: SA's future leaders', Student Marketing, 2015, retrieved 10 July 2016, <http://www.studentmarketing.co.za/afrillennials-sas-future-leaders/>.

South African Graduate Employers Association (SAGEA), *The SAGEA candidate insights 2015*, High Fliers Research, Cape Town, 2015.

Unilever,' A brighter future: A better business', retrieved 1 August 2016, https://www.unilever.co.za/about/who-we-are/our-history/

Additional readings

Jones, G, *Unilever: Transformation and tradition*, Harvard Business School, 28 November 2005, retrieved 10 July 2016, http://hbswk.hbs.edu/item/unilever-transformation-and-tradition.

Rayapura, A, *Millennials most sustainability-conscious generation yet, but don't call them 'environmentalists'*, Sustainable Brands, 11 March 2014, retrieved 10 July 2016, <http://www.sustainablebrands.com/news_and_views/stakeholder_trends_insights/aarthi_rayapura/millennials_most_sustainability_conscious>.

CHAPTER 17

FROM POTENTIAL TO PERFORMANCE
Lisa Ashton and Jacques Haworth

One of the most difficult tasks facing leaders and talent managers in organisations is the ability to identify potential leadership or specialist talent, and to do this within the framework of a talent and succession strategy. The identification of potential provides the basis for most other talent processes, such as

- selection
- succession
- deployment
- development.

The incorrect assessment of potential, resulting in inappropriate appointments, can have devastating consequences for an organisation and the individuals concerned. An understanding of the potential of an individual, timeous appointments and effective development can significantly contribute to the successful engagement and retention of talent. By understanding the collective potential in an organisation, strategic decisions can be made about the capability of the organisation to execute its strategy.

In this chapter, Lisa Ashton and Jacques Haworth provide a framework to enable organisations to assess individual and organisational potential. They define many terms that are used interchangeably, but which actually have specific meanings. Using the stratified systems framework developed by Elliot Jacques, they show the relationship between different levels of work and the competencies required to perform at each level. This is positioned within the context of succession management as well as other talent management processes.

This chapter provides essential insights into the assessment of potential – the core of any talent management system. It is a privilege to have this contribution by two authors with extensive experience in the field, gained through working with organisations across the world in almost all sectors. Their wealth of experience, combined with their rigorous research base, makes this chapter a powerful contribution to any talent management strategy.

Introduction

During tough times, there is increased pressure on every business function to demonstrate a direct (positive) impact on business performance. The functions that successfully demonstrate business measures (revenue, time-to-market, market share, profit) receive the majority of the attention and available resources.

Functions that cannot demonstrate such impacts suffer through endless budget cuts, outsourcing evaluations and budget freezes. In most organisations there is a relatively clear dividing line between the "haves" and the "have-nots". Unfortunately, HR is generally on the side of the "have-nots". The world of sport understands the importance of identifying, nurturing and developing potential, and successful corporations now also understand that identifying potential and appointing the right leaders/specialists in an organisation will ensure that the organisation gets a high return on its investment in its people and on the high cost of developing its people.

Measuring an individuals' current performance can be relatively straightforward, but assessing whether they have the potential to take on greater responsibility in the future is far more difficult. On the one hand, potential partly has to do with an individual's desire/ambition to lead – or at least to move up the organisational hierarchy. But, on the other hand, we have to ask: Do they have the ability to do this?

For organisations, this is a critical question to ask, and one which is directly related to the human resource return on investment (and therefore also the business performance). Whether appointing new employees or developing existing employees (both of which come at a significant cost), the incorrect identification of potential could lead to non-performance/a waste of human resources as well as a poor return on investment when it comes to training spend.

Individuals with potential are not necessarily ready to step into leadership roles or to take on more responsibilities straight away. They need a capacity to learn and grow, demonstrated either in their day-to-day work or their performance on learning programmes. We know that as roles become more complex, the work environment becomes increasingly uncertain. This means that the nature of the judgement required will differ, making this a very important quality to look at when identifying future leaders.

Mistaking a high-performing employee for a high-potential employee can be a very costly affair. This happens all the time: a top-performing salesperson might be promoted to sales manager, and may struggle to transition from attaining sales goals to helping a team of more junior salespeople achieve their goals.

Performance and potential are not mutually exclusive; people always possess a combination of both. But a manager who understands the difference will be more effective in engaging and retaining employees who exemplify aptitude in one or both. To this end, this chapter outlines strategies any manager can apply to identify, assess and develop high potentials and high performers. Should this be done consistently and successfully, it can result in greater individual effectiveness and performance, and therefore also improved organisational performance and sustainability.

Defining concepts

High-potential individuals can be difficult to identify, for two reasons: 1) high performance is so blindingly easy to observe that it drowns out the less obvious attributes and behaviours that characterise high potential, such as leadership, change management, or strategic/learning capabilities; and 2) few organisations codify the attributes and competencies they value in their ideal employees. This means that managers do not know precisely what to look for when trying to assess potential. As a result, most managers focus exclusively on performance, and that can be a problem.

This section is focused on clarifying the concepts we will be using in this chapter to define leadership and its relationship to performance and potential. We also need to understand the concepts of potential and competence – important concepts in the assessment of potential and our understanding of talent management and succession planning.

Potential

Potential is what you can do in the future, while performance is about what you can do at present. Potential refers to innate capacities in the form of aptitudes, cognitive abilities and personality styles – factors that are usually innate to an individual. If the potential is there it can be developed, but if it is not intrinsically part of an individual it cannot easily be changed or developed. For example, successful professional athletes all have an innate athletic potential which is further developed through practice.

Implicit in the definition of potential is a reference to a future state of success, i.e., it is a prediction of whether an individual could succeed in future. In addition, one also has to ask: potential for what? In organisations, this is often broadly determined either as leadership or as specialist potential.

Indicators of potential can also change when employees' context changes, e.g., a young high-performing supervisor may be seen by the organisation as having excellent potential to become a middle manager, but s/he may choose instead to become a specialist as this seems more interesting.

Competence

Unlike potential, competence can be taught or developed. Competence is usually defined as a combination of knowledge, skills and attitudes. While knowledge and skills are easy to teach or develop, the same does not apply to attitudes. It is, however, possible to develop behaviours.

Talent management

The literature is full of convoluted definitions for talent management, but we define it simply as follows: "Having fully performing individuals, doing the right work, at the right level, now and in the future."

It may sound simple, but it involves many parallel systems, process and interventions (see Figure 17.1). We view a manager or leader's role as a function of three tasks: tasking, trusting and tending. This means that individuals need to be clear about what is expected of them, what they are going to be measured by, and their job descriptions need to be appropriate, necessary and aligned to best practice (tasking). Individuals need to be entrusted with those responsibilities and must be allowed to use their own judgement (trusting). Finally, managers and leaders have to create the conditions for their employees to be successful by ensuring that they have the resources, knowledge and skills to perform, by coaching and developing them, and by managing their performance.

Talent management is about potential AND performance, where performance is used to identify what the individual has already successfully achieved, and potential is used to identify what they may still be capable of achieving in the future.

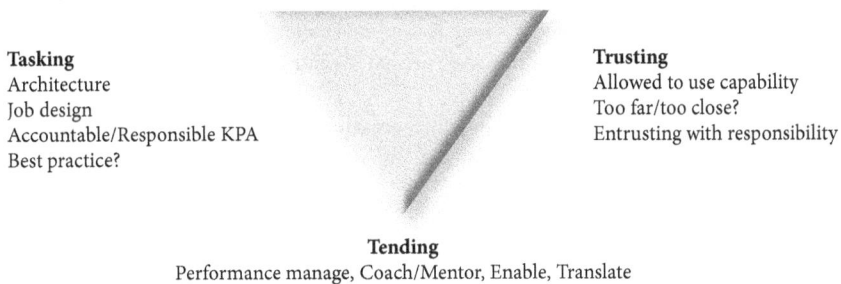

Tasking
Architecture
Job design
Accountable/Responsible KPA
Best practice?

Trusting
Allowed to use capability
Too far/too close?
Entrusting with responsibility

Tending
Performance manage, Coach/Mentor, Enable, Translate

Figure 17.1   Talent management and the Tripod of Work[1]

Succession planning

Succession planning can be defined as "filling a job quickly with a high level of confidence". Organisational sustainability is (amongst other things) dependent on having succession plans in place and ensuring that a person is ready to take over a new role as soon as it becomes vacant. Here the key questions to be asked are: Do we have successors for critical positions? Will they be ready when we think they will be needed? If the answer is no, it may be necessary to identify external successors in advance, especially for critical leadership or technical positions.

Effective succession planning enables the organisation to know which strategy to apply to certain roles: buy, borrow, bind, build, boot or boost.

The next section focuses on a framework that will help us understand work, potential, competencies and leadership at each level.

A framework for understanding leadership at all levels

Elliott Jacques developed a model that outlines the work and accountabilities needed in each organisation to clarify the expectations a company has of its people.[2] He described Stratified Systems Theory, also known as Levels of Work, which will assist us in understanding leadership and specialist potential at all levels in an organisation.

Level 1: Quality

Work at this level is about making or doing things where the output is completely specified beforehand, and where delivery requires set procedures to be followed. Problems are addressed using previously learned methods. There is practical watchfulness for any variations in process, however subtle, and the use of discretion and initiative to decide how to rectify these within clearly set boundaries. If set methods do not work or are inappropriate, the response is to report back and seek guidance. There is significant impact on organisational quality and costs through work performed at this level, because information is gathered on the spot.

People at this level are responsible for task execution, driving immediate response times, solving operational problems and using information to deliver excellence. They are typically "hands-on" and value accuracy and precision.

Level 2: Service

This level is traditionally known as first-line management or first-level specialist work. People have full authority for their teams and for providing service to customers and clients, or in given situations, and also to staff in response to individual needs. Issues or problems are addressed on a case-by-case basis, with each situation examined and a known solution applied. People work within given frameworks of policy, processes and systems, although they do make suggestions for improvement. They outline effective procedures to enable those working at a quality level to provide quality goods and services.

People at this level can be specialists supporting others to achieve their goals, or they could be managers/supervisors who put rules, procedures and specifications in place so that quality can happen at the level below them.

Level 3: Practice

This level of work is about managing effective operations with accountability for operating systems and processes rather than individual incidences, cases, issues or problems. Work is about ensuring that systems and processes represent best practice, that annual ongoing planning and budgeting are undertaken based on operational trends, patterns and cycles, and accountability for all resources – people, raw materials, services, technology and money. Recommendations for changes to services or products are based on analysing trends and patterns identified through real-time operational performance data and innovation, and fine-tuning in line with changing work practices. This theme provides the context for the operational themes of work.

People at this level construct and improve systems for the optimal utilisation of resources, and their work has a direct impact on profitability. They are also responsible for establishing best practices.

Level 4: Strategic development

This level involves anticipating possible future scenarios based on what is known about current and future competitors, modelling these against each other and against what is known, and contributing to the overall strategic intent of the organisation. Work is about turning that strategic intent into operational reality through the termination of old and/or design and the development of new systems, products and services that impact the organisation, it is about integrating systems, services or projects in alignment with overall objectives.

People at this level are responsible for positioning the organisation within its market context and creating the strategy and business models that will move the organisation from its current reality to its strategic intent. They are transformational leaders who are competent when it comes to integrating new futures, new products, services and markets.

Level 5: Strategic intent

Leaders at this level take accountability for the viability of entire organisations as long-term financial and social entities, shaping organisations' external socio-economic, national environments and corporate strategies and direction. Maintaining the organisation's reputation with stakeholders through clearly stating and adhering to overall intent is paramount.

People at this level are responsible for shaping the organisational strategic intent to ensure long-term sustainability.

From the discussion above it is clear that the requirements for success change from level to level (see Figure 17.2).

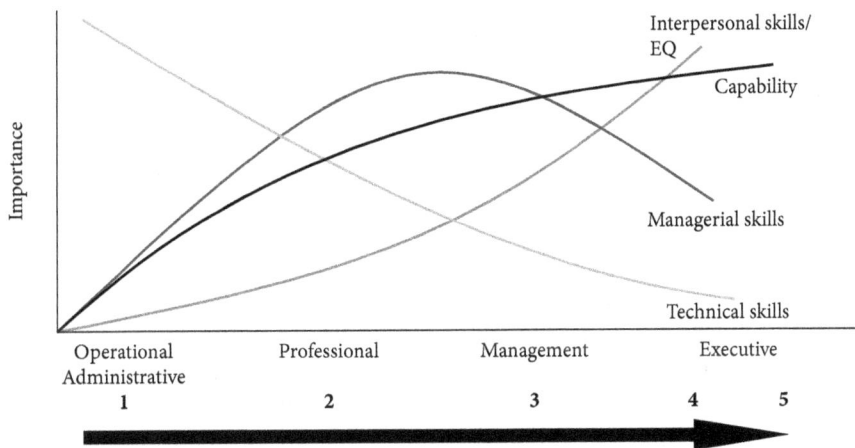

Figure 17.2   *The changing requirements for success*[3]

Potential

Assessing potential

Assessing potential takes us back to the question of "potential for what?" For operational roles, this means that the organisation should first specify the job description, before specifying the requisite knowledge, skills and attitudes for the role. This allows for a definition of what competencies individuals should be assessed against when determining their potential for either more complex managerial or specialist roles.

For strategic roles, where the role is by definition less clearly defined, track record and key competencies (stakeholder management, values, emotional intelligence, comfort with uncertainty) are usually assessed.

When assessing operational potential the following are often considered:

- **Knowledge:** usually assessed through having a recognised prerequisite qualification;
- **Experience:** this could be in the form of having the prerequisite experience in performing certain activities; when assessing potential, experience can also substitute for select qualifications in certain instances;
- **Values:** factors that will impact an individual's motivation and engagement, e.g., it might be an important value for an individual to have a high degree of autonomy in their work;
- **Competencies:** these often relate to three major aspects, namely
  - performing tasks
  - engaging with people
  - self-management.

Performing tasks comprise thinking (cognitive) skills, planning and executing skills and decision-making skills or judgement. At different levels of work complexity, these skills and behaviours may look different.

a) Cognitive competencies: typically this has to do with the ability to solve problems and process information effectively. At high levels of work it might comprise conceptual thinking, whereas at less complex work levels it might comprise detailed problem solving;

b) Capability: this is defined as the potential to apply judgement in a more complex work role in the future; and

c) Planning: at more complex work levels this is strategic, longer-term planning and at less complex levels it is detail planning making use of deadlines and milestones.

Engaging with people relates to the individual's ability to maintain good relationships and, in a leadership context, to realise and maintain performance in individuals.

a) Interpersonal competencies: this entails establishing good relationships with others, communicating effectively, dealing with conflict, stakeholder relationships, and at higher work levels may even include political skills; and

b) Leadership: this involves structuring work for others, delegating effectively and coaching individuals towards effective performance.

Self management relates to the effective use of emotional intelligence, as well as stress management. Effective self-management increasingly encompasses aspects of physical health (sufficient sleep, exercise, hydration); this is as a result of recent neuroscience research which shows the effect of these factors on brain performance.

Once the competencies have been specified (what must be assessed), a choice has to be made about the "how". Here, a myriad options are available, including interviews, psychometric assessments and simulation exercises.

Validity when assessing potential

An important consideration is the validity of the technique, both in terms of the reassurance that it does indeed measure what we need it to measure (construct validity), as well as some reassurance that the technique is able to predict with a reasonable degree of accuracy how someone is likely to behave in future (predictive validity). In addition, we need to ensure that the technique does not unfairly disadvantage certain groups of individuals and that the assessment process is conducted in a fair and unbiased manner.

Figure 17.3 shows which techniques tend to be better predictors of future performance.

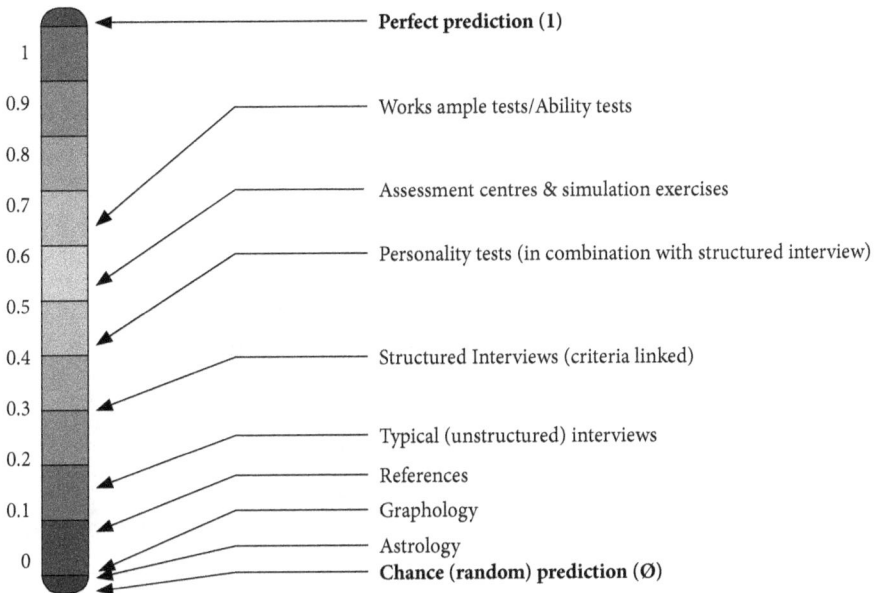

Figure 17.3   Techniques for predicting future performance[4]

Considering Figure 17.3, ability tests and assessment centres clearly tend to be better predictors of future operational job performance in general, whereas unstructured interviews (which are popularly used as a sole basis for recruitment by many organisations) are very poor predictors of future performance.

This indicates that one should think carefully about what tools and assessments to use to assist in identifying future potential. The cost of more rigorous, structured assessment methods with better predictive power would certainly outweigh the cost of an incorrect placement.

How to identify potential at different levels

In Figure 17.3 it is clear that research has shown that not all assessment techniques are good predictors of future potential. In general, the most predictive kind is that of cognitive potential, however, in today's world a leader who cannot get things done through others is unlikely to attain success in the long term.

For this reason, various types of potential are assessed, using techniques with the highest predictive value (usually a combination of simulation exercises, cognitive assessments and style/value indicators). In many companies, determining an individual's future potential is left to the judgement of the immediate manager. There are two problems with this:

1.   It is dependent on the manager's ability to successfully identify potential as well as the manager's own potential, which makes it a less objective assessment; and
2.   Managers confuse current performance with future potential, and current performance does not necessarily translate well into/accurately predict potential at the next level of work.

Table 17.1 provides an overview of the potential that needs to be assessed at different levels, as well as the techniques that can be used to assess this. Where an external applicant may not meet minimum requirements, this can be used as a guideline. In addition, when determining potential for the next level of work, the table offers a framework of critical potential that needs to be assessed.

Table 17.1   Techniques for determining critical potential at various levels

Management level	Critical potential	Techniques					
		Interview	Simulation exercise	Psychometric assessment	Situational judgement tests	360	Complexity/judgement assessment
Executive	Stakeholder management	X	X	X	X	X	
	Strategic thinking	X	X			X	X
	Strategic planning	X	X				X
	Self-management			X			
Senior Manager	Leadership	X	X	X	X	X	
	Emotional intelligence			X			
	Values	X		X			
	Judgement						X
Middle Manager	Leadership		X	X	X	X	X
	Operational planning	X	X	X	X		
	Cognitive ability			X			
	Judgement						X
	Values	X		X			
Supervisor	Leadership	X	X	X	X		
	Resilience			X			
	Cognitive ability	X		X			
	Values	X		X			
	Operational planning						
Operator	Speed and accuracy		X	X			
	Attention to detail		X	X			
	Interpersonal skills	X	X	X		X	
	Self-management	X		X			
	Learning potential			X			

Developing potential

In order to develop potential, a well-defined leadership or development framework should be in place. This means that organisations should be clear about what skills, capabilities, competencies and knowledge need to be developed at each level. Development processes should directly link to a competency framework, as well as the outputs of an assessment process.

In addition to having a clearly defined leadership or development framework in place, organisations are urged to consider the performance of their employees. Many a successful manager has learnt that "there can be no potential without performance". It would therefore be fair to consider the development of potential within the context of levels of work and performance. Figure 17.4 depicts potential on the Y-axis and performance on the X-axis. Four categories of employee are depicted: Stars, Problem Children, Icebergs and Backbones.

Stars: High performance and higher potential

The best way to develop these employees is to agree on challenging, stretching work opportunities for them. Examples include projects, career development, greater responsibility and experiential learning. Such opportunities are important, as these employees are likely to leave the organisation should they not be offered career advancement opportunities.

They could also be provided with appropriate mentoring and coaching. It is advisable to explore and encourage them to take up leadership opportunities during which they can set standards for other staff, or raise standards.

Backbone: High performance and suitable potential

It is important to acknowledge the effort and contribution of these employees, as they are very valuable to the organisation. They may be specialists or may even have reached their ceiling in the organisation, but they still need to be developed. Specialised training and personal development are usually recommended. One of the ways to develop these employees is to offer them new challenges and responsibilities, as appropriate to their work and level, or to stretch them to the extent that they are comfortable.

It is also wise to utilise them as coaches for Icebergs at the same level, or to ask them to coach/mentor Backbones at the level below them.

It is advisable to look for any hidden high potential – these individuals may, for example, become excellent trainers who are capable of transferring their skills to younger people in the organisation.

Problem Children: Low performance despite higher potential

These employees often have the potential, yet they do not perform. In such instances it is vital to find out what may be hindering their performance. The recommendation is that you confirm and acknowledge their potential, understand their performance issues, counsel them and build trust.

Explore and agree on ways to improve their performance. They may require technical skills, training, experience, on-the-job training/coaching or perhaps just appropriate tools and resources.

Icebergs: Low performance and suitable potential

These employees may have the appropriate potential or may be a bit stretched in their roles, but they are not performing. In cases such as these, appropriate performance management and counselling are crucial. Again, it would be prudent to consider why these employees are not performing and then to take corrective action, i.e., training and development. The other alternative may be to facilitate more fitting roles for these individuals – roles in which they can perform or which will be better suited to their skills and competencies. Linked with performance improvement is the need to provide them with direction, purpose and opportunities.

At times it may be necessary to assist or enable them to move one level lower – or out of the organisation, if it is best for all concerned.

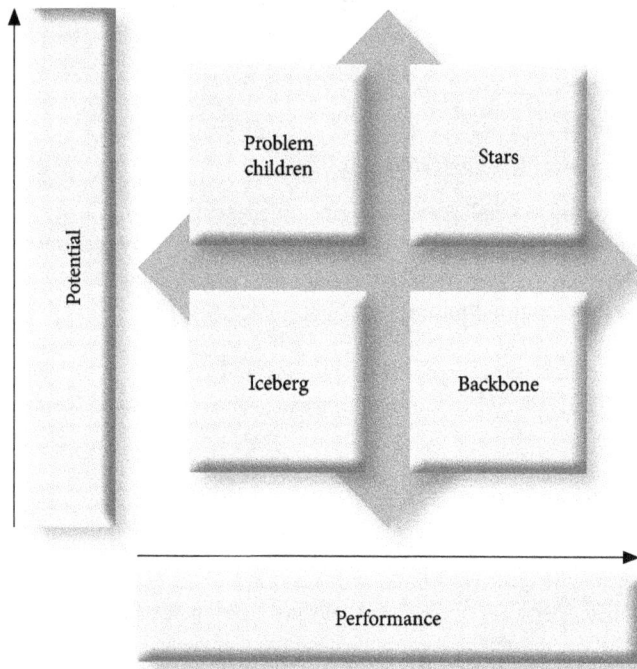

Figure 17.4   Categories of employee[5]

Remember that training is not the only solution to developing human resources. The following interventions can be very powerful, yet inexpensive:

- Constant encouragement;
- Challenging assignments;
- Soft skill development;
- The granting of autonomy;
- Pairing a low performer with a high performer;
- Providing new roles which are better aligned with skills;
- Coaching;
- Mentoring;
- Performance management; and
- Experiential learning.

Conclusion

Management plays a bigger role in building a pipeline of thriving talent than organisations and managers themselves may realise, and it is important that they are empowered to do this successfully. While employee development is not as easy as it seems, failure to assess performance versus potential is a very real business problem. The good news is that the problem can be solved. It simply requires dedication to identify your high-potential and high-performing employees, to assess their competencies and attributes, and put them on the path to success. Doing so, will be time well spent.

Just like winning football teams select and develop the best players, organisations can select and develop the right people in order to ensure that they remain ahead of the competition, while satisfying external customer demands as well as meeting internal shareholder expectations.

Endnotes

1   Adapted from G Stamp, 'The Tripod of Work'. Bioss, retrieved 24 July 2016, http://bioss.com/gillian-stamp/the-tripod-of-work/. [Accessed 24 July 2016].

2   E Jacques, *Requisite organization: A total system for effective managerial organization and managerial leadership for the 21st century*. Gloucester, MA: Cason Hall. 1998.

3   RW Eichinger and M M Lombardo. 'Twenty-two ways to develop leadership in staff managers', The Center for Creative Leadership, 1990, retrieved 1 August 2016, <http://govleaders.org/22ways.htm>.

4   FL Schmidt & JE Hunter. 'The validity and utility of selection methods in personnel psychology: Practical and theoretical implications of 85 years of research findings'. *Psychological Bulletin*, 1998, 124, pp. 262–274.

5   Businessballs.com. This model has uncertain origins, being variously claimed by and/or attributed to the Boston Consulting Group, George Odiome, Jack Welch, Doug Stewart and Nicholas Barnes, among others. The pdf diagram is based on an interpretation by John Addy, 2004. Clarification and evidence relating to authorship, ownership and origins are welcome. © Alan Chapman 2007–2013, retrieved 1 August 2016, <http://www.businessballs.com/people_performance_potential_model.htm#authorship-referencing>.

6   Ibid.

References

Eichinger, RW, & MM Lombardo, 'Twenty-two ways to develop leadership in staff managers', The Center for Creative Leadership, 1990, retrieved 1 August 2016, <http://govleaders.org/22ways.htm>.

FL Schmidt & JE Hunter. 'The validity and utility of selection methods in personnel psychology: Practical and theoretical implications of 85 years of research findings'. *Psychological Bulletin*, 1998, 124, pp. 262–274.

Jacques, E. *Requisite organization: A total system for effective managerial organization and managerial leadership for the 21st century*. Gloucester, MA: Cason Hall. 1998.

Stamp, G. 'The Tripod of Work', Bioss. retrieved 24 July 2016, <http://bioss.com/gillian-stamp/the-tripod-of-work/>.

CHAPTER 18

COACHING FOR LEADERSHIP IMPACT: FOUR MODELS TO ALIGN COACHING AND LEADERSHIP DEVELOPMENT PROGRAMMES
Sarah Babb

Coaching, whether with individuals or teams, plays a prominent part in leadership development in most organisations. More and more it is becoming central to new forms of performance management, while providing leaders and other talent with enhanced capabilities to perform in an increasingly challenging environment.

Too often, though, coaching is applied in relative isolation, rather than as part of an integrated talent and leadership development strategy.

This chapter by Sarah Babb demonstrates how coaching should be incorporated into a leadership development strategy. She demonstrates the importance of clarifying the required leadership framework for an organisation to execute its future strategy and how the use of coaching contributes to leadership culture.

Babb provides four models that enable organisations to decide on the best form of alignment to meet their specific needs.

Coaching on its own can be a powerful developmental process for individuals, but when applied within a leadership development strategy which is aligned to the organisation's business strategy, it becomes an important contributor to building a high-performance, organisation-wide leadership culture. Such a culture is essential if organisations are to survive and compete in a fast-changing, connected world.

As a component of a leadership development strategy, coaching can play an essential role in building Africa's future leadership talent. Sarah has extensive leadership development experience and is highly skilled and passionate about the role of coaching within this and related scenarios.

The wisdom incorporated into this chapter makes it essential reading for any talent manager or person responsible for leadership development in their organisation.

Introduction

Over the past 20 years I have witnessed and experienced the growth of both coaching and leadership development programmes across companies. Coaching and training are purported to provide a return on investment based on increased spend. Yet despite this, many companies bemoan the fact that their leadership pipeline is insufficient and that they do not have high-calibre leaders to guide them into the future. How is it that we are spending more on developing leaders, yet we still have too few? When we do have them, why are they not deemed effective? This chapter seeks to partially address how companies can align their interventions to make a greater impact on leadership development.

It is not a case of simply ticking off a list what companies have done for leaders, but more importantly it is about how companies align their efforts towards creating an overall leadership strategy. In companies where great leaders are developed there is a holistic view of the desired leadership capabilities and characteristics. These companies have an overarching picture of the nature of the leadership they require to take their business into the future. When meeting a leader from these companies, they can be recognised by their brand and style of leadership, and they all "sing off the same song-sheet", so to speak. Although unique and authentic, these leaders work towards attaining the common goals of the company by living the organisation's values and working towards a common strategic direction not only in terms of what they do, but importantly how they do things.

Such companies channel their leadership development interventions towards building and reinforcing sought-after characteristics and capabilities in leaders. They have a company story, and each leader understands his/her role and contribution in building on this leadership story and on the style of a great company.

No single training programme can craft a new leadership style or capacity. However, aligning efforts can reinforce and provide multiple platforms for leaders to step up in new ways. Training programmes can build capabilities, and coaching programmes can develop the character and style of leaders who are able to understand complexity, grapple with defining clear goals in uncertain times, confidently move forward and exhibit the reflexive capability to course-correct as needed. Building leaders of the future requires building not only technical management skills, but also ways of thinking and being which foster confidence and establish the connections needed to take the company in a new direction.

Of late, Africa has been capturing the attention of foreign and eastern investors – China in particular. Often, investment in infrastructure and even in companies themselves does not lead to the sustainable and lasting success of local businesses or leaders. In many instances, expats are imported to complete projects or lead multinational corporations, while local talent goes unnoticed or is even undermined.

Our challenge in Africa is to recognise (by ourselves) and lean into our unique capabilities – assets which are in great demand across the globe. Our leaders have learned to lead and grapple with minimal and declining resources, they have learnt to lead with resilience, to be creative in meeting business goals, to lead multicultural teams in challenging markets, and to do all of this in a tumultuous and uncertain political and social climate. The very capabilities we have as African leaders are sought-after in the West, where countries are also grappling with economic and social challenges (think of the refugee and migrant crises). We have a youthful, resilient, creative leadership pool which requires internal nurturing, feedback and recognition to shine and to be able to lead in impactful ways. The more we integrate our interventions, the more we can focus our efforts to allow our leaders to step up to lead organisations across Africa.

I am amazed by how seldom, when training and coaching across countries, I hear repeated the success stories of African leaders who are appointed to international boards and global companies. Surely it should come as no surprise that we have the capabilities and capacities to do so – I, for one, bear witness to this every day. Rather than replicate outdated models of scientific leadership, our companies need to leverage their unique capacities of leading amidst complexity and change. Leadership, too, needs to build its capacity of awareness, adaptability and enhanced cognitive capabilities. This can be done through experience, coupled with reflection, which is precisely what coaching provides. When combined with targeted learning programmes, the result is that leaders can become increasingly impactful.

This chapter aims to provide the reader with a range of models to choose from, to integrate coaching into leadership development strategies. Integrating leadership development and coaching focuses interventions on providing applications and growing leaders. If we seek to align effort and energy, the impact of our programmes will be so much greater.

Latest findings on HR trends

In 2015, Deloitte[1] completed a survey involving over 3 300 respondents globally, to identify key HR trends. They found that leadership tops the list of challenges (86% of respondents identified this issue)[2] facing organisations:

- Organisations around the world are struggling to strengthen their leadership pipelines, yet over the past year businesses have fallen further behind, particularly in their ability to develop Millennial leaders;
- A focus on leadership at all levels, coupled with consistent year-over-year spending in this area, is key to building sustainable performance and engaging employees in the new world of work.

If nearly every company recognises leadership as a critical talent problem, why are so few organisations making any progress in addressing the issue? Recent research shows that only 32 per cent of organisations have a steady supply of leaders at the top levels, while only 18 per cent regularly hold their leaders accountable to identify and develop successors.[3] The short answer is that many companies treat leadership sporadically, confining development to a select few employees, while failing to make long-term investments in leadership and neglecting to build a robust leadership pipeline at all levels. For all the talk about leadership as a CEO-level priority, too many companies do not consistently invest in this area.

One of the solutions proposed in the research report is to develop or leverage a capability model, i.e., to build a framework for assessment, development and coaching. New models are now available, but companies can benefit by keeping the model simple and focusing on implementing existing leadership models and programmes.[4] Here is what the current chapter proposes: keep the models integrated, simple and aligned, and persist in their implementation over time as you work towards building your leadership framework.

The next section defines coaching and leadership development, before outlining four different models for aligning interventions to greater effect. A number of benefits can be derived from aligning coaching and leadership development interventions: it

- focuses effort and energy on a single, common strategy for leadership across the business;
- supports the application of leadership on an individual basis for maximum impact by each individual;
- ensures a longitudinal, holistic view of personal leadership development over time;
- deepens learning on a personal level to ensure the long-term application of the business leadership framework;
- aligns budgetary expenditure, thus preventing unnecessary wastage and fruitless expenditure;
- provides a frame of reference for coaching and leadership programmes; and
- allows for greater learning, as feedback is experienced in three forums – coaching, learning programme and application.

Coaching

Defining coaching

Coaching can be interpreted in many different ways, and makes use of a variety of models. This chapter does not seek to favour one or the other, as each has unique benefits – when implemented well. For the purposes of this chapter a single definition of coaching is given, namely that of the International Coaching Federation

(ICF): "Coaching is partnering with clients in a thought-provoking and creative process that inspires them to maximize their personal and professional potential."[5] As such, coaching can be defined as a focused series of engagements between a coach and coachee, with a view to attaining personal and professional goals. This leaves the goals to be defined and owned by the coachee. In many cases, businesses invest in leadership development, citing their investment as a sign that they support that executive or leader's development. Often the process is left to the individual to contract and follow through on.

Although there are many ways to highlight the success of coaching, there are not as many signs of it being integrated into an overall business leadership strategy. For that reason, the overall impact of coaching is somewhat confined to personal growth and not necessarily business success.

The impact of coaching

There is no doubt that coaching offers personal impact and growth opportunities, even if the goals are not common or shared across leadership levels of the business. Only seven per cent of respondents claim that coaching interventions are "not successful".[6] Based on a survey of nearly 200 executives who were asked to self-report on how they believed they learned, McCall, Lombardo and Eichinger found that "[l]essons learned by successful and effective managers are roughly:

- 70% from tough jobs
- 20% from people (mostly the boss)
- 10% from courses and reading".[7]

Leaders learn from experience, and coaching helps them reflect on, embed and improve on practical and day-to-day decisions which are made to overcome specific dilemmas. Of course, practical application is what brings the practical success of coaching.

The benefits of coaching for the organisation include increased productivity, better quality of product and deliverables, improved customer service and a more questioning culture. Individuals benefit from heightened self-awareness, improved communication skills, better relationships with others in the workplace, increased empowerment, a better quality of life and an improved ability to set goals.[8]

The ICF claims professional coaching brings many wonderful benefits: fresh perspectives on personal challenges, enhanced decision-making skills, greater interpersonal effectiveness, and increased confidence.[9] But the list does not end there. Those who undertake coaching can also expect an appreciable improvement in productivity, greater satisfaction with life and work, and the attainment of relevant goals.[10]

> I now see how my leadership has prevented my team from performing well. Before I would blame them, and now I see clearly what role I have played. This is a hard pill to swallow at times. But at least I have a way forward now. I can also see more clearly how to work with my colleagues and the benefits of working more collaboratively. The irony is that the less it is about "me", the better my teams achieve. *Coachee 1*[11]

These are goals worthy of pursuit. Coaching – if properly designed and implemented – has a profound impact on both the leaders and the leadership pool of a company. In turn, changing and building leaders across all levels impact on how the organisation is run and how teams perform. There is no doubt that having effective leadership leads to greater results for a company. And coaching has been found to be most impactful when it aligns with the overall leadership framework of a company.

Integrating coaching for leadership development

There is a growing trend to use coaching as a key source of leadership development. However, when it is applied ad-hoc and not linked to an overall leadership development strategy, its benefits and impact are often lost to the organisation. Research shows that 75 per cent of organisations do not integrate coaching into their performance management system, yet it is most commonly used for performance enhancement (93%) and management development (90%).[12] This indicates a lack of overall alignment with a common leadership strategy. Each business needs a unique leadership strategy which will define, in essence, how to recognise a leader. A leadership strategy should include the following:

- Business values, and behavioural descriptors of how leaders display these values;
- A leadership footprint or a way to measure how leaders' impact is experienced across the business;
- The levels of leadership, as well as the style, culture, roles; and
- The character of leadership (including values and ethics) and leadership capabilities.

A leadership strategy provides a touch-point against which any leadership interventions must be aligned, be they performance management, rewards, coaching or development programmes.

> I just never believed before that I could claim that I was a good leader, that I added value as much as I could. I now see how I have managed to turn things around and am so proud of my contribution. My wife even says to me how I have grown in confidence and assertiveness in being able to say what I want to. I would never have thought a year ago that I could be where I am today. *Coachee 2*[13]

Given the need to be more impactful and focused on leadership development approaches, the range of models (discussed below) is considered more impactful in a corporation. Yet businesses differ in respect of how they achieve this, given that there are a range of models to choose from (depending on the sector in which an organisation operates, its culture and its budget). Of course one could argue that leadership development is broader than this.

The aim of leadership development in Africa is to build local leadership capacity across race and gender. Naturally, there are additional considerations, given the cultural differences prevalent in African companies. As a point of departure, the intent of the transformation objectives in each company needs to be clear: organisations must be upfront about the aim to develop women, as well as local black Africans, into leadership positions. They must also be clear on selection and assessment criteria, as all appointments must be based primarily on capability and character, as articulated in the strategic leadership framework. This way there can be no allegations of favouritism or nepotism in the appointment of organisational leaders. While preference may be given to women and people of colour to assist in the transformation process, this should not be the only consideration when promoting or selecting candidates for development opportunities.

The greater the pool of leaders, the better the odds of finding the best leaders for the future. Organisations should build for the long term and for the benefit of the nation. They should bear in mind that talent retention these days does not revolve around retaining talent for the tenure of their lifetimes: new millennials and other top talent are globally mobile, and often choose to join companies which have proven that they develop their people and provide real opportunities for growth and advancement, while contributing to society as a whole. Ironically, talent is so mobile globally that many high-performers find their way back to the companies that initially invested in them.

Of the executives I have met across Africa, many have worked across borders (both in and outside of the continent), only to return to their home countries. Members of the diaspora reinvest in their home countries and often return when the right opportunities present themselves. Organisations should therefore not limit their development and coaching opportunities to the top inner circle, but rather focus on the broader middle and first-line management pool.

Much of the spend in leadership development goes into programmes and coaching, but these are viewed separately. If aligned, the results will be more seamless, experiential, impactful and no doubt more enjoyable. Four alternative ways of aligning coaching and leadership development are outlined here.

Four models of aligning coaching and leadership development

These four models represent a continuum of aligned coaching and development interventions.

- One-on-one coaching
- Horizontal tier coaching
- Vertical team coaching
- Group coaching

Coaching model 1: One-on-one coaching

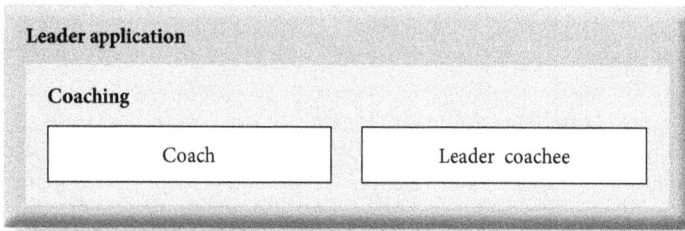

Figure 18.1   Individual/one-on-one coaching

In this model, coaching is available to leaders on an individual basis. A formal coaching process is sponsored by the business, for an agreed period. This represents a minimal level of intervention, thus it is the least directed and aligned model. While it reduces costs, it limits the potential impact and returns. Nonetheless, there are significant gains to be had from coaching individual leaders.

The communication and implementation of this process are key to its success. If poorly communicated or implemented, leaders see one-on-one coaching as remedial, an attempt to manage performance, an unappreciated incentive or even a wasteful perk. Not all leaders perceive the value of coaching or their immediate need for it. It should be declared upfront whether the coaching is compulsory or voluntary. It is also preferable to frame coaching as compulsory for a minimum number of sessions within a constrained time period. The benefits and needs should be clearly communicated beforehand, as well as who is eligible to enrol or to be nominated to participate in the programme.

The aim of one-on-one coaching is to provide leaders with an opportunity to develop their personal leadership goals, raise their self-awareness and make their leadership more impactful. This is an opportunity for a business to invest in leaders and to respect that individual leaders are on their own journeys of discovery and growth. It helps leaders to set personal goals and accomplish these within a six to 12-month period. Organisations should maintain a central database of leaders and coaches, and should keep record of any sessions completed as this could provide useful data for analysis when planning for the second round of the coaching programme.

Coaching works well if

- benefits are defined upfront, with clear communications;
- it is compulsory for a core group or cohort of leaders;
- it entails confidential coaching sessions, without coachee report-backs;
- it involves an easy enrolment process;
- a time-bound start and end date are established, with minimum six sessions per leader over a six to 12-month period;
- scheduled at leaders' convenience, with a minimum time interval between sessions;
- the immediate manager of the coachee signs off on his/her participation; and
- it aligns with the values and leadership strategy framework of the organisation.

Using external coaches

In most cases, leaders source their own coaches externally. It is recommended that they consider qualified and accredited coaches, either through a local body such as Comensa or an international body such as the ICF. The company may then agree to fund a six to 12-month coaching cycle, depending on the level of leadership.

In some instances the business has a list of coaching sources/coaches approved through its procurement processes, from amongst whom a leader can source a coach. In both cases it is imperative that there be a matching process whereby a leader can select the best match for him/her in terms of approach, and whether they foresee the two of them building rapport, trust and a relationship. The leader always has the choice of selecting a coach, and without exception to end or terminate the coaching process should it not be working for him/her. In situations where the coach is preselected or chosen for the leader, the latter can still exit the relationship. For the process to be impactful, an open, trusting rapport and coaching relationship need to be established between coach and leader.

I am often asked whether the race, religion, ethnicity, image, age or gender of the coaches and coachees has an impact. Because of the matching process, I find that coachees tend to select the coach who best meets their needs and suits their temperament. This is not always race, age or gender based. Be sure to have a range of different coaches' profiles on hand to select from, so that those who are sensitive to these dynamics have the option to select similarly profiled coaches.

I suggest there must be an option for coaches, since there is no evidence that the coach must be an exact match (in terms of profile) with the coachee. Do not dictate this in the coaching programme, but always ensure there are options for coachees. I have coached across gender, race and countries as far afield as Saudi Arabia, as well as across ages and have not found my profile to limit or hinder the impact of the coaching. Sometimes men may find it easier to be more open (and even more vulnerable) with women. Some find it easier to talk to an older coach, while others prefer to speak to someone of a different race/culture in order to glean different perspectives. There is no hard and fast rule about matching. What it does boil down to is personal preference, which ensures that a range of coaching profiles can be offered to coachees. In this way, companies can track their own data and matching patterns and see whether there is anything noteworthy for them from this, which will help them improve in their second year of implementation.

Using internal coaches

Some companies develop in-house professional coaches from whom the leader can select a candidate. There are pros and cons to using internal coaches: the benefits include the fact that these coaches are familiar with the company context, culture and dynamics. Internal coaches may be able to share insights into "blind spots" or the impact of the leader, and may contribute to the conversation from an organisational perspective, if required. The disadvantages include the fear that confidentiality will be breeched – the leader may consequently not trust the internal coach as much. Internal coaches are employed by the same company, even if they come from a different department, and may be perceived to have hidden agendas, manipulate the power dynamics or have vested interests. These may limit the coachee's learning possibilities, as s/he may be reluctant to share deeply for fear of reprisal or career repercussions.

If an internal coach is 'contracted', then the professional rules of coaching ethics and etiquette apply, namely to uphold confidentiality and to enable the leader to terminate the coaching relationship at any stage, without prejudice or consequence. Both parties should declare any potential conflict of interest prior to entering the coaching relationship, and this could determine whether or not the leader selects a specific coach. Another con is that an internal coach does not always have the experience or credibility to be a professional coach. It is for the organisation to determine, if it opts to go the internal route, standards for coaches and coach selection in line with professional standards.

A further benefit of using internal coaches is that their approach will be consistent with that of the company. Should the company use external coaches, there needs to be some consistency in terms of approach and objectives, as part of the selection criteria. All coaches – whether internal or external – should adhere to an overall framework of objectives.

Whether the coach is sourced internally or externally, no form of feedback on the content of the coaching sessions should be required. The upfront and overall coaching goals may be shared, but should the coach share anything further this would compromise the privacy, confidentiality and trust relationship, and hence the impact of the coaching conversations. As a professional coach I find it surprising that many corporates still ask for feedback, even though the issue was resolved upfront and agreement was reached that there would be no feedback as a condition for entering the coaching relationship. This should be upheld, even if the coaching is sponsored by the business.

Overall, the coaching relationship is impactful in that it guides the leader towards setting and achieving personal and professional goals. However, these goals do not necessarily contribute to the overall leadership needs and goals of the business. Coaching relationships and interventions are often ad hoc and driven by the individual. For this reason, an integrated model of coaching and leadership development is deemed more comprehensive and focused. The second model under discussion here, offers a more holistic approach by aligning coaching with development programmes.

Coaching model 2: Horizontal tier coaching

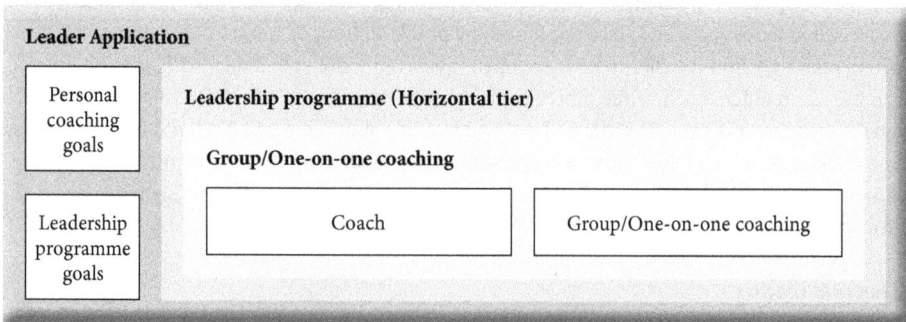

Figure 18.2 The horizontal model of coaching

This model begins to enhance the impact and integration between leadership development and coaching. First, the top tier 50–100 leaders (from the same tier of management across the business, but below the executive committee) are selected to participate in a leadership development programme. This allows for cross-divisional learning, relationship building and reflection. Leaders build an appreciation for the business as a whole, but from the same horizontal level.

There are two components to this programme: the leadership programme modules and coaching (which could take the form of one-on-one events). Each leader may, for example, be sponsored to enter a coaching relationship with a pre-selected external coach for six coaching sessions, to be held between each module of the programme. In such instances, the leaders enter into a coaching contract for one-on-one coaching, to run in conjunction with the programme.

Alternatively, the coaching component could be broken down into group coaching where smaller syndicates work with the same coach. Each syndicate then comprises a horizontal slice of leaders across functions within the organisation, who work with a group coach for the duration of the programme. Syndicates may be allocated projects which they need to implement in the business. In either case, each leader applies personal goals and leadership programme goals at his/her own discretion, back in the workplace.

The leaders work with coaches, either one-on-one or in groups, for a period of a year. This gives them an opportunity to learn, engage and produce results with the coach's feedback, insight and support. While the syndicate engages around a project, the coach observes and provides team coaching on the behavioural and team aspects of the leaders. The group engages the organisation as well as internal expertise to deal with the content and results of the project.

Such group coaching offers each individual an opportunity to reflect on, engage with and witness their leadership behaviours in a group setting. This reinforces the insights gained and provides a platform for each coachee to apply any practices and actions resulting from their one-one-one coaching sessions. The group experience is viewed as a safe environment in which to apply newly acquired competencies/insights, prior to engaging with the broader organisational context. Learning is thus reinforced and goal directed, to balance the learning for the individual and the organisation.

The benefits of integrating leadership and coaching include

- focused personal learning and coaching;
- aligned coaching and learning goals;
- opportunities for real-time practice and feedback;
- deeper relationship building; and
- the building of a strong tier of leadership.

Coaching model 3: Vertical team coaching

The third model provides the coaching component in the leadership programme. In addition, each leader has a coach working with the vertical team. Each leader applies his/her learning with their team/direct reports, and has a coach working with these teams. Therefore, whereas the horizontal model works with the same tier of leaders, this model proposes working additionally with leaders with their direct team, in a vertical slice of the organisation.

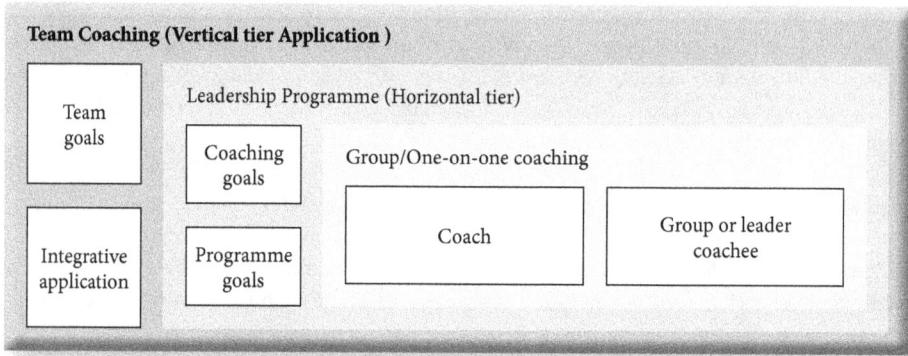

Figure 18.3   *Vertical team coaching*

The first two elements of the alignment are the same as in model 2, i.e., coaching and the leadership programme. The third element comprises a coach offering team coaching to the leader's team (direct reports). This is a vertical tier application, as the leader has the opportunity to be coached with his/her team, to directly apply new-found insights and capabilities, and thus to see the direct results of his/her leadership development.

> We like our leader better now – we understand him and why he has led us in this way. We can see how we have dropped balls between us. We for the first time have agreed how we want to and need to be as a team. Its exciting. We work better together and are able to take on more without our manager telling us all the time. He is a different person, we've seen a new side to him. *Team comments.*[14]

The coach provides insight for the leader and the team as regards their goals, achievements and further areas of development in working towards achieving enhanced results. Each team establishes a team charter and its own results for that year, in line with the overall strategy. For the duration of the programme, the coach observes the leaders in action, with their teams, at regular intervals.

This model provides almost immediate results and follow-through on the outcomes of the leader's coaching and development sessions. This makes the results tangible and easily measurable. Leaders apply their learnings directly back into the business, by working with their teams, who form part of their direct sphere of influence. The results of individual learning and coaching are directly evident in the leaders' teams.

The return on investment is experienced by both for the individual leader and the team, in tangible and immediate ways. The team does not hear what the goals of the leadership coaching sessions are, but team members do experience the application of the chosen behaviours, as well as the values and heightened awareness of the leader. The leader has a way of directly applying his/her learning and insight gained from the coaching sessions. In turn, the team agrees and sets goals to be achieved through team coaching sessions.

This model integrates the benefits of coaching with the overall business needs for enhanced leadership and leadership development. The impact is felt throughout the organisation. In one organisation which applied this model, positive results were seen six months into the programme, with improved employee engagement surveys and leadership 360° feedback improving dramatically over this period. In this case, the improved leadership starts to have a positive impact on the culture of the company, resulting in greater faith in the future success and sustainability of the business. Employees are more engaged, as they experience their leader's growth.

Coaching model 4: Group coaching

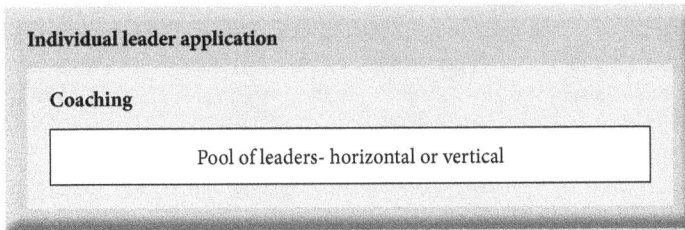

Figure 18.4   The group coaching model

In this model, group coaching is applied: a coach is assigned only to a group, i.e., either a vertical or horizontal group of leaders. The advantage of this approach is that more leaders can be reached, with fewer coaches.

The one-on-one element is precluded, thus costs are reduced both in terms of the leaders' time away and financially (fewer coaches are needed). At best, the team improves its dynamics and outputs. At worst there is a limited, lasting change in the individual leaders since they do not receive personalised attention and support in applying their learning. The change on an individual level is not as deep and profound, nor necessarily long lasting. However, through this process organisations reach teams and scores more leaders who learn practical and improved ways of working together, as well as how to lead more effectively. This contributes to deepening the pool of leaders.

Whichever model the business chooses depends on the leadership strategy. Of course this could entail a combination of the above models. It is important to consider specific criteria when selecting a model.

Choosing a model

The choice of which model to adopt depends on the following:

- The business leadership strategy;
- The budget for choice of coaches, programme and team sessions;
- The number and level of leaders included in the leadership strategy;
- Access to internal and external professional coaches;
- The internal coaching culture;
- The design of the leadership programme; and
- Vertical or horizontal integration leadership gaps.

Hints and tips to align coaching and leadership development

- Have a clear leadership framework and leadership strategy;
- Know the company coaching culture and choose a coaching approach;
- Design a holistic leadership development framework with application points for the leader to take back their learning;
- Agree the principles and rules of engagement with coaches;
- Allow for confidential personal coaching goals;
- Articulate the links between personal, development and team goals;
- Allow time and be consistent over a cycle of at least three years to embed an approach and begin to see results;
- Recognise and reward leaders' efforts to pass on their leadership to the next tier; and
- Reflect on learnings and return on investment against the overall business strategy.

Case study

Of course the overall approach must support the business strategy. One start-up bank, for example, faced the challenge of building a more creative and collaborative culture in order to continue its steady growth. Within this business strategy it defined the need to enhance the capacity of leaders to work together and lead their teams in an empowered way, so as to foster creativity and independent thought.

It followed that their leadership development programme worked with the horizontal tier of leaders who participated in team coaching sessions. Parallel to this, they interspersed coaching sessions with each leader and his/her teams, over the year-long programme. They selected a version of Model 3: Vertical team coaching, which allowed them to build leadership competencies and cross-silo relationships, while allowing each leader to apply their new learnings with their own teams. It was a change from their existing top-down competitive approach, therefore support was needed to bring about cultural and strategic changes aimed at collaboration and teamwork.

Beforehand, the considerations for this company were: What is the end picture of our leadership interventions? How do we want leaders to be? What will leaders be doing and how will they be working differently? How do we empower leaders to be the best they can be, while also working towards a common business strategy? This company found an approach which balances the competitive, personal needs of individuals with those of the collaborative business. Each person is unique, therefore retaining top leaders is key to achieving future success.

The more top talent have the leeway to apply their personal learnings to achieve direct results and success (both personally and professionally), the better. Aligning coaching and leadership development assists leaders to experience the benefits directly. Leaders also want to justify their personal investment in time and effort expended, through participating in the programmes – therefore, the more benefits they derive, the better.

It goes without saying that support is required from the top. Each leader needs to be visibly supported by his/her team as regards any changes they make. There needs to be an overall monitoring of participation and completion of the programme, with some form of evaluation and interpretation of the findings on both a personal and an aggregated leadership level. Sharing the positive findings of the overall programme is, in itself, a self-reinforcing cycle as the leaders receive positive recognition for their change and growth endeavours. In turn, this contributes to their success and that of the business.

Conclusion

Leaders reflect and create the culture of a business. They are key to the sustainable future of any business. Coaching has the capacity to unleash the characteristics of great leaders, and combined with development programmes, build the necessary capabilities and competence for future success.

> There's no question that future leaders will need constant coaching. As the business environment becomes more complex, they will increasingly turn to coaches for help in understanding how to act. The kind of coaches I am talking about will do more than influence behaviors; they will be an essential part of the leader's learning process, providing knowledge, opinions, and judgment in critical areas.[15]

Coaching and leadership development need to be integrated to support leaders in navigating these trying and challenging times.

APPENDIX 1

What can coaches do for you?[16]

HBR conducted a survey of 140 leading coaches and invited five experts to comment on the findings

Did you know ...

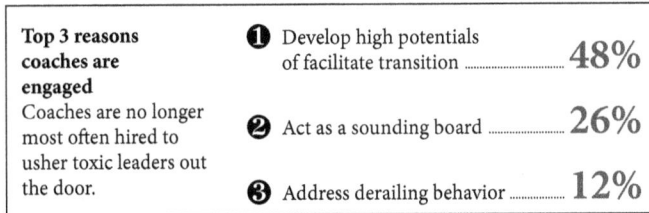

Top 3 reasons coaches are engaged
Coaches are no longer most often hired to usher toxic leaders out the door.

❶ Develop high potentials of facilitate transition **48%**

❷ Act as a sounding board **26%**

❸ Address derailing behavior **12%**

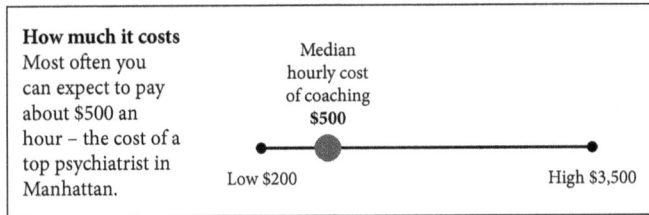

How much it costs
Most often you can expect to pay about $500 an hour – the cost of a top psychiatrist in Manhattan.

Median hourly cost of coaching
$500
Low $200   High $3,500

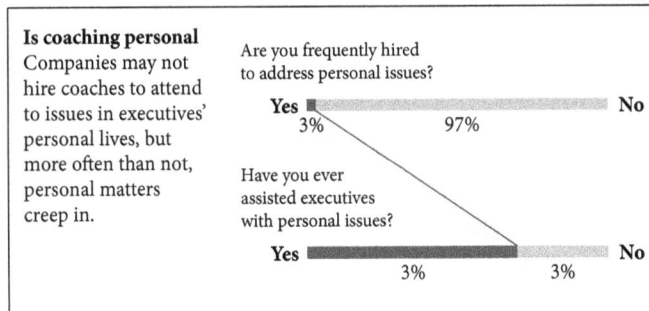

Is coaching personal
Companies may not hire coaches to attend to issues in executives' personal lives, but more often than not, personal matters creep in.

Are you frequently hired to address personal issues?
Yes 3%   **No** 97%

Have you ever assisted executives with personal issues?
Yes 3%   **No** 3%

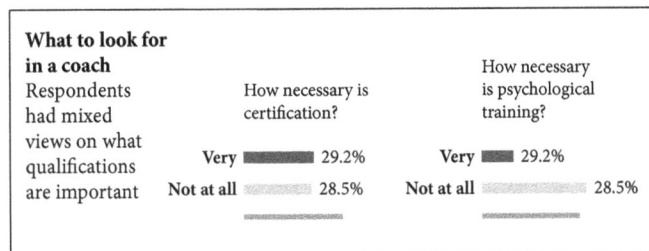

What to look for in a coach
Respondents had mixed views on what qualifications are important

How necessary is certification?
Very 29.2%
Not at all 28.5%

How necessary is psychological training?
Very 29.2%
Not at all 28.5%

Who is involved?
Though they acknowledge that confidentiality was central to successful coaching, respondents said that in most cases, they gave updates on coachees' progress to other stakeholders in the organization.

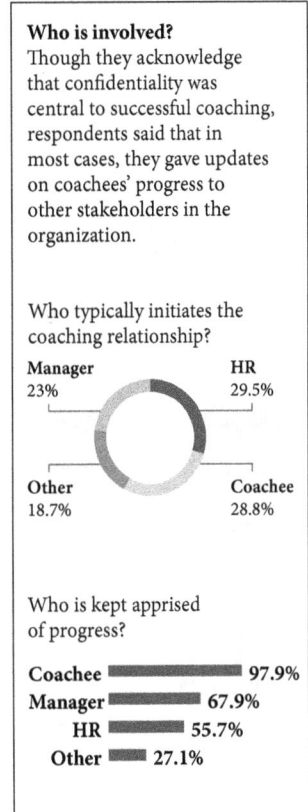

Who typically initiates the coaching relationship?
Manager 23%   HR 29.5%
Other 18.7%   Coachee 28.8%

Who is kept apprised of progress?
Coachee 97.9%
Manager 67.9%
HR 55.7%
Other 27.1%

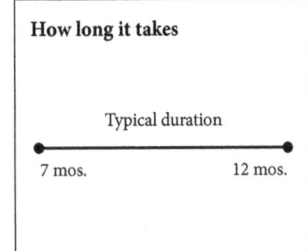

How long it takes

Typical duration
7 mos.   12 mos.

Buyer's guide

We asked the coaches what companies should look for when hiring a coach. Here's how various qualifications stacked up

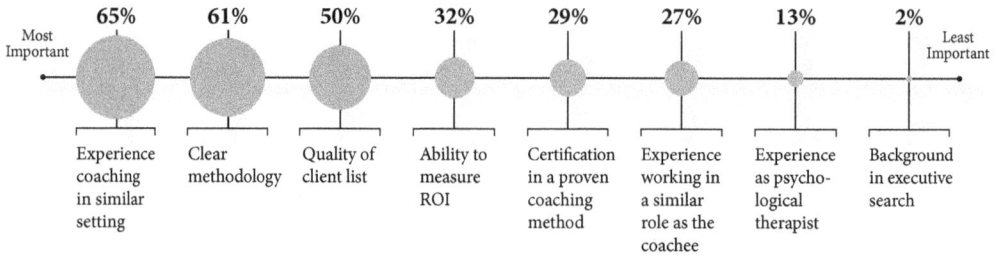

Most Important	65%	61%	50%	32%	29%	27%	13%	2%	Least Important
	Experience coaching in similar setting	Clear methodology	Quality of client list	Ability to measure ROI	Certification in a proven coaching method	Experience working in a similar role as the coachee	Experience as psychological therapist	Background in executive search	

(Percentages of respondents who ranked these qualifications as "very important")

Consulting		Coaching		Therapy
Paid to come up with answers	Advises individual leaders on business matters	Focuses on the future	Paid to ask the right questions	Focuses on the past
Focuses on organizational performance	Involves management in goal setting	Fosters individual performance in a business context	Tackles difficult issues at work and home	Diagnoses and treats dysfunctionality
Strives for objectivity	Based on organizational ethics	Helps executives discover their own path	Focuses on individual behavioral change	Based on medical ethics
Provides quantitative analysis of problems	Paid for by the company		Explores subjective experience	Paid for by the individual

Endnotes

1   Deloitte University Press, 'Global human capital trends 2015: Leading in the new world of work', 2015, retrieved 1 August 2016, <http://www2.deloitte.com/content/dam/Deloitte/at/Documents/human-capital/hc-trends-2015.pdf>.
2   Ibid, p. 17.
3   Ibid, p. 18.
4   Ibid, p. 17.
5   International Coaching Federation (ICF), 'What is coaching?', retrieved 1 August 2016, <http://www.icf-cleveland.org/content.aspx?page_id=22&club_id=508298&module_id=132814>.
6   MM Lombardo & RW Eichinger, *The career architect development planner*, 1st ed., Lominger, Minneapolis, p. iv.
7   Ibid.
8   'What is coaching?', op. cit.
9   Ibid.
10 International Coaching Federation, 'Benefits of using a coach', retrieved 1 August 2016, <http://coachfederation.org/need/landing.cfm?ItemNumber=747>.
11 Interview with Sarah Babb.
12 M Hudson, 'Coaching and mentoring South Africa', December 2011, Comensa research findings on coaching in SA, Leadership Solutions, retrieved 1 August 2016, <http://www.leadershipsolutions.co.za/comensa-research-findings-on-coaching-in-sa.html>.
13 Interview with Sarah Babb.
14 Interview with Sarah Babb.
15 D Coutu & C Kauffman, 'What can coaches do for you', *Harvard Business Review*, January 2009, retrieved 1 August 2016, <https://hbr.org/2009/01/what-can-coaches-do-for-you>.
16 Ibid.

References

Coutu, D & C Kauffman, 'What can coaches do for you', *Harvard Business Review*, January 2009, retrieved 1 August 2016, <https://hbr.org/2009/01/what-can-coaches-do-for-you>.

Deloitte University Press, 'Global human capital trends 2015: Leading in the new world of work', 2015, retrieved 1 August 2016, <http://www2.deloitte.com/content/dam/Deloitte/at/Documents/human-capital/hc-trends-2015.pdf>.

Hudson, M, 'Coaching and mentoring South Africa', December 2011, Comensa research findings on coaching in SA, Leadership Solutions, retrieved 1 August 2016, <http://www.leadershipsolutions.co.za/comensa-research-findings-on-coaching-in-sa.html>.

International Coaching Federation, 'Benefits of using a coach', retrieved 1 August 2016, <http://coachfederation.org/need/landing.cfm?ItemNumber=747>.

International Coaching Federation, 'What is coaching?', retrieved 1 August 2016, <http://www.icf-cleveland.org/content.aspx?page_id=22&club_id=508298&module_id=132814>.

Lombardo, MM & RW Eichinger, *The career architect development planner*, 1st ed., Lominger, Minneapolis, 1996.

CHAPTER 19

LEARNING PATHS – REDUCING SCRAP LEARNING
Lydia Cillie Schmidt

One of the greatest priorities of organisations in Africa is the need to build skills and to do so quickly. For most organisations training is a significant cost, and when cost cutting is necessary it is frequently the first thing to be sacrificed. Increasingly, leaders are questioning the effectiveness of training and the costs involved.

This chapter on learning paths examines what organisations can do to increase the application of training, on the part of learners, to minimise the "scrap" or ineffective training activities that add to training costs. Through the application of Learning Paths Methodology, organisations can improve the efficiency of learning interventions and increase their impact. This is achieved through improved skills retention and transfer of learning, as well as reduced time to achieve proficiency.

Lydia's knowledge of learning theory, combined with her extensive practical experience, provides much more than a methodology: it gives the reader an extensive background to learning theory, while providing practical principles and solutions to improve the effectiveness of training interventions. This is supplemented with a number of case studies demonstrating the application of Learning Path Methodology in a variety of occupations and organisations, with tangible cost and other benefits.

For those tasked with ensuring the effectiveness of training in their organisations, this chapter is essential reading.

Introduction

Organisations increasingly spend a great deal of money on the training and development of their staff. South African organisations spend, on average, four per cent of payroll on training,[1] which is significantly above the one per cent required by the *Skills Development Levies Act*. Deloitte estimates that even if the South African government only spends one per cent of the wage bill on training, that amounts to R4.5 billion.[2] Bersin found that American spending on corporate training grew by 15 per cent in 2013 to over $70 billion in the US and in excess of $130 billion worldwide.[3]

This massive investment in learning and development does not, however, always translate into better business results or even employee proficiency. Many employees who attend training never apply, back at work, what they have effectively learnt during the training – this is called scrap learning.[4] Wick et al., who coined the term "learning scrap", note that it has a high cost.[5] They list the direct cost for instructional designers, trainers, travel, material, venues, etc., as well as the lost opportunity costs of having people spend time learning things they will not use – an example is continued customer dissatisfaction, where training has failed to improve employee behaviour.

It is clear that scrap learning is closely related to training transfer – an aspect that has received a great deal of attention in training literature. The "transfer of training" is the effective and continuing application, by learners, to their jobs, of knowledge and skills gained during training.[6] The transfer of training involves two interdependent actions: 1) that learners immediately apply all they learned in training to their jobs (at least as well as they could demonstrate those skills at the end of the training programme),[7] and 2) the maintenance of the learnt behaviour. Michalak defines the maintenance of training as keeping a learnt skill or knowledge at a required standard.[8] Such maintenance cannot take place if training transfer did not take place, and the transfer of training is meaningless without maintenance. Scrap learning is the result of a failure of both training transfer and maintenance.

According to an analysis by the Corporate Executive Board, the average organisation has a scrap learning rate of 45 per cent.[9] Robert Brinkerhoff, an expert in training evaluation, estimates that scrap learning rates can be as high as 50–80 per cent of all learning delivered.[10] It is clear that organisations cannot tolerate this situation. Cohen states that a reactive approach to learning and development leads to a significant cost to employee engagement and organisational capability.[11] Mattox stresses that research shows a strong correlation between decreasing scrap learning and increasing job performance.[12]

It stands to reason, then, that organisations need to do training and development differently, to realise a positive return on investment in learning and development. The main question is: What can organisations do to be more proactive in delivering the desired business results, reducing scrap learning and ensuring the transfer of learning to the workplace?

One possible solution is to use Learning Path Methodology to ensure that learning and development are focused on application in a work situation. When designing a learning path, the first step is to identify exactly what a person must be able to do to be proficient in the role. The proficiency definition provides the basis for the design of a learning path which will outline all the necessary interventions. In turn, these interventions will ensure that the person is able to deliver all the required outputs demanded of the role, within the shortest possible time.

According to Williams and Rosenbaum, a learning path is a chronological series of activities, events and experience peformed or undergone from Day 1 to proficiency.[13] These authors define proficiency as the measurable outcomes and observable behaviour of doing a job or task correctly, at the desired level of performance.When a learning path is designed based on proficiencies, there is no room for scrap learning as all learning interventions are aimed at helping the person to apply the learning on the job. The learning path is not completed until the person demonstrates proficiency in all the required outputs of the role.

The focus of this article is on how to utilise Learning Path Methodology in reducing scrap learning. I begin by exploring the concept of training transfer and maintenance, as well as the measurement of scrap learning. Next, I discuss the foundational principles of the Learning Paths Methodology and the process followed in designing a learning path.

Training transfer and maintenance

According to Wick et al., the job of training is not done and training will not be rewarded with continued investment unless learning is transferred and applied in a way that improves performance.[14] Wick et al. found that scrap learning mainly occurs during the post-training period or what they refer to as "learning transfer".[15] Also known as training transfer, Mabotha defines this as the application and maintenance of the knowledge, skills and attitudes – learned from training – to do the job.[16] As mentioned in the introduction, in many instances the learning from a training intervention is not applied or maintained in the work situation and thus becomes scrap learning. For this reason, King is of the view that before an organisation goes back to the drawing board to address a flaw in the training itself, it would be wise to examine what is happening during the learning transfer phase.[17]

Broad and Newstrom identify the lack of reinforcement on the job as the main barrier to transferring training to the workplace, followed by interference from the immediate environment (work, time pressures, insufficient authority, ineffective work processes, inadequate equipment and facilities) and a non-supportive organisational culture.[18] King identifies a lack of measurement, a non-conducive culture, participants with limited training readiness, sub-optimal systems and procedures, and a lack of management and peer support as the main causes of a poor learning transfer environment.[19]

Clearly, many similarities exist between the barriers to the transfer of training and the root causes of scrap learning:[20]

- Ineffective delivery
- Content not directly relevant
- Low learner motivation
- Content quality issues
- Wrong learners attend
- No opportunity to apply
- Examples don't connect
- Misalignment with priorities

- Low organisational support
- Insufficient practice
- Inadequate support materials
- Learners already know information
- Lack of manager support
- Delivered at wrong time
- Insufficient time to apply

Wick et al. state that if organisations want to ensure that training leads to improved performance on the job, training professionals must treat training as a process; drive follow-through, transfer and application; and better engage managers and participants.[21]

To support these prescriptions, Wick et al. designed a six-step process (the so-called six disciplines) to ensure that the transfer of training takes place and that training leads to business results on the job.[22] Jefferson and Pollock[23] summarise the six disciplines as follows:

- **Discipline 1**: Make sure that the business needs that training is meant to address are fully and clearly understood. When designing learning paths, the first step is to understand the goals of a role within the broader objectives of the organisation and this is captured in what is called a proficiency definition;
- **Discipline 2**: Design the learner's complete experience. Don't stop with the training event; the ultimate results depend as much or more on the learner's experience before and after the training. A learning path specifies what should happen before, during and after a learning event that forms part of the path. Each stakeholder's role during all these phases is described in detail in, for example, coaching guides;
- **Discipline 3**: Deliver training in ways that enhance the learner's ability to apply the training. That means paying attention to the findings of learning research and, in general, delivering a lot less content and a lot more practice with feedback. A learning path will always include and specify the practising of the required behaviour and outcomes;
- **Discipline 4**: Take responsibility for driving learning transfer by developing strategies, systems, and structures that keep learning the priority. Also, hold learners accountable for using what they learned. Learners have the responsibility to implement the various activities in a learning path and follow-up and review with the line manager/coach are built into the path at regular intervals;
- **Discipline 5**: Make developing and deploying performance support an integral part of training. This might include job aids, online support, help desks, or any other means of support that help optimise success when learners try new approaches for the first time. Performance support also forms an integral part of a learning path and assists in accelerating the learning;

- **Discipline 6:** Evaluate the outcomes in ways that are relevant, credible, and compelling. The evaluation should not only show that the programme is contributing to the desired business results, but also provide insights to support continuous improvement. The effectiveness of a learning path is measured by performance in the role. If a person is not proficient and cannot deliver the desired outputs, the learning path is not completed.

The Learning Paths Methodology, as implemented by Williams and Rosenbaum, incorporates these ideas to a large extent, as it is based on a process view of learning rather than a single event/series of courses.[24] Williams and Rosenbaum are of the view that most learning happens on the job and is usually informal, highly unstructured and highly variable.[25] By viewing learning as a process, they are able to apply process improvement tools to improve learning by cutting down on time, doing away with waste and limiting variability. This method also provides tools to restructure and re-sequence the process in a way that improves retention and transfer to the job.[26]

The measurement of scrap learning

The extent to which training efforts and the resulting learning that (hopefully) took place have been transferred to the workplace, is the focus of many training evaluation models and research projects. Scrap learning was not a focus of these efforts until recently, when Brinkerhoff started to look at training evaluation in a different way.[27]

Kirkpatrick's four-level evaluation model (reaction – level 1, learning – level 2, behaviour – level 3 and results – level 4)[28] formed the basis for others to build on or use as a reference point in creating their own training evaluation models. King is of the view that scrap learning is the casualty of achieving level two (intended skills have been gained), but not level three (application of the skills to the job).[29] Jack Phillips added a fifth level, namely return on investment (ROI), which is designed to quantify performance improvements, measure financial benefits and compute precise investment returns.[30]

Brinkerhoff argues that performance results cannot be achieved by training alone, thus training should not be the object of evaluation.[31] As multiple variables contribute to the impact of a learning opportunity (be it training, performance support or another solution), multiple stakeholders own these results. Brinkerhoff therefore recommends that a systems approach to training evaluation be followed.[32] As arguably one of the first professionals to actually measure scrap learning, Brinkerhoff documented training that was both applied and not applied.

King suggests the following quick method to evaluate scrap learning:[33]

Step 1: Ask learners how quickly they were able to apply what they learned to the job.

The response options that are typically used include:

- 1 week
- 2–4 weeks
- 5–6 weeks
- "I have not applied the learning yet."
- "I don't intend to use what I learned."

Step 2: Once the survey responses are compiled, sum the results of the first three response options together as a percentage of all responses, and then subtract that figure from one hundred. As an example, if the sum of a programme's first three responses represented forty per cent, then the scrap learning rate is sixty per cent.

According to the CEB, the typical organisation is able to reduce the average rate of scrap learning from 45 to 33 per cent, by starting to measure scrap learning and making continuous improvements to programmes based on such an analysis.[34] This could lead to organisations generating millions in annual savings, as confirmed by this 12 per cent drop in scrap learning.

Learning Paths Methodology as a solution to reduce scrap learning

In this section the Learning Paths Methodology, as conceptualised by Williams and Rosenbaum, is discussed further in terms of underlying principles, core concepts and methodology.

Underlying principles

The Learning Paths International Methodology is based on the following main principles:

Principle 1: Learning is a process, not an event

Rosenbaum and Pollock[35] state that as the goal of corporate training is to improve performance, it cannot be achieved in a one-off event and should include elements of practise, coaching and reinforcement. Learning that improves performance needs to be thought of as a path that extends from Day 1 until a predetermined level of performance is reached. Everything along that path is critical, and a well-designed path shortens the learning process and ensures that learning actually transfers to the job: "When you adopt the 'learning is a process principle', you ensure that both the formal and the informal learning happen by design".[36]

Principle 2: Knowing is not the same as doing

In embracing this as a core learning principle, the focus of training shifts to knowledge application instead of knowledge acquisition – training objectives look very different when this principle is applied.[37] Words like "know", "list", "understand", "define" or "be aware of" are replaced by business-oriented action verbs such as "plan", "lead", "sell", "develop" or "execute" – terms that require learners do something meaningful with their new knowledge and skills. The measures of training effectiveness change to indicate a required level of performance, such as "less than a 1% error rate", "on every sales call" or "$100,000 in new business".[38]

When applying this principle, training includes more hands-on training, practice sessions, and on-the-job coaching as it migrates from the classroom and computer screen to live situations on the job.[39]

Principle 3: Passing is not good enough

In practice, this principle means that successful training is measured by the extent to which learners achieve the performance standards of the job. Applying this principle involves a movement away from a curriculum-based training approach. According to Rosenbaum and Pollock, curricula tend to teach topic by topic rather than integrating everything that needs to be learned in order to perform on the job.[40] "Instead of a series of courses, you design a complete Learning Path that includes a variety of formal and informal learning opportunities and rigorous evaluation along the way. The best learning paths mirror the way work is done."[41]

Principle 4: Time is money

Fridman states that given the pace at which society progresses, companies have to do whatever it takes to stay relevant.[42] Speed is required to stay competitive and grow. Similarly, Rosenbaum and Pollock aver that training speed – how quickly people new to a role become independently productive – delivers real bottom-line value for companies.[43] They stress that achieving speed in training does not mean arbitrarily cutting training time or skipping steps, but requires organisations to treat training as a process, eliminating wasted steps and time, and seizing every opportunity in and out of class to accelerate learning.[44] For example, one study found that re-imagining the learning path has enabled customer service agents to answer customer questions completely and accurately within three weeks, rather than three months.[45]

Principle 5: Training is everybody's responsibility

In a culture where this principle is the norm, managers, employees, the Learning & Development Department and subject matter experts actively participate throughout the process.[46]

Learning path core concepts

This section describes two core concepts in Learning Path Methodology: proficiency and the learning path

Proficiency

Proficiencies form the basis of the Learning Path Methodology as they determine what learning activities should be included. Rosenbaum and Williams define proficiency as the measurable outcomes and observable behaviour of doing a job or task correctly at the desired level of performance.[47] A person is viewed as proficient when s/he is independently productive and able to deliver required outputs according to set standards. An example of a proficiency statement for a Call Centre Agent could be: "Handles an average of 40 outbound calls per day so that the Call Centre's target for outbound calls is achieved".

The idea is to get an overall view of all the outputs and deliverables expected in a role, so that the learning activities can focus on teaching role incumbents to be able to deliver those outputs at the desired level of performance, as quickly as possible. According to Rosenbaum it is more effective to focus on proficiency, than competencies.[48] He explains his view as follows:

> A competency model breaks things down into three parts: Skills, Knowledge and Attitudes. When you build a competency model you end up with a long list of items to include in training. The downside of this approach is that it often misses how competencies work together in different combinations to produce a desired result. For example, knowing the features and benefits of your products is part of how a salesperson makes a presentation, answers questions and even fills out an order. A proficiency model, on the other hand, looks at the world from a completely different point of view. Proficiency is both a measure of performance and a set of observable behaviours that describe what a proficient employee produces and how the employee must work to achieve those results. Think of proficiency as a picture or snap shot of what success looks like on the job.[49]

In Rosenbaum's view, the important difference is that with a competency model, you can master all the competencies and not produce the desired results on the job; with a proficiency definition, the end result is completely spelled out and training does not end until the employee becomes proficient.[50]

Various sources are used to determine proficiencies – job descriptions, performance agreements, balanced scorecards, business strategy, interviews with line managers and incumbents, etc. All the proficiency statements are summarised in a proficiency definition, which usually consists of between 30 and 60 proficiency statements. An extract from a proficiency definition for an HR Director is provided in Table 19.1.[51]

The aim of a learning path is to accelerate the time to proficiency. Once the proficiency definition has been developed, the next step is to determine the time to proficiency. This is an important concept in the Learning Paths Methodology, as the main metric used with learning paths is the number of days it takes to reach proficiency.[52] Williams and Rosenbaum provide the following example of how accelerating the time to proficiency could add to the organisation's bottom line: "Taking sixty days out of a Learning Path for one hundred employees equals 6,000 extra days of productivity. If this were a transaction processing function, where each employee did fifty transactions that could mean up to 300,000 additional transactions".[53]

Table 19.1   Extract from the proficiency definition of an HR Director

Done	Category	Proficiency statement	Milestone	Evaluation
	Leadership and strategy	1. Analyse industry/market trends and identify/anticipate future needs so as to provide value-add business input into the organisational strategy sessions and executive meetings	1 month	Review of needs anticipated to ensure alignment with actual trends
	Leadership and strategy	2. Participate in executive and board meetings so as to input HR trends and industry best practice into strategic decision making	4 months	Observation
	Functional HR leadership	3. Monitor the implementation of the HR policies and procedures so as to identify and report incidents of non-compliance by senior management	1 month	Review of incidents escalated
	Functional HR leadership	4. Calculate and demonstrate the potential ROI of HR projects, initiatives and processes introduced into the business	3 months	Feedback from directors
	People management	5. Set key performance areas and standards for direct reports that are agreed to by the incumbents and contribute to achievement of the HR objectives	1 month	Review of documentation
	People management	6. Monitor achievements of direct reports against set standards and take action to correct deviations and ensure that individuals meet their targets	1 month	Review actions taken
	HR value chain management	7. Develop and maintain key critical HR processes such as accurate staff resources forecasting, recruitment and selection, career management, learning and development, remuneration and employee relations so as assist the business to achieve its goals	1 month	Review of HR processes
	HR value chain management	8. Influence senior management to ensure that HR objectives are aligned at both corporate and divisional levels	2 months	Director feedback

Once a baseline of time to proficiency has been established, the learning path will be designed in such a way that the time to proficiency is reduced drastically.

Learning path

A learning path is defined as the total sequence of training, practice and experience from Day 1 to independence day,[54] when proficiency is achieved and the employee is able to perform without constant supervision or assistance.[55] A learning path therefore maps the ideal sequence of learning activities that helps a person from Day 1 in a new role or task, to proficiency. Graphically, it may be depicted as follows:

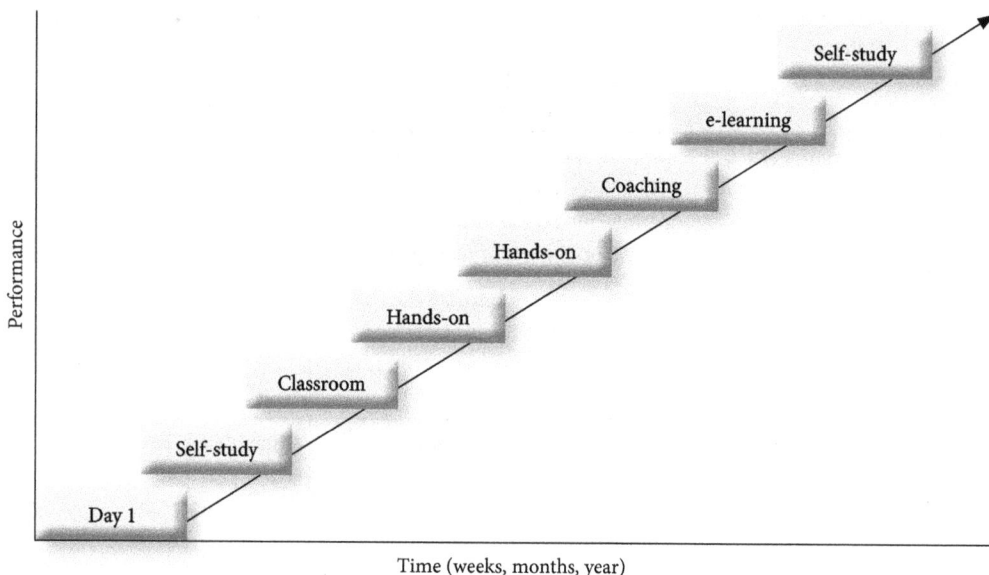

Figure 19.1   The learning path[56]

When developing a learning path, nothing that is necessary to make a person proficient, is left to chance. A learning path is mapped by considering each proficiency statement, as well as the total proficiency definition, to determine what type of learning activity will assist the employee in reaching proficiency.

Usually the current learning path (often informal and not documented) is mapped first. This process in general reveals a great deal of variation in respect of how people are upskilled to become proficient. Different supervisors, regions and trainers do their learning interventions differently, with the result that there is no single effective method of ensuring proficiency. The mapping of the current learning path also reveals gaps where it is uncertain how employees really become proficient – Rosenbaum calls this the "mystery period".[57]

The aim is to develop a learning path that will ensure consistent results across all areas of the business with the same role and proficiency definition. Another objective is to structure the entire timeline from start to proficiency so that it is complete, cost-effective and shorter.[58] When revising the current learning path, a major consideration is the elimination of waste, i.e., anything that does not add value or transfer to the job, and could therefore lead to scrap learning. To enhance the current learning path, Rosenbaum recommends identifying "quick hits"[59] or improvements that are easily identified when a current path is laid out for the first time. "Examples of Quick Hits often include deleting old and out of date information; adding missing or relevant information; structuring the mystery period with practice activities, checklists and evaluations; adding more practice and experience to the formal training; and aligning the training with current practices and business goals."[60]

A learning path structures all types of learning activities (formal, informal, self-directed, mobile, coaching, mentoring, practice sessions, etc.) into one document. As it is so comprehensive, a summary of the learning path (or learning-path-at-a-glance) is provided to form a picture of the detail to be included in the actual learning path, as evident in Figure 19.2.

CSR Call centre learning path at a glance

Month 1 – Week 1

1	2	3	4	5
1. Welcome and overview 2. Human resources 3. Learning path overview 4. Company overview 5. Product overview and demonstration	6. Work rules 7. Types of calls 8. System basics	9. Phone basics 10. Customer greeting 11. Order status calls 12. Order look-up 13. Order status screens	14. Order status situations 15. Shipping tour	16. Order status call evaluation 17. Live practice with a coach

Week 2

1	2	3	4	5
18. Order status live call debrief 19. Live practice with a buddy	20. Introduction to the team 21. Billing 22. Billing look-up 23. The billing screens	24. Billing situations	25. Billing department tour 26. Billing call evaluation 27. Live practice with a coach	28. Order status live call debrief 29. Live practice with a buddy

Week 3

1	2	3	4	5
30. Week 3 review 31. Order status and billing call live practice	(Live practice continued)	(Live practice continued)	(Live practice continued)	(Live practice continued)

Week 4

1	2	3	4	5
32. Week 4 review 33. Initial set-up	34. Initial set-up situations	35. Initial set-up call evaluation 36. Live practice with a coach	37. Initial set-up call debrief 38. Live practice with a buddy	39. Order status, billing and initial set-up call live practice

Week 5

1	2	3	4	5
40. Week 4 review (Live practice continued)	(Live practice continued)	(Live practice continued)	(Live practice continued)	(Live practice continued)

Week 6

1	2	3	4	5
41. Week 6 review 42. Basic troubleshooting calls	43. Troubleshooting situations	44. Troubleshooting call evaluation 45. Live practice with a coach	46. Troubleshooting call debrief 47. Live practice with a buddy	48. All call live practice

Week 7   **Week 8**

1	2
49. Week 7 review (Live practice continued)	50. Week 8 review (Live practice continued) 51. Final evaluation

Figure 19.2   Detailled example of an actual learning path[61]

Below is a snapshot of a three-month learning path for an HR Director. This particular snapshot, shown in Figure 19.3, describes the headlines of activities that should take place in week 2 of month 3.

Month 3 – Week 2

Done	Day	Activity	Type	Comment	Proficiency nr
	1	1. **Coaching in Company X project management software** HR Director to be coached on the Company X project planning software by IT Specialist so as to be able to use all the commands and screens to perform planning function.	Coaching/ demonstration	Scheduled through IT	5,4
	2	2. **Review of strategic HR projects and plans over past year** HR Director to review past HR projects and plans completed by predecessor and HRBPs.	Document review	Past plans can be accessed on the company's Project Management System	5,4
	3	3. **Review of current project plans for allocated projects of direct reports** HR Director to work through all current project plans of direct reports to critique the planning format and content and determine status against plan.	Practical/ working session	The approved company project plan template as on the system is used as the basis of assessment	5,4
	4	4. **Development of a draft project plan for a newly allocated strategic HR project** HR Director to draft project plan, using the Company X software, for a newly allocated strategic HR project and check in with CFO to discuss and amend.	Practical/ working session	IT Specialist to provide coaching during this process	4
	5	5. **Week 10 review** A weekly meeting with the CFO/coach to evaluate progress to date and to plan out the next week. It includes reviewing progress on the proficiency definitions and the Learning Path.	Evaluation/ planning		

Figure 19.3   *Snapshot of learning path for an HR Director*[62]

All activities in the learning path are supported by a detailed activity description. There is usually a learner file with all the activity descriptions and templates needed during the implementation of the learning path. Mentors, line managers and trainers also receive manuals/toolkits describing their roles in the implementation of the learning path and providing them with detailed activity descriptions for their roles in each learning activity.

As is evident in the example, the proficiency that is addressed by a particular activity is also indicated. Ultimately, there is no scrap learning when a learning path is designed well, as each learning activity leads to proficiency in the role and must be applied on the job. Transfer of learning is therefore not an issue, as the learning path (through built-in practice) ensures that all learning is applied in the workplace. Without such practice, proficiency cannot be attained.

The process of developing a learning path

Individual learning paths projects start by targeting a critical job, function or task. Ideally, learning paths are created for every function within an organisation, so as to establish a common approach to learning and promote the sharing of best practices. A learning path project mirrors the process used for successful quality improvement initiatives. Projects follow five steps:[63]

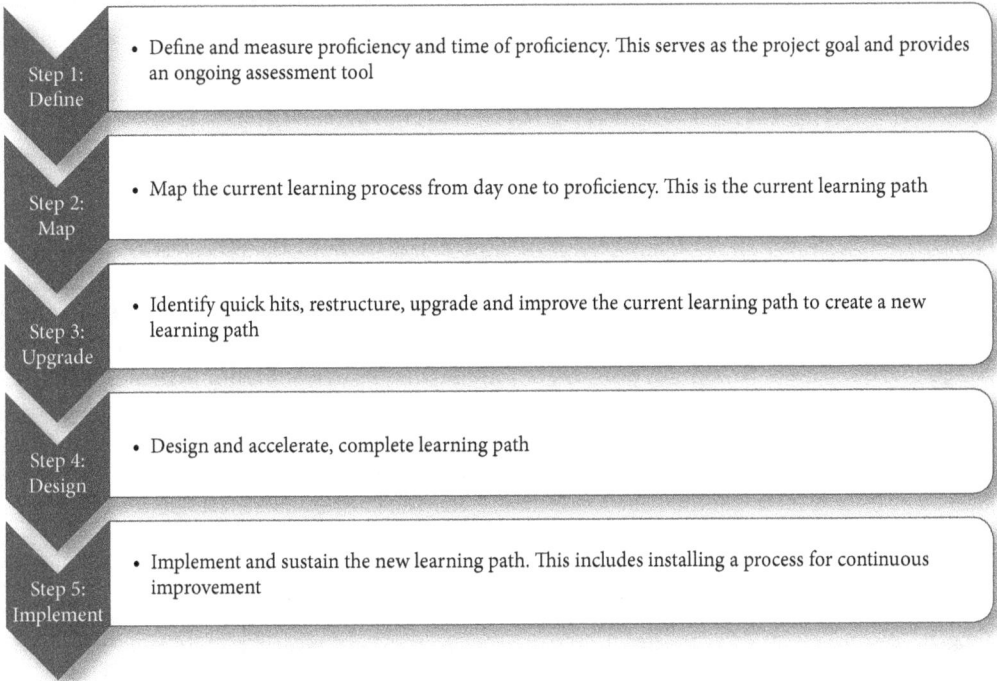

Step 1: Define
- Define and measure proficiency and time of proficiency. This serves as the project goal and provides an ongoing assessment tool

Step 2: Map
- Map the current learning process from day one to proficiency. This is the current learning path

Step 3: Upgrade
- Identify quick hits, restructure, upgrade and improve the current learning path to create a new learning path

Step 4: Design
- Design and accelerate, complete learning path

Step 5: Implement
- Implement and sustain the new learning path. This includes installing a process for continuous improvement

Figure 19.4   The steps of a learning path project[64]

Conclusion

Scrap learning is a major problem in many organisations, as the majority of employees who attend training apply very little of what they effectively learnt during such training, once they are back in the workplace. Scrap learning has a high direct and indirect cost to the organisation, as well as the learner. As a solution to reduce scrap learning, it is recommended that learning paths form the basis of an organisation's training efforts.

As the learning path is based on measurable results and observable actions, the required learning is automatically embedded in the workflow of the role, and transfer of learning to the workplace is thus guaranteed. The effective implementation of a learning path also requires total management involvement: the line manager plays a major role in the delivery of the learning activities and in acting as mentor, coach and monitor, to ensure the effective implementation of learning activities. A well-designed learning path should therefore lead to zero scrap learning, as all learning activities are linked to proficiency and must be demonstrated on the job, thus ensuring that all learning is ultimately applied in the workplace. For examples of two case studies, see the Annexure.

Annexure: Some case studies

These case studies[65] illustrate how the use of learning paths assisted in the effective transfer of training to the workplace, and as a result reduced scrap learning.

Case study 1

CLIENT	Pharmacy network of five contact centres with 2 000 employees
SITUATION	Hiring 30 new employees a month followed by six weeks of classroom training before on-the-job coaching
INSIGHT	The need to improve time to proficiency, ensure consistency of training and improve the link between the training and the on-the-job experience
ACTION	A proficiency definition and a learning path solution were implemented and applied consistently across the business. Implemented shorter and more effective classroom training and established processes that ensure ongoing assessment and support. Focused on two key roles/functions: Prescription Entry Technician and Customer Service Representative
OUTCOME	Decreased classroom time from six weeks to four Reduced time to proficiency from 12 months to eight, and reduced attrition Increased sales volume Increased profits

Case study 2

CLIENT	Leading international chemical manufacturer with approximately 7 000 employees
SITUATION	Significant catastrophic risks to employees, the environment and the product, due to inconsistently trained batch operators. Variability, inconsistency and repetition between 70 business units increased on-boarding costs
INSIGHT	Variable training had led to inconsistent product offering, the risk of serious incidents and costly retaining. A consistency of offering, training and development is key to the ongoing viability of the business
ACTION	A proficiency definition and a learning path solution were implemented and applied consistently across the global operations that incorporated just-in-time safety training. Focus on supervisors, as key business functions across 70 plants
OUTCOME	Accidents decreased by 20 per cent Time to proficiency was reduced by a minimum of 40 per cent across 70 plants A decrease of supervision costs of US$750k p.a. This had an additional impact on future acquisitions in the post-merger integration process

Endnotes

1   R Probart, 'State of the South African training industry', ATD, 2014, <retrieved 25 July 2016>, <https://www.td.org/Publications/Magazines/TD/TD-Archive/2014/05/Intelligence-State-of-the-South-African-Training-Industry>.

2   Deloitte, 'Managing the Public Sector Wage Bill' 2015, retrieved 25 July 2016, <http://sabudgetspeech.deloitte.co.za/featured/6.html>.

3   J Bersin, 'Spending on corporate training soars: Employee capabilities now a priority', *Forbes*, 2014, retrieved 25 July 2016, <http://www.forbes.com/sites/joshbersin/2014/02/04/the-recovery-arrives-corporate-training-spend-skyrockets/>.

4   A May, 'How to avoid scrap learning', Dashe & Thomson, Inc., 2014, retrieved 25 July 2016 <http://www.dashe.com/blog/at-the-time-learning/avoid-scrap-learning/>.

5   C Wick, RVH Pollock & A Jefferson, *The six disciplines of breakthrough learning: How to turn training and development into business results*, second edition, Pfeiffer, San Francisco, 2010.

6   Friesen, Kaye and Associates, 'Training transfer: A corporate strategy for applying skills and knowledge in the workplace', 2009, retrieved 25 July 2016, <http://www.fka.com/files/TrainingTransfer09.pdf>.

7   Ibid.

8   DF Michalak, 'The neglected half of training', *Training and Development Journal*, vol. 35, no. 5, pp. 22–28, May 1981.

9   Corporate Executive Board (CEB), 'Confronting scrap learning: How to address the pervasive waste in talent development', Comdev 2014, retrieved 25 July 2016, <http://comdev.osu.edu/sites/comdev/files/imce/Metrics_that_Matter_Whitepaper_-_Confronting_Scrap_Learning.pdf>.

10 JR Mattox, , 'Manager engagement: Reducing scrap learning', Training Industry Quarterly, Fall 2010, retrieved 20 July 2016, <www.trainingindustry.com/ezine>.

11 E Cohen, 'Learning at the point of need: Chief Learning Officer, Clomedia, 2015, retrieved 25 July 2016, <http://www.clomedia.com/blogs/9-your-career/post/6454-learning-at-the-point-of-need>.

12 J Mattox II, 'Are you using the best metrics to evaluate your skills training?', *Training Industry Magazine*, Spring 2015, retrieved 25 July 2016, <http://www.nxtbook.com/nxtbooks/trainingindustry/tiq_2015spring/#/38>.

13 J Williams & S Rosenbaum, *Learning paths: Increase profits by reducing the time it takes employees to get up-to-speed*, Pfeiffer, San Francisco, 2004.

14 C Wick, R Pollock, & A Jefferson, 'The new finish line for learning', *T+D Magazine*, July 2009.

15 Wick et al 2010, op. cit.

16 AK Mabotha, 'The relationship between attitudes towards supervisory support and work performance of employees in an education department in Mpumalanga', Master's dissertation, University of South Africa, 2012, retrieved 25 July 2016, <ir.unisa.ac.za/bitstream/handle/10500/9356/Dissertation_Mabotha_Ak.pdf?sequence=1>.

17 K King, 'Guide to reducing scrap learning: Scrap learning – the failure of learning transfer', Skillsoft, 2015, retrieved 25 July 2016, <http://www.skillsoft.com/assets/white-papers/ScrapLearning_Guide.pdf>.

18 ML Broad, & JW Newstrom, *Transfer of training: Action-packed strategies to ensure high payoff from training investments*, Addison-Wesley Publishing Company, New York, 1992.

19 King, op. cit.

20 Corporate Executive Board, op. cit.

21 Wick et al. 2009, op. cit.

22 Wick et al. 2010, op. cit.

23 A Jefferson, & R Pollock, 'Learning transfer: Come to Las Vegas and stop gambling', Blog posted 12 November 2014, ATD website, <https://www.td.org/Publications/Blogs/L-and-D-Blog/2014/11/Learning-Transfer-Come-to-Las-Vegas-and-Stop-Gambling>.

24 Williams and Rosenbaum, op. cit.

25 Ibid.

26 Ibid.

27 RO Brinkerhoff, 'The success case method: A strategic evaluation approach to increasing the value and effect of training', *Advances in Developing Human Resources*, vol. 7, no. 1, 2005, pp. <page extent>.

28 DL Kirkpatrick, *Evaluating training programs: The four levels*, Berrett-Koehler, San Francisco, 1998.

29 King, loc. cit.

30 J Phillips & P Phillips, 'ROI: Results enhancer, value adder', ROI Institute, 2007, retrieved 25 July 2016, <http://www.roiinstitute.net/wp-content/uploads/2014/12/ROI-Results-Enhancer-Value-Adder.pdf>.

31 Brinkerhoff, op. cit.

32 Ibid.

33 King, loc. cit.

34 Corporate Executive Board, loc. cit.

35   S Rosenbaum & R Pollock, 'Creating & maintaining a positive learning culture', white paper, Learning Paths International, 2015.

36   Ibid.

37   Ibid.

38   Ibid.

39   Ibid.

40   Ibid.

41   Ibid.

42   A Fridman, 'Four reasons speed is everything in business', 2015, retrieved 25 July 2016, <http://www.inc.com/adam-fridman/4-reasons-speed-is-everything-in-business.html>.

43   Rosenbaum and Pollock, loc. cit.

44   Ibid.

45   S Rosenbaum, 'Competencies versus proficiencies', Learning at light speed, Weblog, 2011, retrieved 6 June 2016, <http://learningatlightspeed.wordpress.com/>.

46   S Rosenbaum, & R Pollock, 'Creating & maintaining a positive learning culture', white paper, Learning Paths International, 2015.

47   J Williams, & S Rosenbaum, *Learning paths: Increase profits by reducing the time it takes employees to get up-to-speed*, Pfeiffer, San Francisco, 2004.

48   Rosenbaum, loc. cit.

49   Ibid.

50   S Rosenbaum, 'Learning paths: The evolution of training', a Learning Paths International white paper, 2011, retrieved 25 April 2016, <www. learningpathsinternational.com>.

51   © Learning Paths International, internal document.

52   Williams and Rosenbaum, op. cit.

53   Ibid.

54   Rosenbaum, loc. cit.

55   Williams and Rosenbaum, op. cit.

56   Ibid.

57   Rosenbaum, loc. cit.

58   Ibid.

59   Ibid.

60   Ibid.

61   © Learning Paths International, op. cit.

62   Ibid.

63   S Rosenbaum, 'How we bring employees up to speed in record time using the Learning Path Methodology: Case D2.6', in RVH Pollock, A Jefferson, and C Wick, *The field guide to the 6Ds*. John Wiley & Sons, Hoboken, 2014.

64   Rosenbaum. loc. cit.

65   Ibid.

References

Bersin, J, 'Spending on corporate training soars: Employee capabilities now a priority', *Forbes*, 2014, retrieved 1 August 2016, <http://www.forbes.com/sites/joshbersin/2014/02/04/the-recovery-arrives-corporate-training-spend-skyrockets/>.

Brinkerhoff, RO, 'The success case method: A strategic evaluation approach to increasing the value and effect of training', *Advances in Developing Human Resources*, vol. 7, no. 1, 2005, pp. <page extent>.

Broad, ML & Newstrom, JW, *Transfer of training: Action-packed strategies to ensure high payoff from training investments*, Addison-Wesley Publishing Company, New York, 1992.

Cohen, E, 'Learning at the point of need: Chief Learning Officer, Clomedia, 2015, retrieved <date>, <http://www.clomedia.com/blogs/9-your-career/post/6454-learning-at-the-point-of-need>.

Corporate Executive Board (CEB), 'Confronting scrap learning: How to address the pervasive waste in talent development', Comdev 2014, retrieved <date>, <http://comdev.osu.edu/sites/comdev/files/imce/Metrics_that_Matter_Whitepaper_-_Confronting_Scrap_Learning.pdf>.

Deloitte, 'Managing the Public Sector Wage Bill' 2015, retrieved 1 July 2016, <http://sabudgetspeech.deloitte.co.za/featured/6.html>.

Fridman, A, 'Four reasons speed is everything in business', 2015, retrieved 4 July 2016, <http://www.inc.com/adam-fridman/4-reasons-speed-is-everything-in-business.html>.

Friesen, Kaye and Associates, 'Training transfer: A corporate strategy for applying skills and knowledge in the workplace', 2009, retrieved 1 July 2016, <http://www.fka.com/files/TrainingTransfer09.pdf>.

Jefferson, A & Pollock, R, 'Learning transfer: Come to Las Vegas and stop gambling', Blog posted 12 November 2014, ATD website, <https://www.td.org/Publications/Blogs/L-and-D-Blog/2014/11/Learning-Transfer-Come-to-Las-Vegas-and-Stop-Gambling>.

King, K, 'Guide to reducing scrap learning: Scrap learning – the failure of learning transfer', Skillsoft, 2015, retrieved 1 May 2016, <http://www.skillsoft.com/assets/white-papers/ScrapLearning_Guide.pdf>.

Kirkpatrick, DL, *Evaluating training programs: The four levels*, Berrett-Koehler, San Francisco, 1998.

Mabotha, AK, 'The relationship between attitudes towards supervisory support and work performance of employees in an education department in Mpumalanga', Master's dissertation, University of South Africa, 2012, retrieved 15 May 2016, <ir.unisa.ac.za/bitstream/handle/10500/9356/Dissertation_Mabotha_Ak.pdf?sequence=1>.

Mattox II, J, 'Are you using the best metrics to evaluate your skills training?', *Training Industry Magazine*, Spring 2015, retrieved 15 May 2016, <http://www.nxtbook.com/nxtbooks/trainingindustry/tiq_2015spring/#/38>.

Mattox, JR, 'Manager engagement: Reducing scrap learning', *Training Industry Quarterly*, Fall 2010, retrieved 20 July 2016, <www.trainingindustry.com/ezine>.

May, A, 'How to avoid scrap learning', Dashe & Thomson, Inc., 2014, retrieved 5 February 2016 <http://www.dashe.com/blog/at-the-time-learning/avoid-scrap-learning/>.

Michalak, DF, 'The neglected half of training', *Training and Development Journal*, vol. 35, no. 5, pp. 22–28, May 1981.

Phillips, J & P Phillips, 'ROI: Results enhancer, value adder', ROI Institute, 2007, retrieved 8 April 2016, <http://www.roiinstitute.net/wp-content/uploads/2014/12/ROI-Results-Enhancer-Value-Adder.pdf>.

Probart, R, 'State of the South African training industry', ATD, 2014, 1 August 2016, <https://www.td.org/Publications/Magazines/TD/TD-Archive/2014/05/Intelligence-State-of-the-South-African-Training-Industry>.

Rosenbaum, S, 'Competencies versus proficiencies', Learning at light speed, Weblog, 2011, retrieved 6 June 2016, <http://learningatlightspeed.wordpress.com/>.

Rosenbaum, S, 'Learning paths: The evolution of training', a Learning Paths International white paper, 2011, retrieved 25 April 2016, <www. learningpathsinternational.com>.

Rosenbaum, S, 'Put your sales force on the fast track', a Learning Paths International White paper, 2011.

Rosenbaum, S, 'How we bring employees up to speed in record time using the Learning Path Methodology: Case D2.6', in RVH Pollock, A Jefferson & C Wick, *The field guide to the 6Ds*. John Wiley & Sons, Hoboken, 2014.

Rosenbaum, S, & R Pollock, 'Creating & maintaining a positive learning culture', white paper, Learning Paths International, 2015.

Wick, C, R Pollock & A Jefferson, 'The new finish line for learning', *T+D Magazine*, July 2009.

Wick, C, Pollock, RVH & Jefferson, A, *The six disciplines of breakthrough learning: How to turn training and development into business results*, second edition, Pfeiffer, San Francisco, 2010.

Williams, J & Rosenbaum, S, *Learning paths: Increase profits by reducing the time it takes employees to get up-to-speed*, Pfeiffer, San Francisco, 2004.

Additional Readings

Eades, J, 'Why microlearning is HUGE and how to be a part of it', e-learning industry, 2014, retrieved <   >, <http://elearningindustry.com/why-microlearning-is-huge>.

Gram, T, 'Evaluating with the Success Case Method', 2011, retrieved 25 April 2016, <https://performancexdesign.wordpress.com/2011/02/24/evaluating-with-the-success-case-method/>.

Grossman, R & E Salas, 'The transfer of training: What really matters', *International Journal of Training and Development*, vol. 15, no. 2, 2011, retrieved 25 April 2016, <http://www.uio.no/studier/emner/matnat/ifi/INF3280/v14/pensumliste/additionalliterature/grossmansalas2011transfertraining.pdf>.

Mandel Communications, <https://www.mandel.com/blog/measuring-training-effectiveness-is-your-scrap-learning-rate-too-high>.

Mattox II, JR, 'Scrap learning and manager engagement: Chief Learning Officer', Clomedia 2011, retrieved 25 April 2016, <http://www.clomedia.com/articles/scrap-learning-and-manager-engagement>.

Pascale, C. Competency development best practices. MapHR, <http://maphr.com/editorial-corner/vado-competency-development-best-practices>.

Pollock, RVH, A Jefferson, & C Wick, *The field guide to the 6Ds*, John Wiley & Sons, Hoboken, 2014.

Skillsoft, Guide to reducing scrap learning: scrap learning—The failure of learning transfer, 2011, <http://1stclass.com/images/stories/Guide-to-Reducing-Scrap-Learning.pdf>.

CONCLUSION

Terry Meyer

This book began with the assertion that, for Africa to realise its potential, it needs to develop and mobilise the rich diversity of talent, skills and potential that exists across the continent.

The book began with an overview of the current state of the continent, using the available information which is so insightfully presented by Wilhelm Crous, based on research by Knowledge Resources.

This was followed by various perspectives on strategic issues in talent management, as addressed by a number of thought leaders in the field. Examples of holistic talent frameworks were provided, and the importance of effective talent management governance was emphasised. Also discussed was the context of a technology-dominated world and the challenges associated with designing "social" organisations that will attract and retain not only millennials, but all those who thrive in a world characterised by collaboration and connectivity.

The strategic issues focused on include the development of an executive and leadership pool that will enable African organisations to compete in a connected and disruptive world, the importance of building organisations that are sustainable and provide social value beyond a narrow shareholder return, and the power of thinking processes that challenge conventional thinking and facilitate innovative solutions to complex problems. Included is the importance of building an employee value proposition to attract and engage various generations of talent that will enhance the future capability of organisations.

Following on from the strategic issues related to talent in Africa were four corporate case studies. The authors were provided with a totally open mandate – *How has talent management contributed to the execution of your organisation's strategy?* In each case the focus was on the role of culture in supporting the strategy, rather than simply on talent processes that are designed and applied by the HR function. The success of all the featured companies is largely attributable to the creation of a culture that supports the organisation's strategic drivers. These drivers are located in business strategy and organisational design, rather than within an HR process-driven strategy. The processes are certainly there, but they support a higher order of intervention than simple talent processes do.

The final section included examples of tools, interventions and practices that will enable talent acquisition and development to take place. These include assessment processes, graduate development, cost-effective training and the role of coaching in a leadership strategy.

Central to the effectiveness of strategies and processes is the effectiveness of all the role players involved in creating a talent-attractive environment. Numerous role players need to contribute to a talent-attractive culture: first, and most important, is the role of executive management in building a culture that people want to be part of. They do this through their proactive leadership abilities and the creation of an organisational purpose that talent can subscribe to. They also ensure that the leadership pipeline is in place to establish continuity and provide development opportunities for future executives and leaders at all levels.

Line managers at all levels have a similar role at their level, therefore the creation of an organisation-wide culture and pipelines for development is cascaded throughout the company. While leaders are responsible for creating a leadership culture, the HR function has a significant role as custodian of the processes and through the provision of advisory services to leaders.

In my view a significant shift is occurring in the role of HR professionals. First, traditional HR transactional operations will change substantially (most organisations are somewhere on that journey) to provide an exceptional employee experience, increasingly known as HR consumerism.

HR services will be defined by exceptional customer service and could well be run by a service centre professional, rather than someone from HR. It will probably have a different, more user-friendly name such as "My (company)", the "People Zone" or some other term that is both sexy and non-traditional. The analogy will be that of a customer service centre run by a corporate public services facility.

In support of exceptional services, the other defining factor will be new technologies which

- are on the cloud;
- offer self-service options;
- can be used anywhere, anytime, on any device, driven by apps;
- are user-friendly, simple and interactive;
- incorporate multiple media, including video;
- are collaborative and "social" in nature; and
- are linked to external social media and other platforms.

Hence the HR services facility will create a "social" environment that will be a key pillar in attracting and retaining staff, in particular millennials.

Other HR roles will also transform. The role of HRBP, being divested of transactional responsibilities, will increasingly become that of key account manager to internal clients. In this role these individuals will be responsible for grasping the challenges facing the business. They will primarily be charged with improving organisational effectiveness through solution development and strategic problem solving. The role will be defined by convening and facilitating teams of experts to address organisational issues.

The role of specialists will expand: process owners will be required to contribute to organisational effectiveness as members of trans-functional teams which form and disband as the need arises. Importantly, specialists in this context will not be restricted to HR specialisations. Marketing personnel, in particular, will become key players within HR teams. Those employees have the expertise to create and enhance a talent brand in conjunction with HR, and are able to segment and understand the psychographics of different employees or prospective employee markets. They are also responsible for the organisation's brand values, and for ensuring that the culture internally is a reflection of the external brand culture.

IT is another area to which HR should be joined at the hip, so to speak. As technology defines the employee experience and drives a "social" organisation, IT will be a key partner with HR to take employee experiences to a new level.

Finance, operations, legal and many other functions in organisations need to be included in trans-functional project teams aimed at creating a talent-attractive organisation.

Finally, employees themselves are important players in executing the organisation's talent strategy. They need to be open to learn and change within a disruptive environment and must be prepared to develop themselves on an ongoing basis. Increasingly, the focus will be on self-management and self-development. Furthermore, employees will need to take ownership of branding themselves, in order to take advantage of opportunities that arise within the organisation.

These changes to key roles need to be effective: after all, any system is only as strong as its weakest link, and if one player in the system does not fulfil his/her role effectively, the entire system will be sub-optimal at best and dysfunctional at worst. The consequences can be severe.

It is my hope that those who have taken the trouble to read this book and engage with their organisations on the issues dealt with here, will find much that is of relevance and will contribute to building the talent and skills pool that Africa needs, to realise its full potential.

INDEX

network of peers, 110
network of strong coaches and mentors, 215
networks of teams, 64
neurolinguistic, 192
neuroscience, 25
neutralising, 148
next level of growth and effectiveness, 68
next level of performance, 68
nomination process, 31
non-alcoholic ready-to-drink beverages, 176
non-compliance, 253
non-degree programmes, 185
non-existent, 133
norm, 66, 112, 137, 178, 252
  cultural, 116, 175

O

objectives, 65, 100, 140, 238, 253
  business unit, 39
  current business, 121
  experienced-based learning, 128
  quantifiable, 139
  strategic, 116
occupations, 20, 247
OD, *see* Organisational Development
OECD (Organisation for Economic Cooperation and Development), 4
officials, 14
  executive-level, 119
oil, 2–3, 85, 90
  leading international, 89
oil prices, low, 2
on-boarding, relevant, 122
on-boarding programme, robust, 217
on-boarding programmes, 166
one-on-one events, 239
online, 189
  completed, 140
  connected, 212
  target students, 98
online business, 110
online channels, 98
online learning, 67, 188–189
online media, 212
on-the-job assessment, 200
on-the-job training/coaching, 227
open executive education programmes, 185
operating framework, 170
operating practices and principles, 170
opportunities/threats, 59
optimise success, 249
optimum flexibility, 138
option for coaches, 237
organic growth strategies, internal, 120
organisational agility, 49, 84
organisational agility perspective priority setting, 127
organisational behaviour, 58, 147, 182, 188
organisational boundaries, 64

organisational capabilities, 26–27, 91, 248
  sustainable, 125
organisational change, 153
organisational change processes, 185
organisational climate, 151
organisational collaboration, 58, 64
organisational context, 57, 125, 239
organisational culture, 103–104, 147–148, 154–155, 169–171, 177–179
  important role, 148
  non-supportive, 249
organisational culture and executive search, 103–104
organisational culture and external brand values, 79
organisational culture and leadership, 169
organisational culture of transparency, 49
organisational design, 37, 64, 191, 263
organisational design issues, 64
organisational development (OD), 26, 29, 31, 33–35, 144
organisational development team, 136
organisational effectiveness, 24, 26, 264
  improving, 264
organisational management level, 73
organisational performance, 30, 148, 169–170, 181–182
  cultural outcomes drive, 155
  improved, 220
organisational perspective, 237
organisational practices, 110, 170
organisational purpose, 57, 263
organisational quality, 222
organisational quality and costs, 222
organisational strategy, 39, 61, 73–74, 76–77
  brilliant, 148
organisational strategy sessions, 253
organisational structures, 27
organisational success, 72, 148
  measuring, 72, 75
organisational sustainability, 221
organisational sustainability practices, 71
organisational systems, 1, 185
  large, 22
organisational tension, 105
organisational transformation, 27, 133
  company's, 170
organisational turnaround strategy, 147
organisational values, 151, 178
organisation articulates, 87
organisation design, 136
organisation embarking, 169
Organisation for Economic Cooperation and Development (OECD), 4
organisation leverages, 109
organisations
  building, 263
  bureaucratic, 172
  developmental, 28
  effective, 59, 66
  exceptional, 58
  family-based, 173
  family-dominated, 169

[Created with **TExtract** / www.Texyz.com]